ENCYCLOPEDIA OF RACISM IN THE UNITED STATES

ENCYCLOPEDIA OF RACISM IN THE UNITED STATES

Volume Two, I–R

Edited by Pyong Gap Min

GREENWOOD PRESS
Westport, Connecticut • London

Library of Congress Cataloging-in-Publication Data

Encyclopedia of racism in the United States / edited by Pyong Gap Min.
    p. cm.
    Includes bibliographical references and index.
    ISBN 0-313-32688-6 (set : alk. paper) — ISBN 0-313-33249-5 (vol. 1 : alk. paper)
— ISBN 0-313-33250-9 (vol. 2 : alk. paper) — ISBN 0-313-33555-9 (vol. 3 : alk.
paper)   1. Racism—United States—Encyclopedias.   2. United States—Race
relations—Encyclopedias.   3. United States—Ethnic relations—Encyclopedias.
4. Minorities—United States—Social conditions—Encyclopedias.   I. Min, Pyong Gap,
1942-
    E184.A1E773 2005
    305.8'00973'03—dc22   2005008523

British Library Cataloguing in Publication Data is available.

Library of Congress Catalog Card Number: 2005008523
ISBN: 0-313-32688-6 (set)
      0-313-33249-5 (vol. I)
      0-313-33250-9 (vol. II)
      0-313-33555-9 (vol. III)

First published in 2005

Greenwood Press, 88 Post Road West, Westport, CT 06881
An imprint of Greenwood Publishing Group, Inc.
www.greenwood.com

Printed in the United States of America

The paper used in this book complies with the
Permanent Paper Standard issued by the National
Information Standards Organization (Z39.48–1984).

10 9 8 7 6 5 4 3 2 1

CONTENTS

PREFACE

The racial and ethnic diversity caused by the influx of new immigrants, the expansion of ethnic-studies programs in colleges and universities, and the gradual shift since the 1970s in the government's policy from Anglo-conformity to multiculturalism have contributed to the phenomenal increase in the number of high school and college courses relating to immigration, ethnicity, and racial- and ethnic-minority relations. These courses are offered in the disciplines of sociology, urban studies, anthropology, and history, as well as in various ethnic-studies programs. To meet the increasing demand, a number of encyclopedias covering new immigrant and minority groups and multicultural education have recently been published. Many high school and college students who study American history, immigration, ethnicity, and racial and ethnic relations need to understand concepts, theories, issues, and historical events related to racism. However, despite this need, no encyclopedia of racism in the United States existed.

Several recently published books focus on racism.[1] Some of them offer conceptual and theoretical clarifications relating to racism, and others concentrate attention on white racism against blacks, drawing on ethnographic research or public documents. But none of them is a reference work offering a comprehensive list of concepts, theories, and historical events relating to racism in the United States. Information about historical events that reflect prejudice, discrimination, and physical violence against minority racial groups can be found in books that cover the histories of particular minority groups. But none provides a comprehensive list of historical events pertaining to various racial and ethnic minority groups in the United States. Several handbooks and encyclopedias, such as the *Encyclopedia of the Civil Rights Movement* and the *Encyclopedia of Indian Holocaust*, specialize in racial issues relating to particular minority groups, but no comprehensive encyclopedia covering racial victimization for all racial and ethnic minority groups in the United

States had been published before this book, the *Encyclopedia of Racism in the United States*.

SCOPE OF COVERAGE AND CLASSIFICATION OF ENTRIES

To prepare the *Encyclopedia*, I reviewed most of the major books that specialize in race and ethnic relations or that focus on particular minority groups in the United States. In consultation with a five-member advisory board, a list of entries was devised for inclusion in the *Encyclopedia*. The selected entries, whether directly or indirectly related to racism in the United States, can be broadly classified into the following six categories:

1. Social-science terms, concepts, and theories related to racism
2. Historical and contemporary events, figures, and organizations reflecting or supporting racial discrimination and racial violence against minority groups
3. Racial prejudice and discrimination in employment, housing, and other areas
4. Reactions of minority groups to racial discrimination and of minority leaders who have fought against racism
5. Governmental measures, programs, and agencies, and court cases related to either discrimination or prevention of racial discrimination against minority groups
6. Major books either supporting or exposing racism

Most entries also refer to particular racial and ethnic minority groups. The groups are broadly divided into the following eight categories:

1. Native Americans/American Indians (terms used interchangeably)
2. African Americans
3. Hispanics/Latinos (terms used interchangeably)
4. Asian Americans and Pacific Islanders
5. Muslims, Arabs, and Middle Easterners
6. White ethnic groups (e.g., Jews, Italians, Irish)
7. Immigrants and their children
8. All ethnic groups

Many entries, such as Derogatory Terms and Hate Crimes, fall into category 8; that is, they relate to all racial and ethnic minority groups. These two ways of classifying entries, which are clearly reflected in the "Guide to Related Entries," will help users of the *Encyclopedia* trace broad themes and topics across the entries and will also assist readers who are searching for related groups of topics that interest them or that meet their study or research needs.

The *Encyclopedia of Racism in the United States* is heavily cross-referenced. For instance, readers searching for an organization by acronym, such as AIM, will encounter a cross-reference that sends them to the main entry under the full name of the organization—in this case, they will be instructed to *See* the American Indian Movement. A reader searching for the term *all-weather bigots* will be instructed to *See* Bigots, Types of, the entry in which "all-weather bigots" are described and discussed. The ends of most of the entries also feature *See also* cross-references that list other, related entries. Most entries also conclude with a "Further Reading" section that lists references the reader can turn to for more detailed information on the entry subject. A detailed person and subject index offers greater access to terms and concepts within entries. The *Encyclopedia* also includes an introduction that traces the history of American racism, a general bibliography of important and useful works on racism and minority and ethnic groups, a brief chronology of racism in the United States, and a selection of the full text or excerpts of important primary documents relating to U.S. racism.

Of the *Encyclopedia*'s 447 entries, 25 (e.g., Affirmative Action) are longer entries of 2,000–3,000 words covering complex topics or concepts, while about 180 are midsized entries of 500–1,000 words. The remainder are entries on issues, people, events, or organizations for which basic information and importance can be conveyed in fewer than 500 words. Each contributor to the *Encyclopedia* committed to write one long essay and several medium and short entries on topics within his or her particular field of expertise, and a continuity of thought and style across many related entries is the result.

PRACTICAL VALUE OF THE *ENCYCLOPEDIA* FOR MODERATION OF RACISM

Despite all the democratic ideals emphasized in the Declaration of Independence, the U.S. Constitution, and many other government documents, the United States has probably been the most racist country in the world, with the exception of South Africa under apartheid between 1948 and 1994, and Nazi Germany. Although federal and local governments have made significant changes since 1970 in support of multiculturalism, they have done little to achieve racial equality and to moderate institutional racism during the same period. White Americans are receptive to ethnic and racial diversity to a much grater extent than they were in 1970, but they do not always accept African Americans as friends, as members of their social clubs, or even as neighbors.

Given the seriousness of the problem of racism and racial inequality in contemporary American society, it is important for everyone to join the effort to moderate it. To moderate racism and racial inequality, education of the general public, especially high school and college students, about historical cases of racial injustices and contemporary forms of racism is needed. Students can learn as much about racism from researching a chosen topic as from listening to lectures.

I undertook the extremely difficult task of editing the *Encyclopedia* mainly because of its practical value for contributing to the moderation of racism. I hope the *Encyclopedia* will be helpful to high school and college students who are conducting research on race-related and minority issues and that it will serve as a valuable resource for graduate students and faculty members who teach and conduct research on race relations, racial inequality, and particular minority groups in social science, history, and ethnic studies programs.

NOTE

1. See Eduardo Bonilla-Silva, *Racism without Racists: Color-Blind Racism and the Persistence of Racial Inequality in the United States* (New York: Rowman & Littlefield, 2003); Benjamin P. Bowser and Raymond G. Hunt, *Impacts of Racism on White Americans*, 2nd ed. (Thousand Oaks, CA: Sage Publications, 1996); Martin Bulmer and John Solomon, *Racism* (New York: Oxford University Press, 1999); Christopher Bates Doob, *Racism: An American Caludron*, 3rd ed. (New York: Longman, 1999); Joe Feagin and Melvin P. Sikes, *Living with Racism: The Black Middle-Class Experience* (Boston: Beacon Press, 1994); Andrew Hacker, *Two Nations: Black and White, Separate, Hostile, Unequal*, 2nd ed. (New York: Random House, 1995); Paula S. Rotenberg, *White Privilege: Essential Readings on the Other Side of Racism* (New York: Worth Publishers, 2002); Neil J. Smelser, William J. Wilson, and Faith Mitchell, eds., *America Becoming: Racial Trends and Their Consequences*, vol. 2 (Washington, DC: National Research Council, 2001).

ACKNOWLEDGMENTS

I would like to acknowledge my gratitude to a number of people who helped me complete this encyclopedia project. First of all, I am grateful to the contributors, especially the main contributors, who wrote one or two sets of sixteen to eighteen entries, for their commitment to and personal sacrifice in completing their essays. In particular, I feel obligated to express my deep gratitude to Mikaila Arthur and Dong Ho-Cho, who each wrote essays for thirty-six entries, or approximately seventy manuscript pages. Their contribution to the encyclopedia has been enormous. I also appreciate the gracious cooperation of the encyclopedia's contributors during the revision process.

I would like to thank the five members of the advisory board for reviewing the original list of entries. Their suggestions and additions have made the list of entries more comprehensive and balanced. In particular, I am grateful to Charles Jaret for his invaluable assistance in shaping the final list of entries, finding two contributors for me, writing essays on a set of entries, and supporting my career activities, both as my dissertation advisor at Georgia State University and as one of my closest friends.

I received the Queens College Presidential In-Residence Release-Time Award in the 2003 fall semester for my book project comparing Indian Hindus and Korean Protestants. But I spent much of the released time in completing this encyclopedia project. I express my sincere gratitude to the president of Queens College and the award committee for granting me release-time that was indispensable to completing the project.

Four students at Queens College—Keiko Hirota, Tiffany Vélez, Kelly Corcorom, and Soyoung Lee—aided me in creating the original list of entries, editing entries by contributors, collecting original documents, reviewing copy-edited manuscripts, and/or communicating with contributors through e-mail. Their aid was essential because the project was completed with no institutional monetary support.

I started this encyclopedia project three years ago when Wendi Schnaufer, acquisitions editor at Greenwood Press, encouraged me to initiate it. I wish to acknowledge that she helped me create the list of entries and collect primary documents, and she edited the final version of the entire manuscript. I also owe my gratitude to John Wagner, development editor at Greenwood Press, who edited every essay, took care of format and references, and arranged all entries in alphabetical order.

Finally, I need to acknowledge my heartfelt thanks to my wife, Young Oak, for spending a great deal of time and energy editing many essays, classifying entries, and reading page proofs. Moreover, her loving support and encouragement were essential to completing probably the most difficult project in my career in sociology.

INTRODUCTION

THE PREVALENCE OF RACISM IN EARLY U.S. HISTORY

African Americans

In its classic form, racism refers to the belief that on the basis of their genetic difference some racial groups are innately superior to other racial groups in intelligence, temperament, and attitudes. Racist ideology began to develop during the fifteenth century, the Age of Discovery, when white Europeans began encountering large numbers of non-white peoples in the New World, Asia, and Africa. In North America, South America, the Caribbean Islands, and South Africa, European colonial rulers established slavery as an effective way to control and exploit African workers on plantations. White racial supremacy was institutionalized with the establishment of the racial slavery system. To justify this system, European Christian settlers emphasized their cultural and moral superiority to African blacks. To perpetuate the system, Europeans tightly supervised and controlled the behaviors and movements of African slaves.

By far, the most rigid form of racial slavery developed in the American South. It has been noted that the absence of a substantial intermediate group of free people of color set the stage for a sharp dichotomy between whites and blacks in the antebellum South.[1] Meanwhile, less restrictive manumission requirements enabled more sizable and socially significant free colored groups to develop in the slave societies of South America, the Caribbean, and South Africa. The racial caste system characterized the form of slavery in the American South, but it did not fit the other three slave societies, where many free blacks married white settlers and thereby gained higher status.

Black slaves in the American South were liberated from slavery after the Civil War, in 1865. But the white violence and physical intimidation—especially with the rise of the Ku Klux Klan during Reconstruction (1865–1877)—effectively prevented black men from competing with white workers in the labor market. Thus, African Americans endured worse economic conditions during Reconstruction than they had under slavery. Moreover, the failure of Reconstruction in 1877 led to the establishment by Southern states of Jim Crow segregation laws to control the black threat to the economic and social advantages of white Americans. Jim Crow segregation laws and other statutes that disenfranchised blacks helped maintain the de facto racial caste system in the South until the early 1960s. In 1903, when black nationalist W.E.B. Du Bois wrote that "the problem of the twentieth century is the problem of the color line," he was mainly concerned about racial separation and inequality as it existed at the time in the United States. The United States preserved a very rigid racial caste system for more than three centuries, from the time of the agrarian economy of the eighteenth and nineteenth centuries into the industrial economy of the twentieth. Only the apartheid system established in South Africa in 1948 was more rigid than the racial caste system in the United States.

As Michael Roberts points out in his entry Race Riots in this encyclopedia, African Americans are mistakenly understood to be mainly responsible for race riots in the United States because race is usually ascribed to minority groups rather than to whites. However, race riots of the Jim Crow era were almost always white-on-black riots, that is, the attempts of "white mobs . . . to maintain the status quo of Jim Crow." Most of these riots occurred when white workers attacked black workers, who were often used by white business owners or managers as strikebreakers. Approximately 250 race riots occurred between 1898 (Wilmington, Delaware) and 1943 (Detroit), claiming the lives of approximately 4,300 blacks. Also, numerous minorities, mostly blacks, were victimized by lynching, another common form of white-on-minority violence. More than 3,500 instances of lynching occurred in the United States between 1885 and 1914.[2]

Native Americans

Other racial minority groups in the United States, while spared slavery, were subjected to other forms of racial prejudice and discrimination. Ethnocentrism, conquest, and racial domination-subordination strongly characterized the relationship between European whites and Native Americans. From the beginning of their encounters, European white Protestant settlers perceived Native Americans as uncivilized and intellectually and morally inferior. Plantation owners in the South used some Indians as slaves but preferred blacks to Indians because in the case of Indian servitude white physical security and control could not be guaranteed: Indian slaves could obtain help and support from their own, nearby peoples and territories.[3] White settlers initially tried to solve the "Indian problem" by killing them all.[4] When this failed, the U.S. government tried by force to remove Indian tribes from their native lands in the East and relocate them to unfamiliar and barren lands west of the Mississippi. In the process, many Indians died and most Indian tribes lost all or a portion of their lands. In the late nineteenth century, a change in government

Indian policy from separation to assimilation only ended up taking more lands from Indians, who were also left culturally uprooted.

Mexican Americans

Mexican Americans, who account for approximately 60 percent of the Latino population in the United States, also were initially absorbed into American society as a conquered group, a fact that set the stage for the colonial pattern of their race relations with American Anglos. Texas, which won its independence from Mexico in 1836, was annexed, over Mexican objections, by the United States in 1845. About half of the remaining Mexican territory, including California and New Mexico, came to the United States at the end of the Mexican-American War (1846–1848). Under the terms of the Treaty of Guadalupe Hidalgo, which ended the war, the U.S. government guaranteed the Mexican residents of these territories political and property rights and promised to safeguard their culture, especially by guaranteeing the right to use the Spanish language and to practice the Catholic religion. However, English gradually replaced Spanish as the standard language, and Anglos in the Mexican states began to develop and exhibit prejudice against Mexican Catholics. Moreover, Anglos gradually took the property of Mexicans through official and unofficial means and through fraud, thus transforming the Mexicans into a colonial work force.

By virtue of their in-between racial status, Mexican Americans and other Latinos have been treated better than African Americans in terms of selection of residential areas, public accommodation, and access to social-club membership. Yet, their physical and cultural differences and generally low economic status have also subjected them to prejudice, discrimination, police harassment, and racial violence. According to a study of a South Texas community, Anglos believed Mexicans to be unclean, prone to drunkenness and criminality, hostile, and unpredictable.[5] The lynching of Mexicans was common in the mining camps of Los Angeles in the nineteenth century.[6]

Asian Americans

The migration of Asians to the United States started after the California Gold Rush of 1848–1849, when Chinese farmers were recruited to California to work in mining and railroad construction. Initially, Californians praised Chinese immigrants as "hard-working" and "compliant." Yet, white workers came to believe that industrious Chinese immigrants were a threat to their employment; thus, prejudice against and stereotypes of Chinese immigrants quickly developed among whites. Lobbying by white workers, and the overall anti-Chinese sentiment on the West Coast, led to passage of the Chinese Exclusion Act in 1882, which prohibited the immigration of Chinese for more than sixty years.[7] The Chinese Exclusion Act is the only U.S. government measure to ban the immigration of a particular national-origin group.

Enforcement of the Chinese Exclusion Act led to the recruitment of Japanese and other Asian workers in Hawaii and California. But these groups also encountered a series of immigration restrictions by the U.S. government, which culminated in the National Origins Act of 1924.[8] Moreover, Asian immigrants were not allowed to be American citizens until 1952. In 1913, California passed the Alien Land Law to prohibit Japanese immigrants from owning farmland, and other West Coast states passed similar laws targeting Japanese and other immigrants. California and other states later used the law to prevent Asian immigrants from purchasing real estate. As noncitizen residents, Asian immigrants before World War II did not receive legal protection even if they were victimized by racial violence. Finally, all Japanese Americans living on the West Coast (excluding Hawaii), including native-born citizens, were incarcerated in internment camps during World War II for "security" reasons. Because of their incarceration, innocent Japanese Americans in relocation camps incurred not only monetary and property losses but also psychological damage.

White Immigrant Groups

Catholic, Jewish, and Eastern Orthodox Americans of heavily eastern and southern European ancestry have today been incorporated into mainstream white American society. But, when large numbers of these non-Protestant European immigrants arrived in the United States at the end of the nineteenth and beginning of the twentieth century, they were considered physically different from native-born Anglos and thus were subjected to prejudice, discrimination, and racial violence.[9] Southern Italians suffered not only antagonism directed against Catholics in general but also severe anti-Italian sentiments because of their peasant background. Italians suffered physical violence as well as negative images and stereotypes. Killings and lynchings of Italian immigrants occurred in the United States, especially in the South, between 1890 and 1910.[10] Nicola Sacco and Bartolomeo Vanzetti, two Italian immigrants, were charged with and found guilty of murder and armed robbery and executed in 1927, even though numerous witnesses testified that they were not involed in the crime.

For many centuries, Jews suffered negative stereotypes, prejudice, and discrimination, including legal discrimination, in European Christian countries. Although American Jews fared better than European Jews in terms of legal discrimination, they also encountered anti-Semitism in different forms.[11] Anti-Semitism in the United States increased in the 1880s with the influx of eastern European Jewish immigrants and reached its high point in the 1920s and the 1930s. The Ku Klux Klan and some white industrialists, such as Henry Ford, filled the media with anti-Semitic propaganda, spreading the idea of a "world Jewish conspiracy."[12] Jews were often denied accommodation at hotels and admission to social clubs. As the number of Jewish students in prestigious universities and professional schools increased, the latter took measures to restrict Jewish admissions. Jewish Americans were also subjected to discrimination in professional occupations, especially in law, medicine, and academia.

Nativist reactions to and prejudice against Jewish, Catholic, and Asian immigrants in the United States in the first decade of the twentieth century contributed to the development of "biological racism," a racist ideology that sees so-called Nordic races as genetically—and therefore also intellectually and morally—superior to other races, including eastern and southern Europeans, African Americans, Mexicans, and Asians.[13] Such well-known psychologists as Lewis Terman and C. W. Gould argued that based on scores of IQ tests, eastern and southern European immigrants and African Americans had lower levels of intellectual ability but tended to "outbreed" people of "Nordic" races. Their arguments supported the eugenics movement, which emerged after World War I. These ideas also contributed to the passage of discriminatory immigration laws in the early 1920s, which severely reduced immigration from eastern and southern European countries and entirely banned Asian immigration.

THE PERSISTENCE OF RACISM IN THE POST–CIVIL RIGHTS ERA

The passage of civil rights laws, including affirmative action programs, in the 1960s may lead many people to believe that racism is no longer an important factor for the adjustment of minorities in the twenty-first century. The ethnic and racial diversities created by the influx of Third World immigrants, the increasing emphasis on multiculturalism by government and schools, and the increase in intermarriages since the early 1970s may further enhance the belief about the insignificance of racism in contemporary American life. Jews, Italians, and other turn-of-the-century white immigrant groups have been incorporated into mainstream America.[14] However, the social-science literature accumulated since the 1980s reveals that African Americans still suffer high levels of racial prejudice and discrimination in all aspects of their lives, and other nonwhite minority groups also experience different forms of unequal treatment because of their nonwhite status.[15] Based on their findings, the authors of these studies have suggested that the color line continues to divide American society in the twenty-first century, just as it did in the twentieth.

Although legal discrimination against African Americans ended with the civil rights legislation of the early 1960s, enough evidence exists to support the view that African Americans still have to deal with racism—both individual and institutional—on a daily basis. Many people tend to believe that racial prejudice and discrimination are problems confronted only by poor blacks concentrated in inner-city neighborhoods and that well-educated, middle-class blacks do not have to deal with it. However, based on personal interviews with middle-class blacks, two social scientists, Joe Feagin and Melvin Sikes, have challenged this view. They conclude that "racism is the everyday experience" for middle-class blacks as well and that experiences with serious racial discrimination "have a cumulative impact on particular individuals, their families, and their communities."[16] Summing up his view of white-black separation in contemporary America, political scientist Andrew Hacker similarly commented that "America's version of apartheid, while lacking overt legal sanction, comes closest to the system even now being overturned in the land of its invention" (South Africa).[17]

Sociological studies show that the high level of segregation for African Americans has not been moderated since the 1970s.[18] Housing discrimination by real estate agents, commercial banks, and local white community leaders, and the racial gap in socioeconomic status are partly responsible for what has been called "American apartheid."[19] But racial prejudice against blacks on the part of white Americans is mainly responsible for racial segregation. Residential isolation, in turn, further enhances antiblack racial prejudice and creates further socioeconomic disadvantages for African Americans.[20] Segregated black neighborhoods are characterized by all kinds of social ills, such as high poverty and unemployment rates, high mortality and crime rates, and poor educational and health-care facilities.

Since the 1978 publication of his controversial book, *Declining Significance of Race*, William Wilson has paid keen attention to the class division within the African American community and focused on poverty among residents in inner-city black neighborhoods.[21] He has argued that the disappearance of blue-collar jobs from black neighborhoods, which is a result of deindustrialization rather than racism, is the main cause of poverty among inner-city black residents. However, various studies reveal that regardless of their class background, blacks experience racial discrimination in the labor market.

No doubt, deindustrialization, along with the poor school performance overall of black children, is an important contributing factor to the exceptionally high unemployment and poverty rates among young blacks. But the preference of employers for Latino legal and illegal workers over black workers is also responsible for the difficulty young blacks have finding employment. Studies by Roger Waldinger and Michael Richter have found that regardless of industry, employers and managers prefer Latino immigrants to blacks because they perceive the former to be more "subservient" and "docile."[22] Moreover, Feagin and Sikes have shown that black professionals also encounter discrimination in finding employment and in salaries, evaluations, and promotions.[23] According to an analysis of census data by Hacker, black men with a bachelor's degree earned $764 for every $1,000 earned by their white counterparts.[24] It can be argued that the racial gap in earnings is caused mainly by racial discrimination.

The influx of immigrants from the Caribbean Islands since the 1970s has contributed to a phenomenal increase in the black immigrant population.[25] Unlike African Americans whose ancestors were brought to the United States by force for economic exploitation, Caribbean immigrants are voluntary migrants who came here for better economic and educational opportunities. An interesting question is: will the adaptation of Caribbean black immigrants and their descendants follow the pattern taken by voluntary minority groups or by colonial minority groups?[26] Mary Waters' 1999 study of Caribbean immigrants in New York City reveals that the children of lower-class immigrants assimilate quickly, becoming African American children.[27] This finding indicates the importance of race as well as class for the racialization of Caribbean immigrants.

Although Latinos in the United States are currently better accepted than African Americans, they are also subjected to prejudice, stereotypes, and discrimination. Their in-between physical characteristics and their generally lower economic class and immigrant backgrounds enhance the negative image of Latinos. The influx of legal and illegal Mexicans immigrants during recent years has led to stereotypes of native-born Mexican Americans as undocumented residents and manual laborers.[28] Because of a long history of Anglo-Mexican racial stratification, Mexicans in Texas, in particular, still experience semi-involuntary segregation in using public facilities and racial harassment by the police similar to that experienced by African Americans.[29] Probably because of their darker skin, Puerto Ricans experience residential segregation from white Americans that is more similar to that of African Americans than to other Latino groups. Moreover, Puerto Ricans, regardless of generational status, exhibit low educational and occupational levels and a high poverty rate comparable to African Americans.

Most Asian-American groups currently have a higher socioeconomic status than whites.[30] Moreover, approximately 40 percent of U.S.-born Asian Americans engage in intermarriages, in most cases with white partners.[31] These facts have led some social scientists to predict that Asian Americans are likely to be incorporated into white society in the near future.[32] However, contemporary Asian immigrants are socio-economically polarized, with one group representing professional and business classes and the other group consisting of poor refugees from Indochina and working-class migrants.[33] Moreover, the social-science literature on Asian Americans indicates that not only Asian immigrants but also U.S.-born Asian Americans encounter racial violence, racial discrimination, and rejection because of their nonwhite racial characteristics. In the past two decades, dozens of incidents of racial violence against Asian Americans have occurred in many U.S. cities, killing a dozen people. Studies based on personal interviews with or personal narratives by second-generation Asian Americans reveal that most informants experienced rejection, with such taunts as "Go back to your country" or "What country are you from?"[34] Third- and fourth-generation white Americans have an option to choose their ethnic identity or not, because they are accepted as full American citizens.[35] However, one ethnographic study showed that society forces most third- or fourth-generation Japanese and Chinese Americans to accept their ethnic and racial identities, even though they, like multigeneration white Americans, are thoroughly acculturated to American society.[36]

The influx of large numbers of Latino, Caribbean, and Asian immigrants into a predominantly white society since the 1970s has increased anti-immigrant prejudice and actions, including a resurgence of white supremacist groups.[37] In particular, Mexican immigrants, accounting for about one-fifth of total immigrants, have been subjected to nativist attacks for serving the interest of their homeland, not being assimilable, and taking welfare monies.[38] In the late 1980s and early 1990s, California, Florida, and other states passed referenda making English the standard language, which partly reflects anti-immigrant attitudes toward Latino immigrants. In 1994, Californians also passed Proposition 187, which was intended to make the children of illegal residents ineligible for free medical treatment and education. Although the proposition was invalidated, it targeted mainly Mexican illegal residents.

Although the separation of church and state and the emphasis on religious pluralism have helped many ethnic groups preserve their ethnic traditions through the practice of religious faith and rituals, white racism and Protestantism, as the foundational elements of American culture, have served each other since the colonial era (see the entry Religion and Racism, by Khyati Josh). At the end of the nineteenth and beginning of the twentieth century, Jewish and Catholic immigrants from eastern and southern Europe suffered prejudice and racial discrimination by native Protestants. At the beginning of the twenty-first century, Muslim, Sikh, and Hindu immigrants from South Asia and the Middle East are experiencing prejudice and discrimination by white Christians, especially by white evangelical Protestants. As documented in detail by Bozorgmehr and Bakalian in this encyclopedia, many Middle Eastern and South Asian Muslims and Sikhs have been subjected to two types of discrimination and physical violence in the post–September 11 era. First, they have become targets of hate crimes and bias incidents, such as arson, assaults, and shootings perpetrated by ordinary American citizens. Second, they have been subjected to supervision, detentions, and other forms of civil rights violations carried out by the U.S. government at the federal and local levels. Although Jewish Americans have successfully assimilated into white society, they are not safe from hate crimes either. Several white supremacist organizations, such as the Ku Klux Klan, the Christian Identity Movement, and skinheads, target Jews as well as other racial minority groups.[39]

CONTEMPORARY FORMS OF RACISM

To better understand the contemporary forms of racism in the United States, we need to make a series of distinctions among different types of racism. Until the 1960s, social scientists focused on individual racism, the belief that some racial groups are morally, intellectually, or culturally superior to other races. However, following the path-breaking book *Black Power* (1967) by Stokely Carmichael and Charles Hamilton, two black-nationalist leaders, social scientists now usually distinguish between individual racism and institutional racism. Institutional racism means that social institutions are arranged in such a way that they are disadvantageous to minority racial groups.[40] According to one source, "Institutional racism, unlike individual racism, is not an immediate action but the legacy of a past racist behavioral pattern."[41] Specifically, institutional racism refers to "the discriminatory racial practices built into such prominent structures as the political, economic, and educational system."

Racial minority groups in the United States, especially African Americans in the post–civil rights era, suffer more from institutional racism than from individual racism. As shown by Francois Pierre-Louis in his essay on this topic (Institutional Racism) in this encyclopedia, there are many examples of institutional racism, such as cultural biases in intelligence tests and the low quality of schools in inner-city black neighborhoods that keep children of lower-income black families at a disadvantage. The 1973 Rockefeller Drug Laws in New York state are another salient example of institutional racism. The laws have imposed severe penalties on those who have sold or possessed narcotic drugs and crack cocaine, and as a result of these laws, the state's prison population has increased rapidly. Most of the prisoners are African American men because users of crack cocaine are heavily concentrated in this population.[42]

Social scientists also tend to divide individual racism into two types: biological racism and symbolic racism.[43] As previously noted, biological racism, which emphasizes the intellectual superiority of northwestern Europeans, was popular in the first decade of the twentieth century. By contrast, symbolic racism focuses on a racial minority group's purported behavioral deficiencies, such as being welfare dependent, lazy, and criminally oriented, which conflict with traditional American values such as hard work and self-reliance.[44] Individual racism against minority groups in the post–civil rights period usually takes the form of symbolic racism. That is, white Americans generally attribute the lower socioeconomic status and poverty of African Americans and other minority groups to the latter's lack of motivation and work ethic, and to their unstable families. Most white Americans seem to accept the culture-of-poverty thesis endorsed by conservative scholars and policymakers.

Given the contemporary knowledge of human development, few people could persuasively argue for the genetic basis of the intellectual superiority of particular racial groups. Nevertheless, biological racism has reemerged among academics in contemporary America. In his controversial 1969 article, Arthur Jensen, an educational psychologist, argued that Asians have the highest level of cognitive abilities, blacks have the lowest, and whites are in the middle, and that these differences were largely determined by biology. Based on his findings, Jensen suggested that the Head Start program that was created at that time to boost the IQ of minority children would have a limited impact. About twenty-five years later, Richard Herrnstein and Charles Murray made a similar argument for biologically determined differences in cognitive abilities among Asians, whites, and blacks.[45] They further claimed that the differences in the cognitive abilities account for some of the social stratification among the three groups.

Joel Kovel made a distinction between dominative racism and aversive racism.[46] This distinction is also of great use for understanding the nature of racial separation in contemporary America. While dominative racism involves unfair treatment of minority members, "aversive racism" refers to the tendency to try to avoid contact with blacks and other minority members. This form of racism is the main cause of the high level of residential segregation of African Americans from white Americans and the lack of white-black social interactions at the personal level. Since the unwillingness of white Americans to contact minority members at the personal and neighborhood levels does not involve civil rights violations, the government cannot use any short-term measures to facilitate interracial friendship and dating.

Finally, most contemporary Americans can be said to commit color-blind racism, which is a form of racism that serves to maintain the racial dominance of whites by ignoring the continuing effects of historical prejudice on the life chances of minority members.[47] Many whites believe that because minority members have enjoyed equal opportunity since the enforcement of the civil rights laws the racial category should no longer be considered as a factor in college admission or employment. They claim that the United States should be a color-blind society that gives reward only based on individual merits. Those who embrace color-blind racism argue that race-based affirmative action programs are not only unfair to white Americans, they are also demeaning to minority members of society because they imply that minorities are not equal to white Americans. The main problem with their argument is that they ignore how minorities' opportunities for socioeconomic attainment have been affected by past and current racial discrimination.

Color-blind racism can be said to be "unintentional racism" in that some white Americans do not pay attention to the current status of racial inequality and the special needs of American society's minority members mainly because they are ignorant of the lingering effects of past racial discrimination and of different forms of current racial discrimination. But many other white conservatives intentionally avoid discussion of racial issues and vaguely emphasize meritocracy to protect their racial privileges.

The "California Ballot Initiative to Ban Racial Data," or California Ballot Proposition 54, was the most exemplary public expression of color-blind racism. This proposition, made by University of California regent Ward Connerly in 2002, would have prohibited state and local governments in California from classifying students, contractors, or employees by race, ethnicity, or national origin. This initiative was an effort to block researchers' and policymakers' access to racial data in employment, public education, and governmental contracts. California voters defeated the proposition in October 2003. If it had been approved, researchers and policymakers would not have information about how underrepresented blacks or Latinos are, for example, in the Los Angeles Police Department or in the student body of the University of California system.

Opponents of racial data collection argue that any kind of racial classification is arbitrary because the human species is biologically and anatomically diverse, and that it "foments separatist racial identities and promotes practices of ingroup/outgroup inclusion and exclusion."[48] But the ulterior motivation of many of the opponents is to control information about the levels of direct and indirect racial discrimination taking place in employment, education, heath care, law enforcement, and other public settings. Racial classification in public documents, however arbitrary it may be, is necessary to understanding the level and nature of racial discrimination and racial inequality, because "race serves as a basis for the distribution of social privileges and resources."[49]

NOTES

1. George Frederickson, *White Supremacy: A Comparative Study of American and South African History* (New York: Oxford University Press, 1981).

2. Terry Ann Knopf, *Rumors, Race and Riots* (New Brunswick, NJ: Transaction Books, 1975).

3. Pierre van den Berghe, *The Ethnic Phenomenon* (New York: Elsevier, 1981).

4. Russell Thornton, *American Indian Holocaust Survival: A Population History since 1492* (Norman: University of Oklahoma Press, 1987).

5. Ozie G. Simmons, "The Mutual Image and Expectations of Anglo-Americans and Mexican-Americans," in *Chicanos: Social and Psychological Perspectives,* ed. Nathaniel N. Wagner and Marsha J. Haug (St. Louis, MO: Mosby, 1971).

6. Carey McWilliams, *North from Mexico: The Spanish-Speaking People of the United States* (New York: Greenwood Press, 1968).

7. Alexander Saxton, *The Indispensable Enemy: The Labor and the Anti-Chinese Movement in California* (Berkeley, CA: University of California Press, 1971); Ronald

Takaki, *Strangers from a Different Shore: A History of Asian Americans* (Boston: Little, Brown, 1989).

8. Bill Ong Hing, *Making and Remaking of Asian America through Immigration Policy* (Stanford, CA: Stanford University Press, 1993).

9. Noel Ignatiev, *How the Irish Became White* (New York: Routledge, 1995).

10. Richard Gambino, *Vendetta* (Garden City, NY: Doubleday, 1977).

11. Frederic Cople Jaher, *A Scapegoat in the New Wilderness: The Origins and Rise of Anti-Semitism in America* (Cambridge, MA: Harvard University Press, 1994); Louise A. Mayo, *The Ambivalent Image: Nineteenth-Century America's Perception of the Jew* (Rutherford, NJ: Fairleigh Dickenson University Press, 1988); Stephen L. Slavin and Mary A. Pratt, *The Einstein Syndrome: Corporate Anti-Semitism in America Today* (New York: World Publishers, 1982).

12. Martin Marger, *Race and Ethnic Relations: American and Global Perspectives*, 5th ed. (Belmont, CA: Wadsworth, 2000).

13. Madison Grant, *The Passing of the Great Race* (New York: Charles Scribner's Sons, 1916); John Higham, *Strangers in the Land* (New York: Atheneum, 1955).

14. Nancy Foner, *From Ellis Island to J.F.K. Airport: Immigrants to New York City* (New Haven, CT: Yale University Press, 2001); Ignatiev, *How the Irish Became White*.

15. Benjamin P. Bowser and Raymond G. Hunt, *Impacts of Racism on White Americans*, 2nd ed. (Thousand Oaks, CA: Sage Publications, 1996); Joe Feagin, "The Continuing Significance of Race: Anti-Black Discrimination in Public Places," *American Sociological Review* 56 (1991): 101–116; Joe R. Feagin and Karyn D. McKinney, *The Many Costs of Racism* (Lanham, MD: Rowman & Littlefield, 2003); Joe Feagin and Melvin P. Sikes, *Living with Racism: The Black Middle-Class Experience* (Boston: Beacon Press, 1994); Andrew Hacker, *Two Nations: Black and White, Separate, Hostile, Unequal*, 2nd ed. (New York: Random House, 1995); Douglas S. Massey and Nancy Denton, *American Apartheid: Segregation and the Making of the Underclass* (Cambridge, MA: Harvard University Press, 1993); Paula S. Rotenberg, *White Privilege: Essential Readings on the Other Side of Racism* (New York: Worth Publishers, 2002); Howard Schuman, Charlotte Steeh, Lawrence Bobo, and Maria Krysan, *Racial Attitudes in America: Trends and Interpretations*, rev. ed. (Cambridge, MA: Harvard University Press, 1997); Stephen Steinberg, *The Ethnic Myth: Race, Ethnicity, and Class in America*, 2nd ed. (Boston: Beacon Press, 1988); Roger Waldinger, *Still the Promised City? African Americans and New Immigrants in Postindustrial New York* (Cambridge, MA: Harvard University Press, 1996); Cornel West, *Race Matters* (New York: Vintage Books, 1994).

16. Feagin and Sikes, *Living with Racism*, 15–16.

17. Hacker, *Two Nations*, 4.

18. Reynolds Farley, Charlotte Steeh, Maria Krysan, Tara Jackson, and Keith Reeves, "Stereotypes and Segregation: Neighborhoods in the Detroit Area," *American Journal of Sociology* 100 (1994): 750–780; Massey and Denton, *American Apartheid*.

19. Massey and Denton, *American Apartheid*.

20. Ibid.

21. William Wilson, *The Declining Significance of Race* (Chicago: University of Chicago Press, 1978); Ibid., *The Truly Disadvantaged: The Inner City, the Underclass, and Public Policy* (Chicago: University of Chicago Press, 1987); Ibid., *When Work Disappears: The World of the New Urban Poor* (New York: Knopf, 1996).

22. Waldinger, *Still the Promised City*; Roger Waldinger and Michael I. Richter, *How the Other Half Works: Immigration and the Social Organization of Race* (Berkeley: University of California Press, 2003).

23. Feagin and Sikes, *Living with Racism*.

24. Hacker, *Two Nations*, 101.

25. Philip Kasinitz, *Caribbean New York: Black Immigrants and the Politics of Race* (Ithaca, NY: Cornell University Press, 1992); Mary Waters, *Black Identities: West Indian Immigrant Dreams and American Realities* (New York: Russell Sage Foundation, 1999).

26. Robert Blauner, *Racial Oppression in America* (New York: Harper and Row, 1972); John Ogbu, "Immigrant and Involuntary Minorities in Comparative Perspective," in *Minority Status and Schooling: A Comparative Study of Immigrant and Involuntary Minorities*, ed. Margaret Gibson and John Ogbu (New York: Garland Publishing, 1991).

27. Waters, *Black Identities*.

28. Min Zhou, "The Changing Face of America: Immigration, Race/Ethnicity, and Social Mobility," in *Mass Migration to the United States: Classical and Contemporary Periods*, ed. Pyong Gap Min (Walnut Creek, CA: AltaMira Press, 2002), 82.

29. Leo Grebler, Joan W. Moor, and Ralph C. Guzman, *The Mexican-American People: The Nation's Second Largest Minority* (New York: Free Press, 1970).

30. Arthur Sakamoto and Chomghwan Kim, "The Increasing Significance of Class, the Declining Significance of Race, and Wilson's Hypothesis," *Asian American Policy Issue* 12 (2003): 19–41; Arthur Sakamoto, Jeng Liu, and Jessie Tzeng, "The Declining Significance of Race among Chinese and Japanese American Men," *Research in Social Stratification and Mobility* 16 (1998):225–246.

31. Sharon Lee and Marilyn Fernandez, "Trends in Asian American Racial/Ethnic Inter-Marriage: A Comparison of 1980 and 1990 Census Data," *Sociological Perspectives* 41 (1998): 323–342.

32. Herbert Gans, "The Possibility of a New Racial Hierarchy in the Twentieth-First Century United States," in *The Cultural Territories of Race: Black and White Boundaries*, ed. Mechele Lamont (Chicago: University of Chicago Press, 1999).

33. Pyong Gap Min, "An Overview of Asian Americans" in *Asian American: Contemporary Trends and Issues* (Thousand Oaks, CA: Sage Publications, 1995).

34. Pyong Gap Min and Rose Kim, eds., *Struggle for Ethnic Identity: Narratives by Asian American Professionals* (Walnut Creek, CA: AltaMira Press, 1999); Pyong Gap Min, *The Second Generation: Ethnic Identity among Asian Americans* (Walnut Creek, CA: AltaMira Press, 2002).

35. Mary Waters, *Ethnic Options: Choosing Identities in America* (Berkeley: University of California Press, 1990).

36. Mia Tuan, *Forever Foreigners or Honorary Whites? The Asian Ethnic Experience Today* (New Brunswick, NJ: Rutgers University Press, 1999).

37. Charles Jaret, "Troubled by Newcomers: Anti-immigrant Attitudes and Action During Two Eras of Mass Immigration to the United States," *Journal of American Ethnic History* 18 (1999): 9–39.

38. Richard D. Lamm and Gary Imhoff, *The Immigration Time Bomb: The Fragmenting of America* (New York: Truman Talley, Dutton, 1985).

39. Amy Ferber, *White Man Falling: Race, Gender, and White Supremacy* (New York: Rowman & Littlefield, 1998); Slavin and Pratt, *The Einstein Syndrome*.

40. Christopher Bates Doob, *Racism: An American Cauldron*, 3rd ed. (New York: Longman), 8; Joe Feagin, *Discrimination, American Style* (Englewood, NJ: Prentice Hall, 1978); Feagin and Sikes, *Living with Racism*, 3; Thomas Pettigrew, ed., *Racial Discrimination in the United States* (New York: Harper and Row, 1975), x.

41. Doob, *Racism*, 8.

42. Aaron Wilson, "Rockefeller Drug Laws Information Sheet," Partnership for Responsible Drug Information, 2000.

43. Doob, *Racism*, 15; Hacker, *Two Nations*, 23–27; David Sears, "Symbolic Racism,"

in *Eliminating Racism: Profiles in Controversy*, ed. Phyllis Katz and Dalmas Taylor (New York: Plenum, 1988).

44. Sears, "Symbolic Racism."

45. Richard J. Herrnstein and Charles Murray, *The Bell Curve: Intelligence and Class Structure in American Life* (New York: Free Press, 1994).

46. Joel Kovel, *White Racism: A Psychohistory* (New York: Pantheon, 1970).

47. Eduardo Bonilla-Silva, *Racism without Racists: Color-Blind Racism and the Persistence of Racial Inequality in the United States* (New York: Rowman & Littlefield, 2003).

48. Yehudi Webster, "Racial Classification: A Wrong Turn," *Footnotes* 31 (January 2003): 8–9.

49. American Sociological Association, "The ASA Statement on the Importance of Collecting Data and Doing Social Science Research on Race," American Sociological Association, February 2002.

LIST OF EDITORS, ADVISORY BOARD MEMBERS, AND CONTRIBUTORS

EDITOR

Pyong Gap Min

Professor
Queens College and CUNY Graduate Center

ADVISORY BOARD MEMBERS

Steven Gold

Professor and the Acting Chair
Department of Sociology
Michigan State University

Ramon Gutierrez

Professor and Endowed Chair
Ethnic Studies Department
University of California at San Diego

Charles Jaret

Professor
Department of Sociology
Georgia State University

Ronald Taylor

Professor
Department of Sociology
Vice Provost, Multicultural and International Affairs
University of Connecticut

Min Zhou

Professor
Department of Sociology
Chair, Asian American Studies Interdepartmental Degree Program
University of California at Los Angeles

MAIN CONTRIBUTORS

Each main contributor wrote a series of at least 14 entries of varying lengths, including one long essay on a broad topic of special significance. Each contributor's long essay topic is listed below.

Daisuke Akiba

Assistant Professor
Elementary and Early Childhood Education
Queens College
Japanese American Internment

Mikaila Mariel Lemonik Arthur

Doctoral Student
Department of Sociology
New York University
Anti-Semitism in the United States

Anny Bakalian

Associate Director
The Middle East and Middle Eastern American Studies Center
September 11th (2001) Terrorism, Discriminatory Reactions to

Sandra L. Barnes

Assistant Professor
Department of Sociology
Purdue University
Culture of Poverty Thesis

Mehdi Bozorgmehr

Associate Professor
Co-Director, The Middle East and Middle Eastern American Studies Center
Hunter College and the Graduate Center of City University of New York (CUNY)
September 11th (2001) Terrorism, Discriminatory Reactions to

Dong-Ho Cho

Adjunct Professor
Department of Sociology
Queens College of CUNY
Civil Rights Movement

Tracy Chu

Doctoral Student
Sociology Program
The Graduate Center of CUNY
Colonized (Involuntary) vs. Immigrant (Voluntary) Minorities

John Eterno

Assistant Professor
Department of Criminal Justice
Molloy College
White Supremacist Movement in the United States

Carmenza Gallo

Associate Professor
Department of Sociology
Queens College of CUNY
The Declining Significance of Race Debate

Kenneth J. Guest

Assistant Professor
Department of Sociology and Anthropology
Baruch College of CUNY
Chinese Exclusion Act of 1882

Tarry Hum

Assistant Professor
Department of Urban Studies
Queens College of CUNY
Black Nationalist Movement

Charles Jaret

Professor
Department of Sociology
Georgia State University
Housing Discrimination

Khyati Joshi

Assistant Professor
School of Education

Fairleigh Dickenson University
Multiculturalism

Kwang Chung Kim

Emeritus Professor
Department of Sociology and Anthropology
Western Illinois University
Immigration Act of 1965

Shin Kim

Professor Emeritus
Department of Economics
Chicago State University
Immigration Act of 1965

Heon Cheol Lee

Associate Professor
Department of Sociology
University of North Carolina at Ashvillle
Nativism and the Anti-Immigrant Movements

Rebekah Lee

Assistant Professor
Department of Sociology
University of London
Derogatory Terms

Romney S. Norwood

Assistant Professor
Department of Sociology
Georgia State University
Residential Segregation

Sookhee Oh

Doctoral Student
Milano Graduate School of Management and Urban Policy
New School University
Jim Crow Laws

Francois Pierre-Louis

Assistant Professor
Department of Political Science
Queens College
Institutional Racism

Etsuko Maruoka-Ng

Doctoral Student
Department of Sociology
State University of New York (SUNY)—Stony Brook

Victoria Pitts

Associate Professor
Department of Sociology
Queens College of CUNY

Tiffany Vélez

Graduate Student
Department of Speech Pathology
Queens College

Barbara J. Webb

Associate Professor
Department of English Literature
Hunter College and the Graduate Center of CUNY

CHRONOLOGY OF RACE AND RACISM IN THE UNITED STATES

1790	Congress passes the Naturalization Act establishing the first rules and procedures to be used in granting citizens to immigrants
1800	Gabriel Prosser leads slave uprising in Virginia
1820	Congress enacts the Missouri Compromise by admitting Missouri as a slave state but prohibiting slavery in Louisiana Purchase territories north of Missouri's southern boundary
1822	Denmark Vesey leads a slave insurrection in Charleston, South Carolina
1824	Bureau of Indian Affairs (BIA) is created as part of the U.S. War Department to manage encounters and interactions with Native Americans
1831	In *Cherokee Nation v. Georgia*, the U.S. Supreme Court declares Georgia laws confiscating Cherokee lands unconstitutional
1831	Nat Turner leads a slavery uprising in Virginia
1833	American Anti-Slavery Society is formed in Philadelphia
1835	Publication of Alexis de Tocqueville's *Democracy in America*, an analysis of the nature of American democracy in the early nineteenth century
1836	New Philadelphia, the earliest known black town, is established in Pike County, Illinois
1838–1839	Trail of Tears: U.S. government forcibly removes the Cherokee from their lands in Georgia to Oklahoma
1845	Publication of the *Narrative of the Life of Frederick Douglass*, the autobiography of ex-slave abolitionist Frederick Douglass

1845	Term *Manifest Destiny* is coined by journalist John L. O'Sullivan in the July–August edition of the *United States Magazine and Democratic Review*
1845	United States annexes Texas
1848	Signing of the Treaty of Guadalupe Hidalgo, ending the Mexican-American War
1849	Bureau of Indian Affairs (BIA) is transferred to the U.S. Department of the Interior
1850	Congress passes a new Fugitive Slave Act as part of the Compromise of 1850
1850	Know-Nothing Party, a nativist, anti-immigrant political party, is founded
1852	Publication of Harriet Beecher Stowe's novel *Uncle Tom's Cabin*
1852	California enacts the Foreign Miners License Tax to protect white miners from foreign competition, especially from Chinese immigrants
1854	Kansas-Nebraska Act repeals the Missouri Compromise and opens all territories to the possibility of slavery
1857	In the Dred Scott Decision, the U.S. Supreme Court strikes down the Missouri Compromise (1820), declaring that Congress has no power to prohibit slavery
1859	Abolitionist John Brown raids the federal arsenal at Harper's Ferry, Virginia, in an effort to initiate a slave uprising
1862	President Abraham Lincoln issues the Emancipation Proclamation
1863	Believing they are being forced to fight and die for African Americans, with whom they are in competition for jobs, Irish immigrants riot against the Civil War draft in New York City
1865	Thirteenth Amendment is ratified, abolishing slavery in the United States
1865	Freedmen's Bureau is established by Congress to oversee all matters relating to war refugees and freed slaves
1865	Ku Klux Klan is founded in Tennessee
1866	Race riots erupt in Memphis, Tennessee, when white mobs attack African American soldiers and residents
1868	Fourteenth Amendment is ratified, requiring equal protection under the law for all citizens
1871	Anti-Chinese race riot erupts in Los Angeles after a white man is accidentally killed while trying to stop a dispute between two Chinese men
1877	To settle the disputed presidential election of 1876, the Democrats concede victory to Republican Rutherford B. Hayes, who

in turn withdraws federal troops from the South, thereby allowing white governments to overturn the political and social advances made by blacks during Reconstruction

1877–1950s   Southern states and municipalities pass and enforce a series of enactments known as Jim Crow Laws, which are designed to create and maintain racial segregation and to discriminate against blacks

1882   Congress passes the Chinese Exclusion Act, which prohibits Chinese laborers from entering the United States and denies naturalized citizenship to Chinese already in the country

1884   Publican of Mark Twain's novel *Adventures of Huckleberry Finn*

1887   Congress passes the Indian Allotment Act, known as the Dawes Act, to distribute parcels of tribal land to each tribal member or family on the reservation

1890   U.S. troops massacre Lakota Sioux Indians at Wounded Knee, South Dakota

1894   Immigration Restriction League is founded in Boston to protect the American way of life from and influx of "undesirable immigrants," mainly Jews and Catholics from southern and eastern Europe

1896   In *Plessy v. Fergusson*, the U.S. Supreme Court declares the separate but equal doctrine constitutional

1898   United States annexes Hawaii

1903   Publication of W.E.B. Du Bois's classic work, *The Souls of Black Folk*

1905   Asiatic Exclusion League, originally called the Japanese and Korean Exclusion League, is formed by white nativist labor unions

1905   Niagara Movement is founded by W.E.B. Du Bois to advocate full civil rights and full manhood suffrage for African Americans

1906   San Francisco School Board orders the segregation of Japanese and Korean children in the city's schools

1907   Bellingham Riots begin when a mob of white men, who fear the loss of their jobs to immigrants, attacks a Hindu community in Bellingham, Washington

1908   Japan accepts the so-called Gentlemen's Agreement, agreeing to issue no passports for immigration to the United States except to relatives of Japanese workers already in the country

1909   National Association for the Advancement of Colored People (NAACP) is founded by an interracial group of citizens in Springfield, Illinois

1911   Dillingham Report on immigration to the United States is issued by the U.S. Commission on Immigration, a congressional commission chaired by Senator William P. Dillingham

1913	Alien Land Law is passed in California to prevent immigrants from owning or leasing land for more than three years
1913	Anti-Defamation League of B'nai Brith is founded to combat prejudice, discrimination, and violence against Jews
1915	Release of D. W. Griffith's film, *Birth of a Nation*, a racist view of U.S. history that is instrumental in the revival of the Ku Klux Klan
1915	Leo Frank, a Jew convicted of murdering a girl in Georgia in 1913, is abducted from prison and lynched, despite the existence of evidence that casts doubt on his guilt
1915	Ku Klux Klan is refounded in Georgia by William J. Simmons
1916	New York chapter of the Universal Negro Improvement Association (UNIA) is established by organization founder Marcus Garvey
1916	Publication of Madison Grant's widely read *The Passing of the Great Race*, which argues that race is a primary factor in differences in intelligence, work ethic, and social and psychological characteristics
1917	Congress prohibits all immigration from the "Asiatic Barred Zone," which includes various parts of Asia and the Middle East
1917	Competition for jobs leads to a deadly white-on-black race riot in St. Louis, Missouri
1920	American Civil Liberties Union (ACLU) is established
1922	In *Ozawa v. United States*, the U.S. Supreme Court declares that a Japanese person is not eligible for citizenship in the United States
1923	In *United States v. Thind*, the U.S. Supreme Court denies citizenship to Asian Indian immigrants
1924	Congress passes the National Origins Act, severely restricting the flow of immigrants to the United States
1924	Congress passes the Indian Citizenship Act, granting U.S. citizenship to all Native Americans who are not already citizens under some other law or treaty
1927	Execution of Nicola Sacco and Bartolomeo Vanzetti, two Italian American anarchists convicted, on largely circumstantial evidence, of two murders committed during a robbery in 1920
1928	Meriam Report on Indian reservations is issued to the Secretary of the Interior
1929	League of United Latin American Citizens (LULAC) is founded to advocate for Hispanic civil rights
1930	Japanese American Citizens League (JACL) is founded to protect the civil rights of Japanese and other Asian Americans
1930	Nation of Islam (Black Muslims) is founded in Detroit by Wallace D. Fard

1932–1972   U.S. Public Health Service conducts and funds the Tuskegee Study of Untreated Syphilis in the Negro Male, which exploits and misleads hundreds of African American men in the name of science

1934   Federal Housing Administration (FHA) is created

1934   Congress passes the Indian Reorganization Act, also known as the Wheeler-Howard Act, to increase Native American self-governance and to foster tribal economic independence

1934   Congress passes the federal Anti-Lynching Law in response to the racially motivated murders of African Americans

1935   Congress passes the Wagner Act, also known as the National Labor Relations Act, giving workers the right to independent, union representation for purposes of collective bargaining with their employers

1942   Emergency Labor Program, popularly called the Bracero Program, is established to allow Mexican workers into the United States to meet the labor needs of southwestern agriculture growers during World War II

1942   Congress of Racial Equality (CORE) is founded as a pacifist group seeking to fight racism, integrate public facilities, and work for civil rights for African Americans

1942   President Franklin D. Roosevelt signs Executive Order 9066, clearing the way for internment of Japanese Americans

1942   War Relocation Authority (WRA) is established by executive order of President Roosevelt as the government agency responsible for removing persons believed to be threats to national security

1943   Detroit Race Riot comprises a series of violent encounters, sparked by competition for jobs and housing, between whites and African Americans in Detroit, Michigan

1943   Zoot Suit Riots, consisting of white attacks on Mexican American youths, erupt in Los Angeles

1944   In *Korematsu v. United States*, the U.S. Supreme Court case upholds the internment of Japanese Americans during World War II

1944   National Congress of American Indians (NCAI) is founded to lobby for Native American rights and causes

1946   Congress creates the Indian Claims Commission (ICC) to hear and determine claims against the U.S. government made by any Native American tribe or group

1947   Jackie Robinson joins the Brooklyn Dodgers, becoming the first African American player in major-league baseball

1948   President Harry S. Truman issues Executive Order 9981 racially integrating the U.S. military

1948	In *Shelley v. Kraemer*, the U.S. Supreme Court rules that the equal protection clause of the Fourteenth Amendment prevents racially restrictive housing covenants from being enforceable
1948	American GI Forum, an organization devoted to securing equal rights for Hispanic American veterans, is founded by Hector P. Garcia
1948	In *Oyama v. California*, the U.S. Supreme Court strikes down California's Alien Land Laws as unconstitutional
1952	Congress passes the McCarran-Walter Act, which eases certain restrictions on immigrants of particular national origins
1954	In *Brown v. Board of Education of Topeka*, the U.S. Supreme Court declares racial segregation in schools unconstitutional
1954	Publication of Gordon Allport's *The Nature of Prejudice*, an influential work examining and defining the nature of racial prejudice
1954	U.S. Immigration and Naturalization Service launches the controversial paramilitary repatriation program, "Operation Wetback," which targets Mexicans working "illegally" in the agricultural industry of the Southwest
1955	African American Rosa Parks refuses to give up her seat on a Montgomery, Alabama, bus to a white passenger, thereby initiating the Montgomery Bus Boycott
1955	Publication of John Higham's *Strangers in the Land*, a classic analysis of nativism in the United States
1956	Publication of Kenneth Stampp's *The Peculiar Institution*, which views slavery as a coercive and profit-seeking regime, a significant revision in the way historians have previously seen the institution
1957	Southern Christian Leadership Conference (SCLC) is created in New Orleans by a group of ministers, labor leaders, lawyers, and political activists concerned about the impact of segregation on their communities
1957	U.S. Commission on Civil Rights (USCCR) is created by the Civil Rights Act of 1957 as an independent, fact-finding arm of the federal government
1957	President Dwight D. Eisenhower sends federal troops to protect from angry whites nine black students attempting to integrate Central High School in Little Rock, Arkansas
1958	John Birch Society is founded by Robert Welch to advocate limited government, anticommunism, and American isolationism
1959	American Nazi Party is founded by George Lincoln Rockwell
1960	Student Nonviolent Coordinating Committee (SNCC) is founded at Shaw University in Raleigh, North Carolina, to coordinate nonviolent protest actions against racial segregation

1960	Publication of John Howard Griffin's *Black Like Me*, the story of the extensive loss of rights and privileges suffered by a white man who darkened his skin to pass for black
1961	President John F. Kennedy issues Executive Order 10925, which makes first use of the term *affirmative action* in calling on government contractors to treat employees "without regard to their race, creed, color, or national origin"
1961	Freedom Riders, blacks and whites who travel together across the South in buses, protest racial segregation
1961	Release of *West Side Story*, a groundbreaking film about white–Puerto Rican race relations
1962	National Farm Workers Association (NFWA), later the United Farm Workers (UFW), is founded by Cesar Chavez and Dolores Huerta
1963	March on Washington is organized to bring attention to the lack of job opportunities and civil rights for African Americans
1963	Martin Luther King Jr. delivers his "I Have a Dream" speech before the Lincoln Memorial in Washington, DC
1963	Martin Luther King Jr. writes his "Letter from a Birmingham Jail" while incarcerated for his role in antisegregation demonstrations in Birmingham, Alabama
1963	Reies Lopez Tijerina founds the Alianza Federal de Pueblos Libres (Federal Alliance of Land Grant) to reclaim Spanish and Mexican land grants held by Mexican and Native Americans before the Mexican-American War (1846–1848)
1964	Congress passes the Civil Rights Act to end the deeply entrenched practices of racial segregation and other forms of racial discrimination
1964	Bracero Program, which has allowed Mexican workers into the United States since 1942, is ended
1964	Organization of Afro-American Unity (OAAU) is founded by Malcolm X to coordinate political action and self-organization among blacks toward the goal of racial equality
1964	Harlem riot begins when a white police officer shoots and kills an African American youth in Yorkville, New York
1965	Congress creates the federal Department of Housing and Urban Development (HUD)
1965	Publication of Paul M. Siegel's groundbreaking article, "On the Cost of Being a Negro," which examines the true extent of the income gap between blacks and whites
1965	El Teatro Campensino, the Farmworkers Theater, is founded by Luis Valdez as part of the organizing effort of Cesar Chavez's United Farm Workers union

1965	Congress passes the Voting Rights Act, which requires certain state and local jurisdictions to get federal approval before altering their voting procedures
1965	Congress passes the Immigration Act, phasing out national-origin quotas and emphasizing the reunification of families
1965	Race riots erupt in the Watts neighborhood of Los Angeles
1965	Publication of Daniel Patrick Moynihan's *The Negro Family in America: The Case for National Action*, which blames the poverty and social problems afflicting African Americans on the breakdown of the family
1966	Black Panther Party for Self-Defense is formed by Huey Newton, Bobby Seale, and other radical black activists
1966	In *Miranda v. Arizona* (1966), the U.S. Supreme Court establishes suspects' right to an attorney and to be informed of their rights before questioning by police
1966	Maulana Karenga, professor of black studies at California State University, develops Kwanzaa as a cultural holiday to promote the African American experience
1967	Race riot erupts in Newark, New Jersey
1967	Publication of *Black Power: The Politics of Liberation in America* by Stokely Carmichael and Charles V. Hamilton
1967	Discrimination and poor housing for blacks spark violent race riots in Detroit, Michigan
1967	National Advisory Commission on Civil Disorders (the Kerner Commission) is formed by President Lyndon B. Johnson to investigate the causes and implications of the urban riots occurring in black sections of many major cities
1968	American Indian Movement (AIM) is founded
1968	Congress passes another Civil Rights Act to ensure fair housing practices (Title VIII, known as the Fair Housing Act) and confer various civil rights on Native Americans
1968	Bilingual Education Act is passed by Congress
1968	Kerner Commission (the National Advisory Commission on Civil Disorders) issues its report on the series of urban race riots that occurred in 1967
1968	Mexican American Legal Defense and Education Fund (MALDEF) is founded in San Antonio, Texas, to protect the civil rights of Latinos and promote their empowerment and full participation in society
1969	Arthur Jensen publishes a widely cited article in the *Harvard Education Review* attacking Head Start programs and claiming that African American children have a low average IQ that cannot be improved by social engineering

1969	MEChA (Spanish acronym for "The Chicano Student Movement of Aztlán"), a national college student organization for Chicano/as, is founded
1969	Native American activists begin a nineteen-month occupation of Alcatraz Island in San Francisco Bay
1970	National Chicano Moratorium demonstration against the Vietnam War and discrimination against Hispanics at home occurs in Los Angeles
1971	Alaska Native Claims Settlement Act is passed by Congress to resolve Native Alaskan claims to lands appropriated by the federal government
1971	United Farm Workers (UFW) is created from a merger of the Agricultural Workers Organizing Committee, founded in 1959, and the National Farm Workers Association, founded in 1962
1971	Arab Community Center for Economic and Social Services (ACCESS), an Arab American support and advocacy organization, is established
1971	*All in the Family*, Norman Lear's groundbreaking sit-com about bigot Archie Bunker, premiers on CBS
1972	Congress passes the Equal Employment Opportunity Act to amend the 1964 Civil Rights Act, making it more effective in ensuring equal job opportunities
1972	In *Furman v. Georgia*, the U.S. Supreme Court declares the death penalty "capricious and arbitrary" and thus unconstitutional
1972	Publication of Robert Blauner's *Racial Oppression in America*, which challenges the traditional theoretical paradigm of racial relations in the United States, that is, the classical assimilation theory, and proposes instead the internal-colonialism paradigm
1973	Organization of Chinese Americans, Inc. (OCA), a national nonprofit, nonpartisan advocacy organization of concerned Chinese and Asian Americans, is founded
1973	American Indian Movement members occupy Wounded Knee, South Dakota
1973	In *Lau v. Nichols*, the U.S. Supreme court rules that the San Francisco public school system violated the Civil Rights Act of 1964 by denying non-English-speaking students of Chinese ancestry a meaningful opportunity to participate in public education
1974	Publication of Nathan Glazer's *Affirmative Discrimination: Ethnic Inequality and Public Policy*, which argues that affirmative action is actually "affirmative discrimination" against individuals

1974	Asian American Legal Defense and Education Fund (AALDEF) is founded to protect the legal rights of Asian Americans
1975	Aryan Nations, a white-supremacist, anti-Semitic group, is founded by Richard G. Butler
1975	Congress amends the Voting Rights Act of 1965 to protect the voting rights of citizens of certain ethnic groups whose first language is not English
1975	Congress passes the Indian Self-Determination and Education Assistance Act to implement tribal self-determination in matters relating to delivery of educational, health, and other services to Native Americans
1976	In *Gregg v. Georgia*, the U.S. Supreme Court reinstates the death penalty
1976	Publication of Alex Haley's *Roots: The Saga of an American Family*, a semiautobiographical history of Haley's family and their experiences as slaves
1978	In *Regents of the University of California v. Bakke*, the U.S. Supreme Court upholds the concept of affirmative action
1978	Publication of William J. Wilson's influential *The Declining Significance of Race*, a polemic on the relative importance of race and class for life chances of African Americans
1978	Publication of Joe Feagin's *Discrimination, American Style*, which argues that racial discrimination is embedded in institutions and policies designed to address the concerns of white European males
1980	American-Arab Anti-Discrimination Committee is established
1981	U.S. Department of Education formulates a clear policy that Ebonics is a form of English, not a separate language, and thus not eligible for public funding
1982	Vincent Chin is murdered in Detroit, Michigan, by two white autoworkers who mistake him for Japanese and blame him for the loss of American jobs
1983	Publication of Thomas Sowell's *Economics and Politics of Race*, in which a conservative social scientist argues that culture makes a difference in the success of an ethnic group and that racial strife has affected human society throughout history
1984	Publication of Charles Murray's *Losing Ground: American Social Policy, 1950–1980*, a controversial examination of U.S. government social programs
1985	Arab American Institute is established to represent the interests of Americans of Arab descent in politics and to foster their civic and political empowerment
1985	Rainbow Coalition is founded by Reverend Jesse Jackson to unite people of diverse ethnic, religious, economic, and political backgrounds in a push for social, racial, and economic justice

1986	Howard Beach incident occurs, in which Michael Griffith, a black Trinidadian immigrant, is killed after he and two other men are attacked by a gang of white teenagers in the white Howard Beach neighborhood in Queens, New York
1986	Publication of Michael Omi and Howard Winant's *Racial Formation in the United States: From the 1960s to the 1980s*, a groundbreaking work on racial theory
1987	Dot-buster attacks occur, in which Latino gangs in Jersey City, New Jersey, threaten violence and vandalism against Asian Indian residents who do not leave the city
1988	Osama Bin Laden, the son of a Saudi billionaire, forms Al Qaeda, an organization that develops in the 1990s into a global terrorist network that promotes an extremist and militant form of Islam and attacks U.S. global interests
1988	Bensonhurst incident occurs, in which black teenager Yusef Hawkins is beaten to death by white youths in Bensonhurst neighborhood of Brooklyn, New York
1988	Congress passes the Fair Housing Amendments Act to strengthen provisions of the Fair Housing Act of 1968 by giving the Department of Housing and Urban Development (HUD) greater power to enforce the earlier legislation
1988	Congress approves the Civil Liberties Act, authorizing redress payments to Japanese Americans interned during World War II
1989	Publication of Stephen Steinberg's *Ethnic Myth: Race, Ethnicity and Class in America*, which challenges various prevailing ideas about race and ethnicity in the United States
1989	In *City of Richmond v. J.A. Croson Company*, the U.S. Supreme Court rules that a city affirmative action program violates the equal protection clause of the Fourteenth Amendment
1990	Congress passes the Hate Crimes Statistics Act, which requires the Department of Justice to compile annual national data on hate crimes and publish an annual summary of findings
1991	Yankel Rosenbaum, a Jewish yeshiva student, is murdered by a black mob in Crown Heights, New York
1991	Los Angeles police officers are taped beating Rodney King, an African American motorist, after King refuses to be pulled over
1991	Congress passes another Civil Rights Act to reverse recent court rulings that seem to weaken enforcement of earlier civil rights legislation
1992	Riots erupt in Los Angeles after the acquittal of the police officers accused in the Rodney King beating incident
1994	California voters pass Proposition 187, the Save Our State Initiative, which denies publicly funded nonemergency medical care, education, and social services to illegal immigrants and their foreign-born children

1994	Council on American Islamic Relations (CAIR) is to advocate for the civil rights of Muslim Americans
1994	Publication of scholar Cornel West's *Race Matters*, which examines the role of race in shaping the African American experience
1995	Minister Louis Farrakhan of the Nation of Islam sponsors the Million Man March on Washington to support African American families
1995	Publication of *Black Wealth/White Wealth: A New Perspective on Racial Inequality*, a book by Melvin L. Oliver and Thomas M. Shapiro detailing disparities in wealth between whites and blacks
1995	Right-wing extremists bomb the Alfred P. Murrah Federal Building in Oklahoma City
1995	O. J. Simpson, an African American football legend, is acquitted of murdering his wife, Nicole Brown Simpson, and Ron Goldman, who were both white
1995	Publication of John Yinger's *Closed Doors, Opportunities Lost: The Continuing Costs of Housing Discrimination*, examining various housing studies to determine how closely the housing industry is adhering to the Fair Housing Act of 1968
1996	Richard J. Herrnstein and Charles Murray publish *The Bell Curve: Intelligence and Class Structure in American Life*, in which they present statistical evidence that supposedly supports the notion of racial superiority based on IQ
1996	California voters pass Proposition 209, the California Civil Rights Initiative, which repeals affirmative action in public employment, education, or contracting
1996	In *Shaw v. Hunt*, the U.S. Supreme Court declares that race cannot be the sole factor in redrawing congressional districts
1997	California voters pass Proposition 227, the English Language Education for Children in Public Schools Initiative, which eliminates bilingual education in California public schools
1998	James Byrd Jr., a black man, is murdered in Jasper, Texas, by three white racists who slit his throat and drag his body behind a truck
1999	Publication of Mary Waters's *Black Identities: West Indian Immigrant Dreams and American Realities*, an award-winning book that explores the experiences of West Indian immigrants in New York
1999	Amadou Diallo, an immigrant working as a street vendor in New York, is shot by four undercover police officers, who mistake him for a rape suspect
1999	Wen Ho Lee, a Chinese American engineer working at the Los Alamos Research Laboratory, is accused of spying by the government and fired from his job in violation of his civil rights. He is later cleared of all charges

2001   Members of the militant Islamist organization Al Qaeda, acting on orders of the group's leader, Osama Bin Laden, launch terrorist attacks on New York City and Washington, DC, that kill almost 3,000 people

2001   Patriot Act is passed in the wake of the September 11, 2001, terrorist attacks to increase the effectiveness of U.S. law enforcement in detecting and preventing further acts of terrorism

2003   U.S. Supreme Court renders decisions in two University of Michigan affirmation action cases—*Grutter v. Bollinger* and *Gratz v. Bollinger*—declaring that race can be considered in university admissions decisions but cannot be a "deciding factor"

2003   California voters reject Proposition 54, the Racial Privacy Initiative (RPI), which would have banned the use and production of racially coded data by various state and municipal agencies

LIST OF ENTRIES

GUIDE TO RELATED ENTRIES

African Americans

"Acting White" Stage of Life

Affirmative Action

Afrocentrism

All-Black Resorts

Back-to-Africa Movement

Bensonhurst Incident

Black Anti-Semitism

Black Conservatives

"Black English" (Ebonics)

Black Family Instability Thesis

Black-Korean Conflicts

Black Nationalist Movement

Black Panther Party

Black Political Disenfranchisement

Black Power: The Politics of Liberation in America

Black Wealth/White Wealth: A New Perspective on Racial Inequality

Blacks, Wage Discrimination against

Block-busting

Brown v. Board of Education of Topeka

Buffalo Soldiers

Busing

Byrd, James Jr.

Caribbean Immigrants, Attitudes toward African Americans

Carmichael, Stokely

Civil Rights Movement

Color Line

"Cost of Being a Negro"

Culture of Poverty Thesis

Diallo, Amadou

Douglass, Frederick

Driving while Black, Stopping People for

Du Bois, W.E.B.

Expatriation

Farrakhan, Louis

Freedmen's Bureau

Freedom Riders

Free Persons of Color in the Antebellum North

Garvey, Marcus

Harlem Renaissance

Concepts, Beliefs, and Theories

Immigration and Immigrants

Asiatic Barred Zone

Asiatic Exclusion League (AEL)

Black Identities: West Indian Immigrant Dreams and American Realities

California Ballot Proposition 187

California Ballot Proposition 227

Caribbean Immigrants, Attitudes toward African Americans

Caribbean Immigrants, Class Differences in the Second Generation

Caribbean Immigrants, Experience of Racial Discrimination

Chinese Exclusion Act of 1882

Chinese Immigrants, Adaptation of to Female Jobs

Chinese Immigrants and Anti-Chinese Sentiments

Colonized versus Immigrant Minorities

Dillingham Report

Diversities, Ethnic and Racial

Expatriation

Foreign Miners License Tax

Gentlemen's Agreement of 1908

Haitians, Discrimination against in Refugee Policy

Immigrant Preference in Employment

Immigration Act of 1965

Immigration Restriction League of 1894

Irish Immigrants, Prejudice and Discrimination against

McCarran-Walter Act of 1952

Melting Pot

National Origins Act of 1924

Nativism and the Anti-Immigrant Movements

Naturalization Act of 1790

Non-Judeo-Christian Immigrant Groups, Violence against

Operation Wetback

Proximal Host

"Second-Generation Decline"

Strangers in the Land: Patterns of American Nativism, 1860–1925

United States v. Thind

Undocumented Immigrants

U.S. Border Patrol

Individuals

Byrd, James Jr.

Carmichael, Stokely

Chavez, Cesar

Chin, Vincent

Diallo, Amadou

Douglass, Frederick

Du Bois, W.E.B.

Duke, David

Farrakhan, Louis

Ford, Henry

Frank, Leo

Garvey, Marcus

Goddard, Henry H.

Gonzales, Rodolfo "Corky"

Gutierrez, Jose Angel

Jackson, Jesse

Jeffries, Leonard

Jensen, Arthur

King, Martin Luther Jr.

Lee, Wen Ho

Lincoln, Abraham, and the Emancipation of Slaves

Malcolm X

Morrison, Toni

Muhammad, Elijah

Paine, Thomas

Parks, Rosa

Powell, Colin

Randolph, A. Philip

Robinson, Jackie

Simpson, O.J.

Spencer, Herbert

Terman, Lewis

Thomas, Clarence

Thurmond, Strom

Tijerina, Reies Lopez

Wallace, George

Washington, Booker T.

Jews

Anti-Defamation League of B'nai Brith (ADL)

Anti-Semitism in the United States

Aryan Nations

Black Anti-Semitism

Frank, Leo

Jewish-Black Conflicts

Jewish Defense League (JDL)

Zionist Occupied Government (ZOG)

Laws, Treaties, Propositions, Constitutional Amendments, and Executive Orders

Alaska Native Claims Settlement Act of 1971

Alien Land Laws on the West Coast

Asiatic Barred Zone

California Ballot Proposition 54

California Ballot Proposition 187

California Ballot Proposition 209

California Ballot Proposition 227

Chinese Exclusion Act of 1882

Civil Rights Act of 1964

Civil Rights Act of 1968

Civil Rights Act of 1991

Equal Employment Opportunity Act of 1972

Executive Order 9066

Executive Order 9981

Fair Housing Act of 1968

Fair Housing Amendments Act of 1988

Fourteenth Amendment

Guadalupe Hidalgo, Treaty of

Hate Crimes Statistics Act of 1990

Immigrant Act of 1965

Indian Allotment Act of 1887

Indian Citizenship Act of 1924

Indian Reorganization Act of 1934 (IRA)

Indian Self-Determination and Educational Assistance Act of 1975 (ISDEAA)

Jim Crow Laws

McCarran-Walter Act of 1952

Missouri Compromise

National Origins Act of 1924

Naturalization Act of 1790

Voting Rights Act of 1965

Voting Rights Amendments of 1975

Wagner Act

Movements

Abolitionist Movement

Afrocentrism

Americanization Movement

Back-to-Africa Movement

Black Nationalist Movement

Chicano Movement

Civil Rights Movement

English-Only Movement

Eugenics Movement

Expatriation

Freedom Riders

Harlem Renaissance

Organizations, Groups, and Government Agencies

Al Qaeda

American-Arab Anti-Discrimination Committee (ADC)

American Civil Liberties Union (ACLU)

American GI Forum (AGIF)

American Indian Movement (AIM)

American Nazi Party (ANP)

Anti-Defamation League of B'nai Brith (ADL)

Arab American Institute (AAI)

Arab Community Center for Economic and Social Services (ACCESS)

Arab/Muslim American Advocacy Organizations, Responding to the Backlash

Aryan Nations

Asian American Legal Defense and Education Fund (AALDEF)

Asian Americans for Equality (AAFE)

Asiatic Exclusion League (AEL)

Black Panther Party

Bureau of Indian Affairs (BIA)

Congress of Racial Equality (CORE)

Council on American Islamic Relations (CAIR)

Federal Housing Administration (FHA)

Freedmen's Bureau

Freedom Riders

Immigration Restriction League of 1894

Indian Claims Commission (ICC)

Islamic Jihad

Japanese American Citizens League (JACL)

Jewish Defense League (JDL)

John Birch Society

Know-Nothing Party

Ku Klux Klan (KKK)

La Raza Unida

League of United Latin American Citizens (LULAC)

Mexican American Legal Defense and Education Fund (MALDEF)

Muslim Philanthropic Organizations, Closure of after September 11, 2001

Nation of Islam

National Advisory Commission on Civil Disorders

National Association for the Advancement of Colored People (NAACP)

National Congress of American Indians (NCAI)

Organization of Afro-American Unity (OAAU)

Organization of Chinese Americans (OCA)

Rainbow Coalition

Southern Christian Leadership Conference (SCLC)

Student Nonviolent Coordinating Committee (SNCC)

Texas Rangers

United Farm Workers (UFW)

U.S. Border Patrol

U.S. Commission on Civil Rights (USCCR)

U.S. Department of Housing and Urban Development (HUD)

War Relocation Authority (WRA)

Policies, Programs, and Government Acts

Affirmative Action

Affirmative Action, University of Michigan Ruling on

Anglo Conformity

I

ICC

See Indian Claims Commission (ICC).

Identity Politics

Not limited to activity in the traditionally conceived political sphere, *identity politics* refers to activism, politics, theorizing, and other, similar activities based on the shared experiences of members of a specific social group (often relying on similar experiences of oppression). Many of the groups that engage in identity politics are racially, ethnically, or pan-ethnically organized, but people have also organized around identities such as gender, sexuality, and disability. They engage in such activities as state-oriented social movements, movements for change at colleges and universities, consciousness-raising support groups, and education and awareness in the outside world. The most important and revolutionary element of identity politics is the demand that oppressed groups be recognized not in spite of their differences but specifically because of their differences: it was an important precursor to the emphasis on multiculturalism and diversity in certain facets of modern political and educational culture.

Identity-politics movements have suggested that those who do not share the identity of and the life experiences that it brings to an individual thus cannot understand what it means to live life as a person with that identity—they cannot understand the specific terms of oppression and thus cannot find adequate solutions to the problems that the members of the group face. Thus, identity-politics movements have pushed for self-determinism on the part of oppressed groups. This has meant, for example, that proponents of identity politics believe that ethnic-studies courses should be taught only by those who share the ethnic identity that the course addresses and that faculty and students of color should have sole responsibility for determining the policies of curriculum and faculty hiring in such departments and the admission of students of color to colleges and universities. In spheres of action beyond academia, identity-politics movements have pushed for self-determination in local politics through the institution of community boards controlled by people of color and the establishment of social-service agencies staffed by people of color to deal with the specific problems faced by communities of color.

Conservative politicians and back-to-the-basics academics have criticized identity politics movements as being naïve, fragmenting, essentialist, or reductionist. They have stressed the importance of unified "American" identities in moving away from discriminatory pasts and suggested that focusing attention on the specific histories of identity groups disadvantages these groups by ensuring that they do not possess the cultural capital they will need to get ahead. One important aspect of this debate is that those engaged in identity politics believe that legacies of discrimination can only be overcome by drawing attention to the oppressed difference, while traditional liberal analysis promotes color-blindness as a way to overcome discrimination and believes that paying attention to difference merely highlights its salience in interactions. Additionally, critics worry that multiculturalism brings with it a call to moral relativism, a philosophy that prevents judgment of the practices of other groups that might be found reprehensible. Identity-politics movements counter with the idea that it is possible to preserve cultures and identities without allowing the practice of certain objectionable elements within it.

Criticism does not stem only from critics who do not share the oppressed identity. There are conflicts within identities as well. Of chief importance is the fact that many people's identities are multifaceted, and thus involvement in one identity politics does not suffice. For instance, Asian American gay men often struggle to find a place when their Asian American communities are homophobic and their gay communities are racist. Black women who turn to support organizations to build their identity have found that "all the blacks are men and all the women are white." Those with multiply oppressed identities have sometimes responded by forming new, more specific identity-politics groups (e.g., lesbians of color). This fragmentation counters the original point of identity politics, which is to encourage recognition of the vast numbers of people who share identities that are outside the mainstream. However, these communities can also provide support and consciousness-raising to those who become involved in them.

See also Pan-Asian Solidarity; Pan-ethnic Movements; "Third World Movement" of the 1960s.

Further Reading

Arthur, John, and Amy Shapiro, eds. *Campus Wars: Multiculturalism and the Politics of Difference*. Boulder, CO: Westview Press, 1995.

Giroux, Henry A. *Living Dangerously: Multiculturalism and the Politics of Difference*. New York: P. Lang, 1993.

Heyes, Cressida. "Identity Politics." In *The Stanford Encyclopedia of Philosophy*. Fall 2002 ed., edited by Edward N. Zalta.

Reed, Ishmael. *MultiAmerica: Essays on Cultural Wars and Cultural Peace*. New York: Viking, 1996.

Mikaila Mariel Lemonik Arthur

"I Have a Dream" Speech

As a minister and the most influential leader of the civil right movement, Martin Luther King Jr. delivered hundreds of speeches and sermons. Of all the speeches he delivered, his "I Have a Dream" speech is his most well known and most often quoted. He delivered the speech before the Lincoln Memorial in Washington, DC, on August 28, 1963, as the keynote speech for the March on Washington. Television cameras broadcast him pleading to the entire nation for freedom and justice.

The year 1963 was pivotal for the civil rights movement. It was the centennial of the Emancipation Proclamation (1863). That year, the police used brutal techniques (police dogs and fire hoses) to suppress peaceful black demonstrations in Birmingham, Alabama. A black church in Birmingham was firebombed, killing four black children. The national media broadcast these horrible scenes, and there was much public and governmental support for the civil rights movement. The March on Washington of 1963, in which approximately 200,000 people, including many white sympathizers, participated, was the climax of three years of protests for civil rights. After commenting on the injustices against blacks, King ended his speech with a dream he said was deeply rooted in the American dream: "So I say to you, my friends, that even though we must face the difficulties of today and tomorrow, I still have a dream. It is a dream deeply rooted in the American dream that one day this nation will rise up and live out its true meaning of its creed—we hold these truths to be self-evident, that all men are created equal."

See also Civil Rights Movement; King, Martin Luther Jr.; "Letter from a Birmingham Jail"; March on Washington; Montgomery Bus Boycott.

The Rev. Dr. Martin Luther King Jr. acknowledging the crowd at the Lincoln Memorial during his "I Have a Dream" speech, August 28, 1963.

AP/Wide World Photos.

Further Reading

King, Martin Luther Jr. *I Have a Dream: Writings and Speeches That Changed the World*. New York: HarperCollins, 1992.

Pyong Gap Min

Illegal Aliens

See Undocumented Immigrants.

Illegal Immigrants

See Undocumented Immigrants.

Illegitimacy and Race

In the United States, there has long been concern about children who are born out of wedlock. These children are sometimes called illegitimate. Critics of the term *illegitimacy* argue that it is derogatory and stigmatizing. They also argue that the presence of a father who is legally married to the mother should not be seen as necessary for children to be viewed as legitimate. The term *out-of-wedlock childbirth*, therefore, is often used as a more neutral—and more broadly accepted—description of children born to unmarried mothers.

Rates of out-of-wedlock childbirth vary across racial and ethnic groups. In the United States, blacks have far higher rates of out-of-wedlock childbirth than do whites. For example, in 1992, 68 percent of black children were born outside of marriage, compared with 19 percent of white children.

It is not clear why African Americans have much higher rates of out-of-wedlock childbirth than do whites. One possibility is that this is a legacy of slavery—in which families were intentionally broken up—in the United States. Another possibility is that the economic and social hardships faced by many African Americans have discouraged marriage. It has been argued, for example, that the high rates of unemployment and incarceration among African American men has meant that there are comparatively few "marriageable" black men. Regardless of racial background, adolescents tend to initiate sexual activities at earlier ages than they did thirty years ago. With a much higher proportion of black men who are not ready to get married because of their unemployment or incarceration, many more black unmarried women are likely to deliver babies.

Some social critics, such as Patrick Moynihan and Charles Murray, have suggested that out-of-wedlock childbirth causes social pathology. They argued that children born out of wedlock are more likely to commit crimes and engage in other socially destructive behaviors. But other social critics indicate that although children born out of wedlock do tend to be more disadvantaged than their peers from married families, out-of-wedlock childbearing does not in itself cause these problems. Instead, they argued that high a rate of out-of-wedlock childbearing is a consequence rather than a cause of poverty. Some white Americans have charged that unmarried black women deliberately bore babies for welfare benefits. But welfare monies were too small to be a significant incentive for unwed women to plan to have babies. The fact that the rate of out-of-wedlock births has continued to increase for both whites and blacks since welfare reform in 1996 suggests that welfare programs were not the main cause of out-of-wedlock births in the black community.

See also Black Family Instability Thesis; *Losing Ground: American Policy, 1850–1980*; *The Negro Family: The Case for National Action*.

Robin Roger-Dillon

Immigrant Minorities

See Colonized versus Immigrant Minorities.

Immigrant Preference in Employment

The postindustrial economy in the United States demands a highly educated labor force. It also creates many unskilled entry-level jobs. Immigrant preference in employment is mainly an issue in hiring at low-skilled, low-wage entry-level jobs. Many employers prefer immigrants, particularly Hispanics, because of their willingness to accept lower wages and/or unfavorable working conditions. Hispanic workers are perceived to work hard for low wages and to be the least likely to complain about their poor working conditions. Employing low-skilled immigrant workers at garment sweatshops, private homes, and farms illustrates such a case. One consequence of this preference is the displacement of similarly qualified and willing native workers, especially African American workers.

Native-born and immigrant workers compete for high-skilled jobs as well. In this case, though, employers usually point out the lack of qualified members of the native workforce. Nevertheless, employers' preference for professional immigrants is also a case of employer exploitation of workers in terms of salaries/working condition and legal status. Illegal immigrants will work for substandard wages and in poor conditions for fear of being reported to the INS. One difference between professional and the low-skills is that the training of the high-skilled labor force is not paid for. Thus, it is beneficial to the U.S. economy. If there are enough native-born workers available, it still involves the displacement of native workers by foreign professionals, lowering the wage level.

See also Labor Movement, Racism in.

Further Reading

Waldinger, Roger, and Michael I. Lichter. *How the Other Half Works: Immigration and the Social Organization of Labor.* Los Angeles: University of California Press, 2003.

Shin Kim and Kwang Chung Kim

Immigration Act of 1924

See National Origins Act of 1924.

Immigration Act of 1965

Intended or not, the Immigration and Naturalization Act of 1965 brought a momentous change in the country-of-origin composition of immigrants to the United States. In that sense, the act truly represents a historical shift in U.S. immigration policies. To understand its significance, the history of U.S. immigration laws prior to the passage of the act must be reviewed.

Immigration before 1924

With the opening of the western frontier, the U.S. economy demanded a large influx of workers. This pull factor in America that began in the seventeenth century and remained until the Civil War brought a huge surge in European immigration. Most of these immigrants came from the British Isles and other western European countries and were Protestants. These white Protestant immigrants and their descendants emerged as the dominant group in the United States. Their dominance generated the image of America as a white, Protestant society.

As expected, there was a lull in immigration during the Civil War. Immediately afterward, though, the industrialization of the U.S. economy again required large numbers of workers. Once again, America obtained the needed labor force from immigrants. But the immigrants of this period came mostly from eastern and southern European countries. A great majority of these new immigrants were not only illiterate but also brought religious traditions—Catholicism, Judaism, and Eastern Orthodoxy—different from those of the dominant group. They suffered prejudice, discrimination, and even physical violence by the dominant white Protestant group. For a long time, these immigrants and their children were treated as second-class citizens at best. World War I eventually halted immigration from eastern and southern European countries. Then, as blacks began migrating to the North in significant numbers, these white immigrants and their descendants were gradually assimilated into mainstream America.

Several groups of non-Europeans began arriving in the United States in the middle of the nineteenth century. For example, as the United States acquired Texas and what would become California, New Mexico, and other western states from Mexico through an annexation or war between 1845 and 1848, a large number of Mexicans became members of U.S. society, but they were treated as immigrants. In the early part of the twentieth century, many Mexican migrant workers moved to the United States as well. As a whole, though, Mexican Americans were relatively small in number and concentrated in the former Mexican territory.

Beginning in the mid-nineteenth century, a limited number of Chinese immigrants arrived in Hawaii and California. When the Chinese Exclusion Act of 1882 prohibited the Chinese from immigrating to the United States, the immigration of the Japanese to Hawaii started. A small number of Korean immigrants also arrived to the United States between 1903 and 1905. Then, Japanese labor migration was stopped by the Gentlemen's Agreement in 1908 and Filipino workers immigrated in substantial numbers. But most of these Asian immigrants and their descendants, numbering about a half million, were confined to the Hawaiian Island and the West Coast. As expected, these non-European immigrants were too small in number to dent the image of the United States as the land of white men.

This short review of American immigration history bespeaks the racial stratification in the United States that existed in the nineteenth century and in the early part of the twentieth century. The native-born whites, the descendants of western European immigrants, enjoyed a highly respected racial position and were regarded as the dominant group. Although the immigrants from eastern or southern European countries and their descendants were eventually accepted as white Americans, they were not socially well respected. Nonwhite and non-European immigrants were in the worst situation, at the bottom. They were brought to meet the need for cheap labor, but the United States did not want to accept them as a part of America. Even their U.S.-born descendants were not allowed U.S. citizenship for a long period of time.

National Origins Act of 1924

The U.S. government began a sweeping regulation of the immigration flow in the early part of the twentieth century. The immigration law that faithfully reflected this regulation was passed in 1924. The 1924 National Origins Act spelled out the national origins of immigrants the United States would like to accept. As reflected in its name, it stipulated that the number of immigrations allowed from European countries should be based on the race/ethnic composition of the U.S. population. This law heavily favored immigration from the British Isles and other western European countries, as western European Americans maintained a numeric dominance among the U.S. population.

The 1924 immigration law did allow for immigration from eastern and southern European countries. But their number was limited because of a small proportion of the native-born population of eastern- and southern-European ancestry. The number of immigrants from these parts of Europe was further reduced when the calculation of the ethnic composition of the population was made on the basis of the 1880 census, instead of the 1920 census, as originally conceived. The 1924 immigration law virtually prohibited immigration from non-European countries, with the exception of Mexicans. It also had a special provision that completely banned immigration from Asian countries. With the enforcement of the 1924 National Origins Act, no Asian country, with the exception of the Philippines, a U.S. colony at that time, was able to send immigrants.

Immigration Reform in 1965

The 1924 immigration law was enforced until the end of World War II in 1945. Afterward, the United States was forced to critically review the immigration laws for several reasons. First, the experience of World War II made Americans more tolerant of racial and religious differences. Second, the civil rights movement in the 1950s and 1960s sensitized the issue of racial equality. Viewed with this perspective, U.S. immigration laws clearly violated the principle of racial equality. Third, in the early 1960s, the heart of the cold war period, the United States had to abolish its racist immigration policy for the diplomatic purpose of gaining more support from Third World countries at the United Nations. Fourth, the escalation of cold war tensions rendered the racist U.S. immigration policy problematic. Along with the escalation of the cold war, U.S. military involvement in various parts of the world greatly expanded the numbers of refugees. Fifth, the growing globalization of mass media spread the American way of life throughout the world and increased the number of people in the other parts of the world eager to move to the United States. Sixth, there was a growing need for foreign professional workers, especially foreign medial professionals, in the 1960s, which could not have been met by the native workforce alone.

Even though a couple of small-scale changes had already been made to the 1924 National Origins Act, the McCarran-Walter Act of 1952 was the first attempt to address to these issues. Nevertheless, it was a reluctant transitional response at best. This law reaffirmed the national origins system of the 1924 law but eased some restrictions, such as the ban on non-European immigrants and their descendants acquiring U.S. citizenship. It also legally accepted some non-European immigrants and refugees. Since this law had maintained the main tenet of the 1924 National Origins Act, however, U.S. immigration policies remained racially restrictive until 1965.

President John F. Kennedy sent his immigration reform law to Congress in July 1963; it was intended to eliminate the racially biased national-origins system. This bill called for an abolition of the national-origins system over a five-year period but retained the nonquota system for the Western Hemisphere. It also specified that the total number of immigrants outside the Western Hemisphere be only 165,000 annually, with no one country permitted to have more than 10 percent of the total. Visas were expected to be granted on the basis of preference categories in which one-half of immigrant visas would be granted to persons with special skills, training, or education advantageous to the U.S. economy and the rest to close relatives of U.S. citizens.

The Johnson administration also stressed admitting persons with skills, education, and desirable occupations and wanted to grant half of the visas to such people. Preferences to those with close family ties in the United States came second. Congressman Edward Feighan won his battle with the Johnson administration and reversed these preferences, though. Congressman Feighan's preferences heavily favored immigration based on family reunion. As a result, the final proposal contained only two preference categories—the Third and Sixth Preferences—and allowed 20 percent maximum of total immigrant visas to be granted for those with professions, skills, occupations, and special talents needed in the United States.

The act phased out the national-origin quotas over a three-year period. Effective July 1, 1968, the act provided 170,000 visas for persons from the Eastern Hemisphere and 120,000 from the Western Hemisphere per year. No one country in the Eastern Hemisphere was to have more than 20,000 visas. However, immediate family members, such as spouses, minor children (under 21), and parents of American citizens, and a few others such as ministers were exempt from the numerical limits. In 1978, the U.S. Congress passed a law providing for a worldwide immigration cap of 290,000 without differentiating Eastern and Western Hemispheres.

Post–1965 Immigrants from Non-European Countries

After the Second World War, the United States experienced rapid suburbanization and high rates of interethnic marriages among descendants of various white immigrants. Eventually, various white ethnic groups merged into one single group: white Americans, or European Americans. As the U.S. Congress amended immigration laws to abolish discrimination based on national origin and to open the door for immigration to non-European countries, many legislators nonetheless preferred to have more European immigrants. As a way to facilitate European immigration, they supported the legal device that stressed family reunion. Legislators thought that heavy emphasis on family reunion would definitely favor immigration from European countries, because a great majority of Americans were descendants of past European immigrants.

However, contrary to policymakers' expectations, emphasis on family reunification has instead facilitated immigration in large numbers from Asian, Latin American, and Caribbean countries. Right after the passage of the act, Greece, Italy, Portugal, and some other southern European countries sent more people than before to the United States, while fewer immigrants came from northern and western European countries. By the mid-1970s, however, immigration from southern European countries, except Portugal, also decreased. While European immigration declined, immigration from Asian countries, Mexico, the Caribbean Basin, and Latin American countries increased. These non-European Third World countries accounted for three-quarters of the four million immigrants of the 1970s. Since then, the immigration flow in the United States has consisted dominantly of immigrants from two areas of the world: Mexico and other Latin American countries, and Asian countries.

To explain the dominance of non-European immigrants in the post–1965 era, the following factors need to be considered. First, immediately after the full enforcement of the 1965 Immigration Act, many Asian and Middle Eastern professionals, especially medical professionals, immigrated as beneficiaries of occupational immigration preferences. But western European professionals were not motivated to come here because they were paid well in their native countries. Soon, these occupational immigrants from Asian and Middle Eastern countries became naturalized citizens and brought their parents and married brothers and sisters. Since there were few Latino and Asian naturalized citizens in 1965, policymakers did not realize the "multiplier effects" of family-based immigration.

Second, the U.S. military and political involvement in Asian, Latin American, and Caribbean countries has brought in huge numbers of refuges and women who are married to U.S. soldiers. After the fall of South Vietnam, more than one million South East Asian refugees have come to the United States. Large numbers of refuges have also originated from Cuba, El Salvador, Ecuador, Haiti, and even China, and the presence of the U.S. forces in the Philippines, South Korea, and Vietnam has brought many Asians married to U.S. service men and women. These refugees and U.S. soldiers' spouses have brought many more married brothers and sisters and their own family members, using family-union preferences that grant eligibility for naturalization after only three years. Many Jews from the former Soviet Union and many people from other eastern European countries have entered the Unites States as refugees since the early 1990s, but no significant number of refugees has originated from the politically stable northwestern European countries.

Third, the 1965 Immigration Act has gone through some revisions, and two revisions have affected the dominance of non-European immigrants as significantly as the original law did. The 1986 Immigration Reform and Control Act provided for an amnesty program for illegal residents. As a result, about three million illegal residents became permanent residents at the end of the 1980s and the early 1990s. Two-thirds were Mexicans, and the vast majority originated from non-European countries. They have brought their immediate family members and many of them have invited their brothers and sisters and parents through naturalization.

The Immigration Act of 1990 further revised the 1965 Immigration Act, which has had a strong effect on the increase in the number of Asian professional immigrants as well as in the total number of annual immigrants. It increased the total number of immigrants per year by about 40 percent, to 700,000 through 1994 and thereafter to 675,000. It also increased employment-based visas (heavily professionals) by three times, to 140,000, to meet the shortage of professionals, especially in the information technology (IT) field. So many Asian professionals, especially those in the IT industry, have come as beneficiaries of the occupational immigration since the early 1990s. Many of these professional Asian immigrants have become naturalized citizens and brought their family members. Computer specialists and other professionals from India, China, and the Philippines are strongly motivated to immigrate to the United States because of a big gap in their earnings potential, but professionals from northwestern European countries have little motivation because they do well in their own countries.

Effects of the 1965 Immigration Act

There were several intended and unintended effects of the act. First, the overall number of immigration increased dramatically. In fact, the United States would have experienced a population decrease without the increased immigration. According to U.S. censuses, the major population growth in the last several decades was coming from either immigration itself or children of immigrants. In that sense, without substantial increases in immigration, the U.S. economy could not have maintained its robustness. Second, the racial/ethnic composition of the U.S. population has altered drastically due to a large influx of non-European immigration. In 1970, Hispanics (4.5 percent) and Asian Americans (.07 percent) composed only tiny fractions of the population. The 2000 census reports a huge increase in both minority groups, with Hispanics accounting for 13 percent of the U.S. population and Asian Americans 3.5 percent. The proportion of white Americans decreased from 87 percent in 1970 to 70 percent in 2000, and it will continue to decline to the extent that white Americans will turn into a numerical minority. Most experts predict that whites will account for a little more than a half of the U.S. population by the mid-twenty-first century. The vast influx of non-European immigrants since the mid-1960s has changed the United States from a black-white, biracial society to a multiracial society.

Third, a large proportion of the post–1965 immigrants from non–European countries, particularly Asian countries, brought human capital in the form of high education and professional skills, as well as vast amounts of money to the United States. Although these middle- and upper-middle-class immigrants struggle to adjust to life in the United States, a great majority of their children are likely to receive a college education and will work as professionals. They will be highly visible and active in the mainstream American society. This is seen today, and, in the future, their visibility will only increase. One consequence of this is the high out-marriage among children of immigrants. It will only accelerate the race/ethnic multiplicity of the U.S. population.

By contrast, the 1990 Immigration Act has brought a heavy influx of Latino and Caribbean immigrants from lower socioeconomic groups, which is very different than the post–1965 immigrants. Compared with Asian immigrants, immigrants from Mexico, other Latin countries, and the Caribbean Islands include more political refugees, many low-skilled workers, and many undocumented workers. Researchers have indicated that because many of their families are poor and have settled in minority neighborhoods, the children of Caribbean black and many Latino immigrants generally have poor performance in school, and many have failed to complete high school. Given racial discrimination and a lack of blue-collar jobs owing to deindustrialization, these children have bleak prospects for jobs without a high school diploma. Researchers cautiously predict that they may fill the low layers of the racial hierarchy in the United States in the future.

Fourth, the influx of Third World immigrants in the post–1965 era has contributed to cultural and religious diversity. Because of transnational ties, the children of post–1965 immigrants have advantages over European immigrants from the early twentieth century and before in preserving their ethnic cultural traditions and language. The children of Latino immigrants have a huge advantage in retaining their mother tongue because many Latinos speak the same common language. According to one analysis of data from the 1989 Current Population Survey that provides monthly labor force data, the majority of second-generation Latinos aged twenty-four to forty-four are perfectly bilingual (Lopez 1996, 200). The mass migration of Third World immigrants has also contributed to religious pluralism in the United States. The influx of immigrants from Asia and the Middle East has brought several non-Judeo-Christian religions—Islam, Buddhism, Hinduism, and Sikhism—into the mix of American culture. Also, the mass migration of Catholics from Latin America, the Caribbean Islands, and Asia has contributed to the diversification of American Catholics as well as the substantial increase in the Catholic population.

See also Chinese Exclusion Act of 1882; Diversities, Ethnic and Racial; Gentlemen's Agreement of 1908; McCarran-Walter Act of 1952; National Origins Act of 1924; Naturalization Act of 1790.

Further Reading

Bryce-Laporte, Roy S. *Sourcebook on the New Immigration*. New Brunswick, NJ: Transaction Books, 1980.

Hing, Bill Ong. *Making and Remaking Asian America through Immigration Policy, 1850–1990*. Stanford, CA: Stanford University Press, 1993.

Keely, Charles B. *The Immigration Act of 1965: A Study of the Relationship of Social Science Theory to Group Interest and Legislation.* New York: Keely Publishers, 1978.

King, Desmond S. *Making Americans: Immigration, Race, and the Origins of the Diverse Democracy.* Cambridge, MA: Harvard University Press, 2000.

Min, Pyong Gap, ed. *Mass Migration to the United States: Classical and Contemporary Periods.* Walnut Creek, CA: AltaMira, 2002.

Reimers, David M. *Still the Golden Door: The Third World Comes to America.* New York: Columbia University Press, 1986.

Shin Kim and Kwang Chung Kim

Immigration Restriction League of 1894

During the 1890s, for the first time, more new immigrants came from southern and eastern Europe than from northern and western Europe. The most prominent group of newcomers at this time were Italians, followed by Jewish immigrants. During this second great immigrant wave, many "native" Americans thought that their American way of life, especially based on Protestantism, was threatened by these "undesirable immigrants." Under this perceived threat, the Immigration Restriction League was founded in 1894 by Charles Warren, Robert DeCourcy Ward, and Prescott Farnsworth Hall. It was founded in Boston but quickly spread to many other cities across the country. The constitution stated the following as the main objectives of the League:

> To advocate and work for the further judicious restriction, or stricter regulation, of immigration, to issue documents and circulars, solicit fact and information, on that subject, hold public meetings, and to arouse public opinion to the necessity of a further exclusion of elements undesirable for citizenship or injurious to our national character. It is not an object of this league to advocate the exclusion of laborers or other immigrants of such character and standards as fit them to become citizens.

With such intention, the League proposed that all immigrants should pass a literacy test before entering the country. The League remained active for nearly twenty years and made a significant impact on the enactment of the so-called National Origins Act of 1924. After Hall's death, the league's influence waned, and it eventually disbanded.

See also National Origins Act of 1924.

Heon Cheol Lee

Indentured Servants

Indentured servitude is defined as the repaying of a debt through human bondage. It was a common strategy employed by early European immigrants who settled in America during the colonial period in the seventeenth and eighteenth centuries. It is estimated that one out of every two European immigrants was an indentured servant who sold his or her labor for three to seven years in exchange for passage to the New World and housing upon arrival. Around the middle of the seventeenth century, colonial laws began to differentiate between the races of indentured servants and associated "servitude for natural life" with people of African descent.

In contemporary times, human trafficking is a form of indentured servitude and, many argue, a form of modern slavery because migrants are often unable to pay the exorbitant debt incurred as the cost of their transportation. Modern-day indentured servants are made to labor under slavelike conditions in restaurants, factories, agricultural fields, homes, and the sex industry. According to the U.S. State Department, eighteen thousand to twenty thousand individuals have been trafficked into the United States annually during recent years. People are snared into trafficking by various means, including physical force, coercion or false promises that a legitimate job or marriage awaits them. Victims are subjected to physical and emotional abuse, rape, threats against self and family, passport theft, and physical restraint. The horrific discovery in the summer of 1995 of seventy-two Thai women who had been held as virtual slaves in an El Monte, California, apartment complex focused public attention on the continued practices of indentured servitude in the United States. Some of these women had been held for up to seventeen years, and they labored for more than eighteen hours a day to sew clothes for some of the nation's top manufacturers and retailers. Armed guards and barbed wire around the apartment complex ensured that the women would not escape.

In 2000, anti-trafficking legislation—the Victims of Trafficking and Violence Protection Act (TVPA)—was enacted to strengthen penalties for trafficking-related offenses, create new programs and outreach efforts to combat worker exploitation, and offer new protections and expanded services to trafficking victims. The act also authorized the establishment of the Office to Monitor and Combat Trafficking in Persons and the President's Interagency Task Force to Monitor and Combat Trafficking in Persons. Moreover, the U.S. State Department prepares an annual Trafficking in Persons (TIP) Report to assess governmental efforts to combat human trafficking. Upon the release of the first TIP Report, former secretary of state Colin Powell stated "It is incomprehensible that trafficking in human beings should be taking place in the twenty-first century—incomprehensible, but it's true, very true. The only way to effectively address the worldwide problem of trafficking is through collective efforts by all countries, whether they are countries of origin, transit or destination."

See also Powell, Colin.

Tarry Hum

Index of Dissimilarity

The index of dissimilarity (D) is a common measure that expresses quantitatively the degree of difference between two groups' distributions among residential areas of a community or across occupational categories. Its most common use is to measure the residential segregation of racial/ethnic groups. Social scientists use the index of dissimilarity more than any other alternative measure in research on segregation.

For any city or metropolitan area, the D score for the segregation of any two groups is obtained by computations that compare the percentages of group A and group B residing in each subarea of the community (e.g., census tracts or blocks). The more *dissimilar* the two groups' distribution through these subareas is, the *higher* the index of dissimilarity. Computing the D score produces a number ranging from zero (indicating maximum residential *integration* of the two groups) to 100.0 ([1.00 if proportions are used] indicating complete *segregation* of the two groups). For example, in 2000, the index of dissimilarity between blacks and whites in Atlanta is 66, in Chicago is 81, and in Norfolk-Virginia Beach is 46. From this it can be concluded that blacks and whites are most separate in their residential patterns in Chicago and most integrated in Norfolk-Virginia Beach. In addition, if D scores for blacks and whites (or any other pair of groups) are computed for the same area at different times (e.g., 1970 and 2000), it shows how much increase or decrease in residential segregation has occurred. The index of dissimilarity is also used to compare segregation levels of several pairs of groups. For example, in metropolitan Miami the D scores for blacks and whites (74), Hispanics and blacks (74), and Hispanics and whites (44) show clearly that blacks are most segregated. Although the index of dissimilarity gauges how high or low segregation is, by itself it does not tell the cause of the segregation (e.g., Is it mainly voluntary? Is it because of racial steering? Or does intergroup economic inequality drive the segregation?), so in this sense it is like a thermometer that tells how hot or cold it is, but not *why* it is hot or cold.

See also Exposure Index; Residential Segregation.

Charles Jaret

Indian Allotment Act of 1887

Also known as the Dawes Act, the Indian Allotment Act was passed in 1887 to distribute allotments or parcels of tribal lands—up to 160 acres on a reservation—to each individual tribal member or family. It was intended to create a system of private land ownership that would make the American Indians into farmers or ranchers and to absorb the tribes into American mainstream culture. The act went on to offer Indians the benefits of U.S. citizenship if they took an allotment, lived separate from the tribe, and became "civilized."

For the first twenty-five years after an individual Indian or Indian family received an allotment, the United States held the land in trust for the benefit of the family or individual. During this time, the land could not be taxed, mortgaged, sold, or otherwise burdened with a lien without the express approval of the government. After that time, the allottee could apply for a land patent. If the patent was given, the owner could sell the land without restriction and it could be taxed, just like real estate anywhere else. After allotting reservations to tribal members, federal officials sold the surplus tracts to non-Indians, and Congress amended the allotment act to facilitate the sale of allotments.

As a result, reservation lands were reduced from 138 million acres in 1887 to 48 million acres in 1934 (about a 65 percent decrease). Most Indians resisted assimilation to the American capitalist system of private ownership and lost their allotted lands rather than being farmers and "civilized." Politically, the allotment policy hampered tribal sovereignty in that federal agents began to deal primarily with individual Indians rather than with their tribal govern-ments. The recognition of the failure of the Indian Allotment Act led the U.S. government to change its Indian policy in 1934 with the passage of the In-dian Reorganization Act (IRA).

See also Indian Citizenship Act of 1924; Native Americans, Conquest of; Na-tive Americans, Forced Relocation of; Native Americans, Prejudice and Dis-crimination against.

Sookbee Ob

Indian Citizenship Act of 1924

The Indian Citizenship Act that was passed in 1924 granted citizenship to all American Indians who were not already citizens under other provisions of fed-eral law or treaties. By the time the 1924 Citizenship Act was passed, two-thirds of all Indians had already gained citizenship. Before this act, Indians obtained citizenship through two ways: separate treaties and special federal statutes. Treaties often provided that a person must either accept U.S. citi-zenship or retain tribal membership. Those who did not accept U.S. citizen-ship under the terms of treaties could retain sovereign nationhood. By the Indian Allotment (Dawes) Act of 1887, Indians could obtain citizenship if they chose to adopt the terms. Some federal laws granted citizenship to all mem-bers of a tribe who served in the military during a particular time of war or individual Indians who complied with special statutes' terms. The 1924 act was an all-encompassing act that granted citizenship, including the right to vote in national elections, to all Indians born within the U.S. territory. This act did not impair the trust relationship in any manner that Indians had with the U.S. government; gaining the status of a U.S. citizen did not affect Indians' ex-isting rights of membership within a tribe.

See also Indian Allotment Act of 1887; Native Americans, Conquest of; Na-tive Americans, Forced Relocation of; Native Americans, Prejudice and Dis-crimination against.

Sookbee Ob

Indian Claims Commission (ICC)

The Indian Claims Commission (ICC) was created as an independent agency by an act of 1946 to hear and determine claims against the United States on behalf of any tribe, band, or other identifiable group of American Indians re-siding in the United States. The ICC Act created a three-person commission to hear and determine claims from the Indian tribes who had been deprived of their land and economic resources by the federal government without com-pensation. Indians had no tribunal under U.S. law in which to present their claims until the ICC Act was passed in 1946.

Settlement of such claims often dealt with as many as 142 different statutes. The commission docketed 605 individual claims cases, nearly half of which resulted in monetary awards. Between 1946 and 1975, the commission awarded $534 million to Indian claimants, $53 million of which was paid in attorney's fees. Compensation, however, was not based on current market value but on the land's value at the time of the taking. No compensation was given for land if more than one tribe used the area. After the commission determined the land's value, the government subtracted the cost of preparing the case, and the tribe had to pay 10 percent of its award as attorney's fee. The commission had originally been created for five years but was extended four times. The commission was finally abolished in 1978, and the 102 cases remaining on its docket were transferred to the U.S. Court of Claims.

See also Indian Allotment Act of 1887.

Sookhee Oh

Indian Occupation of Alcatraz Island

Hundreds of young, urban Indian college students and American Indian supporters led by Richard Oakes, a Mohawk, occupied Alcatraz Island in San Francisco Bay for nineteen months beginning in November 1969. In 1964, five Sioux had occupied the former federal prison on the island. They claimed that under the terms of the 1868 Fort Laramie Treaty between the Sioux and the United States, an abandoned federal facility must be returned to Indian ownership. The 1969 occupation reclaimed the ownership in the name of Indians of all tribes to establish an educational and cultural center in the abandoned prison. The underlying goals of the occupation included awakening the American public to the plight of Native Americans, to the suffering caused by the federal government's broken treaties and broken promises, and to the need for Indian self-determination and autonomy.

Even though the protesters could not obtain title to the island or build an American Indian culture center, they achieved their underlying goals by attracting a great deal of public attention to the Native American issues of identity, self-determination, autonomy, and respect for Indian cultural heritage. As a result, either directly or indirectly, the U.S. government had to adopt a policy of Indian self-determination.

Group of Native Americans occupying the former prison at Alcatraz Island, November 1969.

AP/Wide World Photos.

This protest was different in that before this event, Indian activism was generally tribal in nature, centered in small geographic areas, and focused on specific issues such as illegal trespass on Indian lands or violation of Indian treaty rights for access to traditional hunting and fishing sites. Thus, the Alcatraz occupation is recognized as the springboard for the rise of new Indian activism, which is more organized and more pan-ethnic in nature.

See also American Indian Movement (AIM); Pan-ethnic Movements; Red Power Movement.

Sookhee Oh

Indian Reorganization Act of 1934 (IRA)

The Indian Reorganization Act of 1934 (IRA), also known as the Wheeler-Howard Act, was the centerpiece of the Indian New Deal during the administration of President Franklin Roosevelt and Indian Commissioner John Collier. The act was intended to increase self-governance and to foster the economic independence of Indian tribes. Prior to this act, the Indian General Allotment Act of 1887 and the eventual massive breakup of Indian landholdings severely undermined the general well-being and self-determination of Indian tribes. When the Meriam Report (a federally sponsored survey on the state of Indian reservations, published in 1928) revealed the appalling state of Native Americans in the reservations, the voice of Indian reformers gained support for a major change of Indian policy, which led to the passage of the IRA.

The objectives of the IRA included conserving and developing Indian lands and resources; extending to Indians the right to form businesses and other organizations; establishing a credit system for Indians; granting certain rights of home rule to Indians; and providing for vocational education for Indians. The IRA gave the tribes two years to vote on whether they wanted to adopt it. About half of the federally recognized Indian tribes chose to accept the IRA constitution. As a result, the national policy of allotment of Indian lands ceased, and the land that had been divided began to be consolidated. The act also restored some measure of self-governance, made federal loans for economic development available to tribes who adopted the IRA, and mandated, for the first time, an Indian hiring preference within the Bureau of Indian Affairs. Although the act did not systematically incorporate existing Indian conceptions of authority, it at least provided an opportunity and a legal basis for Indian tribes to formulate their own tribal government and constitutions.

See also Indian Allotment Act of 1887; Indian Citizenship Act of 1924; Meriam Report.

Sookhee Oh

Indian Reservations

Indian reservations are land set aside for the use, possession, and benefit of an Indian tribe and its members by the president and Congress. Ordinarily, such reservations are considered to be Indian land where the exercise of some measure of self-government is allowed. In reality, reservations frequently represent a struggle on the part of Indians for autonomy, self-sufficiency, religious freedom, and cultural identity as being eroded by the path of white settlement.

Continuing the seventeenth-century English colonizers' reservation tradition, the U.S. government controlled Native Americans by forcing them to live within clearly defined zones based on treaties, executive orders, or congressional decrees. These treaties involved promises to provide food, goods, and money and to protect them from attack from other tribes and white settlers, but these treaties were often broken. The reservation policy also reflected the view that forcing the Indians to live in a confined space with little opportunity for nomadic hunting would make it easier to "civilize" them. Indians on reservations, however, have preserved many of their traditional values, beliefs, and customs rather than being assimilated to American ways of life.

The passage of the General Allotment Act in 1887, which began dividing reservation lands into individual parcels, had a profound impact on reservations. Many Indian nations lost most of their land because reservation residents had to sell their allotments for income or to pay delinquent state taxes or mortgages. In addition, the allotment policy undermined tribal sovereignty on reservations because federal agents began dealing primarily with individual Indians rather than with their tribal governments.

By the time Congress passed the Indian Reorganization Act (IRA) in 1934, Indian tribes began to reassert their authority over reservation lands. The IRA was significant in that it discontinued the allotment policy, allowed reservation residents to form their own governments, protected Indian culture, and promoted traditional arts and crafts.

Today, Indian reservations make up less than 2 percent of their original area. These reservations also vary in size and demographic composition. In 1990, the federal government recognized 278 Indian land areas as reservations. The Navajo (Diné) Reservation consists of some 16 million acres in Arizona, New Mexico, and Utah; others contain fewer than a hundred acres. The 2000 U.S. census reported that 921,322 people lived on reservations and 52 percent of the reservation residents were American Indians. About half of the land on reservations belongs to Indians; significant portions are owned and inhabited by non-Indians. The Indian-owned land is usually held in trust by the federal government, meaning that this property is exempt from state and country taxes and can be sold only in accordance with federal regulations.

See also Indian Reorganization Act of 1934 (IRA); Meriam Report; Native Americans, Forced Relocation of; Sioux Outbreak of 1890.

Sookhee Oh

Indian Self-Determination and Education Assistance Act of 1975 (ISDEAA)

In 1975 Congress passed the Indian Self-Determination and Education Assistance Act (ISDEAA) to implement tribal self-determination policy. Before passage of this law, the Bureau of Indian Affairs (BIA) and other federal agencies regulated and maintained federal control over the delivery of educational, health, and other services to American Indians. Congress recognized the obligation of the United States to respond to the strong expression of Indian people for self-determination by assuring maximum Indian participation in the educational services as well as other federal services to Indian communities. This recognition would enable Indian communities to assume their rightful role in control of their own lifeways. Although this Act deals primarily with the delivery of educational services, nearly all other federal support to Native Americans is also within the extent of the act. Such services include agriculture, health care, law enforcement, and other programs in support of tribal government.

The ISDEAA permits the tribes or any group chartered by the tribe's governing body to take the responsibility for delivering federal services to tribal members. Contracting organizations must meet certain requirements before they are eligible to enter into such agreements with the federal government. Elementary and high schools located on a reservation are among the most common organizations. Although tribes and allied organizations now deliver these services using their own employees, buildings, and equipment, the federal government still retains significant oversight over these contracts.

Sookhee Oh

Indians, Conquest of

See Native Americans, Conquest of.

Institutional Racism

Definition

Social institutions are organized in such a way that they discriminate against minority members. This type of discrimination, or racism, is referred to as institutional racism. In their 1967 book *Black Power*, Stokely Carmichael and Charles Hamilton first used the term *institutional racism* to differentiate individual acts of racism from institutional policies that affect blacks and other minorities in all spheres of life. Institutional racism encompasses discriminatory mechanisms and policies that adversely affect minorities, even though the institution itself may have an official policy against discrimination. Institutional racism can also involve actions where those who work for the institution have no intention to discriminate against minorities but result in doing so because of the policies that are already in place (Feagin 1978). Sometimes rules and regulations that were established over time to protect the institution may result in discrimination against minorities today because they are outdated and no longer reflect current racial and social attitudes.

Race expert Joe Feagin identified two types of institutional racism. The first is direct institutional discrimination, which includes actions or policies that are consciously devised by an institution to discriminate against people on the basis of their race, color, religion, or national origin. The employees who are aware of its discriminatory policy usually carry out direct institutional racism. The second is indirect institutional racism, which includes practices and policies that have a negative impact on a group of people even though there is no official policy to discriminate against that group. As Carmichael and Hamilton note, "When five hundred black babies die each year because of the lack of proper food, shelter, and medical facilities and thousands more are destroyed and maimed physically, emotionally and intellectually because of conditions of poverty and discrimination in the black community, that is a function of institutional racism" (1967, 4).

Another important difference between direct and indirect forms of institutional racism is that the former has been legally banned in our society so that even private institutions such as clubs, golf courses, and universities that practice direct institutional racism have been under tremendous pressure to end these practices. However, indirect institutional racism still exists today, fifty years after the passage of the Civil Rights Act by Congress in 1964. Indirect institutional racism takes place through mechanisms and policies that have an impact on minorities in the community where they live in the areas of employment, health, housing, education, and other spheres of life.

There are several reasons why indirect institutional racism continues to exist in society today. First, most of the people who write the rules and regulations for these institutions are often whites who have little or no knowledge of the distinct needs of the particular minority communities. Second, it is more difficult to root out indirect institutional racism because it is difficult to pinpoint who is responsible for discrimination. The structure of the organization or the agency that is implementing a set of policies may be guilty of indirect racism without knowing it. Unless certain practices or policies are challenged, the institution may not be aware that it is engaged in indirect institutional racism.

Examples of Institutional Racism

The health-care industry is an example of how institutional racism adversely affects African Americans. According to data from the 2000 census, a white person born today can expect to live to 79 years, while a black person is expected to live only to 69 years. Diseases and conditions such as prostate cancer, high blood pressure, stroke, and diabetes that can be controlled when caught early are often the leading killers of African Americans (Williams 2003, Acevedo-Garcia et al. 2003, Williams and Williams-Morris 2000). The U.S. government supports institutions that do research on health issues through grants and tax exemptions. However, there is no requirement that they include minorities in their research design. These institutions may already have white researchers who were hired at a time when black and other minority scientists were denied employment in these fields because of official discrimination policies. Therefore, when these researchers create their research design, there may not be any black or other minority group present to provide the viewpoint of their community. As a result, the major illnesses that the minority populations suffer from may be omitted from the research design.

According to law, anyone who shows up in an emergency room has to be treated. However, studies have shown that white doctors tend to perform fewer tests on black patients who show up in emergency room than on whites.

In a study of asthma among racial and ethnic groups that use Medicaid, Lieu et al. (2002) concluded that black and Latino children had a more severe asthma status and less use of preventive asthma medication than white children within the same economic group. Even though white and black children have access to the same insurance group, black children tend to use inhalers less often than whites and are more likely to go to the emergency room whenever they have an asthma attack. The authors note that the disparity between the white and black children in obtaining care for their asthma because of communication barriers between doctors and patients and the lack of cultural understanding on the part of those who are providing care to the patients.

In a 2000 study of racism and the mental health of African Americans, Williams and Williams-Morris concluded that institutional racism can have an adverse effect. This is due to the level of crime and violence that African Americans are exposed to, the noise and overcrowding that exists in their neighborhoods, and the level of anxiety they live with as they experience various forms of discrimination in their daily encounter with white institutions. Moreover, since racism is an internalized assumption of superiority over another group, when blacks are treated in an institution, the providers may already assume that the treatment will not be effective since they have already a set of stereotypes against blacks. The authors noted that black clinicians have long argued that the popular misconceptions and inaccuracies of the psychology of African Americans could lead to the misdiagnosis of black patients. "The over-diagnosis of paranoid schizophrenia and the under-diagnosis of affective disorders are the most frequent types of misdiagnoses for Blacks" (Williams and Williams-Morris 2003, 256).

Many people may assume that black children have enjoyed equality in education since official segregation in education ended in 1954 with the Supreme Court's ruling that separate schools for blacks and whites were unequal and unconstitutional. Yet, institutional racism still persists in the education system. Institutional racism is manifested in how school districts are funded, the policies that authorities adopt to address education issues, and cultural and social stereotypes of blacks that are often found in books and the media. School districts are usually supported by property taxes. Citizens who live in affluent communities receive more money for their schools than do minorities who live in the inner cities or poor communities. Despite the rhetoric on quality of education for every child in the United States, most blacks attend mostly segregated schools in this society. Most of these schools do not have adequate funding to meet the needs of their students, and fewer of these children attend graduate schools. Of the minority children in the United States, 40 percent attend inner-city schools, and more than half of these children are poor and fail to achieve basic achievement levels (*Washington Post* March 1, 1998). In 2000, about one-sixth of blacks attended schools in which 1 percent of their fellow students were white (Orfield and Eaton 2003).

Residential segregation remains one of the most enigmatic problems that U.S. society faces today, because most communities are divided primarily between those who live in predominantly white neighborhoods and others who live in predominantly black or mixed neighborhoods. Institutional racism continues in the housing market when those who do not have significant savings or a history of credit are asked to come up with a large down-payment to obtain a mortgage. Blacks and other minorities are often unable to raise the money or find family members who can cosign a mortgage application for them because they do not have a history of credit or collateral to support the mortgage.

Mortgage lenders and insurance companies can also be involved in the politics of redlining. Redlining is a practice where banks and other financial institutions denied mortgage or home improvement loans to homeowners who live in certain geographic areas, regardless of the physical condition of the home or the credit worthiness of the potential buyer (Perle and Lynch 1994; Center for Urban Studies 1977).

In a report published by the Federal Office of Thrift and Supervision, Feagin (1999) notes that "Black mortgage loan applicants have been rejected by savings and loan associations twice as often as White applicants." Other researchers noted that "White Americans made a series of deliberate decisions to deny blacks access to urban housing markets and to reinforce their spatial segregation" (Massey and Denton 1993, 19). More than thirty-five years after the adoption of the Fair Housing Act, institutional racism still exists in the housing sector, and it forces African Americans to live in ghettos that have substandard housing, few opportunities for employment, and inadequate health care and education.

On June 16, 2003, a Texas judge freed twelve African Americans in the town of Tulia after they had spent almost four years in jail on accusations brought by a lone white undercover narcotics agent (Davey 2003). At the time of the arrests, the law-enforcement agent was hailed as a hero and decorated as the state's lawman of the year. Subsequently, it was discovered that the agent not only lied about the people he had arrested, but his methods of gathering the evidence were dubious. The most impressive aspect of this story is the rapidity of law-enforcement associations in the state of Texas in believing the charges that the agent brought against the defendants. The eagerness of whites to accept official police accusation of blacks has been the most pernicious effect of institutional racism in society today.

Institutional racism is manifested in the way that law enforcement, the courts, and the prison system disproportionately convict African Americans and other minorities for crimes. Blacks, who account for only 12 percent of the population, make up 45 percent of the people who are in prison (Hacker 1992). Law enforcement officials profile African Americans more than any other racial or ethnic group in America. For example, the Civil Rights Commission and the New York City Council reported recently that police officers in New York City tended to profile blacks at a higher rate than any other group in the city (*New York Times* June 18, 2003).

One of the most famous examples of institutional racism is New York state's Rockefeller Drug Laws. In 1973, Governor Nelson Rockefeller pressed the state legislature to pass a series of stringent anti-drug laws. These laws were the most severe in the country at the time. Their goal was to deter citizens from using or selling drugs and to punish and isolate from society those who had engaged in this enterprise. The laws required judges to impose a mandatory sentence of fifteen years to life for "any one convicted of selling two ounces or possessing four ounces of narcotics drug." In 1973, the laws were amended by the legislature to include crack cocaine and to increase the amount of drugs needed to be convicted. As a result of these laws, the population of the state's prison system increased from 20,000 in 1980 to almost 62,000 in 1992. By the end of 2002, the prison population was expected to exceed 73,000 prisoners (Wilson 2000). Most of the prisoners are African American males, because crack cocaine is likely to be used by the poor and is found mostly in communities that are heavily populated by minorities. Of those convicted and incarcerated for drug offenses today in New York state, 94 percent are African Americans (NYCLU 2000).

The fear of crime is not the exclusive purview of whites. Blacks are as much afraid of crime as whites and are more often the victims of crime. However, the deployment of police officers in black communities depends on the policies and priorities that are established by city officials. African Americans often find themselves underserved when it comes to having police officers patrol their community. Moreover, even when officers are deployed in their community, they are often ignorant of the needs of the community. As far back as 1968, the Kerner Commission, which investigated the causes of the riots of the summer 1967, reported that most police officers deployed in black neighborhoods had little knowledge of the community and therefore were unable to communicate effectively with residents. Police officers, who are often white because of past departmental hiring practices, have been seen to regard blacks no matter how good a citizen, in the role of the enemy.

Whether in private or public institutions, blacks often confront institutional racism in employment. This is expressed in the form of denial of promotion, paying them less than their white workers, or hiding information that could enhance their chances of being promoted. Although well-known African Americans, such as Colin Powell, Condoleeza Rice, Richard Parsons, and Kenneth Chenault, have occupied high-powered positions in government and the private sector, the reality is that there are fewer African Americans in the position of power in corporate or government institutions than it appears. Corporate and government policies, such as the seniority system, exams, and tenure, often work against blacks and other minorities who are just entering these institutions.

Since the 1960s, there have been many efforts to end institutional racism in corporate and public institutions. Citizens have sued the police, fire, sanitation, parks, and private agencies over their testing policy, their recruitment practices, and their requirements, such as height, weight, or racial backgrounds, to force them to end institutional racism. There have been numerous victories since these lawsuits have been filed. However, there is still a long way to go before institutional racism is eliminated.

See also Black Power: The Politics of Liberation in America, Carmichael, Stokely; Racism, Aversive versus Dominative.

Further Reading

Carmichael, Stokely, and Charles Hamilton. *Black Power: The Politics of Liberation in America*. New York: Random House, 1967.

Davey, Monica. "Texas Frees 12 on Bond after Drug Sweep Inquiry." *New York Times* (June 17, 2003).

Feagin, Joe R. "Excluding Blacks and Others from Housing: The Foundation of White Racism." *Cityscape* 4, no. 3 (July 10, 1999).

Fletcher, Michael A. "Prophecy on Race Relations Came True" *Washington Post* (March 1, 1998): A06.

Lieu, Tracy A, Hacker, Andrew. *Two Nations: Black and White: Separate, Hostile, Unequal.* New York: Scribners, 1992.

Lieu, Tracey, et al. "Racial/Ethnic Variation in Asthma Status and Management Practices among Children in Managed Medicaid." *Pediatrics* 109, no. 5 (May 2002).

Orfield, Gary, and Eaton Susan. "Back to Segregation." *Nation* 276, no. 8 (March 3, 2003).

Perle, Eugene D., and Kathryn Lynch, "Perspectives on mortgage lending and redlining" *Journal of the American Planning Association* 60, no. 3 (Summer 1994): 344.

West, Cornel. *Race Matters.* New York: Vintage Books, 1993.

Williams, David R. "The Health of Men: Structured inequalities and opportunities." *American Journal of Public Health* 93, no. 5 (May 2003): 724.

Williams, David R., and Ruth Williams-Morris. "Racism and Mental Health: The African-American Experience." *Ethnicity and Health* 5, no. 3/4 (2000): 243–268.

Francois Pierre-Louis

Intelligence and Standardized Tests, Cultural Biases in

The earliest intelligence tests, the precursors of the IQ test, were developed in Europe in the late nineteenth century to classify mentally retarded children. Although Alfred Binet, the man most generally associated with these early tests, believed that intelligence was a learnable and culturally specific feature of an individual that could only be truly understood through in-depth observation, the tests that developed from his early work did not take these views into consideration. Instead, they drew heavily on the pseudoscience of eugenics, which held that intelligence was a racially specific characteristic, with northern and western Europeans (especially Protestant upper-class males from these regions) genetically predisposed to the highest IQ levels and people of African descent falling lowest on the scale. Other test creators, such as G. S. Brett in 1904, worked on the project of test development because they wanted to create an instrument that would let them select individuals who would not be able to adjust to urban life, therefore giving the test an urban bias.

Because the individuals who designed IQ tests held these beliefs, the tests they designed came to reflect them. In other words, the test designers administered their tests to a sample of individuals, and if the results did not come out as expected, they modified the tests to reflect reality as they themselves perceived it, rather than using the tests as tools of discovery to understand how intelligence really works. Early versions of the tests were often tried out on soldiers or army enlistees to see whether the desired results would occur.

Even when test creators do not approach their work with the specific goal of making a test that is stratified racially (as in standardized tests for college admission or school placement), the tests often come out stratified. This is because there is a middle-class white cultural bias inherent in how the tests are written. For instance, the test may ask its takers to draw analogies from culturally specific proverbs; test takers who are familiar with the proverbs will have an advantage over those who are not. These biases are not limited to the verbal section of tests. Math questions can also be culturally biased; for instance, a word problem about car speeds or airplanes may be unfamiliar to an inner-city child who has never been in one of these vehicles. Even more important, the skills tested by IQ tests, and to an even greater degree by standardized achievement tests, are ones that are heavily dependant on what an individual has learned at home or in school. Underfunded schools, attended primarily by inner-city black, Latino/a, and immigrant children, do not have the same resources to teach vocabulary words, reading skills, and math in small groups with individualized attention. The IQ and standardized tests also measure specific facets of intelligence (most commonly vocabulary, reading comprehension, mathematical reasoning, and spatial reasoning) that may not be the ones emphasized in a particular culture (which may instead emphasize physical aptitude, knowledge of the natural world, understanding of tradition, artistic creativity, or problem solving). Finally, the math and science sections on these tests sometimes permit or require the use of a calculator. Poor students may not be able to afford a calculator, especially one of the scientific or graphing models used for higher-level tests, thus putting them at a disadvantage. When the use of a calculator is required, the test administrators must provide it. However, students who have not had a chance to become familiar with calculators before are, again, disadvantaged.

Given that IQ and achievement tests do have cultural biases that result in differential achievement based on race, black and Latino/a students are prone to see themselves as individuals who will not perform as well on the tests. This process is called the "stereotype threat," which means that in a racially charged test-taking circumstance, those students who believe that individuals of their race perform poorly on the test will worry so much about this stereotype that it will have a negative impact on their test-taking skills. Tests that claim to measure intelligence or aptitude rather than learned skills, tests taken in a majority-white setting, and tests that ask for the race of the taker before beginning are especially likely to provoke this response.

Some test-making companies are beginning to address the issues of cultural biases in their tests. There are two main ways that companies do this. First, they may rigorously evaluate each individual test question (as well as the entire test) to try to eliminate the source of the bias. This involves gathering data about the race of each test-taker and comparing the performance of different racial groups on test questions, as well as administering experimental test sections and abandoning those questions that show wide, or at least the widest, racial gaps. Second, they (or independent test-tutoring companies) can create free or low-cost educational seminars for black and Latino/a children or inner-city school classes to help them learn the skills that the test requires. Although these methods have been successful in narrowing the performance gaps on some tests, the gaps remain wide.

See also Education and Racial Discrimination; Intelligence Tests and Racism.

Further Reading

Fischer, Claude S., et al. *Inequality by Design: Cracking the Bell Curve Myth*. Princeton, NJ: Princeton University Press, 1996.

Jencks, Christopher, and Meredith Phillips, eds. *The Black-White Test Score Gap*. Washington, DC: Brookings Institution Press, 1998.

Lehmann, Nicholas. *The Big Test: The Secret History of the American Meritocracy*. New York: Farrar, Straus and Giroux, 1999.

Mikaila Mariel Lemonik Arthur

Intelligence Tests and Racism

The development of standardized tests designed to measure intelligence (like the IQ test), along with those designed to evaluate scholastic ability and achievement (like the SAT) is closely linked to the ideologies of race that were in effect at the time of their creation, and these legacies remain. There are persistent differences in test scores based not only on race but also on gender and socioeconomic class. These tests were created based on a number of important psychological ideas: that intelligence could be measured through the administration of a simple multiple-choice test that tested a limited set of skills, that the distribution of intelligence in society matched the classic statistical bell curve, that success on the tests could not be taught, and that intelligence was at least predominantly hereditary and, thus, different racial and ethnic populations varied genetically in their ability to perform well on the test.

The first intelligence test, the IQ test, was invented in 1905 by Alfred Binet, a French psychologist. Over the years, others improved on and altered the test into the shape that it takes today and developed tests such as the SAT, the GRE, and the ACT as derivations of it. When these tests were developed, the norms for scoring them were established through experimental administration on subjects who were primarily middle-class Protestant males of northern European descent. Therefore, those who were not members of this specific cultural and racial group had not been taken into account in the development of the test and performed poorly on it. These poor performances cemented the inferior intelligence of women and individuals who were not of northern European descent in the minds of the psychologists who developed and administered the tests. During the earlier years of their use, IQ tests were used by persons involved in the eugenics movement to decide who to sterilize. Additionally, they were used to keep immigrants from southern and eastern Europe, especially Jews, from entering the United States. Similar ideas derived from the eugenics movements were a part of the ideology of the Nazi party in Germany, and it is perhaps this association that led to their decline in the United States.

Despite the decline in the practice of eugenics, intelligence and aptitude tests continue to show differential performance on the basis of race. Some of the sources of these differences today are the use of culturally coded language and situations in test questions, exposure to situations similar to the test in the past, stereotype anxiety due to the knowledge that people of one's race or gender tend to perform less successfully on the test, and lack of access to the expensive coaching courses that offer promises that they can raise performance on the tests—often by more than 200 points on the SAT. Additionally, studies done on multiracial children have demonstrated that the social and cultural context of the child's family has more to do with performance on the tests than how much of their ancestry was European.

Despite the fact that numerous studies have demonstrated racial gaps in standardized test performance and certain efforts have been made to correct the problem, it has not been eliminated. Test makers have developed a number of evaluative techniques that are supposed to detect and eliminate bias in tests and in specific questions, but the gaps still persist. Almost four hundred colleges and universities in the United States have chosen to deemphasize standardized testing in admissions decisions, but many of the most selective state university systems continue to rely on test scores in their admissions decisions, often because it is easier to make decisions in this purely numeric fashion. Some colleges and universities continue to use a minimum cut-off score: if applicants score below this cut-off, they cannot be admitted, regardless of the merits of their other qualifications. In addition, the National Collegiate Athletic Association (NCAA) uses a cut-off score in determining eligibility to participate in intercollegiate athletic competition. These cut-off scores mean that thousands of otherwise-qualified black, Latino/a, and Native American students have been denied opportunities in higher education. Additionally, IQ tests are used in elementary education to classify children as special-education students or even as so developmentally disabled that they are in need of institutionalization, and this has contributed to the fact that a higher proportion of children of color have been placed in special-education programs or have been institutionalized.

See also Biological Racism; Education and Racial Discrimination; Eugenics Movement; Intelligence and Standardized Tests, Cultural Biases in.

Further Reading

Fischer, Claude S., et al. *Inequality by Design: Cracking the Bell Curve Myth*. Princeton, NJ: Princeton University Press, 1996.

Jencks, Christopher, and Meredith Phillips, eds. *The Black-White Test Score Gap*. Washington, DC: The Brookings Institution Press, 1998.

Lehmann, Nicholas. *The Big Test: The Secret History of the American Meritocracy*. New York: Farrar, Straus and Giroux, 1999.

Mikaila Mariel Lemonik Arthur

Intermarriage

Intermarriage refers to a marriage between two partners of different groups. There are three forms of intermarriage: interethnic, interfaith, and interracial. Interethnic marriage is commonly used to refer to a marriage between partners of two different national-origin or language groups, whereas interracial marriage indicates a marriage between persons who belong to two different racial groups. Interfaith marriage refers to a marriage between members of

Interracial couple.

Getty Images/PhotoDisc.

two different religious backgrounds. In the United States, interethnic marriages are more common than interfaith marriage, which are more common than interracial marriages. It suggests that physical differences are more difficult to overcome for friendship and intimate relations than are differences in national origin or religion, which indicates the tenacity of racism in the United States.

The most widely known and studied cases of interethnic marriages are those among descendants of European immigrants. More than 75 percent of third-generation and higher white Americans are involved in interethnic marriages across national origin. Before World War II, interethnic marriages among different white ethnic groups were at a considerably high level, but interfaith marriages were exceptionally few. This trend led to the triple-melting-pot hypothesis proposed in 1944, which claimed that intermarriage was occurring between various nationalities but only within the three major religious groupings (Protestants, Catholics, and Jews). But interfaith marriage rates have gradually increased since 1960, to the extent that the majority of Protestants, Catholics, and Jews now marry members of different religions.

Interethnic marriages among white Americans are now so common that most white Americans have difficulty tracing their ancestries. Intermarriage indicates the highest level of assimilation, so a high level of intermarriage among white ethnic groups means their high level of assimilation into American society. Interethnic marriages among different Asian, Latino, and/or black groups within each racial minority group have also increased since the 1980s as these minority populations have rapidly increased as a result of mass migration from Asian, Latin American, and Caribbean countries. But it remains to be seen whether third- and fourth-generation racial minority members will have high levels of intermarriage within each pan-ethnic or racial group, comparable to multigeneration white Americans. It is anticipated that their high level of intermarriage will not lead to assimilation into American society because they belong to racial minority groups.

Interracial marriages are generally less common than the other two forms of intermarriages. African Americans in particular have had an exceptionally low intermarriage rate. During the periods of slavery, unions between whites and blacks were prohibited legally in almost all states, although many white slave owners raped black slaves and mixed-race children resulted. In the Jim Crow system, almost all Southern states established the antimiscegenation laws that banned interracial marriages between whites and members of other racial minority groups. Various antimiscegenation laws lasted until 1967, when the U.S. Supreme Court declared them unconstitutional. Such formal segregation and related discrimination certainly discouraged interracial marriage between whites and African Americans. Children of black-white interracial marriages were treated as black. In fact, according to the one-drop rule, one drop of African American blood identified a person as black.

Since the Supreme Court struck down antimiscegenation laws in 1967, black-white intermarriages have steadily increased. Nevertheless, a tiny proportion of African American marriages are interracial marriages. In the mid-1990s, only 1 percent of black women and 3 percent of black men were married to persons other than blacks, mostly to whites. Given the great social distance between African Americans and whites and a high level of residential segregation of African Americans, this extremely low rate of interracial marriage is not surprising. Of white-black interracial marriages, about 75 percent are marriages between black men and white women. Often, it is occupationally successful African American men who marry white women. This kind of interracial marriage is often interpreted as an exchange of black men's high occupational status with white women's superior racial status.

In 1990, about 40 percent of native-born Asian Americans had intermarried, most of them with white spouses. Their high intermarriage rate may be the result of a low level of social distance between Asian and white Americans and Asian Americans' high socioeconomic status. But it is also a result of their small population size. As its native-born adult population increases in the future, more and more Asian Americans may be able to marry members of their own ethnic group and other Asian Americans. Even though Hispanics are shown to have married interracially as often as (if not more than) Asian Americans, racial origins of their marriage partners are much more diverse, including both white and black. This is because of their diverse racial characteristics.

Native Americans have always shown a high rate of interracial marriage, which is due to their small population and a low level of segregation. Today, most Native Americans are children of interracial marriages between Native Americans and other racial groups. Children of interracial marriages between Native Americans and others have a wider option as far as their ethnic identification is concerned. In spite of this possibility, a high proportion of children of such interracial marriages tend to identify themselves as Native Americans.

Further Reading

Kennedy, R.J.R. "Single or Triple Melting Pot? Intermarriage Trends in New Haven, 1870–1940." *American Journal of Sociology* 49 (1984): 331–339.

Mathabane, Mark, and Gail Mathabane. *Love in Black and White: The Triumph of Love over Prejudice and Taboo.* New York: HarperCollins, 1992.

Qianm Zhenchao, Sampson Lee Blair, and Stacey Ruf. "Asian American Interracial and Interethnic Marriages: Differences by Education and Nativity." *International Migration Review* 35 (2001): 557–586.

Rosenblatt, Paul C., Terri A. Karis, and Richard Powell. *Multiracial Couples: Black and White Voices*. Thousand Oaks, CA: Sage Publications, 1995.

Shin Kim and Kwang Chung Kim

Internal Colonialism

Internal colonialism is a theory of interethnic relations based on the analogy of the relationship between the colonizers and the colonized. This theory gained significant currency in the 1960s and the 1970s when national liberation movements proliferated both within and without the U.S. border. Just as the Vietnamese and Algerians would fight for the independence of their nations, Native Americans, African Americans, Chicanos, and Puerto Ricans would demand their own autonomous nation-states.

The social situation of the colonized minorities in Africa differs from that of the immigrant minorities such as the Irish and the Germans of the Unites States in many aspects. The colonized minorities were indigenous and numerically a majority but forcefully subjugated to the domination of alien colonizers in their own homelands. Thus, they were minorities in terms of power. The colonial interethnic system usually allocated the most degrading jobs to the natives. Social mobility, if there was any, was extremely limited. Assimilation into the mainstream culture was impossible. The only hope lay in the overthrow of colonial domination and the establishment of an independent government of the indigenous people. The aspiration of the colonized for liberation took the form of nationalism. Political struggle for national liberation required solidarity as a nation based on the presumed common root of national history and identity and pride in the national language, religion, and culture.

Some tried to apply this colonial paradigm to the interethnic relations of the United States. Robert Blauner, author of *Racial Oppression in America* (1972), thought that the peoples of color in the United States shared essential conditions with the colonized peoples abroad: economic underdevelopment, a heritage of colonialism and neocolonialism, and a lack of real political autonomy and power. Indeed, as many argued, the historical experience of Mexican Americans could be better understood within the paradigm of internal colonialism than with that of assimilation. At first, Mexicans were colonized by the Spaniards and then by the Anglo Americans. The Anglo elite frequently intermarried or became *compadres* ("god-relatives") with the landowning Mexican families. Many of traditional Mexican landowning elite lost their titles by the legal and illegal actions of the Anglo administration. The conquered people were kept at the bottom of the occupational structure as a cheap and controlled labor force, always filling the dead-end jobs. Unlike European immigrants, Mexican Americans confronted strong racial discrimination and found little opportunity for upward social mobility through the generations. In the 1960s, the protest movement of Mexican Americans developed into the Chicano nationalist movement fighting against Anglo imperialism. It called for the unity of the people of La Raza, who supposedly shared the cultural heritage from the Aztec, Inca, and Toltec, as well as the Spanish, civilizations. They sought community control in the hope that it would assure political and economic equity and preserve their cultural identity.

The theory of internal colonialism draws attention to the historical experience of African Americans, Mexicans, and Puerto Ricans, in contrast to that of European ethic immigrants. They were forcefully incorporated into the U.S. society and remain the subordinated "others" instead of being assimilated into the mainstream American culture. Native Americans have suffered near extermination since the "discovery of America" in the fifteenth century and have survived with few resources, forced into in reservations. Africans were forcefully brought to the United States only to be slaves at the discretion of the white masters, while the African continent became colonized by the European empires. Mexicans and Puerto Ricans became Americans through conquest.

See also Black Power: The Politics of Liberation in America; Racial Ghettoes; Racial Oppression in America.

Further Reading

Acuna, Rodolfo. *Occupied America*. 2nd ed. New York: Harper & Row, 1981.

Blauner, Robert. *Racial Oppression in America*. New York: Harper & Row, 1972.

Montejano, David. *Anglos and Mexicans in the Making of Texas, 1836–1986*. Austin: University of Texas Press, 1987.

Moore, Joan W. *Mexican Americans*. 2nd ed. Englewood Cliffs, NJ: Prentice Hall, 1976.

Dong-Ho Cho

Internalized Racism

Internalized racism is a product of the socialization process in the United States exhibited by many people of color at some point in their lives. People of color exhibit internalized racism when they collude with the racist ideas of the dominant white society. Internalized racism has both a conscious and an unconscious component. Conscious collaboration occurs when people of color knowingly (but not always voluntarily) accede to their own mistreatment to survive or maintain some status, livelihood, or other benefit, as when a person of color silently endures racist jokes told by a boss. The more insidious form of internalized racism is unconscious. It occurs when people of color do not even know they are collaborating in their own dehumanization. Often, this occurs because they do not recognize that racism occurs at an institutional level; rather, they see prejudice and discrimination only at the individual level. An example of unconscious internalized racism is when a person of color who has been repeatedly passed over for promotions at work feels that the problem is his own—for example, that he needs to work harder—rather than recognizing his plight as a manifestation of his superiors' racist attitudes. Another form of internalized racism is denial of one's ethnic or cultural background, such as not wanting to speak one's native language or eat one's ethnic food. This denial of one's ethnic or racial background is also known as the "acting white" or "wanting to be white" stage of ethnic and racial identity development.

See also "Acting White" Stage of Life.

Khyati Joshi

International Slave Trade

See Slave Trade.

Involuntary Minorities

See Colonized versus Immigrant Minorities.

Involuntary Segregation

See Segregation, Voluntary versus Involuntary.

IRA

See Indian Reorganization Act of 1934 (IRA).

Iran Hostage Crisis and Anti-Iranian Stereotypes

The Iran hostage crisis began on November 4, 1979, when a group of Iranian students seized the U.S. Embassy in Tehran, taking its employees hostage. Ayatollah Khomeini, the charismatic leader of the Iranian Revolution (1978–1979), denounced the United States for its longtime support of the deposed leader Reza Shah Pahlavi. When the exiled Shah entered the United States in October for medical care, many Iranians feared a repetition of the U.S.-assisted coup that had put him back on the throne in 1953. At Khomeini's encouragement, fifty-two Americans were taken hostage as a preventative measure. President Jimmy Carter immediately applied economic and diplomatic pressure on Iran; Iranian diplomats in the United States were expelled, oil imports from Iran were stopped, and around $8 billion of Iranian assets in the United States were frozen. At the same time, he began several diplomatic and military initiatives to free the hostages, all of which failed. Then, in exchange for the hostages, the United States agreed to unfreeze almost all the Iranian assets. Finally, on January 20, 1981—only a few hours after Carter left office— all hostages were released, after 444 days in captivity. Clearly, the hostages were used as pawns to deal a blow to Carter's incumbency. The hostage crisis occurred right after the revolution in Iran, which led to a massive influx of Iranian exiles into the United States. Ironically, these exiles faced unfair targeting and scapegoating, despite their opposition to the new Iranian regime.

The hostage crisis prompted a presidential order referred to as the "Iranian Control Program." The program screened, on a case-by-case basis, almost

57,000 Iranian students—the single largest group of foreign students—to make sure that they were in the United States legally. After holding 7,177 deportation hearings, 3,088 students were ordered to leave the United States, and the departure of 445 was verified. The program was not aimed at students only, but in the words of the Immigration and Naturalization Service (INS), the new policy "effectively prohibited the entry of most Iranians into this country." In light of the permanent closure of the American Embassy in Iran, even a quarter of a century later Iranians seeking a U.S. visa must first travel to another country.

Iranian Americans become scapegoats every time conflict erupts between Iran and the United States. This started with the Iranian revolution, with its vehemently anti-American slogans, it peaked during the hostage crisis, and it flared up again in the post–9/11 era, when President George W. Bush included Iran in the "axis of evil" and the U.S. Department of Justice ordered the "special registration" of recent immigrant men, eventually leading to the detention of some in Los Angeles. There have also been widespread allegations that the Iranian government is acquiring the raw materials and technology to build an atomic bomb, although these have been toned down since June of 2004 because of the Iranian government's cooperation with the International Atomic Energy Agency's standards.

Iranian Americans are perceived as Islamic fundamentalists and, by analogy, terrorists. However, significant proportions of Iranians in the United States are not even Muslims; they overrepresent Iran's religious minorities—Christians (mostly Armenians and Assyrians), Bahais, Jews, and Zoroastrians. In general, Iranian Americans are one of the most educated and skilled immigrant groups and present few social problems. They have suffered disproportionately and inadvertently from widespread American stereotypes dating back to 1978–1979.

See also Middle Easterners, Historical Precedents of Backlash against; Middle Easterners, Stereotypes of.

Mehdi Bozorgmehr and Anny Bakalian

Irish Immigrants, Prejudice and Discrimination against

The great potato famines of the 1840s pushed very large numbers of the Irish to immigrate to the United States. Their mass migration, which peaked in the 1850s with almost one million, continued until 1930. Irish farmers produced enough food to feed the country's people, but English rulers were exporting the product to England in hopes that the Irish would be left with no other choice but to migrate to North America. This made the Irish feel as if their immigration was a forced exile instead of a willing move to another country.

Irish immigrants settled mainly in large East Coast cities such as New York, Boston, and Philadelphia and were forced to live in overcrowded, filthy slums. They suffered from poverty, unemployment, high infant death rates, and disease. They were often sent to live in buffer zones between Anglos and Native

Americans and forced to participate in the scalping of Native Americans. The Irish were discriminated against in similar ways as the African Americans were, but the Irish were often in competition with African Americans for employment opportunities. Members of the dominant group often depicted the Irish newcomers as a separate racial group ("black Caucasians").

Early Irish immigrants were openly discriminated against in the job market with labor advertisement signs reading "Help Wanted. No Irish Need Apply." They could only get low-paying, often health-hazardous jobs, such as in railroad construction, coal mining, logging and ditch digging, that mainstream Americans did not want. After the emancipation of black slaves in 1865, Irish immigrants often competed with African Americans for the same menial jobs, and so they became antiblack.

Even though America was founded on the basis of religious freedom, Irish Americans faced religious discrimination. Early English settlers were mainly Protestant and were prejudiced against Irish Catholics. During early immigration, laws were passed that forced Irish children to be baptized as Protestants instead of Catholics. In some instances, Irish Catholics were not allowed to worship or vote. Also, during early immigration, Irish Catholics were taxed heavily upon entering the United States so as to dissuade future Irish immigration. There were also anti-Irish or anti-Catholic riots in which Catholic churches were burned and Irish homes were destroyed.

Irish Americans also faced prejudices in the media. During the 1840s and 1850s, local press depicted the Irish as apelike characters to show the Irish as inferior. They were portrayed as criminals and dangerous and rowdy drunks. Irish Americans were also blamed for some of the "dirty politics" that occurred in the United States.

It was not until the twentieth century that the Irish began to shed their undeserving negative image and came to be seen as intelligent and progressive citizens. Irish Americans can currently be found in many professions, including business, politics, law enforcement, and the fire department. The United States has had two Irish American presidents in the twentieth century: John F. Kennedy and Ronald Reagan. The Irish are also credited with the foundation of the Catholic school system in the United States. Many Americans, not just Irish Americans, celebrate St. Patrick's Day on March 17, when "everyone is Irish" and all wear green, the color of Ireland.

See also Anti-Catholicism in the United States; Know-Nothing Party; Nativism and the Anti-immigrant Movements.

Further Reading

Callahan, Alethea. 1999. " 'No Irish Need Apply': A Critical Perspective of the Irish in America." http://www.presidioinc.com/newsletter/99newsarchive/99march_irish need.htm.

Free the Children. "Irish Americans." 2002. http://www.freethechildren.org/cultures/ html/map/european/european-american.html#IrishAmericans.

Moynihan, Daniel Patrick, and J. F. Watts. *The Irish Americans.* IpictureBooks, Inc., 1996.

Tiffany Vélez

Irish Riot of 1863

See Draft Riot of 1863.

ISDEAA

See Indian Self-Determination and Education Assistance Act of 1975 (ISDEAA).

Islamic Jihad

The Palestinian Islamic Jihad (PIJ) is a group of Islamist radicals based in Syria who operate primarily in Israel, the West Bank, and the Gaza Strap. Islamic Jihad is committed to the creation of an Islamic Palestinian state and to the destruction of the state of Israel. It was designated by the U.S. State Department as a "foreign terrorist organization" in October 1997. The PIJ allegedly has received funding from Iran and conducted attacks against Israeli military and civilian targets, including many suicide-bombing missions. For example, in June 2001, twenty-one people were killed in a suicide bombing at a Tel Aviv disco.

Since September 11, 2001, the U.S. government has more aggressively pursued possible American-based links to the organization as part of its War on Terror. In February 2003, the U.S. Justice Department indicted PIJ head Ramadan Shallah as well as other PIJ leaders for conspiring to plan, finance, and coordinate international terrorist activities using locations and facilities within the United States. Included in this group was Palestinian Sami Amin Al-Arian, forty-five, a professor at the University of South Florida's College of Engineering. In this indictment, it was alleged that the Tampa-based Islamic Committee for Palestine (formerly Islamic Concern Project) and the World and Islam Studies Enterprise (WISE) were used to fund militant Islamic Palestinian groups. Muslim American advocacy groups have criticized the treatment of Al-Arian since his arrest and warn that his arrest is but one example of how Muslims in America have become increasingly and unfairly targeted due to mounting public concern over terrorism.

The Islamic Jihad has been linked to Hamas, the Palestinians' major Muslim fundamentalist movement. However, unlike Hamas, Islamic Jihad does not support any social-service activities (such as schools, hospitals, and mosques) and has no defined social or political role. Its purpose appears to be exclusively to conduct terrorist activities as part of the "holy war" against Israel and Western influence in the Middle East. *Jihad* refers to the Muslim term for a "righteous struggle" waged on behalf of Islam.

See also Jihad; Muslims, Terrorist Image of; September 11, 2001, Terrorism, Discriminatory Reaction to.

Rebekah Lee

Italian Americans, Prejudice and Discrimination against

There has been a constant stream of immigrants from Italy, primarily the northern regions, to the United States, since the early 1800s. A large number of southern Italians, who were typically Catholics, arrived in the United States between 1880 and 1920, and accounted for approximately 90 percent of immigration from Italy during that period. Most non-Protestant immigrant groups at the time encountered prejudice and discrimination upon arriving in the United States, but Italian Americans faced harsher prejudice and discrimination than most.

The religious and physical distinctiveness of southern Italians greatly contributed to the initial perception of Italian Americans in the United States. They were Catholics like the Irish, so the Protestant mainstream considered them morally and intellectually inferior. Moreover, the darker physical features of many southern Italians enhanced the perception that Italian Americans, more so than Irish Americans, were people of color, incapable of becoming constructive members of the mainstream society.

The occupational and educational characteristics of Italian immigrants also contributed to their negative reception. A large majority of the immigrants from southern Italy were farmworkers with little education and intended to stay here temporarily and save money for their return migration. As such, most became low-wage manual workers without any prospect of advancing. Also, schools were not friendly places for many Italian Americans, partly because of the devaluation of Catholicism and non–northern European cultures in the U.S. public schools. In addition, Catholic schools had already been serving as the refuge for Irish Americans, who had arrived nearly a half century before the Italians. Although they shared the same religion, Irish Americans did not welcome the arrival of Italians. Hence, Italian Americans often chose not to pursue schooling. These occupational and educational characteristics impeded the advancement of Italian Americans, which may have further contributed to the widely held stereotype that Italian Americans were unsophisticated and intellectually incapable.

Such negative beliefs about the moral characteristics and intellectual capabilities of Italian Americans are also reflected in the Mafia stereotypes with which they have long been associated. According to these stereotypes, Italian American men, who are often portrayed as being illogical and dim-witted, seek economic and social gain through organized crime. By contrast, their female counterparts support their efforts by serving the men in the family as hyper-emotional homemakers. These perceptions have survived well into the twenty-first century. The popular media today continue to perpetuate the stereotypical representation of Italian Americans. Despite these blatant stereotypes and prejudices, Italian Americans have made many advances in many arenas over the decades.

World War II marked the dramatic beginning of a changing outlook for Italian Americans. Aside from the war related political climate in which all Americans of European descent were prompted to unite as Americans, this war systematically expanded the white-collar jobs and educational opportunities, particularly in urban areas, where most Italian Americans resided. Today, on average, Italian Americans are occupationally and educationally comparable to other European Americans, although there are considerably fewer Italian Americans at top executive levels. Still, scholars argue that fourth-generation Italian Americans are on par professionally and educationally with Americans of either British or German descent. This trend of mainstreaming both reflects and is reflected in the prevalence of intermarriage; currently, only one-third of Italian Americans marry intra-ethnically. In sum, despite the fact that the lives of Italian Americans have become comparable to those of other European Americans in many ways, they continue to face devaluation in this country.

See also Italian Americans, Violence against.

Further Reading

Alba, Richard. *Italian Americans: Into the Twilight of Ethnicity*. Englewood Cliffs, NJ: Prentice Hall, 1985.

———. "Italian Americans: A Century of Ethnic Change. *Origins and Destinies: Immigration, Race and Ethnicity in America*, edited by Silvia Pedraza and Ruben G. Rumbaut. Belmont, CA: Wadsworth, 1996.

Lopreato, Joseph. *Italian Americans*. New York: Random House, 1970.

Daisuke Akiba

Italian Americans, Violence against

Italian immigrants to the United States were different culturally, linguistically, religiously, and physiognomically from those who were already living in the country. Additionally, many Italian immigrants came from extremely poor backgrounds, making them eager to work menial jobs for low pay so that they could make new lives for themselves in the United States or save some money for their families back home. Earlier European arrivals, most of British, German, Dutch, or Scandinavian origin, regarded the Catholic, southern European Italians with suspicion because of who they were and because they were ready to take away jobs from native-born Americans. Italians did come to the United States in early immigration periods (before 1880), but they were mostly from northern Italy. After 1880, the mass migration of southern Italians began, particularly of Sicilians. These immigrants came from a part of Italy that was behind in industrialization, their language differed from that of the earlier immigrants, they were phenotypically distinct, less urbanized, less educated, and more devoutly Catholic. Indeed, it was not only non-Italians who felt prejudice towards the southern Italian immigrants—northern Italians did as well.

Mob violence, including group lynchings, was common against Italian Americans as early as the 1870s, particularly in areas where the occupational choices of the immigrants were seen as threatening by residents. Perhaps the worst incidence of violence against Italian immigrants occurred in New Orleans in 1891, when six alleged members of the Mafia were acquitted after a trial and several thousand individuals responded by breaking into the jail and shooting eleven Italian Americans held there, including one who had no relation to the Mafia charges. Later, a jury retroactively justified the murders, and the national news media editorialized that the citizens of New Orleans had no other recourse against "the Italian outlaws."

Mob violence also continued into the early part of the twentieth century, particularly in the South and West as immigrants spread out from the urban centers where they had first settled. For instance, in 1920, in the town of West Frankfort, Illinois, mobs rioted for three days in the Italian quarter of town, attacking anyone in sight and burning down homes. The violence only stopped when the rioters were faced with five hundred state troopers. Additionally, during the twentieth century, Italian American youth in many urban areas were involved in gang violence, often fighting against Irish or Latino gangs. This sort of gang violence often moved beyond mere battles for dominance and control of turf into ethnically motivated fighting.

In the 1920s, Italian Americans were held accountable for the influx of communism in the United States. The most notable example of this was the execution of Nicola Sacco and Bartolomeo Vanzetti, two Italian immigrant men convicted of a violent robbery in Massachusetts in 1920. It is still not known whether the men were actually guilty, though it is clear that their trial was not fair and that they were involved in radical politics before their arrest. Later, during Prohibition, Italian Americans became associated with gangster boot-legging activity, although people of every conceivable ethnic background took advantage of the regulation of alcohol to make money. And during World War II, thousands of Italian Americans were subjected to scrutiny and imprisonment because of Italy's involvement in the war as an enemy of the United States.

See also Italian Americans, Prejudice and Discrimination against.

Further Reading

Gambino, Richard. *Blood of My Blood: The Dilemma of the Italian-Americans*. Garden City, NY: Doubleday, 1974.

————. *Vendetta: The True Story of the Worst Lynching in America, the Mass Murder of Italian-Americans in New Orleans in 1891, the Vicious Motivations behind It, and the Tragic Repercussions That Linger to This Day*. Garden City, NY: Doubleday, 1977.

Mikaila Mariel Lemonik Arthur

J

Jackson, Jesse (1941–)

Born on October 8, 1941, in Greenville, South Carolina, as Jesse Louis Burns, Jesse Jackson took his stepfather's surname in 1956 and became Jesse Louis Jackson. A civil rights activist since the early 1960s, Jesse Jackson was an acolyte of the Rev. Martin Luther King Jr. and directed the economic division of the Southern Christian Leadership Conference (SCLC), known as Operation Breadbasket. Jackson went on to establish several organizations, including Operation PUSH (People United to Save Humanity), the National Rainbow Coalition, and the Rainbow/PUSH Action Network (a merger of the two organizations). Through these organizations, Jackson has mobilized voter-registration drives and successfully registered millions of new voters. He gave many minority voters a reason to go to the polls with his presidential runs in 1984 and 1988, and he won the Democratic primary in Michigan during his second presidential run.

Jackson's current projects focus on remedying persistent inequities in education and the economy. Jackson launched the Wall Street Project in 1997 to promote minority participation in corporate America, and corporate investment in minority entrepreneurial development by negotiating "covenants" with major corporations, including 7-Eleven, Coors, Coca-Cola, Texaco, and Denny's. The Rainbow/PUSH 1,000 Churches Connected program seeks to educate parishioners of member churches about economic responsibility through training in debt and credit management, homeownership, and consumer purchasing. The Push for Excellence (EXCEL) program strives for educational excellence and competitiveness among students of color.

Jackson is also an international figure and mediator. An active opponent of apartheid, Jackson pushed for American companies to divest from South Africa. During the Kosovo war in April 1999, Jackson negotiated the release

The Rev. Jesse Jackson, president and CEO of the Rainbow/PUSH Coalition, at a 1997 press conference in New York.

AP/Wide World Photos.

of three U.S. POWs who were captured on the Macedonia border while patrolling with a UN peacekeeping unit.

Jackson is, however, a controversial figure. He has been criticized for his actions after the 1968 assassination of Martin Luther King Jr. Only hours after King was slain in Memphis, young Jesse Jackson, wearing a bloodied shirt, appeared on national television saying that he had been at King's side when he died and was the last person with whom King spoke. Several aides protested that Jackson was not near King when he died and objected to Jackson's self-promotion. This dispute created a rift between Jackson and SCLC leaders, such as Ralph Abernathy and King's widow, Coretta Scott King. During the 1984 presidential run, Jackson made an anti-Semitic reference to New York City as "Hymietown," for which he apologized. While consoling the Clinton family over the Lewinsky affair, it was later revealed that Jackson had engaged in an extramarital relationship with a Rainbow/PUSH staff member and consultant and had fathered a child out of wedlock in 1999. Despite controversy, Jackson remains a formidable contemporary civil rights activist and an articulate spokesperson for the needs and issues of poor people.

See also Jewish-Black Conflicts; King, Martin Luther Jr.; Rainbow Coalition.

Tarry Hum

JACL

See Japanese American Citizens League (JACL).

Japan Bashing

As the U.S. economy suffered a decline in the 1980s and early 1990s, some politicians and media outlets blamed cheap imports, especially Japanese cars, for the failure of American industries. This fueled anew anti-Japanese sentiments among Americans and the scapegoating of Japanese Americans. Examples of Japan bashing include the brutal 1982 murder of Vincent Chin, a twenty-seven-year-old Chinese American in Detroit. The assailants, two autoworkers (one recently laid off), called him a "Jap" and blamed him for the loss of their jobs. In 1992, a Japanese businessman was stabbed to death in his home in Ventura, California. Two weeks earlier, two white young men, who blamed Japan for the economic crisis in the United States, had threatened him. There were also instances of graffiti on Asian American stores and crank phone calls to individuals or institutions with Asian names. A striking feature of Japan bashing is the inability of some Americans to differentiate among diverse ethnic/nationality groups of Asian Americans. This mistaken identity results in pan-ethnic prejudice, discrimination, and racism every time one of these groups is involved.

In the past, the policies of the U.S. government were the chief source of anti-Japanese racism. At the turn of the twentieth century, Japanese immigrants were severely restricted from entering the United States and from bringing their spouses and also barred from owning agricultural lands. Many observers believe that racist acts of Congress set the stage for the internment of 120,000 Japanese Americans in western states for a period of four years during World War II. Against all odds, though perhaps because of these occurrences, Japanese Americans mobilized and succeeded in American society. Along with the Jews, they are considered the most successful of American ethnic groups. They were elevated to "model-minority" status in the 1960s and 1970s. This phase came to an end when Japan emerged as an industrial giant and a serious competitor to the United States, once again triggering the malicious, if highly remote, association between Japan and Japanese Americans.

See also Asian Americans, Discrimination against.

Mehdi Bozorgmehr and Anny Bakalian

Japanese and Korean Exclusion League

See Asiatic Exclusion League (AEL).

Japanese American Citizens League (JACL)

The Japanese American Citizens League (JACL) is the nation's oldest and largest Asian American civil rights organization, with more than 30,000 members. The JACL was established in 1930, growing out of several local and re-gional organizations of the *nissei* (second-generation Japanese Americans). As a citizens league, the *issei* (immigrants) were excluded from joining JACL. On the other hand, the issei community leaders did not approve JACL's emphasis on Americanization. Japan's attack on the U.S. naval base at Pearl Harbor on December 7, 1941, changed the lives of both the issei and the nissei. Under Executive Order 9066, signed by President Franklin D. Roosevelt in 1942, all men, women, and children of Japanese descent in western coastal regions, in-cluding about two-thirds of the U.S.-born nissei, were rounded up and taken to guarded camps in the interior. The JACL wired President Roosevelt imme-diately after Pearl Harbor, demonstrating its loyalty to the United States, even if it meant agreeing to this mass evacuation and relocation.

After the war, however, the major political activities and legislative efforts of JACL were directed at eradicating anti-Japanese discrimination. In 1946, the JACL embarked on a hard-fought campaign to repeal California's Alien Land Law, which prohibited all Japanese immigrants from purchasing and owning land in the state. In 1948, it supported the passage of the Evacuation Claims Act, the first of a series of efforts to rectify the losses and injustices of the World War II internment. In 1949, efforts by Japanese immigrants to become naturalized U.S. citizens, a right denied them for more than fifty years, were initiated. In 1978, the membership and board of JACL decided to focus the or-ganization's efforts on the recognition of, and reparations for, the interments during World War II. The Commission on Wartime Relocation and Internment of Civilians was formed, and in 1982 it found the government's actions un-justified and unconstitutional. The redress campaign culminated in the Civil Liberties Act of 1988, which provided monetary compensation of $20,000 to each victim if alive, or an heir if deceased, and a formal apology.

While the JACL's founding mission was to protect the civil rights of Amer-icans of Japanese ancestry, since 1982 this organization has extended its serv-ices to protecting the rights of all segments of the Asian Pacific American community. This change came about when Vincent Chin, a young Chinese American, was murdered by two laid-off Detroit autoworkers who mistook him for being Japanese. Since 9/11, JACL has also become a vocal defender of the civil rights of Arab and Muslim Americans who have become victims of the government's initiatives. JACL has realized that the civil rights of one group can only be guaranteed by ensuring the rights of all Americans.

See also Japanese American Internment; Japanese Americans, Redress Move-ment for.

Mehdi Bozorgmehr and Anny Bakalian

Japanese American Internment

Following a highly choreographed plan, the Japanese military attacked the naval station in Pearl Harbor, Hawaii, in December 1941. After this incident, individuals of Japanese descent living in the United States faced a great deal of sociopolitical tension. Executive Order 9066, signed by President Franklin D. Roosevelt, resulted in the mass incarceration of Japanese Americans. Although some consider this injustice an aberration in American history, others point out that Japanese Americans had long faced similar discrimination—though not as drastic—throughout their residence in the United States, and that many people of color are currently facing similar political scrutiny.

The Anti-Asian Climate

The arrival of a wave of farmworkers in Hawaii and California in the late 1880s marked the beginning of Japanese immigration to the United States. Although many immigrant groups, including Italians and the Irish, faced hostility upon their arrival, the anti-Asian climate had already been heightened when the Japanese began arriving. The Chinese first arrived on the West Coast in the mid-1800s, during the Gold Rush, and rapidly expanded their labor presence there, primarily because they were willing to work diligently under harsh conditions for lower wages than were their European American counterparts. The presence of low-wage Chinese laborers challenged the job security of American laborers. White Americans and institutions grew extremely prejudiced against them while continuing to exploit their labor. In 1882, Congress passed the Chinese Exclusion Act to prevent the Chinese from entering the United States, despite the fact that the Chinese represented a negligible portion of the population—fewer than 100,000. This reflects the racist nature of the law; white American policymakers were concerned not about the number of Chinese people in the United States but instead about the ever-growing labor participation of the Chinese. Although the Chinese and the Japanese did not share a common language, customs, or food, nor did they consider each other allies, they appeared to be indistinguishable, from the European American point of view. It is therefore not surprising that the preexisting resentment toward the Chinese communities was quickly transferred to the Japanese communities in the United States.

Much like the Chinese had done decades earlier, Japanese immigrants began to contribute to the U.S. economy soon after their arrival, particularly in agriculture and business. Their economic participation was highly welcomed in Hawaii, perhaps because it stimulated the local economy and because diversity had always been a fact of life in Hawaii. Similarly, the economic participation by the Japanese was not considered threatening on the East Coast, where the presence of Asians in general was minimal. By contrast, their economic participation was considered a threat on the West Coast, where European Americans already held extreme resentment toward Chinese immigrants. European American politicians and labor organizations on the West Coast unwarrantably feared that Asians were conspiring to invade and overtake the United States, and the media actively circulated such literature. Subsequently, Japanese Americans, like other Asian Americans, encountered legal exclusions, whereby they were prevented from becoming citizens or landowners. Japanese Americans were thus not granted the same rights and privileges enjoyed by European Americans. It was in this discriminatory context that the internment of Japanese Americans took place.

Days Following the Attack on Pearl Harbor

The Second World War had permeated most of Europe by 1940. While Japan and the United States had initially maintained neutrality, it was clear that they were supportive of opposing sides, which further aggravated the existing tension between the two countries. For example, the U.S. government had intervened against the Japanese efforts to expand their occupation of China and Korea, and there were also trade-related conflicts between Japan and the United States. When the Japanese military attacked Pearl Harbor in Hawaii on December 7, 1941, it was clear that the heightened tension between the two countries had become a major conflict. Almost instantaneously, blatant anti-Japanese American movements began to emerge in the United States.

Immediately after Pearl Harbor, FBI agents raided the residences of Japanese Americans in search of evidence of espionage, only to find nothing to substantiate their suspicion. The primary target of these raids included more than 1,000 prominent members of the Japanese American communities (e.g., community leaders, teachers, and journalists), who had immigrated to the United States but who had been legally prevented from becoming citizens. Thousands of them were arrested without due process; their families were not informed of the nature of the charges, nor were they aware of the location or the duration of the detention.

With similar swiftness, secretary of the navy and publisher of the *Chicago Daily News*, Colonel Frank Knox, launched his own campaign against Japanese Americans by falsely reporting that Japanese American fifth columnists had been found to be responsible for arranging the attack on Pearl Harbor as saboteurs and spies. Although the government investigation quickly found this accusation, along with other, similar allegations, unwarranted, government agencies reportedly suppressed such findings of innocence, arrested the accused despite the complete lack of evidence, and remained silent on these issues. Not surprisingly, these actions served to confirm the suspicion against Japanese Americans in the eyes of the public. This, combined with the general anti-Asian sentiment, prompted the War Department to advise the army commander in Hawaii to imprison all Japanese Americans in Hawaii. However, the commander, General D. C. Emmons, adamantly rejected this advice, citing that Japanese Americans represented a significant segment of the population in Hawaii and that the United States needed them to effectively recover from the damages from the attack. Emmons's view was not shared by other Americans, particularly those on the mainland.

Efforts toward Internment

President Roosevelt declared the Japanese, German, and Italian nationals residing in the United States to be "enemy aliens" and imposed restrictions on their daily activities. However, the experiences of the Japanese differed greatly from those of Germans and Italians. First, whereas many of the noncitizen Germans and Italians residing in the United States were sojourners who had elected not to pursue U.S. citizenships, the Japanese had been prevented by law from doing so, even thought a large majority desired to live and die in the United States as patriotic Americans. Because of this, their status as noncitizens should not have been interpreted as a lack of commitment to the nation. Second, U.S. citizens of Japanese descent were subject to the same constraints facing the noncitizens. The same was not the case for German

Americans or Italian Americans. The most important event that set the experience of Japanese Americans apart from that of other Americans was the internment.

General John DeWitt of the U.S. Army filed a report entitled "Final Report: Japanese Evacuation from the West Coast," which urged the government to remove all individuals of Japanese descent from the West Coast; this report later became known for its dubious logic. In the report, DeWitt stated that individuals of Japanese descent needed to be relocated from the West Coast, because the very fact that they had not engaged in any sabotaging efforts to that date was a "disturbing and confirming indication that such action will take place." Despite this logical flaw, his recommendations gained overwhelming support, largely because European American civilians began to consider Japanese Americans a menace; this attitude spread rather quickly, given the preexistence of an anti-Japanese climate, owing to their labor participation. In fact, many labor and trade organizations supported the removal of the Japanese, not primarily because they were concerned about national security but because they saw it as an opportunity to regain their labor and business monopoly.

Reflecting these public opinions, the anti-Japanese sentiment and push toward the mass removal of Japanese Americans were prevalent in the media. It is therefore not surprising that the War Department eventually approved DeWitt's recommendations; this series of events ultimately led to Executive Order 9066, signed by President Roosevelt on February 19, 1942, authorizing the army to establish internment camps to coercively imprison certain individuals on the West Coast. Although the order did not specify any nationality—perhaps fearing the clear constitutional infirmity of the inclusion of such a clause—its intended target was clear to everyone involved: only individuals of Japanese ancestry were subject to internment.

The collaborative efforts among President Roosevelt and various governmental agencies facilitated the mass incarcerations of Japanese Americans from the West Coast, without any criminal investigations or the filing of charges. Such efforts were welcomed by European Americans—particularly farmers and businesspeople—who had long resented the success among their Japanese American peers. It is crucial to note that in Hawaii and on the East Coast, where the anti-Japanese sentiment was less drastic, Japanese Americans did not face internment. In Hawaii in particular, Japanese Americans were considered productive and integral members of the community, while their number was too small to be considered a threat on the East Coast.

The Relocation

Within a month of the signing of Executive Order 9066, the War Relocation Authority (WRA) was formed to carry out the internment of Japanese Americans living on the West Coast. Over a period of eight months, the mass removal of more than 110,000 Japanese Americans was executed. Japanese Americans found posters throughout their communities alerting them to the immediate "evacuation" to take place in as little as two days, without specifying either the location or duration. They were informed of the curfew, which restricted their mundane activities, and were instructed to sell their properties, including real estate and

A Japanese family arriving at Manzanar relocation camp, April 1942.

Courtesy Library of Congress.

businesses, on very short notice. Thus, they were in essence forced to abandon their properties. They were only allowed to bring the staples they could carry and were transported in packed buses and trains for hours without knowing what lay ahead—only to find themselves in inhumane living conditions.

The severity of the economic and psychosocial devastations associated with leaving home was matched only by the harsh conditions the Japanese Americans faced during the internment. They were initially taken to prisonlike "assembly centers," which had been converted from racetracks and fairgrounds located primarily in California. There, crowded and unsanitary tarpaper barracks and horse stalls without privacy or plumbing, surrounded by barbed wire, become their temporary homes, where they were provided only with minimal services necessary to survival. Within a few months, incarcerated Japanese Americans were transferred from the temporary camps to ten permanent WRA camps in inhabitable remote areas, such as deserts or swamps on the West Coast.

Although the notion of permanent camps may imply improved living conditions, the detainees found themselves instead in unsanitary living quarters consisting of overcrowded small rooms with cots, with no other furniture or plumbing. In many ways, the life at the permanent camps was far worse than it had been at the assembly centers. For example, organized activities gradually separated children from their families both physically and psychologically, which challenged the traditional family structures and parental authority. No immediate hope of escaping the inhumane living conditions was provided. Still, the detainees attempted to make the best of the situation. Many families constructed pieces of furniture from scraps. Adults kept themselves busy with farming and enjoyed brief moments away from the harsh realities through sports, while children attended barrack schools—although they had inadequate supplies. Some families were blessed with babies, among whom was Carole Doi, who later married another child detainee, Jim Yamaguchi. Americans were proud in 1992, when these Japanese American internment survivors' daughter, Kristi Yamaguchi, won the gold medal for the United States in figure skating at the Olympics in Albertville, Norway, slightly outskating a competitor from Japan, Midori Ito.

Resistance against Injustice

Back in the camps, protests, strikes, and riots, sometimes not so peaceful, began emerging among the anguished detainees, in response to the inhumane conditions within which they were constrained and to the injustice they faced. In February 1943, detainees seventeen years and older received a questionnaire, "Statement of U.S. Citizenship of Japanese American Ancestry," ostensibly to identify loyal Americans who could be released from the camps under the condition that they move out of the West Coast or join the army. Although the very notion of testing the loyalty offended many, two of the questions were especially troublesome.

Question Number 27: "Are you willing to serve in the Armed Forces of the United States, in combat duty, wherever ordered?"

Question Number 28: "Will you swear unqualified allegiance to the United States of America and faithfully defend the United States from any or all attack by foreign or domestic forces, and forswear any form of allegiance or obedience to the Japanese emperor or any other foreign government, power, or organization?"

They wondered why they should fight for the United States, which was interfering with the basic human rights of their people and their families. Also, *isseis*, Japanese-born immigrants—most of whom had been denied U.S. citizenship because of their ethnicity—were reluctant to renounce their Japanese citizenship, as that would have meant that they would become people without a country. *Nisseis*, or second-generation Japanese-Americans—who were granted citizenship by virtue of their birth in the U.S.—were also angered because the government would not question the loyalty of other citizens, such as German Americans and Italian Americans. Detainees were classified according to their answers to a series of loyalty questions, and many were relocated as a result. The most "disloyal" and defiant were sent to Tule Lake in northern California, where a mass riot transpired among its eighteen thousand residents. Army tanks were brought in to contain the riot in November of 1943.

Another wave of resistance came when the Nisseis residing in the camps began to receive draft notices in 1944 to fight for the United States. The "Fair Play Committee" was established at a Wyoming internment camp, and, in the end, more than three hundred nisseis refused to comply with the draft order and demanded a clarification and reexamination of the U.S. treatment of Japanese Americans. Many of them were subsequently convicted of draft resistance and sentenced to three years in federal prison—as if they were not already living in prisons. However, most nissei men chose to participate in the American military efforts. The U.S. armed forces were, at that time, organized by race and ethnicity, and the 442nd Regimental Combat Team was designated to house nisseis, who worked closely with the 100th Infantry Battalion, which consisted of Japanese Americans from Hawaii. Although the contributions made by soldiers of Japanese descent were significant, many nissei soldiers protested by refusing to participate in daily training while their families were being detained.

Others challenged the internment in the courts of law. The case of *Korematsu v. United States* (1944) is notorious. Fred Korematsu defied the evacuation order in hopes of joining his fiancée, who lived on the East Coast, and was arrested in 1942 and convicted. After his conviction, he was sent to an assembly center. Korematsu unsuccessfully appealed his case to the Ninth Circuit Court of Appeals and subsequently to the U.S. Supreme Court. In 1944, a conservative Supreme Court upheld the conviction, stating that internment of Japanese Americans was constitutional. It was not until the early 1980s that Korematsu gained some sense of redemption; a team of attorneys filed a petition on behalf of Korematsu and others for a *Writ of Error Coram Nobis*—a request to acknowledge gross legal injustice in cases in which earlier Supreme Court decisions cannot be reversed. Their efforts successfully negated the legality of the incarceration of Japanese Americans.

After the Internment

The WRA had become increasingly aware of the legal implications of the internment, partly as a result of a wave of lawsuits filed on behalf of the incarcerated. Some detainees were allowed to relocate out of the West Coast to find freedom. Eventually, fearing court decisions challenging the constitutionality of the internment, the government announced in December 1944 that the internment program was to be terminated. In the subsequent three months, all detainees were released from camps. Although Japanese Americans welcomed the freedom, resettlement proved to be a challenge for many. Their businesses and properties had been taken over by new owners, severely vandalized, or terribly neglected. Their communities had been diminished and had lost many of their members. They also faced the reality of racism in their own neighborhoods and endured housing and employment discrimination. Their lives as Japanese Americans, thus, continued to be harsh after the war.

Eventually, however, fueled by the civil rights movements initiated by African Americans and their supporters in the 1950s and 1960s, Japanese American communities found their way toward empowerment. The redress movement chronicles such efforts. The Japanese American Citizens League (JACL) initiated a movement in 1970 seeking both acknowledgement of and compensation for the injustice of the World War II internment of Japanese Americans by the U.S. government. In response, the government established the Commission on Wartime Relocation and Internment of Civilians in 1980 to investigate the matters. The commission conducted a thorough investigation, through such means as public hearings in a number of U.S. cities, interviews with remaining survivors and their families, and extensive reviews of documents.

The commission concluded that the internment programs were indeed reflective not of justifiable national security concerns but of racism and hysteria, a conclusion that had been reached by many constitutional scholars decades earlier. Furthermore, the devastating psychosocial, professional, and economic consequences in the Japanese communities as a result of the internment were meticulously documented. The commission recommended that the surviving internees or their heirs, who numbered approximately 60,000, be granted compensatory payments of $20,000 each, that a statement of apology be issued by the U.S. Government, and that a presidential pardon be granted for the Japanese Americans who were unjustly convicted during the war. In 1988, the redress payments were finally approved by the Congress, and in 1990, the first redress payments were made, accompanied by letters of apology, marking a major milestone in the history of ethnic oppression in the United States.

Six decades after the Internment of Japanese Americans ended, the threat of a war again caused some hysteria among citizens and government officials that resulted in the compromising of civil rights of certain members of U.S. society. On September 11, 2001, thousands of civilians were killed in a series of attacks in the United States by the supporters of Al Qaeda, an Islamic extremist group. After these attacks, in the name of the War on Terror, the U.S. government quickly began detaining Muslims and individuals who appeared to be of Middle Eastern descent, frequently without a determination of individual guilt, in an attempt to prevent further attacks against the nation.

Various federal laws (e.g., the Law of Secret Evidence) were passed to allow the incarceration of individuals based simply on suspicion, without due process or disclosure of the charges. National security is a significant concern for most Americans, but some Americans are even more alarmed by the government practices, greatly compromising the civil rights and right to due process of the targeted individuals and their families. Although these detentions appear to have been false alarms, polls indicate that most Americans remain uncritical of these civil rights violations by the government. Although the Japanese American experiences during the Internment cannot necessarily be equated with the current civil rights violations against Muslim Americans, one may argue that any compromise, stemming from hysteria, in civil rights of the members of a particular social group may signal the history of injustice being repeated.

See also Executive Order 9066; Japanese American Citizens League (JACL); Japanese Americans, Redress Movement for; *Korematsu v. United States*; War Relocation Authority (WRA).

Further Reading

Commission on Wartime Relocation and Internment of Civilians. *Personal Justice Denied: Report of the Commission on Wartime Relocation and Internment of Civilians.* Washington, DC: U.S. Government Printing Office, 1982.

Cooper, Michael L. *Fighting for Honor: Japanese Americans and World War II.* New York: Houghton Mifflin, 2000.

Daniels, Roger. *Prisoners without Trial: Japanese Americans in World War II.* New York: Hill and Wang, 1993.

Daniels, Roger, Sandra C. Taylor, and Harry H. L. Kitano. *Japanese Americans from Relocation to Redress.* Salt Lake City: University of Utah Press, 1986.

Hansen, Arthur A. *Japanese American World War II Evacuation Oral History Project.* Westport, CT: Meckler, 1991.

Inada, Lawson Fusao. *Only What We Could Carry: The Japanese American Internment Experience.* Oakland: Heyday Books, 2000.

Yamamoto, Eric K., and Susan Kiyomi Serrano. "The Loaded Weapon." *Amerasian Journal* 27/28 (2002): 61–62.

Daisuke Akiba

Japanese Americans, Redress Movement for

Japanese Americans won a major victory when the Civil Liberties Act of 1988 was passed by the Congress, authorizing a redress program for the internment of Japanese Americans during World War II. However, this victory did not transpire overnight; it was a product of decades of discussions, protests, and negotiations by individuals and groups across the nation.

Following the civil rights movements initiated by the members and supporters of the African American communities across the nation in the 1950 and 1960s, civil rights awareness began to intensify among other minority communities. This gradually fueled the movement to demand redress for Japanese American internment. The Japanese American Citizens League (JACL) approved a resolution in 1970 to seek both acknowledgement of and compensation for the injustice imposed on the World War II internment of Japanese Americans by the U.S. government. Although the framework for the redress movement was formed at this time, JACL's resolution was initially received with apathy, skepticism, and disagreement within the Japanese American communities.

For instance, many community members thought that their communities would benefit more by forgetting the dark past and focusing on creating a bright future. They frequently cited the notable success among Japanese Americans in the post–war United States. For instance, in 1974, Japanese Americans Norman Mineta and George Ariyoshi had been elected a congressman of California and the governor of Hawaii, respectively. Others expressed their skepticism by stating that the American government would never apologize or compensate for its actions three decades before, and they feared that seeking redress was not the best use of their resources. Yet others thought that demanding monetary compensation would tarnish the legacy of their suffering in the internment camps, by reducing their collective experiences of injustice to a finite dollar amount.

Partly because of these ideological differences, it took JACL several years to launch a major campaign to demand redress from the U.S. government. In 1978, JACL unanimously voted to seek monetary compensation in two forms: a $25,000 payment to each individual who had been interned, or to his or her heirs; and a trust fund to help reestablish the Japanese American communities that were destroyed as a result of the internment programs. It initially sought to pursue these goals through a series of legal actions. However, recognizing the time-consuming nature of such processes, JACL followed the advice of Japanese American senator Daniel Inoue of Hawaii and decided instead to recommend that a federal commission be established. As with most political movements, this decision prompted some members of the communities to branch out and establish their own organizations to tackle the redress issue differently. Such organizations included the National Council for Japanese

American Redress (NCJAR) and the National Coalition for Redress Reparations (NCRR), both of which disapproved of having a governmental commission address their concerns.

In the midst of these disagreements, President Jimmy Carter signed a bill to establish the Commission on Wartime Relocation and Internment of Civilians in 1980. This commission was designed to investigate whether the U.S. government had committed any human rights violations through their relocation programs involving Japanese Americans and to suggest any applicable remedies if such violations had indeed taken place. The commission conducted a series of public hearings across the nation, interviewed remaining survivors and their families, and reviewed documents. In 1983, the Commission concluded, in its report entitled "Personal Justice Denied," that the internment programs were indeed reflective not of justifiable security considerations but of racism and wartime hysteria created by government officials.

The commission recommended that the surviving internees or their heirs, approximately 60,000, be granted compensatory payments of $20,000 each, that a statement of apology be issued by the U.S. Government, and that a presidential pardon be granted for the Japanese Americans who were unjustifiably convicted of violating the curfew and internment orders. In 1988, the redress payments were finally approved by the Congress; in 1990, the first redress payments were made, accompanied by letters of apology. Although these terms did not fully comply with its original resolution, JACL nevertheless endorsed these recommendations, citing that this marked a major milestone in the lives of Japanese Americans, as it concluded one of the darkest episodes in the constitutional history of the United States.

See also Executive Order 9066; Japanese American Citizens League (JACL); Japanese American Internment; War Relocation Authority (WRA).

Further Reading

Daniels, Roger, Sandra C. Taylor, and Harry H. L. Kitano. *Japanese Americans from Relocation to Redress.* Seattle: University of Washington Press, 1991.

Hatamiya, Leslie T. *Righting a Wrong.* Stanford, CA: Stanford University Press, 1993.

Hohri, William Minoru. *Repairing America, Account of the Movement for Japanese American Redress.* Seattle: Washington State University, 1988.

Daisuke Akiba

JDL

See Jewish Defense League (JDL).

Jeffries, Leonard (1937–   )

Revered by some as a crusader for black empowerment and African-centered education, and condemned by others who regard his views as anti-Semitic, Leonard Jeffries is a controversial leading thinker on black politics and racial affairs. Jeffries was born in Newark, New Jersey, in 1937 and attended

Lafayette College, during which time he made his first trip to Africa. Jeffries received his PhD from Columbia University, and his dissertation focused on economic and political development in the Ivory Coast. He is currently a professor of Africana studies at City College, City University of New York (CUNY), where he has been since 1972, and was formerly chairman of the Black Studies Department. He was the founding director of the Association for the Study of Classical African Civilizations and a former president of the African Heritage Association. He has written on and researched widely West African politics and history, as well as race in education and politics, and is a frequent and sought-after public speaker.

Jeffries entered the public spotlight in August 1991 after the publication of what later became known as the "Albany speech," given at the Empire State Black Arts and Cultural Festival. In this speech, he defended his views that "rich Jews" were influential in the media and in Hollywood and had historically played a major role in the slave trade. His speech generated widespread controversy and media coverage. In March 1992, the CUNY Board of Trustees voted to remove Jeffries from his position as chairman of the Black Studies Department. After numerous appeals and counterappeals, which eventually led to his case appearing before the U.S. Supreme Court, the decision to remove Jeffries from the chairmanship was upheld. Jeffries continues to be regarded as a leading black intellectual and has advocated for a renewed pan-Africanism in the black community, reparations for slavery, and heightened black activism, particularly in education and curriculum development. Critics, however, argue that Jeffries' rise to prominence can be seen as part of a trend toward increasing anti-Semitism within the black community and have questioned his ideological links with the Nation of Islam and its leader, Louis Farrakhan.

See also Black Anti-Semitism; Farrakhan, Louis.

Rebekah Lee

Jensen, Arthur (1923–   )

Arthur Jensen was born in 1923. An educational psychologist, Jensen received his PhD from Columbia University in 1956 and went on to teach at the University of California at Berkeley. A controversial figure, Jensen wrote that intelligence is primarily an inherited trait that is only slightly influenced by environmental factors. Based on tests that he performed in the 1960s on school children, Jensen divided cognitive ability into two groups, level 1, simple functioning, and level 2, higher-level thinking. Based on these tests, which he considered to be culturally unbiased, Jensen argued that level-1 abilities were distributed across racial groups but that level-2 abilities were not. According to Jensen's research, Asians as a group have the highest level-2 abilities, followed by whites. Blacks on average, according to Jensen, had the lowest level-2 scores.

Jensen argued that the differences he found reflect a fundamental biological difference only slightly affected by environmental factors. Critics, such as Stephen Jay Gould, argue that Jensen and other hereditarians make a fundamental mistake in equating observed differences with inborn, immutable differences. Critics of Jensen and other hereditarians note that even if it were accepted that the test scores are true reflections of intelligence—a leap that many, including Gould, are not willing to make—that does not mean that the scores reflect inborn ability that could not have been changed through environment. How much intelligence is mutable and how much it is inborn remains a controversial question.

See also Biological Racism; Hereditarians vs. Environmentalists; Intelligence Tests and Racism.

Robin Roger-Dillon

Jewish-Black Conflicts

Jewish-black conflicts manifest the intricacy of race relations in the United States, because both Jews and blacks have long been the victims of racial discrimination and thus have a better chance of sympathy, if not of solidarity, in the struggle for racial justice. In fact, there have been efforts toward sympathy and solidarity between the two groups, particularly in the era of the civil rights movement. But several polls conducted in the 1990s found a noticeable increase of anti-Semitism in the Black population to a greater extent than among any other ethic groups. It is surprising because since the 1960s, negative Jewish stereotypes have clearly declined among the general American public. On the other hand, most Jews were found to not support government spending for the benefits of blacks. Jews, more than other white ethnic groups, another poll found, disliked having blacks in their neighborhoods and black students in the same school with their children.

Black anti-Semitism may be traced back to the tradition of medieval Christian anti-Semitism that holds Jews as killers of Christ and shrewd money handlers. It was, however, socioeconomic disparity between two groups that reinforced the negative images of Jews. In spite of ethnic bigotry, most Jews as a group achieved an impressive upward mobility only with the span of two generations in the United States, while most blacks have remained at the bottom. Many saw the evidence of the inflated notion of Jewish control of the United States in the incredible success of Jewish Americans, combined with their disproportionate presence in media, film and retail industries, and their influence in national politics. Blacks in large cities, particularly in New York City, often found themselves in financial deals with Jews because Jews owned a substantial number of small businesses and apartment buildings in black communities. Such transactions frequently turned Jews into the closest and most visible symbol of white oppression and they became an easy target of black resentment.

Among other factors contributing to black anti-Semitism was the radicalization of the black freedom struggle toward Black Nationalism beginning in the mid-1960s. One extreme example was Louis Farrakhan, the leader of black Muslims, who, in his fiercely anti-Semitic rhetoric, bluntly condemned Jews for their supposed role in white domination. Black advocates of community control accused Jewish-owned small businesses in black neighborhoods of being parasitical. Militant black civil rights leaders did not want Jewish activists in their organizations, where they had once played active roles. In addition, the policies of the Israeli government toward Palestine also tended to strengthen the negative attitude against Jews among blacks, whose experience of racial oppression led them to identify with Palestinians.

Jews' racism toward blacks can be partially explained as a result of their successful assimilation into mainstream American culture. As they assimilated into U.S. society, some also adopted mainstream racism. The actual contact with poor blacks through their business activities could reinforce the negative stereotypes of blacks. Many Jewish intellectuals were wary of Black Nationalism, just as many black intellectuals were uncomfortable with Zionism. Jewish Americans also found that affirmative action worked against them, even though it was intended to compensate for the harms caused by past racial discrimination. Around 1920, many discriminatory quota systems had been introduced to curb the number of Jews in schools, occupations, and neighborhoods, and Jews had fought against those measures. Given the disproportionate concentration of Jews in higher education and high-ranking occupations, they argued, affirmative action acted in reality as reverse discrimination against Jewish Americans.

See also Anti-Semitism in the United States; Black Anti-Semitism; Jeffries, Leonard.

Further Reading

Anti-Defamation League. *Survey on Anti-Semitism and Prejudice in America*. New York, 1998.

Nathan, Glazer. *Affirmative Discrimination: Ethnic Identity and Public Policy*. New York: Basic Books, 1975.

Salzman, Jack, Colin Elman, and Mirium Fendius Elman, eds. *Bridges and Boundaries: African Americans and American Jews*. New York: George Braziller, 1992.

Smith, Tom W. *Jewish Attitude toward Blacks and Race Relations*. New York: American Jewish Committee, 1990.

Dong-Ho Cho

Jewish Defense League (JDL)

This organization was founded in 1968 to defend Israel and Jews worldwide from discrimination and from violence by "whatever means necessary," including violent reprisals. Its tactics have ranged from nonviolent actions such as sit-ins, takeovers of facilities, and demonstrations to terrorism, including bombings, theft, threats, and shootings. It is considered a terrorist group by the U.S. government, and its targets include U.S. and UN facilities, Arab terrorist groups, and Jewish groups that the JDL believes are not doing their part in the struggle. While disapproving of the Palestinian cause and of intermarriage between Jews and African Americans, the JDL's ideology suggests that just as Jews should be free from hate, so should other groups. As of December 2002, most of the JDL's leadership was either dead or imprisoned, so its future activities are uncertain.

A member of the Jewish Defense League trains with a rifle.

© David H. Wells/CORBIS.

See also Anti-Defamation League of B'nai Brith (ADL); Anti-Semitism in the United States; Black Anti-Semitism; Jewish-Black Conflicts.

Mikaila Mariel Lemonik Arthur

Jihad

Although *jihad* has popularly come to mean "holy war" in the West, the Arabic root of the word can be translated into "struggle" in the path of God and Prophet Muhammad, as prescribed by the holy Qur'an of Islam. Jihad has at least two broad historical interpretations: a violent and a nonviolent one. The "greater" jihad involves the individual struggle to live a righteous and moral life and to submit to God's will. *Islam* literally means "submission to Allah or God." The "lesser" jihad refers to the duty of all Muslims to defend Islam and the *umma* (the worldwide community of Muslim believers). This may involve the use of armed struggle or holy war if necessary. The references in the Qur'an to jihad fall into two additional categories of defensive and offensive (expansionist) connotations. Defensive jihad refers to fighting back aggression against Muslims. Offensive or expansionist jihad encourages Muslims to spread the message of their faith and convert "infidels" (non-Muslims), a central component of Islam in its formative years.

The early followers of Muhammad believed that their jihad—devout sub-mission to the teachings of the Qur'an—would be rewarded with prosperity and the multiplication of the umma. The reverse was also true. Assaults against the believers were blasphemous and should be stopped by jihad. These diverse interpretations of jihad were subject to distortion and abuse during various periods in the history of Islam. As recently as the 1950s, Sayyid Qutb, one of the leaders of the Muslim Brotherhood in Egypt—a social movement that embraced religious piety with political mobilization and social-service programs—called for jihad in the sense of armed struggle. He argued that Muslims had the duty to overthrow corrupt, Westernized governments as violators of Islamic law. This line of thinking was later appropriated by extremist Islamist groups. As early as 1996, Saudi-born Al Qaeda leader Osama Bin Laden issued a declaration of jihad against the United States and its allies.

See also Al Qaeda; Islamic Jihad; Muslims, Terrorist Image of.

Mehdi Bozorgmehr and Anny Bakalian

Jim Crow Laws

Jim Crow laws are a set of segregation and discrimination laws against blacks enacted by Southern states and municipalities in the United States between the end of the Reconstruction period (1877) and the beginning of the civil rights movement (1950s). The term *Jim Crow* stems from a character in popular minstrel shows of early-nineteenth-century America. A white performer, Thomas "Daddy" Rice, blackened his face with charcoal and then danced and sang in mockery of a shabbily dressed rural black. Before the American Civil War, some Northern railroad lines had been called Jim Crow cars, meaning segregated cars. How this minstrel show character became synonymous with the segregation laws is unclear, but Jim Crow came to signify both formal segregation laws and practices of customary and informal segregation as a way of life.

Emergence of Jim Crow Laws

Segregation laws for blacks in the South began immediately after the American Civil War. Most Southern states tried to restrict the economic and physical freedom of the formerly enslaved blacks by adopting laws known as Black Codes. Although varying from state to state, Black Codes were designed mainly to secure a steady supply of cheap labor and continued to assume the inferiority of the freed slaves. For example, many Southern states had vagrancy laws that declared a black person to be vagrant if unemployed and without permanent residence; blacks who had no employment and permanent residence could be arrested, fined, and bound to a term of labor if unable to pay the fine. Apprentice laws provided for the "hiring out" of orphans and other young dependents to whites. Some states limited the type of property blacks could own, and in other states blacks were excluded from certain businesses or from the skilled trades. Former slaves were forbidden to carry firearms or to testify in court, except in cases concerning other blacks. Legal marriage between blacks was provided for, but interracial marriage was prohibited. A

South Carolina law prohibited black people from taking any job other than agricultural or domestic work, unless they obtained a special license from the local judge. That license could cost from ten to one hundred dollars, a fortune for a postwar worker. In Opelousas, Louisiana, African Americans needed written permission from an employer to enter the city.

During Reconstruction, Congress reacted to these laws by imposing military rule over the South and passing civil rights legislation. Black Codes also motivated Republican Congressmen to promote the Fourteenth and Fifteenth Amendments to the U.S. Constitution, extending citizenship to all African Americans and suffrage to black males. During this period of congressional Reconstruction (1866–1876), the passage of the Fourteenth and Fifteenth Amendments and the various enforcement acts of the early 1870s limited Southern whites' attempts to curtail blacks' civil rights. These governmental supports, however, did not continue. When the Compromise of 1877 gave the presidency to Rutherford B. Hayes in return for the promise to end Reconstruction, the federal government essentially abandoned all efforts at protecting the civil rights of Southern blacks.

Jim Crow Era

The following decade, the 1880s, was characterized by mob lynchings and a variety of laws that discriminated against blacks. Jim Crow laws began to be enforced legally to separate blacks in public spaces and to prevent adult black men from exercising the right to vote. Most Southern states imposed segregation on public transportation, especially on trains. Some states also passed antimiscegenation laws, banning interracial marriages. In the 1890s, starting with Mississippi, legislators in most Southern states began to rewrite state constitutions to deprive black men of voting rights by adopting complex voting requirements. For example, they imposed voter-registration requirements, such as proof of residency, payment of a poll tax, no criminal convictions, and literacy tests. These requirements were easily met by whites if they understood the state constitution when it was read to them. Louisiana introduced a grandfather clause in 1898, which stated that only men who had been eligible to vote before 1867, or whose father or grandfather had been eligible to vote prior to that year, were qualified to vote. Some states also passed the so-called white primary, which limited voting in the Democratic Party primaries to whites. These disfranchising measures excluded virtually all black men from Southern politics and circumvented the Fifteenth Amendment, which explicitly forbids the denial of the right to vote on account of race, color, or previous condition of servitude.

In addition, segregation was reinforced through intimidation, mob terror, riots, and lynching by such organizations as the Ku Klux Klan (KKK). During the period from 1882 to 1968, 4,730 lynching victims were reported. Of these victims, 3,440 were black men and women. Admittedly, hundreds of other lynching and mob terror cases were not reported. In conjunction with the segregation laws and the KKK's violent actions, there was also Jim Crow etiquette: a set of unwritten rules governing how blacks and whites should interact. Breaking this code could result in lynching. During the Jim Crow era, segregation laws governed nearly every aspect of African Americans' daily lives in the former Confederate states.

The Separate but Equal Principle

The most important court decision that sanctioned various segregation laws was handed down in the infamous 1896 *Plessy v. Ferguson* case. In 1890, Louisiana required that "all railway companies carrying passengers in their coaches in this state shall provide equal but separate accommodations for the white and colored races." The railway companies provided two or more "colored" passenger coaches for each train or divided the passenger coaches with a partition to separate the races.

In 1892, a thirty-year-old "colored" (one-eighth black and seven-eighths whites) shoemaker named Homer Plessy was jailed for sitting in the white car of the East Louisiana Railroad. Plessy went to court and argued that the Separate Car Act violated the Thirteenth and Fourteenth Amendments to the Constitution. The judge at the trial was John Howard Ferguson, a lawyer from Massachusetts who had previously declared the Separate Car Act unconstitutional on trains. In Plessy's case, however, he decided that the state could choose to regulate railroad companies that operated only within Louisiana. He found Plessy guilty of refusing to leave the white car. Plessy appealed to the Supreme Court of Louisiana, which upheld Ferguson's decision. In 1896, the U.S. Supreme Court heard Plessy's case and found him guilty once again. The *Plessy* decision provided the legal foundation to justify other actions by state

An African American man drinking at a segregated water cooler in a streetcar terminal, Oklahoma City, 1939.

Courtesy Library of Congress.

and local governments to separate blacks and whites. Separate facilities for blacks and whites became constitutional as long as these facilities were equal. With the Supreme Court's approval, the separate but equal doctrine was quickly extended to cover many other areas of public life such as restaurants, theater, restrooms, hotels, and public schools.

Moreover, in 1899, the Supreme Court legitimized further in *Cumming v. Richmond County Board of Education* that segregation laws were valid even if they provided no comparable schools for blacks. By 1914, every Southern state had passed laws that created two separate societies in every aspect of people's lives: one black, the other white. Blacks and whites could not ride together in the same railroad cars, sit in the same waiting rooms, use the same restrooms, eat in the same restaurants, or sit in the same theaters. Blacks were denied access to parks, beaches, and picnic areas.

From Jim Crow to Civil Rights

Starting in 1915, victories in the Supreme Court began to chip away at Jim Crow Laws. In *Guinn v. United States* (1915), the Supreme Court supported the position that a statute in Oklahoma law denying the right to vote to any citizen whose ancestors had not been enfranchised in 1860 was unconstitutional. In *Buchanan v. Warley* (1917), the court struck down a Louisville, Kentucky, law that required residential segregation.

It took until 1954, however, for the Supreme Court to find in *Brown v. Board of Education of Topeka* that school segregation was unconstitutional. This landmark decision was the turning point not only for the desegregation of public schools, but also for the push for racial equality that followed. Linda Brown, a black fifth-grader in Topeka, Kansas, was denied admission into a white elementary school. The National Association for the Advancement of Colored People's (NAACP) advocacy effort consolidated this case into another four similar cases from Kansas, South Carolina, Virginia, and Delaware. All five cases were argued together in 1952 by Thurgood Marshall, a black lawyer who headed the NAACP. Under Chief Justice Earl Warren's leadership, the Supreme Court reversed the *Plessy v. Ferguson* case by ruling that separate facilities based on race were inherently unequal in the area of public schools. This finding enabled civil rights advocates to demand and eventually obtain the federal government's assistance in their struggle for racial justice. Indeed, it has been noted that the ruling in the *Brown* case was the nation's most significant social transformation since the Civil War.

The *Brown* ruling inspired Southern blacks to adopt a more aggressive stance. In 1955, blacks in Montgomery, Alabama, began a boycott of city buses to protest Jim Crow seating practices. The boycott began when seamstress Rosa Parks, a long-time NAACP member and well-known member of Montgomery's black community, was arrested for refusing a bus driver's request to vacate her seat for a white male passenger. Park's arrest brought in the massive and well-organized boycott movement led by Martin Luther King Jr. The movement achieved victory in 1956 when a district court ruled segregation of the city buses illegal, and when the Supreme Court affirmed this ruling six months later.

Another nationally recognized protest took place in 1960 in Greensboro,

North Carolina. Black college students took their seats at the Greensboro five-and-dime white's-only lunch counter and staged a sit-in protest. The sit-ins persisted, and within six months, Greensboro blacks could sit down at a lunch counter and be served. All of these civil rights movements in the 1950s and 1960s ushered in the transition from segregation to civil rights and finally brought the end of Jim Crow Laws with the passage of the Civil Rights Act of 1964 and the Voting Rights Act of 1965.

Although African Americans no longer live under Jim Crow laws, the provocative book *American Apartheid* (1998) argues that black segregation (mainly residential segregation) is persistent through an interweaving set of individual actions, institutional practices, and governmental policies. The authors contend that in some cities, the degree of black segregation is so intense and occurs in so many dimensions simultaneously that it develops into "hypersegregation." They argue that segregation's deep roots in Jim Crow laws and the practices of the first half of the twentieth century led to the creation of perpetuated black underclass communities. Under conditions of extreme segregation, black poverty and its geographic concentration are likely to result in a climate of racial isolation, attitudes, behaviors, and practices that further marginalize African American neighborhoods and undermine their chances of success.

See also Brown v. Board of Education of Topeka; Civil Rights Act of 1964; Hayes-Tilden Compromise of 1877; Ku Klux Klan (KKK); Lynching; National Association for the Advancement of Colored People (NAACP); Parks, Rosa; Reconstruction Era; Separate but Equal Doctrine.

Further Reading

David, Ronald. *From Terror to Triumph: Historical Overview*. New York Life History Resources. http://www.jimcrowhistory.org/history/history.htm.

Fredrickson, George M. *Racism: A Short History*. Princeton, NJ: Princeton University Press, 2002.

Humphrey, H. Hubert, ed. *School Desegregation: Documents and Commentaries*. New York: Thomas Y. Crowell Company, 1964.

Kluger, Richard. *Simple Justice: The History of* Brown v. Board of Education *and Black America's Struggle for Equality*. New York: Knopf, 1976.

Massey, Douglas S., and Nancy A. Denton. *American Apartheid*. Cambridge, MA: Harvard University Press, 1998.

Woodward, C. Vann. *The Strange Career of Jim Crow*. 2nd ed. Oxford: Oxford University Press, 1966.

Sookhee Oh

John Birch Society

The John Birch Society was founded in 1958 by Robert Welch. The organization, named after Captain John Birch, a missionary killed in China shortly after World War II, advocates limited government, anticommunism, and American isolationism. It is also strongly associated with conservative Christianity, pro-gun activism, and states' rights. Critics of the organization charge that it is also racist and anti-Semitic. The John Birch Society famously contended that many in the United States government were soft on Communism, including President Dwight D. Eisenhower. The John Birch Society was at its most active in the 1960s, when anticommunist activism was its main focus. The John Birch Society claims that its goal is to defend "American" values, but critics have argued that it is politically too conservative. Among other controversial charges, the John Birch Society claims that the federal government—particularly the Bureau of Alcohol, Tobacco, and Firearms—had advanced knowledge of the Oklahoma City bombing in 1995. They have also claimed the United Nations aims to abolish the family and make all children wards of the state. In 1965, prominent conservative William Buckley Jr. denounced the John Birch Society for its anti-Semitism. Since then, the organization has operated on the fringes of the conservative movement.

See also Anti-Semitism in the United States.

Robin Roger-Dillon

Journalism and Racial Stereotypes

The news industry has changed dramatically in the United States since the early 1990s. Stories cycle in and out at a much faster pace, which leaves little time to delve into details. Stories and the people involved are presented so quickly, but repetitively, that only caricature-like profiles are established. One result is the perpetuation of stereotypes, or unreliable, exaggerated generalizations, about all members of a group that do not take individual differences into account. Stereotypes tend to evolve from statements or facts that are somewhat truthful, until they are stretched beyond their initial scope and applied with a more liberal meaning than they were originally able to support. The repetitive nature of the news industry today means that inaccurate representations have a great number of opportunities to influence the beliefs and perceptions of the audience.

There are several ways in which journalism perpetuates stereotypical attitudes in the United States. First, bad outcomes are most often associated with minority communities. News stories convey the notion that crime happens in certain parts of town, primarily the parts where higher percentages of African Americans and Latinos reside. The full range of economic and social status experienced by racial minorities are not represented. Instead, minority communities are frequently depicted as economically disadvantaged. Local newscasts typically show photographs of whites with an attorney when they are accused of crimes, whereas they typically show African Americans when they are being arrested. Stories about drug abuse, drug-addicted babies, AIDS patients, and homeless people are usually accompanied by photographs of African Americans. The reality is that white Americans are the majority or at least a significant proportion of each of these groups.

For years, the Mexican American population was treated as nonexistent by mainstream media outlets. When the news industry finally offered coverage of the Mexican American community, simplistic and inaccurate images were presented. As media outlets were beginning to recognize the presence of Mexican Americans, farm-labor activist Cesar Chavez and his United Farmworkers Union were highly visible, leading most Americans to identify Mexican Americans as farmworkers and rural dwellers. The reality is that most Mexican Americans and other Hispanics live in urban areas. Other stereotypical images of Mexican Americans that have been hard to dispel are those that represent them as illegal aliens, "wetbacks" who take public assistance without contributing tax dollars, drug dealers, and gang members.

Asian Americans are depicted as recent immigrants rather than citizens, regardless of how long they have been in the United States. A prime example of this is when, during the 1998 Olympics, U.S. news outlets reported that "the American beat Kwan," ignoring the fact that figure skater Michelle Kwan is also an American. The news industry also creates images of Asian Americans as disinterested participants in American society who prefer to remain segregated from mainstream society while benefiting from the resources that are available in the United States.

Muslims are portrayed not only as foreigners but also as undemocratic and unpatriotic. Arab Americans are depicted as threats to national security.

Attempts to offer humanized profiles of Native Americans typically involve concepts of spirituality and closeness to nature. These concepts at first glance seem complimentary, but on closer examination are really strategies for creating a perception of Native Americans as antiquated, behind the times, or out of touch with the modern world. More often than not, images of Native Americans are not present at all.

Jewish Americans have been characterized as wealthy and materialistic. Jewish mothers are depicted as overbearing and asexual.

White Americans are frequently stereotyped as well, but the difference is that most of their stereotypes are positive, as they control the images that are released.

The stereotypes that are promoted by the news industry are dangerous, not only because they are inaccurate and often negative but because the source is powerful. Despite the changes that have transpired in the last decade, journalism is still associated with a significant level of credibility. In the fast-paced twenty-first century newsroom, the lack of time to commit to accuracy often translates into institutionalized stereotyping, which could be a precursor to institutionally sanctioned discrimination.

Further Reading

Enns, Aiden. "Questioning Our Images of Islam." March 2002. http://www.journalism.ubc.ca/thunderbird/2001-02/february/religion.html.

Jones, Jackie. "Stereotypes Don't Change Themselves: Survey on Whites' Misconceptions Shows Need for a New Generation of Minority Journalists." http://newsatch.sfsu.edu/columnists/nabj/080101jones.html.

Lester, Paul M., ed. *Images That Injure: Pictorial Stereotypes in the Media.* Westport, CT: Praeger Publishers, 1996.

Romney S. Norwood

K

Kerner Commission

See National Advisory Commission on Civil Disorders.

Kerner Commission Report

The Kerner Commission Report (1968) refers to the official report of the National Advisory Commission on Civil Disorders, which was headed by Illinois governor Otto Kerner. President Lyndon B. Johnson organized this commission on July 27, 1967 to investigate urban racial disorders of 1967, and he appointed several moderates to the commission. Many critics were skeptical at best of the commission's ability to conduct its investigation responsibly and fairly. However, what came out as the Kerner Commission Report shocked even its critics for the report's comprehensiveness and clarity.

In 1967, more than fifty metropolitan areas in the United States were rocked by violent racial disturbances. The intensity of racial disorder varied by city: while other cities had experienced a moderate form of racial disturbance, Detroit, Michigan, and Newark, New Jersey, experienced the most violent racial disorder. Against this backdrop of the "summer of discontent," Present Johnson specifically raised the following three questions for the commission to inquire into: (1) What happened? (2) Why did it happen? and (3) What can be done to prevent racial disturbance in the future?

In the report's introduction, the commission presented their basic conclusion: "Our nation is moving toward two societies, one black, one white—separate and unequal. . . . Discrimination and segregation have long permeated much of American life; they now threaten the future of every American." It also pointed out that white institutions created and maintained ghettos of mostly African Americans. Thus, moderate, middle-class white Americans ought to accept the responsibility for creating conditions for racial disorders. Unless this deepening polarization was reversed, American society would be destroyed.

The report described in detail what happened to various cities, such as Tampa (Florida), Cincinnati (Ohio), Atlanta (Georgia), Newark, New Brunswick, Plainfield (New Jersey), and Detroit (Michigan). The Kerner Report concluded that even though disorders erupted right after "the final precipitating event," most of the 1967 racial disturbances were not results of a single triggering event. Instead, the continuous and insidious oppression of African Americans by white American society was to blame for their occurrence.

The report also mentioned that not all racial disorders were uniform in their profile. Like most human events, they did not unfold in an orderly sequence. Nonetheless, the twenty-four racial disorders they reviewed exhibited several common patterns. First, most of the riots and triggering incidents occurred in the evening. Riots usually subsided during the daytime and erupted again in the evening or night. Second, the typical participants in the riots were young African American males who were lifelong residents of the city, high school dropouts, and unemployed.

Third, even though African Americans rioters were acting against local symbols of white American society, they sought full participation in the social order instead of destroying the social order. Rather than rejecting the American system, African American rioters were anxious to obtain a place for themselves in it. Yet, the consequences of their participation in riots were physical injuries, death, property damage, and burning of buildings and houses in ghetto neighborhoods. Fourth, how police and other political establishments responded to initial riots determined the course of the disorder. Fifth, African Americans were severely discriminated against economically and socially, and efforts to address the grievances of African Americans were limited and sporadic at best.

To answer the question, why racial disorders had occurred, the commission explored the root cause of riots and reassessed structural conditions of whites and blacks in the United States. After observing that the United States was rapidly descending into two nations, one white and the other black, separate and unequal, the report pointed out whites' attitudes and behaviors toward blacks as the most fundamental root cause. Combined with this white racism were pervasive discrimination and segregation in education and employment, and white exodus due to blacks' migration into inner cities. The expansion of African American ghettos where jobs were scarce and poverty was deep further segregated the American society racially. It was truly a case of a vicious cycle.

What made this vicious cycle explode so violently? Here the commission directed attention to the fact that blacks had been frustrated repeatedly for a long time in redressing their grievances. This frustration and feeling of powerlessness created a climate that tended to approve violence as the only remaining option. This diagnosis indicated that the conditions of African Americans in the central cities reached the level of a crisis characterized by extremely high rates of unemployment and underemployment, high levels of poverty, and family breakdown. With these came a steep devaluation of property and inadequate public services. A deep hostility between ghetto residents and police, accumulation of unresolved grievances by ghetto residents against local authorities, and little confidence in the willingness and ability of local governments to respond to African American grievances contributed to creating a culture conducive to violence.

What could be done to prevent such disorders in the future? Here the report made detailed suggestions to local and federal governments. For example, it recommended that local governments create and maintain channels of communication to the residents of ghetto communities. It also implored local governments to provide opportunities for meaningful involvement of ghetto residents in shaping policies and programs that affected the community. The report stressed the roles of local police and mass media in improving the atmosphere in the community. Cities and states should reform their courts and improve the quality of justice. This enrichment of life conditions in racially segregated ghettoes could not be accomplished without federal government's involvement. Thus, the report implored the federal government to get involved proactively by creating jobs and dismantling discrimination in education and employment.

The commission invited Kenneth B. Clark to read and react to their report before its public release. With his experience of reading reports of past racial riots, he stated that, "I must again in candor say to you members of this commission—it is a kind of Alice in Wonderland—with the same moving picture re-shown over and over again, the same analysis, the same recommendations and the same inaction." After the initial shocks and realization tapered off, only minimal efforts were made to slow down the polarization of the nation. Alas, the long-term response of the United States to the Kerner Commission Report was the same inaction Clark alluded to in his remarks.

See also National Advisory Commission on Civil Disorders; Race Riots.

Further Reading

Campbell, Angus, and Robert M. Fogelson. *Supplemental Studies for the National Advisory Commission and Civil Disorders*. New York: Praeger, 1968.

Meranto, Philip J. *The Kerner Report Revisited: Final Report and Background Papers*. Urbana: Institute of Government and Public Affairs, University of Illinois, 1970.

U.S. Riot Commission. *Report of The National Advisory Commission on Civil Disorder*. Washington, DC: U.S. Government Printing Office, 1968.

Shin Kim and Kwang Chung Kim

King, Martin Luther Jr. (1929–1968)

Martin Luther King Jr., America's renowned leader of the civil rights movement, was a minister, author, social reformer, and intellectual who advocated creating social changes through the use of nonviolent social protest, such as demonstrations, sit-ins, and boycotts. The significance of his contributions to American society was recognized when he received the Nobel Peace Prize in 1964 for his role in the passage of civil rights legislation. He is considered both an African American and an American hero; thus, in 1986, a national holiday was established in his honor.

On January 15, 1929, Martin Luther King Jr. was born to Alberta Williams King and Rev. Martin Luther King Sr. He spent his youth in Atlanta, Georgia, where he witnessed the impact of Jim Crow laws firsthand. Before completing his high school education, King was accepted, at age fifteen, into Morehouse College's advanced-placement program. Three years later King decided to become a minister and began his early training at his father's church, Ebenezer Baptist Church.

King went on to pursue more formal religious training and became an ordained Baptist minister in 1948. He also earned a bachelor's degree in sociology from Morehouse College just before entering the Crozer Theological Seminary. King completed his work at Crozer in 1951. During his time there he became quite interested in the works of Indian independence leader Mahatma Gandhi and studied them in great detail. He continued his quest for knowledge by entering a PhD program in systematic theology at Boston University.

While working on his PhD, King also began to create what some consider his greatest legacy, his family. In 1953, he wed Coretta Scott and the couple had Yolanda, the first of four children in 1955. Their second child, Martin Luther King III, arrived in 1957, followed by Dexter in 1961 and Bernice in 1963. The family's safety was often in jeopardy: bombs were discovered in the family's home on several occasions and other acts of violence were directed toward the family in an effort to discourage his leading role in the civil rights movement.

Upon completing his formal education, King was catapulted into the role of a national civil rights leader when he helped to organize the Montgomery, Alabama, bus boycott in response to Rosa Parks's arrest after her refusal to give up her seat to a white passenger on a Montgomery bus. His role as a religious leader in the community led to him to be elected the president of the Montgomery Improvement Association, which organized a bus boycott and other protest events. In 1957, King met with a group of ministers, labor leaders, lawyers, and political activists who were concerned about the impact of segregation on their communities. This group formed the Southern Christian Leadership Conference, and King was the organization's first president.

Over the next decade, King was entrenched in the battle to end the second-class status of people of color in the United States. On several occasions, he was arrested for his leading role in the civil rights movement. Throughout this period, he continued to establish himself as an authority on race relations and civil rights with his speeches and writings. Notable written works by King include *The Measure of Man*; "Letter from a Birmingham Jail"; and *Why We Can't Wait*. His well-known speeches include "I've Been to the Mountain Top," which was the last speech he delivered before his assassination, and his most famous, the "I Have a Dream" speech, which was delivered during the March on Washington in 1963, on the steps of the Lincoln Memorial.

In 1964, King reached the pinnacle of his influence. At the end of the year he received *Time* magazine's most coveted Man of the Year award, and he was the recipient of the Nobel Peace Prize. Slowly, because of his persistent efforts, laws based on social equality for all were adopted, culminating with the Civil Rights Act of 1964 and the 1965 Voting Rights Act. Still, King continued

The Rev. Dr. Martin Luther King Jr. at the March on Washington, August 28, 1963.

Courtesy National Archives.

to champion social justice. On April 3, 1968, he attended a march to support sanitation workers who were striking in Memphis, Tennessee. The next day, King's life ended when a bullet struck him as he stood outside his hotel room in Memphis. A man who promoted nonviolent social change died in the most violent manner. James Earl Ray was convicted of assassinating King, but many historians question whether the right person was charged with this crime.

There is a consensus that the debates and conversations Martin Luther King Jr. provoked and the awareness of civil rights he stirred in America directly contributed to the passage of several monumental pieces of civil rights legislation. But many young African Americans appreciate more confrontational leaders, such as Malcolm X.

See also Civil Rights Movement; "I Have a Dream" Speech; Jackson, Jesse; "Letter from a Birmingham Jail"; Malcolm X; March on Washington; Montgomery Bus Boycott; Parks, Rosa; Southern Christian Leadership Conference (SCLC).

Further Reading

Fager, Charles. *Selma, 1965.* New York: Scribner, 1974.

Fairclough, Adam. *Martin Luther King, Jr.* Athens: University of Georgia Press, 1995.

Romney S. Norwood

King, Rodney

See Rodney King Beating.

KKK

See Ku Klux Klan (KKK).

Know-Nothing Party

The American, or Know-Nothing, Party was an anti-immigrant party that gained some strength in mid-nineteenth-century America. The party grew out of a secret nativist organization, the Order of the Star-Spangled Banner, which was founded in 1850. The members of the party were often called know-nothings because of their origins as a secret organization whose members insisted, when questioned, that they "know nothing" about it. From 1852 through 1854, the nativist Know-Nothing Party gained surprising strength. In the elections of 1854, those voters who believed that immigration was the greatest threat to the American way of life cast their ballots for the Know-Nothing Party. In that election, seventy-five congressmen and many city, county, and state officials from the party were elected.

Their primary objective was to restrict the flow of immigration to the United States. The Know-Nothings opposed the admission of paupers, criminals, and any other "undesirable immigrants," including Catholics, into the country. They believed that the period required for naturalization should be extended from five to twenty-one years. The party's slogan was "America for the Americans," and its platform urged that only "native"

Portrait of a young man representing Uncle Sam's youngest son, Citizen Know Nothing, 1854.

Courtesy Library of Congress.

white Americans be permitted to hold public office. Throughout the 1850s, nativist hostility against immigrants, especially Irish Catholics, intensified with the Know-Nothing Party's support. The powerless immigrants were exploited as scapegoats for the problems by the politicians to enhance their own political interests. The targeted group at that time was Irish immigrants, but the pattern has been continuing up to today.

See also Anti-Catholicism in the United States; Irish Immigrants, Prejudice and Discrimination against; Nativism and the Anti-immigrant Movements.

Heon Cheol Lee

Korematsu v. United States

Korematsu v. United States (323 U.S. 214 [1944]) was a U.S. Supreme Court case in which the Court upheld the internment of Japanese Americans during World War II. Just after the surprise attack on Pearl Harbor, Hawaii, by the Japanese on December 7, 1941, President Franklin D. Roosevelt issued Executive Order 9066. This order gave vast powers to restrict the movement of Japanese along the coast, due to fears of espionage. Acting under the president's authority, the military forcibly relocated more than 100,000 people of Japanese ancestry to internment camps—including U.S. citizens. By 1944, when the war hysteria had eased, the order was rescinded, and the camps were closed by 1945.

In *Korematsu*, the legality of the internment was challenged. A divided Supreme Court upheld the internment by a 6–3 vote, essentially stating that citizens of the United States have benefits as well as duties and that during wartime, each citizen is expected to do more. Additionally, the Court thought that, at the time they were hearing the case, the situation was calm compared with just after the Pearl Harbor attack. Therefore, they believed it was unfair to judge actions taken after the attack because those making the decisions did not know then that the actions they were taking were obviously unnecessary.

There was, however, a strong dissent. Dissenting Justice Frank Murphy argued that the internment violated the constitution and was blatant racism. Eventually, in 1988, this strong dissent was vindicated as Congress, through the Civil Liberties Act, attempted to remedy the injustices endured by Japanese Americans. Congress apologized and gave $20,000 to each person still alive who had been interned. The issues in *Korematsu* continue to be debated today, especially with respect to terrorism and crime.

See also Executive Order 9066; Japanese American Internment; Japanese Americans, Redress Movement for.

John Eterno

Ku Klux Klan (KKK)

The Ku Klux Klan (KKK) is the most well known and the oldest existing white supremacist group in the United States. The KKK's acts of hate and terror have targeted just about every group other than Southern white Anglo-Saxon Protestants; blacks, Jews, Catholics, and immigrants have all been targets of their hate. The KKK was formed in the 1860s, just after the Civil War, during the Reconstruction period. At this time, whites in the South were unsure of their position in the postwar society. Their fears were exacerbated by two important Amendments to the U.S. Constitution passed at this time. The Thirteenth Amendment outlawed slavery, while the Fourteenth Amendment, among other provisions, prevented any state from depriving any person "of life, liberty or property, without due process of law" and from denying "any person within its jurisdiction the equal protection of the laws."

The KKK can be traced to a small group of six former soldiers from the defeated Confederacy. They initially formed a social club on Christmas Eve in 1865 called "the Pulaski Circle." Robert E. Lee, the Confederacy's famous general, was initially asked to serve as the Klan's leader but declined for health reasons. Another former Confederate General, Nathan Bedford Forrest—known for massacring more than three hundred black soldiers at Fort Pillow, Tennessee, in 1864—became the first "Grand Wizard of the Invisible Empire" (Harris 2003, 9A). Eventually, the Pulaski Circle evolved into the "Ku Klux Klan," which was a violent group that terrorized against blacks. They are known in particular for night rides—riding on horseback carrying torches while wearing white sheets—and for lynching black men. President Ulysses S. Grant, the former Union General, had to send troops to the South to prevent the spread of violence during this period. The Klan of this era, however, deteriorated quickly as it became obvious that whites would maintain their power over blacks. In particular, the passage of Jim Crow segregation laws institutionalized racism, keeping whites in their position of power over blacks, thus making the KKK unnecessary.

The KKK, however, reemerged in 1915. Its numbers soared to over five million by 1925 (Ferber 1997, 17). This was the height of the KKK's mainstream respectability. At this time, the Klan was thought of, more or less, as a fraternal order rather than a hate group. Additionally, some of the popularity of the KKK of this period can be traced to the 1915 film *Birth of a Nation*. This immensely popular film falsely portrayed the Klan of the Reconstruction era as rescuing the South from the ravages of unscrupulous and ruthless Northern businesspeople and protecting Southern women. This film glorified the earlier KKK as heroes rather than the terrorists they actually were. Also, apparently for visual effect, Klansmen are seen burning crosses in the film—something the original Klan never did—and the KKK adopted cross burning following that film. Nearly 500,000 women joined the Klan during this period.

Into the 1920s, however, Klan membership declined enormously. This demise is generally blamed on "economic depression, internal battles, and financial scandals" (Ferber 1999, 18). Membership was reduced to only 350,000 toward the end of the 1920s. Due to the civil rights movement of the 1950s and 1960s as well as the Klan being implicated in acts of terror, their popularity declined. Some of the many atrocities that have been linked to the Klan include the homicides of three young men in Mississippi who had traveled to that state as part of an effort to increase black voter registration; the bombing of a church, in which four young black girls were killed; and the beatings of freedom riders (blacks and whites who rode together on segregated buses in Southern states as protests against the racist Jim Crow segregation laws).

Ku Klux Klan members in a Klan parade in Virginia, 1922.

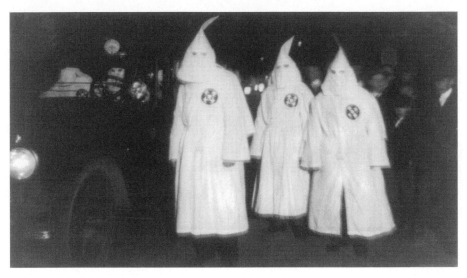

Courtesy Library of Congress.

By the early 1970s, the Ku Klux Klan had only 1,500 members. However, more recently the Klan has seen some increases in their numbers. Current estimates are about six thousand members (Burris et al. 2000, 218) spread out through a number of splinter organizations or chapters. The current Klan has attempted to change its image to appear to be nonviolent and has expanded its message of hate through the Internet. The most well-known Klansman behind this image change is David Duke. He won a seat in the Louisiana legislature in 1989 but has failed to achieve further political office. Duke presents a clean-cut image: he wears a suit and tie and presents himself as an honest, law-abiding person. However, he recently plead guilty to mail fraud and federal tax charges (Knickerbocker 2003). On April 15, 2003, David Duke was sent to a low-security federal prison in Texas. Just before his incarceration, Duke was in the process of presenting his message of hate to other areas of the world. For example, in May 2002, the Anti-Defamation League (ADL) reported that Duke "claimed that Israel had 'aided and abetted' the terrorists in the 9/11 attacks, and that Al-Qaeda was secretly controlled by the Mossad, Israel's intelligence agency."

Although Duke is in prison, the KKK continues its message of hate. Today, Thomas Robb leads the largest chapter, which is based in Arkansas. Although he seems to be steering the group away from its use of racist language, as with Duke, this appears to be merely a facade change; the hatred that drives the Klan's mission remains. Certainly, given its past use of terror and message of hate, law-enforcement and watchdog groups will continue to carefully monitor the KKK's activities.

See also Al Qaeda; Aryan Nations; Duke, David; Lynching; White-Supremacist Movement in the United States; White-Supremacist Underground.

Further Reading

Anti-Defamation League, http://www.adl.org.

Burris, Val, Emery Smith, and Ann Strahm. "White Supremacist Networks on the Internet." *Sociological Focus* 33, no. 2 (2000): 215–235.

Ferber, Abby L. "The White Supremacist Movement in the United States Today." In *Race and Ethnic Conflict: Contending Views on Prejudice, Discrimination, and Ethnoviolence*. 2nd ed., edited by Fred L. Pincus and Howard J. Ehrlich. Boulder, CO: Westview Press, 1999.

Harris, Barbara. "The Ku Klux Klan: From Fear, Anger, Poverty and Disenfranchisement Arose a Terrorist Group." *Jackson Advocate News* 65, no. 19 (2003): 9A.

Knickerbocker, Brad. "Setbacks for White-Supremacist Groups." *The Christian Science Monitor* 10 (January 2003): 2.

John Eterno

Kwanzaa

Kwanzaa is an African American holiday that commemorates and celebrates family, culture, and community. The name *Kwanzaa* means "first fruits" in

Kwanzaa decorations.

Getty Images/PhotoDisc.

Swahili, and the holiday has its origins in African harvest celebrations. Celebrated from December 26 through January 1, Kwanzaa was developed in 1966 by Maulana Karenga, professor and chairperson of the Department of Black Studies at California State University, as a cultural holiday to promote the African American experience. Kwanzaa was appropriated by African Americans in the United States during the Black Freedom movement, but the holiday retains many of its original Pan-African characteristics. Thus, current Kwanzaa celebrations among African Americans incorporate elements from continental Africa as well as aspects of the experiences of Africans in the Americas. The goal is to reaffirm African culture and reinforce bonds between African peoples. Kwanzaa is founded upon seven principles (*nguzo saba*) from African communities: *umoja* (unity), *kujichagulia* (self-determination), *ujima* (collective work and responsibility), *ujamaa* (cooperative economics), *nia* (purpose), *kuumba* (creativity), and *imani* (faith). Gifts (a book and a heritage symbol) are usually given to children and serve to reinforce African traditions and the commitment to African history. The colors of Kwanzaa are red, black, and green, and holiday decorations reflect traditional African items such as harvest symbols, cloth patterns, and African baskets. Although its impetus is in continental Africa, Kwanzaa is now celebrated by millions of persons of African descent in the diaspora, regardless of ethnicity, nationality, or religion.

Sandra L. Barnes

L

Labor Movement, Racism in

The year 1996 was a landmark year for the labor movement because for the first time in its history, most union members were not white and male. Indeed, the labor movement has come a long way from the days when blacks, if not completely excluded from unions, were forced to charter separate "colored" locals. Discrimination, however, does still exist in both the labor movement and employment at large in the United States.

Race has been a fundamental problem for the labor movement since the late eighteenth century, when the first unions were formed in Philadelphia and New York. The question of race in the labor movement has a complex history that can be broken down into three historical eras: from 1780 to the Civil War, from Reconstruction to the 1930s, and from the founding of the Congress of Industrial Organizations (CIO) in 1935 to the post–civil rights era of today. For most of its history, the labor movement was segregated if not outwardly racist. In California, for example, the Workingmen's Party was formed in large part as a means to deport Chinese immigrants. In the cases where blacks were allowed to join unions, they were forced to request separate charters from the American Federation of Labor (AFL) for "colored" locals. It was not until the formation of the CIO in 1935 that any unions pressed for integration as official policy. The United Mine Workers and the United Auto Workers were the most progressive of the CIO unions, and they pushed for interracial solidarity.

Because the labor movement emerged in the United States when slavery was the dominant mode of production in the South, "free labor" and civil rights for workers would come to be defined as being an issue exclusive to white workers. The construction of white identity and racism is intimately bound up with the rise of the labor movement: the concept of "whiteness" was developed during these years, and it would be a major obstacle for the labor movement after the Civil War, because it prevented interracial solidarity. Certain ethnic groups, such as the Irish and Italians, could "become white," but other groups could not. And, writing in 1935, W.E.B. Du Bois argued, "It must be remembered that the white group of laborers, while they received a low wage, were compensated in part by a sort of public and *psychological* wage." Before the Civil War, most white workers opposed ending slavery because they feared that free blacks would take their jobs. White workers suffered under harsh conditions in factories, working twelve- to fourteen-hour days, six days a week for very low wages. But if they were exploited in the factories, white workers could still take pride in knowing that they were free and that another group of workers, namely African Americans, were not. This is what Du Bois referred to as a kind of compensation for their exploitation; white workers could promote themselves by denying job opportunities for blacks. As a result, white workers in the labor movement were more concerned with the supposed "threat" of free blacks than with challenging the power of capital and the erosion of independence created by the wage system and factory labor. The investment in whiteness proved more salient than interracial solidarity among workers.

There were a few exceptions to the predominance of racism among white workers. One union in particular, the Knights of Labor, which was founded in 1869, vowed not to discriminate against blacks, on the principle that integration was necessary to build solidarity among workers and a powerful labor movement that could challenge the growing power of monopoly capital and the newly emerging corporations. Integration of workers and interracial organizing was an early goal of the AFL too, but as early as 1893, the AFL chose to allow racist locals to join the federation, and the AFL began the practice of allowing separate locals for black and white members. Nor did the AFL do anything to stop union members in California from attacking Chinese workers. The policy of tolerating racism among its rank and file is partly explained by the AFL's narrow focus on craft workers, or skilled workers, who were almost exclusively white and male. Blacks, Latinos, and Asians (especially the Chinese in California) were consistently shut out of high-paying, high-skilled jobs by both employers *and* unions. A. Philip Randolph, the president of the all-black union, the Brotherhood of Sleeping Car Porters, appealed to the AFL numerous times to abolish the practice of segregating locals in the AFL, to no avail. As a consequence, the labor movement continued to practice racial discrimination until the AFL was challenged by the CIO in the 1930s.

The CIO, an umbrella group of industrial unions, was founded by John L. Lewis of the United Mine Workers. The CIO was committed to organizing unskilled workers across craft lines and organized more than a million black workers between 1935 and the end of World War II. In many ways, the CIO was a precursor to the civil rights movement in the 1950s, in that many members of the CIO were also activists in the fight for equal rights for blacks. Many of the tactics first implemented by the organization drives of the CIO—including the sit-down strike and various other types of nonviolent civil disobedience—would later be used in the civil rights movements. Although the CIO made significant progress toward ending racial discrimination in the labor movement, many unions did not end the practice of segregation until they were forced to do so by the passage of the Civil Rights Act in 1964. Title 2 of the Civil Rights Act forced labor unions to integrate their locals. But even the CIO leadership did little to challenge Jim Crow in the South. In fact, the CIO suffered a spectacular failure to organize Southern workers when their campaign, Operation Dixie, collapsed under the weight of racism in the South. Still, black workers were able, in spite of the opposition, to form the National Negro Labor Council in 1951, an organization designed to pressure both employers and unions to end racial discrimination.

Today, blacks and other racial and ethnic minorities have risen into the ranks of leadership in many unions across the United States. One of the most progressive unions today is Janitors for Justice (JFJ), which grew out of the Service Employees International Union (SEIU). JFJ is on the forefront of the fight to end discrimination in the workplace, and their union reflects the changing face of the labor movement. Today, the working class is the most diverse it has ever been, and the rank and file of the labor movement is no longer dominated by white men working in the blue-collar industries. Today, union members are more likely to be working in the service sector in hospitals, schools, and retail establishments and are more likely to be African American, Latino, and South Asian than white. There is still progress to be made, however. Minority communities suffer the most when companies downsize or shut down their operations altogether as more and more U.S. jobs are moved oversees in the process of globalization. The new challenge for the labor movement is to become truly international.

See also Capitalism and Racial Inequality; Du Bois, W.E.B.; Economics of Discrimination; Wagner Act.

Further Reading

Draper, Alan. *Conflict of Interest: Organized Labor and the Civil Rights Movement in the South, 1954–1968*. Champaign: University of Illinois Press, 1994.

Du Bois, W.E.B. *Black Reconstruction in the United States: 1860–1880*. New York: Atheneum, 1977.

Marshall, Ray. *The Negro and Organized Labor*. New York: John Wiley, 1965.

Roediger, David. *The Wages of Whiteness: Race and the Making of the American Working Class*. New York: Verso, 1996.

Saxton, Alexander. *Indispensable Enemy: Labor and the Anti-Chinese Movement in California*. Berkeley: University of California Press, 1995.

Michael Roberts

Laissez-Faire Racism

Sociologist Lawrence Bobo and his colleagues use the term *laissez-faire racism* to describe the mechanisms that maintain the uniquely disadvantaged position of African Americans in the American economy and polity even as overt and institutionalized discriminatory practices and beliefs have declined. They argue that racial ideology reflects the particular economic context, prevailing cultural ideas, and politics of a specific historic period and set of actors. The post–World War II period marked a shift in the racial attitudes of white Americans from a Jim Crow racism of overt bigotry, state-enforced segregation and discrimination, and a belief in the intellectual and biological inferiority of blacks to laissez-faire racism, defined as a modern free-market ideology that "involves persistent negative stereotyping of African Americans, a tendency to blame blacks themselves for the black-white gap in socioeconomic standing, and resistance to meaningful policy efforts to ameliorate America's racist social conditions and institutions."

Jim Crow racism was at its height when African Americans were largely a rural, Southern, agricultural workforce. During this period, state policy enforced anti-black biases, and the idea that blacks were inherently inferior was widely accepted. Laissez-faire racism rationalizes antiblack attitudes in a period when African Americans are largely urbanized, dispersed throughout the country, and heterogeneous in terms of occupations. State policy is formally race neutral and committed to antidiscrimination, and biological racism has been replaced by a "more volitional and cultural" explanation for the disadvantaged position of blacks. Laissez-faire racism is premised on a notion of black cultural inferiority that faults blacks for their disadvantaged position. Racial ideology has shifted with the times, meeting the "needs" of a postindustrial economy and modern polity. Rather than state enforced discrimination, lassiez-faire racism is based on the market and informal racial biases that recreate "and in some instances sharply worsen, structured racial inequality."

See also Jim Crow Laws; Labor Movement, Racism in.

Further Reading

Bobo, Lawrence, James R. Kluegel, and Ryan A. Smith. *Laissez-Faire Racism: The Crystallization of a 'Kinder, Gentler' Anti-Black Ideology*. New York: Russell Sage Foundation, 1996. Also see http://epn.org/sage/rsbobo1.html.

Tarry Hum

La Raza Unida

La Raza Unida, "the People United," was a racially based third-party movement of Mexican Americans to challenge the political monopoly of the Democratic and Republican parties in the United States. It grew out of the militant Chicano movement that had proliferated throughout the Southwest and in some parts of the Midwest from 1966 to 1970. Many activists in the Chicano movement found neither of the two dominant political parties adequately responsive to the needs of most Mexican Americans who were living in disproportionate poverty and experiencing racial discrimination. They also saw the traditional civil rights organizations of Mexican Americans, such as the League of United Latin-American Citizens, the GI Forum, and the Political Association of Spanish-Speaking Organizations, as being unwilling to work to bring about the social change demanded by the rising expectations of Chicanos.

The endeavor toward a Chicano political party emerged first in Texas and Colorado and expanded soon to California, New Mexico, Arizona, Utah, and the Midwest in the early 1970s. It could have flowered on the soil of Chicano grassroots social movements of an anticapitalist and nationalist bent, which provided the ideology, leadership, organization, constituency, and financial resources. La Raza Unida party in Texas came out of the Mexican American Youth Organization (MAYO), founded in 1967 under the leadership of Jose Angel Gutierrez. Colorado's La Raza Unida was organized by the Crusade for Justice, founded in 1966 by another prominent Chicano movement leader, Rodolfo "Corky" Gonzales. The explosive political atmosphere of the 1960s, both domestically and abroad, also emboldened Chicano activists. The party mainly appealed to radicalized students and poor Mexican Americans with anticapitalist and nationalist platforms, declaring that it was time for Chicanos' political self-determination to dismantle internal colonialism and systematic inequality.

La Raza Unida party's political success was, however, confined to several counties in Texas during the brief period from 1970 to 1975. Its achievement on state and national levels remained symbolic rather than real. In Texas, the party took over the local school boards and city councils of Cristal, Cotulla, Carrizo Springs, and other places where the Mexican American population predominated. It demonstrated how they could win political power and use it for La Raza. The newly elected Chicano officers had new schools built and old ones refurbished, implemented bilingual, bicultural education from kindergarten through twelfth grade, promoted Chicano pride and multiculturalism, improved city services and infrastructure, and, though less successful, tried to advance Mexican American businesses. The success made Texas an inspiration for Chicano activists in other states. Even though La Raza Unida in Texas was an official political party on the ballot, it never won any statewide election. In the 1978 gubernatorial race, it lost its official party status. The party never regained its lost momentum after that and was defunct by 1981.

La Raza Unida's electoral record in other states did not match even that of Texas. But the political-party movement provided Chicano activists with a chance to put their radical demands on the state- and national-level political agenda, as well as an organizational impetus. No Chicano party movement survived the general turn toward political conservatism that has occurred since the 1970s, which saw the decline of antiwar, civil rights, and Chicano struggles. Restrictive election laws, lack of media access, insufficient financing, Democratic Party cooptation, and law-enforcement infiltration, which led to members being arrested on questionable drug charges, also contributed to the demise of the third-party movement. In addition to these external obstacles, internal strife, particularly the power struggle between two top leaders, Gutierrez and Gonzales, debilitated the movement. The internal conflict reflected the eclectic nature of La Raza Unida's ideology, a mixture of various types of nationalism and Marxism. Also inconsistent was its strategy. Whereas Gutierrez stood for a more pragmatic coalition approach, Gonzales opted for a direct ideological agitation of ultranationalism.

La Raza Unida, although it had little formal structure, never completely disappeared. Some activists have been working to revive El Partido Nacional de la Raza Unida. The increase of the Latino population, expanded financial resources, and Latino mass media, combined with the deteriorating economic and racial situations, may create suitable conditions for its revitalization in the twenty-first century.

See also Chicano Movement; Gonzales, Rodolfo "Corky"; Gutierrez, Jose Angel.

Further Reading

Garcia, Ignacio. *The Forging of a Militant Ethos among Mexican Americans.* Tucson: University of Arizona Press, 1997.

Munoz, Carlos. *Youth, Identity, Power: The Chicano Movement.* New York: Verso, 1989.

Navarro, Armando. *La Raza Unida Party: A Chicano Challenge to the U.S. Two Party Dictatorship.* Philadelphia: Temple University Press, 2000.

Rosales, F. Arturo. *Chicano! The History of Mexican American Civil Rights Movement.* Houston: Arte Publico, 1996.

Dong-Ho Cho

Lau v. Nichols

In 1973, the United States Supreme Court issued its decision in *Lau v. Nichols*, ruling that the San Francisco public school system violated the Civil Rights Act of 1964 by denying non-English-speaking students of Chinese ancestry a meaningful opportunity to participate in the public educational program. The decision stated that "merely by providing students with the same facilities, textbooks, teachers, and curriculum," the school district failed in its obligation to ensure that they received an equal educational opportunity. The *Lau* decision was important because it extended civil rights protections to linguistic minorities, that is, to students who did not speak English, by applying the Civil Rights Act's prohibition on discrimination based on "national origin." If English is the mainstream language of instruction, the high court reasoned, then measures must be taken either to ensure that English is taught to students who have limited English proficiency, or to provide such equal opportunities by holding instruction in students' native language.

Lau was a class-action lawsuit filed on behalf of 1,800 Chinese immigrant students who were not receiving English-language instruction but were forced to attend academic classes offered only in English. It followed meetings between the growing multigenerational Chinese American population and school administrators. Chinese American advocates had conducted studies that demonstrated the needs of non-English-speaking children were not being met, but the school system had not responded with policy changes. At that time, the population of Chinese immigrant students was growing and large numbers of them were becoming disengaged from the educational process because they could not understand the language of instruction.

See also Civil Rights Act of 1964; Education and Racial Discrimination.

Khyati Joshi

League of United Latin American Citizens (LULAC)

The League of United Latin American Citizens (LULAC) is the oldest and largest Hispanic civil rights organization that is still active. It was founded on February 17, 1929, by the merging of four Mexican American organizations: the

Corpus Christi Council of the Sons of America, the Alice Council of the Sons of America, the Knights of America, and the Latin American Citizens League in the Rio Grande valley and Laredo. Although LULAC was created to address racial inequality, discrimination, and injustice Mexican Americans had suffered since the annexation of Mexico's territory after the Mexican War, the founders intended from the outset to include all Hispanics. The organizing efforts by a special task force called the "Flying Squad" frequently met intimidation by the Anglo authorities. By 1932, however, LULAC established local councils in Arizona, Colorado, New Mexico, and California. Today it represents all Hispanics in most of the United States, including Puerto Rico and Guam.

LULAC has always been a multi-issue organization. In 1945, a California LULAC Council successfully sued Orange County to desegregate its school system. In 1954, LULAC won another landmark victory in the Supreme Court case *Hernandez v. State of Texas*, successfully stopping the state's racist practice that had excluded Mexican Americans from jury duty. LULAC also started an early-childhood-education program, called "The Little School of the 400," which later became the model of the federal program Head Start. LULAC was also instrumental in creating Hispanic national organizations such as the American GI Forum, the Mexican American Legal Defense and Education Fund, and SER—Jobs for Progress. It also developed many low-income housing units.

LULAC has been a largely middle-class organization composed of skilled workers and small-business owners, as well as some professionals. Ideologically, it adheres to the mainstream American ideology: liberalism, individualism, free-market capitalism, anticommunism, and U.S. patriotism.

Dong-Ho Cho

Lee, Wen Ho (1939–   )

Wen Ho Lee, a Chinese American engineer, became the victim of racism when the U.S. government accused him of spying and violated his civil rights in 1999. Born in 1939 in Nantou, Taiwan, Wen Ho Lee immigrated to the United States in 1965. Having earned a BS in mechanical engineering from Cheng Kung University, Lee came to the Unites States to pursue graduate studies at Texas A & M University, where he earned his PhD in 1969. He was a naturalized U.S. citizen and a long-time employee of the Los Alamos Research Laboratory when, on March 8, 1999, just months from retirement, he was abruptly fired from his position in the computational fluid dynamics group.

His termination took place after it became known that the Chinese had acquired the technology to the W-88 warhead, on which Lee had worked. On December 10, 1999, Lee was arrested after the U.S. attorney had filed a fifty-nine-count indictment against him. This included ten counts of keeping national-defense information in violation of the law, another ten counts of illegally obtaining national-defense information, and thirty-nine counts of violating the Atomic Energy Act by incorrectly handling classified documents essentially for the purpose of spying. Lee was immediately placed in solitary confinement. He was permitted a one-hour exercise period each day, during which he was separated from other inmates, and a one-hour visit from his family each month. Whenever he left his cell he was shackled. News of the severity of his treatment in prison brought complaints and protests from such groups as the Committee of Concerned Scientists, the New York Academy of Sciences, and the American Chemical Society.

On September 15, 2000, U.S. District Court Judge James A. Parker formally apologized to Lee for the unfair manner in which he was held in custody. The government had never produced a case for a grand jury, and Lee pled guilty to a count of downloading classified information to an insecure computer, which permitted Lee to go free and saved the government embarrassment. In his 2002 book *My Country versus Me*, Lee argued that without doing anything wrong he was singled out mainly because he was a Chinese American, a charge earlier corroborated by the former head of counterintelligence at Los Alamos.

In the nineteenth and early twentieth centuries, Asian immigrants encountered many exclusionary laws and other forms of discrimination in the United States. During World War II, Japanese Americans in the West Coast, including U.S.-born citizens, were incarcerated in relocation camps although there was no evidence that they were helping the Japanese in the war against the United States. Since the end of World War II, Asian Americans have achieved a high level of socioeconomic mobility, but as nonwhite minority members, they are still perceived as perpetual foreigners. The Wen Ho Lee case aptly demonstrates that regardless of their legal or native-born status, Asian Americans can

Support for Wen Ho Lee during his plea hearing in Albuquerque, New Mexico, September 2000.

Photo by Joe Raedle/Getty Images.

be considered foreigners who are more loyal to their home or mother country than to the United States.

See also Asian Americans, Discrimination against.

Benjamin F. Shearer

Legacy of Past Discrimination Argument for Affirmative Action

Affirmative action refers to preferential treatment for racial and ethnic minority members and women. Many white Americans oppose affirmative action for blacks and other racial minority groups on the grounds that they were subjected to discrimination in the past but that it has been forty years since civil rights legislations abolished all forms of discrimination. Of course, this argument is invalid because members of racial minority groups and women, especially African Americans, still encounter different forms of discrimination and disadvantages and lack of opportunity in education and social mobility remain as the legacy of past discrimination.

For example, because of formal racial discrimination in the pre–civil rights era, many black people who are now in their sixties may not have received even a high school education. A limited education limited their chances of finding meaningful, well-paying jobs in the 1960s and 1970s, even after all types of job discrimination were made illegal. As a result, they could not provide a good education to their children, who are now in their thirties and forties, and the pattern is left to be repeated. Thus, disadvantages of grandparents, created by past discrimination, can still negatively affect their grandchildren's chances for education and social mobility. Therefore, to offset the residual effects of past discrimination, minority members and women need to get preferential treatment.

See also Affirmative Action; Affirmative Action, University of Michigan Ruling on; Role-Model Argument for Affirmative Action.

Pyong Gap Min

"Letter from a Birmingham Jail"

During the several years of his active leadership in the civil rights movement, Martin Luther King Jr. was arrested and put in prison several times. In March and April 1963, he played a leading role in sit-in demonstrations in Birmingham, Alabama, to protest racial segregation of eating facilities. He was arrested during the demonstration and put in a jail in Birmingham. On April 16, 1963, while imprisoned, King wrote this famous letter. In it, he was responding to the eight liberal Alabama Jews and other white clergymen who had sent him an open letter. In the open letter, they asked him to allow the battle for integration to continue in the local and federal courts rather than on the streets. They warned him of the possibility that sit-in demonstrations would incite civil disturbances. In this long letter directed to "My Fellow Clergymen," King tried to defend his use of nonviolent resistance as the only effective alternative to negotiations, which had not worked to correct injustices. Responding to the charge that he and his followers were breaking laws, he made a distinction between a just law and an unjust law. He argued that we could disobey unjust laws, such as segregation ordinances, which "are out of harmony with the moral law."

See also Civil Rights Movement; "I Have a Dream" Speech; King, Martin Luther, Jr.; March on Washington; Montgomery Bus Boycott.

Further Reading

King, Martin Luther, Jr. *I Have a Dream: Writings and Speeches That Changed the World*. New York: HarperCollins, 1992.

Pyong Gap Min

Liberal and Conservative Views of Racial Inequality

Racial inequality in the United States indicates an unequal distribution of resources, such as wealth, income, power, and status, between white Americans and racial minority groups. As the influx of immigrants from Third World countries during recent years has transformed the United States from a largely black-white, biracial society to a multiracial society, minority groups include Latinos, Asian Americans, and Caribbean blacks as well as African Americans. Nonetheless, racial inequality in the United States is still present in the disparate levels of ownership of economic and noneconomic powers of blacks and whites.

On the whole, white Americans exhibit an ambivalent and ambiguous attitude toward the existence of this racial inequality. Nonetheless, white Americans' views of racial inequality are commonly placed along a liberal-conservative spectrum. Although somewhat oversimplified, the conservative view of racial inequality stands somewhere between the moderate right to the extreme right on this spectrum. The liberal view can be placed from the middle to the extreme left location. Conservatives and liberals differ in their views about the causes of racial inequality and their proposed remedies for this inequality.

Conservatives believe in the maintenance of the present system as far as racial inequality is concerned. It is neither because they deny the existence of racial inequality in America nor because they regard the present system as the ideal one. It is rather because conservatives trust the present capitalistic system's capability of bringing out the most efficient and fairest reward to individual members of a society. According to conservatives, there is no better alternative to the present system, even with its shortcomings. Said another way, conservatives consider that the current racial inequality has originated from minority members' lack of education and lack of motivation.

According to Hacker (1992), the conservatives reject the suggestion that they bear any *personal* guilt toward the racial inequality in present-day America. Conservatives' response to the critic who points to the system of slavery and its lingering impact usually runs as follows: It is true that the slavery system forbade American blacks for a long time from reaping the fair result of their efforts, but blacks have had ample opportunity for at least one (possibly two) generation since the 1960s to rectify their position in America. After more than one generation of preferential treatment, whatever they achieve is a result of their own efforts and hard work as individuals. The same logic applies to whites as well.

As their perspective is focused on an individual, not on a group, the conservatives tend to advance the high-achieving African American individuals as the evidence for the fair workings of the system. African Americans who lag behind have nobody but themselves to blame. According to the conservative view, social programs that promote racial equality by giving preferential treatment to minorities (e.g., affirmative action programs) could have had beneficial effects initially. That is, these programs had been leveling the playing field between two races for more than one generation. In effect, these programs had outlived their usefulness in eradicating racial inequality. Conservatives thus point out the detrimental effects of these programs to African Americans with high aspirations. Any color-specific programs stigmatize these individuals and kill their incentive. In other words, color-specific programs reduce the efficacy of the whole society. This is conservatives' public rationale for their fierce opposition to any programs that grant preferential treatment on African Americans. They therefore advocate color-blind social programs. It is identical to the leaky basket argument in economics.

On the whole, liberals are critical of the present capitalistic system in the United States. In other words, liberals view the American capitalistic system as a system of institutionalized exploitations in which the dominant, white group has benefited at the expense of African Americans and other minority groups. The racial inequality observed in the United States has its origin in such a system. According to liberals, several decades of social experiments with programs that intended to rectify the wrongs of the slave system and subsequent discrimination were unable to sufficiently level the playing field. This insufficiency (of social programs) originates from either the piecemeal fashion with which these programs are meted out or their short duration, or both. Therefore, liberals contend that American society still owes its African American members some preferential treatment.

Liberals are more sympathetic than conservatives to the stress individual African Americans experience in their daily living. Hacker expresses it in this way: "To be black in America means reining in your opinions and emotions as no whites ever have to do. Not to mention the forced and false smiles you are expected to contrive, to assure white Americans that you harbor no grievances against them" (1992, 49). To the extent that liberals empathize with African Americans, they tend to accept personal responsibility for the racial inequality present in contemporary American society. It must be noted that their acceptance of personal responsibility is not due to their personally harming African Americans but to their recognition that white privilege somehow makes it harder for blacks to reach the level of whites in America. Thus, liberals tend to support the continuation of color (race)-specific governmental programs.

Although both conservatives and liberals admit the existence of racial inequality in contemporary America, the two groups differ radically in analyzing the source of racial inequality. Conservatives believe racial inequality arises from individuals' dissimilar contribution to society. Irrespective of one's race, the one who contributes less receives less in a capitalistic system. In the United States, blacks as a group include a large proportion of lesser-contributing individuals, economically speaking. After several decades of preferential treatment, low-achieving blacks have nobody but themselves to blame, conservatives say. Liberals, on the other hand, believe that the social programs of several decades were not sufficient to eliminate the systemic discrimination African Americans face in America just because of their skin color. With this recognition, they advocate the continuation of race-specific governmental programs.

Further Reading

Clayton, Obie, Jr., ed. *An American Dilemma Revisited: Race Relations in a Changing World*. New York: Russell Sage Foundation, 1996.

Farley, John E. *Majority-Minority Relations*, 4th ed. Upper Saddle River, NJ: Prentice Hall, 2000.

Hacker, Andrew. *Two Nations: Black and White, Separate, Hostile, Unequal*. New York: Ballantine Books, 1992.

Shin Kim and Kwang Chung Kim

Lincoln, Abraham, and the Emancipation of Slaves

Abraham Lincoln was elected president on November 6, 1860, and even before he took office, South Carolina seceded from the Union. The Confederate States of America was born in early February 1861, and by mid-April the Civil War had begun, starting with the Confederate attack on Fort Sumter. Within another month, North Carolina had seceded, thus bring the Confederacy to its full complement. With the Union defeat at Bull Run that July, it became clear that rebellion would not be put down easily.

This quick and dramatic succession of events united the antislavery forces in Congress and the military to act on their convictions. In early August, Congress passed the First Confiscation Act, which nullified all claims to fugitive slaves involved in the South's war effort. These slaves worked in munition factories, produced needed foods, and served as teamsters and laborers in the Confederate Army. At the end of the month, General John Frémont freed the slaves of pro-Confederate owners in Missouri, but Lincoln claimed Frémont had exceeded the intention of Congress in doing so and eventually ordered him to revise his emancipation edict. Likewise, when General David Hunter began recruiting black soldiers in South Carolina in 1862, Lincoln's War Department refused to fund his effort, and when Hunter emancipated all slaves in South Carolina, Florida, and Georgia, Lincoln proclaimed his action null and void.

Lincoln attempted to steer what he saw as a middle ground. He asked Congress to adopt a policy that employed federal funds to entice states to emancipate slaves gradually and compensate owners. Indeed, on March 16, 1862, Congress abolished slavery in Washington, DC, agreed to compensate owners who were loyal to the Union, and funded efforts to colonize freed slaves in places such as Liberia. Lincoln had long been enamored of these so-called colonization plans, which he saw as a legitimate answer to the solution of the race issue. His insistence on compensation to slave owners seemed to him a political imperative at the time based on the belief, imbedded in the Constitution he swore to uphold as president, that slaves were property. However, when Lincoln tried to convince congressmen from the border states that a policy of compensation, colonization, and gradual emancipation was the best way to proceed, he was roundly rejected.

Congress moved quickly on its own agenda. In July 1862, it passed the Second Confiscation Act, which provided for freeing the slaves and seizing and selling the property of anyone involved in or abetting the rebellion. Furthermore, it prohibited military personnel from making decisions on any claims to freedom by fugitive slaves or surrendering any fugitives to those who claimed them. Most significantly, however, Congress authorized Lincoln to employ African Americans to put down the rebellion.

Portrait of Abraham Lincoln.

Lincoln now had to make a decision, which, he later claimed, was a decision between choosing the Constitution or preserving the Union.

Still clinging to the notion of colonization for emancipated slaves and wavering between gradual and immediate emancipation, on September 22, 1862, Lincoln proclaimed that, effective January 1, 1863, slaves in any rebellious state or part thereof would be forever free. He committed the federal government and the military to safeguard the freedom of the former slaves. This preannouncement allowed Confederate states the opportunity to rejoin the Union by sending duly elected representatives to Congress, for the Proclamation defined states or parts thereof in rebellion as those not represented in Congress. When January arrived, however, it was clear that this political gambit failed. Slaves were freed in the following rebellious states: Arkansas, Texas, Mississippi, Alabama, Florida, Georgia, North Carolina, and South Carolina. Slaves in parts of Louisiana and Virginia were also freed.

In his Proclamation, Lincoln asked the newly freed slaves to shun violence except in defense of themselves and, in the Republican Party preference for free soil and free labor, to work faithfully for reasonable wages. He also invited emancipated slaves in good condition to join the Union Army and Navy. This last provision, echoing the previous intent of Congress, proved to be quite important. Lincoln wrote in an 1864 letter that his difficult decision to emancipate the slaves had turned out quite for the good, because it added to the Union military forces 130,000 black soldiers it would not otherwise have had. Even with this additional manpower, however, Lincoln was forced to initiate a very unpopular conscription program.

The Emancipation Proclamation did not, contrary to popular belief, free all the slaves, only those living in areas and states declared to be in rebellion. Thus, for example, slaves in border states that permitted slavery but remained pro-Union, and slaves in Confederate territory already under Union domination were not freed. Although Lincoln claimed that he had found the institution of slavery to be immoral from his earliest memory, he was not a radical abolitionist, as some in his party were, nor was he ever one to miss scoring a political point. By freeing the slaves only in Confederate hands, he managed not only to raise an army but to disrupt plantation lifestyle and production, while avoiding the slavery issue altogether in those areas contributing to the Union cause. Only when the Thirteenth Amendment was ratified on December 18, 1865, was slavery completely abolished in the United States.

See also Abolitionist Movement; Civil War and the Abolition of Slavery; Emancipation Proclamation; Reconstruction Era; Slavery in the Antebellum South.

Further Reading

Fredrickson, George. *The Arrogance of Race: Historical Perspectives on Slavery, Racism, and Social Inequality*. Middletown, CT: Wesleyan University Press.

Guelzo, Allen C. *Lincoln's Emancipation Proclamation: The End of Slavery in America*. New York: Simon & Schuster, 2004.

Benjamin F. Shearer

Literacy Test

The literacy test was one of the techniques used by Southern states to keep blacks from voting during the Jim Crow period. After President Abraham Lincoln signed the emancipation proclamation in 1863, the federal government guaranteed through the support of its troops, the right of blacks to vote in the South. However, when the federal government decided to withdraw its troops from the South in 1896, the white supremacist governments in the Southern states slowly took away most of the civil rights of black residents. One of the first rights taken was voting. Since the Fifteenth Amendment gave blacks the right to vote in 1869, the Southern states could not legally prevent blacks from voting. Therefore, they instituted a literacy test and other measures. The literacy test required that a citizen be able to read to be eligible for voting. Blacks had a much lower literacy rate than whites at that time, so it systematically eliminated them from voting. Moreover, the test was usually arbitrary and depended on the whim of the white registrar. For example, in

Florida, one of the questions included in the test was "How many windows are in the White House?"

Although the law required every voter to take the literacy test, African Americans who were brave enough to face all the intimidations and humiliations would often take the test. When they passed it, they were still denied the right to vote. With the passage of the Civil Rights Act in 1964, the federal government abolished the literacy test as a condition for voting. This decision enabled Southern blacks to exercise their right to vote and to elect their own representatives to local and national offices.

See also Civil Rights Act of 1964; Fourteenth Amendment; Jim Crow Laws; Poll Tax.

Francois Pierre-Louis

Literature

See American Literature and Racism.

Little, Malcolm

See Malcolm X.

Little Rock (Arkansas) Central High School, Integration of

In the 1954 *Brown v. Board of Education of Topeka* case, the U.S. Supreme Court ruled that separate school systems for black and white children were unconstitutional because they violated the equality principle. Following this ruling, the federal government asked state governments to dismantle the segregation system that state governments had established in all aspects of public life, including their school districts. Although the Court ruled on that case in 1954, it took a long time for various states to comply with the ruling. Some states had to be forced into compliance by the federal government, while others took some voluntary steps. Arkansas was one of those states whose leaders took cautionary steps to integrate their school system. Although the University of Arkansas and its law school were officially integrated by 1957, the real test of how whites would comply with the Supreme Court ruling took place in Little Rock Central High School.

In the summer of 1957, the City of Little Rock made plans to integrate its public school system by starting with Central High School. When white parents and residents of the city heard that the governor was planning to integrate the school by admitting nine blacks into the high school, they began to protest. At one point, they threatened to storm the school to physically remove the black students. On September 25, 1957, fearing a riot, state and federal officials asked President Dwight D. Eisenhower to send federal troops to protect the nine students and to assure that the school pursued its integration policy. This was the first time since Reconstruction that the federal government had sent federal troops to protect blacks. The posting of federal troops in Little Rock by President Eisenhower sent a signal to white supremacists in the South that the federal government was serious about implementing school desegregation.

See also Brown v. Board of Education; Civil Rights Movement; Education and Racial Discrimination.

Francois Pierre-Louis

Los Angeles Riot of 1871

On October 24, 1871, in the Chinese section of Los Angeles, two Chinese men, reportedly arguing over a woman, became embroiled in a physical confrontation that became serious enough that a police officer and a white bystander, Robert Thompson, intervened in an attempt to end the fight. In the midst of the conflict, Thompson was accidentally shot and killed. It is unclear whether Thompson had a gun and whether he fired any shots. Word spread quickly about the death of Thompson, and a race riot ensued. Estimates put the number of rioters in the mob in the thousands. Many Chinese residents fled to an adobe building to escape the violence, but once there, they were trapped inside as the angry mob attempted to set the building on fire. Others in the mob, led by a man named Refugio Batello, climbed onto the roof of the building, bored holes in the roof, and opened fire on the unarmed people inside. Other Chinese residents were dragged outside, where some were lynched and others were dragged to death over the cobblestone streets. In all, nineteen Chinese members of the community were killed by the mob, eighteen of whom had no involvement in the conflict that led to Thompson's death. Only a few of those responsible for the murders during the riot served sentences—short ones—at San Quentin prison, and the leaders of the riot were never punished.

The Los Angeles riot of 1871, which some have renamed the Los Angeles *massacre* of 1871, was the beginning of the anti-Chinese movement that pushed for the passage of the Chinese Exclusion Act of 1882. Racial violence against Chinese immigration continued after the massacre of 1871, but the Los Angeles riot was by far the most violent and deadly attack on Chinese immigrants.

See also Bellingham Riots; Chinese Exclusion Act of 1882; Chinese Immigrants and Anti-Chinese Sentiments; Los Angeles Riots of 1992; Race Riots; St. Louis Riot of 1917.

Michael Roberts

Los Angeles Riots of 1992

The Los Angeles Riots, also referred to as a rebellion, uprising, insurrection, and civil disorder or unrest, erupted on April 29, 1992, upon the acquittal of four white police officers who were involved in the beating of Rodney King, an African American motorist. Previously, the twelve-member jury was unable to reach a conclusion regarding one charge against Officer Laurence Powell for using excessive force, and the judge declared a mistrial. Because the brutal beating of Rodney King was videotaped by a bystander and aired repeatedly on television, defense attorneys argued that the police officers could not get a fair trial in Los Angeles County, so the trial was moved to Simi Valley in Ventura County, widely known as a residential community for many Los Angeles police officers.

The reaction to the acquittal was an immediate and explosive unfolding of urban violence, burning, and looting over three days that spread throughout Los Angeles County and other cities and states as well. In the end, sixty people were killed more than two thousand were injured and sixteen thousand people arrested, and property damage was estimated at $785 million to $1 billion, including the destruction of about 2,300 Korean-owned businesses. The toll exceeds that of any major civil disorder of the 1960s, including the Watts riot of 1965. The social and political costs of the riots have been the subject of much public discourse, policy debate, and academic research.

At the time of the verdict announcement, a white truck driver, at the intersection of Florence and Normandie Streets in the historically African American neighborhood of South Central, was pulled out of his truck and beaten; ironically, this was also broadcast on television, to the horror of viewers. Mayor Tom Bradley imposed a city-wide curfew after sunset. Governor Pete Wilson dispatched four thousand National Guard troops to patrol the streets. Other images of the three days of urban mayhem were the participation of Latinos in looting, many for essential supplies necessary for daily life, such as diapers; armed Korean business owners protecting their stores because of the virtual absence of police in rioting neighborhoods; the National Guard stationed in affluent and predominately white neighborhoods, protecting downtown banks and office buildings. On the third day of the riots, Rodney King made a plea during a news conference: "Can't we all get along?"

While the catalysts that set off the Los Angeles rebellion were the prevalence of police brutality and the injustice of the verdict that affirmed for many the failure of the criminal justice system, the problems are more extensive than that and reveal a complex social and economic terrain in multiracial, multiethnic cities. Some scholars contend that this civil unrest was not a riot in the 1960s mode, but rather a rebellion, because the burning and looting was not random or limited to a single neighborhood but

Truck driver Reginald Denny being beaten by an African American youth on April 29, 1992, during the riots in Los Angeles.

Photo by Alan Levenson/Time Life Pictures/Getty Images.

"targeted, systematic, and widespread" (Johnson et al. 1992). As Johnson and his colleagues contend, "The response was not about the verdict in the police brutality trial per se; rather the civil unrest reflected the high degree of frustration and alienation that had built up among the citizens of South Central Los Angeles over the past 20 years," due to a fundamental restructuring of the local and national economy, as well as the demographic transformation of inner-city neighborhoods.

The deindustrialization of numerous industries in Los Angeles, including the automotive and aerospace industries, left many African Americans jobless. A shift to service-sector jobs that rely heavily on immigrant workers led to jobless poverty among blacks and working poverty among Latino immigrants. Disinvestment in South Central Los Angeles by banks and city government contributed to the neighborhood's decline. Conservative policies implemented during the Reagan administration promoted a laissez-faire business environment and the dismantling of a social safety net marked by dramatic reductions in the funding for community-based organizations.

During this period of economic restructuring, the mass influx of Asian and Latino immigrants transformed the urban landscape of Los Angeles. Many Latino immigrants settled in historically African American neighborhoods, which led to racial conflict and competition over jobs, housing, and scarce public resources. The "Latinization" of South Central Los Angeles is evident in the finding that 51 percent of those arrested during the most intense period of rioting were Latinos (Pastor 1993). The retirement of Jewish shopkeepers and the long-standing pattern of disinvestment in poor black neighborhoods created marginal opportunities for Korean immigrants to eke out a livelihood based on small retail businesses such as liquor stores, grocery stores, and swap meets (a cluster of small individual stalls set up to sell a variety of goods). Korean immigrant businesses serve a "middleman" function, as they supply goods manufactured by American corporations to underserved, impoverished minority communities.

The 1992 Los Angeles Rebellion demonstrates how race relations in the United States have moved decidedly beyond a black-and-white dynamic as "Latino immigrants, Korean merchants, African American residents and Whites participated as both victims and assailants" (Chang 1993, 1). Ignited by a sense of outrage that justice was not served in the trial of the four police officers who brutally beat an African American man, this rage was fueled by fundamental societal changes that heightened economic hardships and joblessness among blacks while creating marginal opportunities for immigrants.

See also Black-Korean Conflicts; Los Angeles Riot of 1871; Middleman Minorities; Race Riots; Rodney King Beating.

Further Reading

Chang, Edward T. "From Chicago to Los Angeles: Changing the Site of Race Relations." *Amerasia Journal* 19, no. 2 (1993): 1-3.

Johnson, James H. J., Cloyzelle K. Jones, Walter C. Farrell, Jr., and Melvin L. Oliver. "The Los Angeles Rebellion: A Retrospective View." *Economic Development Quarterly* 6, no. 4 (1992): 356-372.

Ong, Paul, Kye Young Park, and Yasmin Tong. "The Korean-Black Conflict and the State." In *The New Asian Immigration in Los Angeles and Global Restructuring*, edited by Paul Ong, Edna Bonacich, and Lucie Cheng. Philadelphia: Temple University Press, 1994.

Pastor, Manuel, Jr. *Latinos and the Los Angeles Uprising: The Economic Context.* Report for the Tomas Rivera Center, Claremont, CA, 1993.

Tarry Hum

Losing Ground: American Social Policy, 1950–1980

Published in 1984, *Losing Ground: American Social Policy, 1950-1980*, by Charles Murray, was a controversial book on U.S. government social programs. The rationality principle assumes that people almost always act rationally to incentives and disincentives. Using this rationality framework, Murray analyzed government welfare and other social policies and programs from the 1950s to the 1980s, focusing heavily on Great Society programs passed under the Johnson Administration in the 1960s. According to Murray, welfare payments worked as a disincentive in general; that is, the recipients were not motivated to work or study. Moreover, when welfare payments were provided with the tacit assumption of recipients' victimhood, governmental supports had negative consequences such as increasing criminal activities. To motivate people to work hard and to prepare themselves for a normal life, Murray proposed to eliminate the welfare and other safety-net programs. In the absence of any other external supports, he reasoned, people would be motivated to make their way in life on their own.

This book did not take into account the social/structural conditions that existed in the United States during the 1960s and 1970s. The emerging postindustrial U.S. economy during that time period had devastating effects on inner-city minority communities because blue-collar jobs suitable for inner-city residents disappeared. Murray ignored this macro context in his analysis, and without it, the simultaneous occurrence of the Great Society programs and deteriorating social problems does not necessarily imply any cause-and-effect relationship between the two.

Further Reading

Murray, Charles. *Losing Ground: American Social Policy, 1950-1980.* New York: Basic Books, 1984.

Shin Kim and Kwang Chung Kim

LULAC

See League of United Latin American Citizens (LULAC).

Lynching

Lynching may be considered the most brutal form of vigilantism. In a typical lynching, a mob of people physically harms or murders a target individual without due legal process. The lynching victims have typically been people of color—predominantly African Americans, particularly in the Deep South. Lynching has frequently been justified as a means of retaliating for an alleged offense, ranging from the violation of local customs to theft and murder. The question of whether such alleged offenses actually transpired in the first place were usually not an issue, suggesting that lynching was frequently committed for motives other than concern for justice. For example, it is widely acknowledged that the members of Ku Klux Klan have executed many African Americans for no reason except to assert their power and supremacy over people of color. Although lynching became less common as both legal protections (e.g., the 1934 Federal Anti-Lynching Law) and political awareness among many Americans increased, it reportedly continued well into the mid-nineteenth century. Lynching on a smaller scale still occurs to this day.

See also Ku Klux Klan (KKK).

Daisuke Akiba

M

Malcolm X (1925–1965)

Malcolm X was a Nation of Islam leader, public speaker, activist, political thinker, and public intellectual, especially in the 1960s. Malcolm X is possibly the most renowned Black Nationalist in U.S. history and, in some circles, his acclaim is comparable to that of Martin Luther King Jr. Born Malcolm Little in 1925 in Omaha, Nebraska, to Earl and Louise Little, his father was a Baptist preacher and active in Marcus Garvey's Universal Negro Improvement Association. As a child, Little experienced racism, including the burning of his family's home in Lansing, Michigan, by the Ku Klux Klan in 1929. After his father was killed under mysterious circumstances and his mother was subsequently placed in a mental institution, Little and his siblings were separated and placed in foster care. Little again experienced racism while living in a white-run detention center and, by eighth grade, had left school and moved to Boston to live with his half-sister, Ella. During this period, he began to challenge authority and reject mainstream dictates. He would later relocate to Harlem, in New York, where he earned money as a petty hustler, drug dealer, pimp, and gambler. In 1946, Little was arrested for burglary and spent ten years in prison. During his incarceration, he began to study the teachings of the Lost-Found Nation of Islam (NOI), a black Muslim group founded by Wallace Fard and led by Elijah Muhammad. Spurred by a new sense of religious fervor, he began to read the Koran, the Bible, literature, and history and also led a prison debating team.

Upon his release from prison in 1952, Little took a new name—Malcolm X, rejecting what he believed to be a white man's last name—and became spokesperson for NOI on both television and radio, and established NOI's first nationally distributed newspaper, *Muhammad Speaks*. Malcolm X was critical of Martin Luther King Jr. and other civil rights leaders for being assimilationists. He espoused a central tenet of the NOI: black empowerment through building black businesses.

Malcolm X waits at a Martin Luther King press conference, 1964.

Courtesy Library of Congress.

His commentaries, radical for the times, concerned many liberals who wished to approach civil rights issues and integration from a less confrontational approach, as well as conservatives who sought to maintain the status quo.

The separatist ideology espoused by Malcolm X stood in stark contrast to the integrationism of the day suggested by King. Malcolm X believed that black unity was central for social and political action, that whites' treatment of blacks was politically oppressive, economically exploitative, and socially degrading, and that the U.S. Constitution did not give blacks concrete citizenship rights. Rather than seeking to join forces with white America to address racism, Malcolm X believed that blacks themselves could champion the most effective efforts. He also suggested that, if the American government could not protect blacks against white violence and racism, blacks had the right to defend themselves. King's platform of nonviolent protest differed dramatically from Malcolm X's challenge for racial redress "by any means necessary." Although King's demands were palatable to some whites, Malcolm X engendered fear among whites and concern from black liberals who wished to distance themselves from his controversial philosophy. Although he initially focused his activist efforts in the United States, Malcolm X considered black Nationalism to be an African-oriented social movement. He identified with African states and argued that the liberation of Africa was central to liberation of all people of African descent.

Malcolm X married Betty Sanders (Shabazz) in 1958, formed the Muslim Mission in 1964, and made his first pilgrimage to Mecca. This experience altered his views about whites considerably, and Malcolm X acknowledged the true brotherhood of humanity that transcends race and ethnicity. As an activist, political thinker, and public intellectual, Malcolm X directly or indirectly influenced Congress of Racial Equality (CORE), the Student Nonviolent Coordinating Committee (SNCC), and the Black Power movement in general. His doctrine of black self-help was especially influential for inner-city black males who felt cast aside by the system and abandoned by the more conservative arm of the civil rights movement. In addition, Malcolm X's transition from uneducated street hustler to self-educated, internationally known political figure resonated with the myriad poor and near-poor blacks who sought redress from discrimination and inequality. Malcolm X was gunned down in 1965, three months before his fortieth birthday.

See also Black Nationalist Movement; Congress of Racial Equality (CORE); Farrakhan, Louis; King, Martin Luther, Jr.; Muhammad, Elijah; Nation of Islam; Student Nonviolent Coordinating Committee (SNCC).

Further Reading

Myers, Walter Dean. *Malcolm X: A Fire Burning Brightly*. New York: HarperCollins, 2000.

Perry, Bruce. *Malcolm: The Life of a Man Who Changed Black America*. Barrytown, NY: Station Hill Press, 1991.

Reliand, Rabaka. "Malcolm X and/as Critical Theory: Philosophy, Radical Politics, and the African American Search for Social Justice." *Journal of Black Studies* 33, no. 2 (2002): 145–165.

Sandra L. Barnes

MALDEF

See Mexican American Legal Defense and Education Fund (MALDEF).

Manifest Destiny

Manifest Destiny was an ideology prominent in the United States from the mid-nineteenth until the early twentieth century. It was fundamentally an expansionist ideology that attempted to justify American attempts to increase its territorial claims. Manifest Destiny was used to muster political and popular support for events ranging from the annexation of Texas, American entry into war with Mexico and Spain, and the acquisition of territories that make up present-day California, New Mexico, Puerto Rico, Guam, and the Philippines.

The term *manifest destiny* was first coined by John L. O'Sullivan, a journalist. Writing in the July-August 1845 edition of the *United States Magazine and Democratic Review*, O'Sullivan argued for the annexation of Texas. As justification, he asserted that it was America's right and duty to expand its borders westward to the Pacific, to spread its doctrine of liberty and freedom throughout the continent. Though the term was first penned by O'Sullivan, scholars suggest that the ideological origins of Manifest Destiny can also be traced to seventeenth-century Puritan notions of predestination and divine right. Of particular importance was the idea that Puritan settlers were graced by God with a divine mission to create a new "city upon a hill." This sense of a preordained design to settlement in an alien and hostile land was to permeate later American expansionist efforts.

Manifest Destiny rapidly became a driving ideological force in the latter half of the nineteenth century, adopted not only by expansionist politicians but also by a broad cross section of the American population, including settlers, slaveholders, and businessmen. Its power derived from its ability to serve a variety of economic and political agendas. Strategically, the doctrine of Manifest Destiny was seen as helpful in bolstering a fledgling country's position against possible encroachments by the British, which in the mid-nineteenth century still had a foothold on the West Coast and Mexico to the

Allegorical female figure of America leading pioneers and railroads westward.

Courtesy Library of Congress.

south, which was newly independent from Spain in 1821. Commercially, the ability to access valued ports on the Pacific to engage with the lucrative East Asian trade was seen as a highly desirable goal. Expansion was seen as politically expedient for Southern states who sought more leverage in Washington, DC, by working to increase the number of slave states added to the Union. Also, expansion provided a practical and profitable outlet for the burgeoning slave populations in the South. Technological change, such as the development of the telegraph in 1844 and the increasing use of steamboats, made communication and travel to remote places far more possible. Also significant was the view of expansion as a natural solution to excessive urbanization and the unhealthy concentration of political and economic power. Implicit in the concept of Manifest Destiny was this notion that, ultimately, expansion would increase opportunity and allow for the growth of personal freedom and prosperity.

However, Manifest Destiny was decidedly a racialized ideology as well. From its inception, the beneficiaries of expansionism were meant to be white settlers and landowners. Manifest Destiny can be read as an attempt to justify white settler acquisition of land from nonwhite peoples. Land was characterized as essentially "unoccupied" and "cheap," though Native Americans, Mexicans, and other indigenous peoples had to be forcibly removed to make room for American settlement. Manifest Destiny can be likened to the "civilizing mission," which was used to legitimize European colonialism in Africa and Asia.

Because America had the duty to spread the civilizing influence of freedom and democratic culture to "other" people, it could engage in territorial imperialism.

Manifest Destiny was tested almost immediately, with America's engagement in the Mexican-American War from 1846 to 1848. This war was the result of Mexican objection to the annexation of Texas and repeated border disputes along the U.S.-Mexican border. American victory in 1848 meant that California and New Mexico were ceded to the United States. Combined with the acquisition of the Oregon territory through the Oregon Boundary Treaty of 1846 with Great Britain and the Gadsden Purchase in 1854, the borders of what would later be the lower forty-eight states were set. America had attained its goals of expanding westward to the Pacific and south to the Rio Grande. Because of growing sectionalism that culminated in the Civil War, Manifest Destiny retreated to the back of the American political landscape. However, the turn of the century saw a renewed interest in American expansionism, this time beyond the contiguous borders of the United States. As a result of its defeat of Spain in the Spanish-American War (1898), the United States acquired Guam and Puerto Rico and purchased the Philippines for $20 million. In line with American desires to extend its reach into the Pacific, Hawaii was placed under American control in 1898. Hawaii eventually became America's fiftieth state in 1959.

See also Guadalupe Hidalgo, Treaty of; Hawaii, Annexation of; Mexican-American War; Philippine-American War; Spanish-American War; Texas, Annexation of; Texas Rebellion.

Further Reading

Anders, Stephen. *Manifest Destiny: American Expansionism and the Empire of Right*. New York: Hill and Wang, 1996.

Graebner, Norman, ed. *Manifest Destiny*. Indianapolis: Bobbs Merrill, 1968.

Merk, Frederick. *Manifest Destiny and Mission in American History: A Reinterpretation*. New York: Vintage Books, 1966.

Rebekah Lee

March on Washington

Black union and civil rights leader A. Philip Randolph, who had led the March on Washington in 1941, organized the August 28, 1963, March on Washington. It was organized to bring attention to the lack of job opportunities and freedom for African Americans. All major black organizations at that time, such as the Southern Christian Leadership Conference (SCLC), the National Association for the Advancement of Colored People (NAACP), the Congress of Racial Equality (CORE), and the Student Nonviolent Coordinating Committee (SNCC), along with their leaders, participated. Approximately 200,000 participants were whites. While they were marching peacefully, they sang the unofficial anthem of the civil rights movement, "We Shall Overcome." The march is famous especially for Martin Luther King's "I Have a Dream" speech. The

The March on Washington, August 1963.

Courtesy Library of Congress.

next year, the U.S. Congress passed the United States' most comprehensive civil rights legislation, abolishing all forms of legal discrimination against minorities.

See also Civil Rights Movement; "I Have a Dream" Speech; King, Martin Luther, Jr.; March on Washington Movement.

Further Reading

King, Martin Luther, Jr. *I Have a Dream: Writings and Speeches That Changed the World*. New York: HarperCollins, 1992.

Pyong Gap Min

March on Washington Movement

An early civil rights initiative, the March on Washington movement was planned for 1941 to encourage then president Franklin D. Roosevelt to guarantee employment for African Americans in wartime industry. It was organized by A. Philip Randolph, the president of the Brotherhood of Sleeping Car Porters, one of the earliest organized labor groups representing African American workers. The demands and the threat of the march were effective enough that the march itself was called off at the last minute. However, the same organizer was involved in the 1963 March on Washington at which Martin Luther King Jr. spoke. Estimates of attendance of that event, which included members of most civil rights groups (e.g., the Congress of Racial Equality and the Southern Christian Leadership Conference), range from 200,000 to 500,000. The tactic of the March on Washington has since been emulated by many other social movement groups, particularly those fighting for civil rights on the basis of race, gender, and sexual orientation.

See also Congress of Racial Equality (CORE); King, Martin Luther, Jr.; March on Washington; Randolph, A. Philip; Southern Christian Leadership Conference (SCLC).

Mikaila Mariel Lemonik Arthur

Marriage

See Intermarriage.

McCarran-Walter Act of 1952

Retaining a large part of the 1924 Immigration Act, the McCarran-Walter Act regulated the quota system for immigration based on national origin. Under this law, 70 percent of all immigrant slots were allotted to natives of the United Kingdom, Ireland, and Germany, most of which remained unfilled, while only a few quotas were granted to Asian nationalities. Moreover, the Act replaced the 1917 Asiatic Barred Zone with a territorial concept called the Asia-Pacific Triangle. Although this particular statute somewhat liberalized the entry of Asian immigrants, it still included highly racialized provisions against Asians in comparison to northern and western Europeans. It limited the number of immigrants who were indigenous to the Asian-Pacific Triangle to no more than two thousand annually and the number of those who were natives or descendants of each Asian country within the Triangle to a mere one hundred. The McCarran-Walter Act is considered a significant step toward ending the long-standing racial discrimination in the U.S. immigration policy, but it continued to endorse racist practices in immigration law.

Reflecting the shift toward ending racial discrimination, the McCarran-Walter Act repealed all previous exclusion laws against naturalization of Asians. It made Japanese and Korean immigrants eligible for citizenship, whereas special measures taken in the 1940s made Chinese, Filipino, and Indian immigrants eligible for citizenship. The act also provided for family reunification and occupational-skills preferences within the national quotas for immigration. The Immigration and Nationality Act of 1965 finally dismantled the national-origins quota system, but these provisions of the McCarran-Walter Act remained an integral part of the liberalized immigration law of 1965.

See also Asian Americans, Discrimination against; Asiatic Barred Zone; National Origins Act of 1924.

Etsuko Maruoka-Ng

Melting Pot

For many generations the melting pot has served as one of the primary metaphors for describing U.S. racial/ethnic relations, both real and ideal. A melting pot, or crucible, mixes various substances, and if successful, produces a completely new and improved compound. As early as 1845, Ralph Waldo Emerson applied the melting-pot metaphor to American society in an essay promoting the virtues of bringing the world's people together in the United States, "so in this continent—asylum of all nations—the energy of Irish, Germans, Swedes, Poles, and Cossacks, and all the European tribes—of the Africans and of the Polynesians—will construct a new race, a new religion, a new state, a new literature, which will be as vigorous as the new Europe which came out of the smelting-pot of the Dark Ages." By the time Israel Zangwill's play, *The Melting Pot*, opened in Washington, DC, in 1908, the nation was in the midst of the largest wave of immigration in American history, which brought twenty million mostly southern and eastern Europeans to the country between 1880 and 1920. The title of Zangwill's play resonated with the promise that all immigrants, regardless of national origin, culture, or language could be transformed into Americans. In the American crucible, Zangwill's hero and heroine, a Russian Jew and a Cossack, overcome the prejudices and hostilities of the ethnically divided Old World and find love and marriage in a new land. "God is making the American," writes Zangwill, capturing the sense of both destiny and new beginnings in America.

In contrast to the Anglo-conformity model that assumed the unified United States should be an ethnically homogenous society sharing a single culture—English language, English law, English customs and English world view—the American melting pot was imagined to combine its contents into a new and improved American society, bringing out the virtues and strengths of the disparate racial/ethnic groups and eliminating less desirable qualities in the process. In a challenge to white-racist ideologies, the melting pot suggests that mixing racial/ethnic groups would retain the ancestors' positive characteristics and build a stronger, richer, and higher civilization. The fusion of groups would become so complete that the amalgam would become greater than the original components.

Has the melting pot ever been reality in U.S. racial/ethnic relations? While extensive intermarriage and interaction have occurred among immigrants from Europe and their children, American racial attitudes divided the country so that blacks were essentially excluded from the melting pot. Civil rights leader Bayard Rustin argued that for American blacks, "There never was a melting pot, there is not now a melting pot, there never will be a melting pot. . . ." Studies in the mid-twentieth century revealed sharp divisions even among whites, as marriage patterns suggested a triple melting pot along religious lines between white Protestants, Catholics, and Jews. Glazer and Moynihan's *Beyond the Melting Pot* (1963) argued that white Americans were not homogenizing but, on the contrary, still shared strong ethnic ties related to national origin. More recent studies have explored the possible formation of new melting pots among Latinos, Asians, Native Americans, and black immigrants from the Caribbean and Africa as strategic political identities emerge to unite immigrants from distinct nations in response to structural conditions in the United States. For instance, immigrants from South and Central America, Mexico, and the Spanish-speaking Caribbean have established social solidarity through association with and by organizing around a "Latino" or "Hispanic" group identity.

Passage of the Immigrant and Nationality Act of 1965 dramatically transformed the composition of immigrant flows to the United States. Elimination of national-origin-based preferences has led to a marked increase in immigration from Asia, Latin America, and the Caribbean Islands and a decline of European immigration. As a result, the ethnic composition of the United States has rapidly diversified. Today, nearly one million immigrants, legal and illegal, enter the country every year, and only ten percent of them are from Europe. Hispanics are America's largest and fastest-growing ethnic minority group, surpassing African Americans in the 2000 U.S. census. The civil rights movement launched a celebration of ethnic identity that continues to expand, even among whites. Improvements in global communication and transportation facilitate continuous flows of people, money, and ideas between home and host countries. Transnational migratory activities provide alternatives to previous patterns of assimilation. In this rapidly changing context, rising multiculturalism encourages the practice of many different ethnic traditions and the parallel socialization of individuals into the dominant national culture and a particular ethnic culture. As the United States enters the twenty-first century, the melting-pot metaphor is being replaced as the core myth and value for racial/ethnic relations in this "country of immigrants" by the salad, the mosaic, and the kaleidoscope metaphors, in which individuals maintain their unique ethnic identity yet contribute to the construction of a national identity as well.

See also Anglo Conformity; Chinese Exclusion Act of 1882; Colonized versus Immigrant Minorities; Gentlemen's Agreement of 1980; Immigration Act of 1965; Immigration Restriction League of 1894; National Origins Act of 1924; Naturalization Act of 1790; Undocumented Immigrants.

Further Reading

Glazer, N., and D. P. Moynihan. *Beyond The Melting Pot: The Negroes, Puerto Rican, Jews, Italians, and Irish of New York City*. Cambridge, MA: MIT Press, 1970.

Gordon, Milton. *Assimilation in American Life: The Role of Race, Religion, and National Origin*. New York: Oxford University Press, 1964.

Jacoby, Tamar. *Reinventing the Melting Pot*. New York: Basic Books, 2004.

Jaret, Charles. *Contemporary Racial and Ethnic Relations*. New York: HarperCollins, 1995. See esp. pp. 400–416.

Kenneth J. Guest

Memphis Race Riot of 1866

The Memphis Race Riot of 1866 occurred from May 1 to May 3 in Memphis, Tennessee, when Irish American policemen and firemen and other white laborers rioted in the southern part of the city, attacking African American Union troops and African American residents. By May 4, when federal military officials declared martial law in the city, two whites and at least forty-six African Americans had been killed. As many as eighty others had been wounded, at least five African American women raped, and hundreds of African American homes, schools, and churches broken into or destroyed by arson.

There are differing accounts of what incident sparked the riot. During the

Civil War, the African American population in Memphis had quadrupled. Tensions between the white residents, which included a largely Irish American police force, and the African American residents, especially members of the Third United States Colored Infantry, were running high. Black Union troops were acting as provost guards in Memphis and other Southern cities, which infuriated many white Southerners.

Beginning in the evening of May 1, 1866, law-enforcement officials and citizens attacked the black residents of the area, with particular hatred aimed at the black Union troops and those affiliated with them. As the riot continued, all African Americans became targets for the white mob. Some were assaulted or killed for wearing blue, which was the color of the Union troops. Four of the five African American women who were raped by white men during the riot were married or somehow related to black Union soldiers, or had pictures of black Union troops displayed in their homes.

See also Race Riots; Reconstruction Era.

Tracy Chu

Meriam Report

In 1926, the Secretary of the Interior, Hubert Work, commissioned a team of ten social scientists, led by Lewis M. Meriam, to study the conditions of Indian reservations. Meriam was the principal investigator at the Institute for Government Research at Johns Hopkins University. The survey team conducted fieldwork by visiting ninety-five different jurisdictions, including reservations, agencies, hospitals, schools, and many communities to which Indians had migrated. Officially entitled *The Problem of Indian Administration*, the Meriam Report was published in 1928.

The voluminous 872-page report contained a general policy evaluation and recommendations on various aspects of the Indian community, such as health, education, economic conditions, and the legal aspects of the Indian problem. Even though results varied from reservation to reservation, the major findings were that an overwhelming majority of the Indians were not adjusted to the economic and social system of the dominant white society. For example, the study found that Indians had a higher infant mortality rate than any other minority group. Diseases such as measles, pneumonia, tuberculosis, and trachoma (an infectious eye disease) were rampant on the reservations, and material conditions related to diet, housing, health care, and the like were deplorable. These appalling conditions were closely associated with widespread food shortages, poor health, inadequate housing, and a lack of education.

According to the report, the Indians' poverty was caused mainly by the fact that the economic basis of their culture had been largely destroyed by the encroachment of white civilization. The report also pointed out that the U.S. government's effort to assimilate the Native Americans had been a total failure. The report singled out the U.S. government's allotment policy as the greatest contributor to Indian peoples' impoverishment. The allotment policy forced Indians to give up their traditional ways of life and adopt Western ways of living by making them farm the plot of land that was allotted to them.

In the conclusion, the report called for a complete reexamination of the Bureau of Indian Affairs and of national Native American policy, and suggested what remained to be done in terms of improving the socioeconomic condition of Native American communities. The report recommended that the allotment program be stopped and that more funds be available for health and educational programs for Native Americans. It also recommended that the Bureau of Indian Affairs, which was created in 1824, should oversee the operation of the reservations and that the Bureau hire Native Americans as employees.

Thus, the Meriam Report led government leaders to substantially reconstruct the nation's policy toward Native Americans. The Indian Reorganization Act (IRA), passed in 1934 during the Roosevelt administration, was the government's direct response to the call to reform its policy toward Native Americans. Under the impact of the IRA, Native Americans finally gained an opportunity to rebuild their cultural heritage and self-reliance.

See also Indian Allotment Act of 1887; Indian Citizenship Act of 1924; Indian Reorganization Act of 1934 (IRA); Indian Reservations.

Further Reading

Brookings Institution (Institute for Government Research). *The Problem of Indian Administration*. Baltimore: Johns Hopkins University Press, 1928.

Johansen, Bruce Elliott. *The Encyclopedia of Native American Legal Tradition*. Westport, CT: Greenwood Press, 1998.

Sookhee Oh

Mestizo

Mestizo is a term most frequently used in Latin America to designate a person of mixed European ancestry, especially Spanish and indigenous. In the complex hierarchy of color mixture in Latin America, mestizos held greater power and higher social status than Indians or black slaves, but were lower socially than white Spaniards and *criollos* (the Spaniards' descendents born in the colonies). In the eighteenth and nineteenth centuries, mestizos were often defined more by their social status and spatial location than by their racial and ethnic mixture and physical appearance. In Mexico, for example, rural mestizos were called peasants and studied by social scientists with the analytical categories of social class, while more economically and spatially marginal mestizos were called Indians and studied by social scientists with the analytical categories of ethnicity. In Andean countries the differences between mestizos and Indians often hinged on rural or urban location, command of the Spanish language, or dress. Throughout Latin America *mestizaje* denotes the generalized process of white/Indian mixture initiated by the Spanish conquest and colonialism, and in Mexico of the early twentieth century, *mestizaje* came to be seen as the quintessential process of the country's national identity.

See also Mulatto.

Carmenza Gallo

Mexican American Legal Defense and Education Fund (MALDEF)

The Mexican American Legal Defense and Education Fund (MALDEF) was founded in 1968 in San Antonio, Texas, to protect the civil rights of Latinos and promote their empowerment and full participation in society. As a leading national non-profit organization, MALDEF conducts litigation, advocacy, and educational outreach work through multiple regional sites located across the United States, including Atlanta, Los Angeles, Sacramento, San Antonio, Chicago, Phoenix, Albuquerque, Houston, and Washington, DC. MALDEF works to advance public policies, laws, and programs that protect Latino civil rights in employment, education, immigration, political access, and the equitable distribution of public resources.

Modeled after the National Association for the Advancement of Colored People's (NAACP) Legal Defense Fund and started with an initial $2 million Ford Foundation grant, MALDEF's extensive works in civil rights litigation have set precedents in electoral processes (to ensure that Latinos have a fair opportunity to elect representatives of their choice and/or run for elective office), in educational and employment practices, and immigrant rights, including language rights. A recent landmark MALDEF victory was the final settlement of the *Gregorio T. v. Wilson* (1995) case, which essentially struck down California's Proposition 187, the intent of which was to deny public services, including education, health care, and social services, to the state's undocumented population. MALDEF's work in such key areas as census enumeration and political redistricting, equity in public-resource allocation, and community education seeks to fully engage Latinos in advocating for policy changes that protect and advance civil rights and social justice.

See also California Ballot Proposition 187; National Association for the Advancement of Colored People (NAACP).

Tarry Hum

Mexican-American War

In May 1846, the United States invaded the Mexican territories of California, New Mexico, and central Mexico. Mexico surrendered and signed the Treaty of Guadalupe Hidalgo on February 2, 1848, under which the United States took California, New Mexico, Nevada, Utah, Colorado and most of Arizona, in addition to Texas, which had already been annexed before the war. The war completed the westward movement of the Anglo-Saxons in the New World and appeared to bring to fruition the white men's vision of a transcontinental republic spanning from the Pacific to the Atlantic. Mexicans who had lived in those conquered territories entered the U.S. society as a conquered people. The first generation of Mexican Americans found themselves subjugated, discriminated against, and oppressed under the racist domination of the Anglo society, even though they were offered U.S. citizenship. The war is also called the Mexican War, the U.S.-Mexican War, and the U.S. Invasion of Mexico, revealing controversy over the historical understanding of the war. Most contemporary historians agree that the war can be best understood in the context of the U.S. expansionism of the 1840s.

U.S. Expansionism

Territorial expansion had been a contested political agenda in American history before the United States invaded Mexico. The Whig party vehemently warned against the undermining of the Jeffersonian democracy that expansion would inevitably entail. Abolitionists opposed it because the southwestward expansion would add more slave states. Even within the largely expansionist Democratic Party, some argued for a gradual process, while others insisted on a bold move.

In the late 1830s, there was a sudden surge of the expansionist passion. Technological, demographic, economic, and political factors converged to fuel the desire. Even if some may have dreamed of a transcontinental republic since the beginning of the United States, the expansionist vision did not become a viable goal until the 1840s, when innovations in transportation and communications technology conquered enormous physical distances that hitherto looked insurmountable. Steamships connected commercial centers through waterways. Railroad systems integrated eastern markets with cities and towns on the western slope of the Appalachians. In 1844, the telegraph opened up a new world of modern long-distance communication. Urbanization and the ever-increasing immigrants from Germany and Ireland also pressed the need for territorial expansion, although there still remained vast unoccupied lands. Leaders of the Southern slave states were particularly anxious to add new slave states because they would strengthen their political power and also serve as an outlet for the growing slave population. The U.S. control of the Pacific coast would provide American corporations with a greater competitive edge over the formidable rival Great Britain for the Asian trade. The economic crisis of 1837 made U.S. farmers desperate for new foreign markets. Policymakers coveted San Francisco and other coastal ports for their strategic and commercial advantages. All of these aspirations and calculations, combined with the fear of "being hemmed in" by Great Britain, inflamed the expansionist frenzy. In the early 1840s, countless books about California were published, all marveling at its richness, mild climate, and ports.

The U.S. expansionism of the 1840s was marked by an extreme version of Anglo-Saxon racism. In the early 1830s, the use of the phrase *Anglo-Saxon* in a racial sense was rather rare in political discourse. By the mid-1840s, the idea of the Anglo-Saxon race as the noblest stock chosen to dominate the New World had emerged. God had reserved America for a special people of Saxon blood. By the time of the Mexican-American War, the Mexicans who stood in the way of southwestward expansion, were depicted as a mongrel race, adulterated by extensive intermarriage with an inferior Indian race. They were idle, thriftless, and, thus, it was believed, unable to govern such a beautiful land as California. "In the hand of an enterprising people," lamented California missionary and author Richard Dana, "what a country this might be!" Like Indians and Negroes, the Mexicans must have faded away or been subordinated with the destined progress of the Anglo-Saxon race. To John L. O'Sullivan, editor of the *United States Magazine and Democratic Review*, any interference with the U.S. expansion amounted to a futile attempt to reverse a natural process. In the summer of 1845 he boldly criticized other nations that stood in the way of the United States "for the avowed object of thwarting our policy and hampering our power, limiting our greatness and checking the fulfillment of our manifest destiny to overspread the continent allotted by Providence for the free development of our yearly multiplying millions." He also suggested that the United States should claim its right to Oregon, based on the notion of Manifest Destiny. Since Representative Robert C. Winthrop of Massachusetts used the phrase in Congress in 1845, Manifest Destiny became the focal point of political debate on territorial expansion.

Northern Frontiers of Mexico

Following its conquest in 1521 by Conquistador Hernán Cortés, Mexico remained a colony of the Spanish Empire for three hundred years. But the offspring of Spaniards in New Spain aspired to independence, spurred on by the independence of the United States in 1776 and the French Revolution in 1789. On September 16, 1810, Miguel Hidalgo Costilla, a priest from the village of Dolores, Guanajuato, incited a rebellion against Spanish rule, and his compatriots, after eleven years of fighting, gained independence at last in 1821.

The northern regions of Mexico posed a particularly vexing problem to the Mexican government. They were not only far from the center of power, they also bordered with the expansionist America. Also they were sparsely populated, mostly by Native Americans and a smaller number of Mexicans. In an effort to stem the westward movement of Anglo Americans, in 1820 the Spanish crown took a desperate measure and granted foreigners—mostly Anglo Americans—the right to settle in Texas. Moses Austin received the first colonization contract, and in 1821 his son Stephen began to settle in eastern Texas. In subsequent years other families followed. By 1830, about twenty thousand Anglos were living in Texas, constituting a numeric majority. Already in the late 1820s the Anglo settlers became troublesome elements to the Mexican government. Despite their promise to abide by Mexico's laws, they engaged in illegal homesteading, land speculation, smuggling, and support of slavery. They preferred the U.S. federalism and regarded the Mexican government as despotic and the Mexican culture as retarding economic development. They became increasingly rebellious.

During the 1820s, many Anglos also poured into California and New Mexico. It was against the law, but the Mexicans accepted them warmly. The earlier immigrants tried hard to assimilate themselves to the Mexican culture, learning Spanish, converting to Catholicism, and marrying native women. Intermarriage brought them citizenship and legal access to real estate and to political position. Both the Mexican elite and the lower class saw intermarriage with Anglo entrepreneurs as an opportunity to upgrade their social status by "whitening" their families and to improve economically. The later Anglo intruders, however, had no respect for Mexicans, whom they thought descended from a mongrel race and were prone to indolence, immorality, cowardice, filthiness, debauchery, cruelty, and frivolity.

The 1824 Mexican constitution, the first democratic constitution, granted autonomy to states and provinces. But the federalist principle did not apply to the northern frontier regions. New Mexico and California were under direct control of the national congress. Texas was incorporated into the state of

Coahuila. The coup of 1835 by Antonio López de Santa Anna ended federalism throughout Mexico, restricting provincial autonomy. The central government began sending military rulers to the northern regions, which triggered the Texas Rebellion. On March 2, 1836, the Texans declared their independence from the Republic of Mexico and gained it on April 21, 1836, by defeating Santa Anna's troops at San Jacinto, although Mexico did not recognize it yet. In the same year, groups of Californians declared their independence, although by 1837 they had compromised with the Mexican government. New Mexico saw a rebellion among the lower classes in 1837, but it was suppressed by the ruling class.

Toward Armed Conflict

Democrat James K. Polk was elected U.S. president on an expansionist platform in 1844 when the sense of urgency for the U.S. expansion prevailed. Polk quickly moved to invite Texas to be the twenty-eighth state of the United States. The Polk administration held Mexicans in contempt and assumed that firmness would force them to yield to American wishes—the annexation of Texas and the purchase of California—without resorting to physical force. The U.S. minister in Mexico, Wilson Shannon, said in October 1844, "I see it predicted in some of the papers in the U.S. that Mexico will declare war against the U.S.; there is as much probability that the Emperor of China will do so." To Mexico, however, the annexation of Texas was inadmissible because it violated the sovereignty of Mexico over its territory and would create a dangerous precedent threatening Mexico's territorial integrity. Yet Mexico did not want a war with the United States. The Jóse Joaquin de Herrera administration attempted in vain a double-edged diplomacy to avoid both the Texas annexation and a war with the United States. Mexico would even have recognized the independence of Texas if the Texans refused annexation. On July 4, 1845, however, Texas agreed to the annexation. Since its separation from Mexico, Texas had claimed the Rio Grande as the border instead of the traditionally recognized Nueces River, about 150 miles to the north of the Rio Grande.

The Herrera administration had no choice but to deploy federal troops to protect the disputed area between the Nueces River and the Rio Grande. President Polk promised the Texans that if they accepted annexation he would uphold their claim to the Rio Grande. Yet the Mexican government still wanted a negotiation with the United States. Any attempt at a diplomatic solution failed partly because of the lack of internal consensus in Mexican society. But it also failed because the United States sent John Slidell as the U.S. plenipotentiary secretary to demand what Mexico could hardly accept: recognizing the annexation of Texas and ceding the territories of New Mexico and California. Upon the abortion of the Slidell mission, President Polk ordered General Zachary Taylor to move his troops to the Rio Grande. It was obviously provocation of an armed confrontation. To the Mexican government, the deployment of the U.S. troops in the disputed area was an outright attack on Mexico's territorial integrity and a clear demonstration of the U.S. intention not to respect the 1828 border treaty. Mexico's new centralist president, Mariano Paredes, declared a war on April 4, 1846. Battles broke out. The report of a Mexican attack helped persuade Congress to vote for war with an overwhelming majority, 174 to 14 in the House of Representatives and 40 to 2 in the Senate. A handful of antislavery congressmen opposed the war on the grounds that the Mexican war would add to the number of slave states. Joshua Giddings of Ohio called the war measure "an aggressive, unholy, and unjust war." Pacifist Henry David Thoreau refused to pay tax, denouncing the Mexican war, and was put in jail. Based on this experience, he gave a lecture entitled "Resistance to Civil Government" two years later and published it in the famous essay, "Civil Disobedience."

The United States declared war against Mexico on May 11, 1846. In the declaration, President Polk stated: "Mexico had crossed over the U.S. border, had invaded our territory and had caused the shedding of U.S. blood in U.S. territory." This declaration suggested that the purpose of the war was the defense of U.S. territory, which the United States had unilaterally defined. Contradicting the spirit of the declaration, Polk ordered the occupation of the territory south of the Rio Grande, the territories of New Mexico and California. General Stephen Watts Kearny entered Santa Fe on August 18, 1946, meeting no resistance. He headed for California and finally established a provisional government in 1847 after a series of military victories gained with the help of other leaders. Meanwhile, General Winfield Scott entered Mexico City on September 12, 1847. Internal division disabled Mexico to launch a unified and effective military operation. Seven different Mexican presidents led the country during the two years of war.

The war ended with the signing of the Treaty of Guadalupe Hidalgo in February 1848. Mexico ceded California and New Mexico and recognized the U.S. sovereignty over Texas north of the Rio Grande. From 1845 to 1848, the United States added 1.2 million square miles to its territory, a gain of more than sixty percent. In return, the United States paid $15 million to Mexico.

Foreigners in Their Native Land

There were about 75,000 Mexicans living in the conquered territories at the time of the war's conclusion. They were given the choice of either moving to Mexico or staying in the United States. If they decided to stay, they could choose either Mexican or U.S. citizenship. If they did not declare their choice in a year, they would become U.S. citizens automatically. But soon they found themselves foreigners in their native land. The war may have expanded freedom and democracy to some, but it also expanded subordination and racial domination.

The war had been justified by the racist idea of Manifest Destiny: that the Anglo-Saxon race was destined to dominate the whole United States. Now the victorious war proved that was indeed the case. The heightened sense of racial superiority on the part of Anglo Americans reinforced Mexican Americans' ethnic awareness as La Laza. After 1848, the word *barrio* (meaning neighborhood in Spanish) came to denote a discernable section of a town populated by Mexican Americans.

Some Mexican Americans with property and business acumen, of course, found an economic niche in the new situation. But most farmers were dispossessed of their ancestral lands. Once owners failed to pay taxes or debts, county courts under the control of Anglo-Americans sold lands at public auction. Some Anglos used friendships with influential political figures to usurp the land titles from natives. Mexican American farmers, who were not familiar with the U.S. system, were easily victimized by Anglo-Americans' administrative and legal manipulation. Massive land loss made it harder for the lower classes to find jobs as common workers on ranches and farms. Displaced from agriculture and craft occupations, most Mexican Americans found themselves at the bottom of the occupational ladder in the new society. They sought a livelihood as day laborers, cooks, and servants. Racial oppression and discrimination often led to revolt and resistance in the conquered zones.

Many more Mexicans have immigrated to Texas, California, New Mexico, and other parts of the former Mexican territory since the United States took control of those areas in 1848. Thus, only a tiny proportion of Mexican Americans are the descendants of the indigenous Mexican population conquered by Anglo-Americans. However, the legacy of the Anglo conquest of Mexico is the blatant anti-Mexican prejudice that has continuously affected Mexican Americans. Mexican Americans currently living in barrios face many of the problems of poverty and disadvantage that residents of inner-city black neighborhoods do.

See also Barrios; Creation Generation; Guadalupe Hidalgo, Treaty of; Manifest Destiny; Mexican Americans, Prejudice and Discrimination against; Mexican Americans, Violence against; Texas, Annexation of; Texas Rebellion.

Further Reading

Castillo, Richard Griswold del, and Arnold De León. *North to Aztlán: A History of Mexican Americans in the United States*. New York: Twayne Publishers, 1996.

Fraizier, Donald S., ed. *The United States and Mexico at War: Nineteenth Century Expansionism and Conflict*. New York: Macmillan Reference USA, 1998.

Horsman, Reginald. *Race and Manifest Destiny: The Origins of American Racial Anglo-Saxonism*. Cambridge, MA: Harvard University Press, 1981.

Zinn, Howard. *A People's History of the United States: 1492–Present*. New York: HarperCollins, 2001.

http://www.pbs.org/kera/usmexicanwar.

Dong-Ho Cho

Mexican Americans, Prejudice and Discrimination against

Discrimination and prejudice against Mexican Americans and Mexican immigrants by Anglo-Americans are enmeshed in the history of contact between the two groups. Mexico lost most of the Southwest to the United States as a result of the Mexican-American War (1846–1848). The war ended with the Treaty of Guadalupe Hidalgo, by which Mexicans could choose to be either Mexicans or American citizens, and their property was to be protected. After the war, however, the contact between the two groups entailed, for the most part, competition for land, which by the end of the nineteenth century came to be largely in the hands of Americans. For example, between 1840 and 1859, all land that was owned by Mexicans in the county of Nueces, Texas, except for one ranch, was transferred to Americans. In New Mexico, only 30 percent of original owners held their land by 1910 (Moore and Pachon 1985, cited in Hraba 1994). Thus, a large number of Mexican inhabitants became landless workers, forced to work for the new landowners and, with virtually no competition from other ethnic groups, remained concentrated in agricultural jobs until about the 1930s. Further throughout the Southwest, Mexican Americans were employed in gangs, on crews (in farm factories, large fruit and vegetable agribusiness, railroads, copper mines), and by families (in the sugar beet industry), and thus they remained relatively isolated from other workers, and from potential assimilationist forces in the region (McWilliams 1968, 215 cited in Hraba 1994). This pattern of employment—concentrations of large numbers of Mexican Americans in low-paid occupations—generated what some scholars call an occupationally stratified ethnic group that laid the grounds for the development of discriminatory ideologies against them.

To the early American settlers in Mexican lands, Mexicans were lazy, bigoted, superstitious, and backward. For a long time such stereotypes continued to influence the views that Americans have of Mexicans. Mexicans were included among the undesirable groups denoted by the Dillingham Commission in the early 1900s, along with southern and eastern Europeans. But despite this, Mexicans were desirable as a source of cheap labor and were exempted from the restrictive immigration laws that were drafted largely on the basis of the commission's report (Marger 1991, 307). Mexican immigrants then came to the United States, sometimes crossing the border without legal documents, and sometimes as temporal workers (as in the Bracero Program that ran from World War II until the early 1960s), to fill demand for jobs in agribusiness. Serving as labor buffers, Mexican immigrants are laid off during economic downturns and rehired when the economy improves. But in periods of severe recession, Mexicans workers have been subjected to massive deportation. Indeed, during the Great Depression, the U.S. government launched a Repatriation Program in which thousands of Mexicans, both legal and illegal, were indiscriminately deported. And in the depression of the mid-1950s the Immigration and Naturalization office set up Operation Wetback to find and return undocumented Mexicans. It is estimated that about 3.8 million Mexicans were then expelled (Parrillo 1994, 416–417).

Once Mexican Americans migrated to the cities, a process that started in the 1940s, they were concentrated in marginal neighborhoods with substandard schools and high levels of unemployment. In the city of Los Angeles during the 1940s, newspapers adopted and propagated negative stereotypes that associated Mexican Americans with urban criminality and gangs, creating a climate of general hostility and even hysteria against Mexican Americans and against youth in particular. Vigilante attacks against Mexicans in the Zoot Suit Riots of 1943 were condoned in the local press and generated a weak police response (Escobar 1999, 243–246).

Although a considerable number of Mexicans work as operators, laborers, and farm hands, many second- and third-generation Mexican Americans have achieved middle-class status during recent years. The political mobilization during the 1960s, together with urbanization, widened access to economic opportunities that improved the economic and political standing of Mexican

Americans. Negative stereotypes and discrimination have not disappeared. Until the 1960s, for example, movies and advertisements routinely portrayed Mexicans as villains, always cruel and always on the "losing side." When allied with Americans, they were always subservient. More recently, common stereotypes involve being "illegal," and for youth, being involved in gangs. And relations with police continue to be contentious. But overall, negative stereotypes are slowly changing as Mexicans, and in general Latinos, have gained some economic and political power. Significantly, the political mobilization of Mexican Americans, together with that of other minority groups since the 1960s, has generated a greater degree of awareness about the ways in which the larger society constructs negative stereotypes and the impact that these stereotypes have on shaping the contact between Mexican and white Americans. As a consequence, Mexican Americans have become more proactive in constructing their own identity and in consciously influencing the shorthand markers that white Americans adopt to designate them.

See also Bracero Program; English-Only Movement; Hispanics, Prejudice and Discrimination against; Mexican Americans, Violence against; Mexican Illegals, Labor Exploitation of.

Further Reading

Escobar, Edward J. *Race, Police, and the Making of a Political Identity: Mexican Americans and the Los Angeles Police Department 1900–1945*. Berkeley: University of California Press, 1999.

Hraba, Joseph. *American Ethnicity*. Itasca, IL: F. E. Peacock Publishers, 1994.

Marger, Martin. *Race and Ethnic Relations: American and Global Perspective*. Belmont, CA: Wadsworth, 1991.

Parrillo, Vincent N. *Strangers to These Shores: Race and Ethnic Relations in the United States*. Boston: Allyn & Bacon, 1994.

Carmenza Gallo

Mexican Americans, Violence against

Violence against Mexican Americans has been associated with at least three sets of interacting factors: the defeat in the Mexican American War (1846–1848) followed by territorial occupation; the presence of prejudice and discrimination; and the severe control and economic subordination accompanied by relative geographic isolation of many Mexicans working in the agricultural sector. Although this short list is certainly not exhaustive, throughout the twentieth century, violence against Mexican Americans and Mexican immigrants has been associated with a mixture of these three sets of factors and their legacies.

First, the annexation by the United States of large areas in the South and Southwest designated large numbers of Mexicans culturally and politically as a conquered or defeated group, against which economic dispossession, cultural discrimination, and sometimes violence were easy to justify. Indeed, even though the Treaty of Guadalupe Hidalgo in 1848 guaranteed basic rights to

Mexicans residing in the annexed territory, scholars agree that throughout the nineteenth century at least, these rights were not enforced. Systematic land dispossession, particularly of small landowners, followed the annexation, forcing previous owners to become laborers for the new landlords. Ultimately, the annexation converted the bulk of Mexican Americans in this tract of land into a poor, economically exploitable, and politically subordinated group. The struggle for the control of land was, for the most part, carried out by economic, legal, and political means, but violence against Mexicans was not altogether rare. For example, courthouses across the region were burned to destroy Mexicans' land-rights and property documentation, and periodic open warfare erupted between cattlemen (Anglos) and sheep men (Mexicans). On other occasions, violence was mutual, as in the Lincoln County Wars of New Mexico and the Cortina Wars in Texas (Hraba 1994, 255).

Second, discrimination and prejudice against Mexican Americans accompanied urban riots in which Mexican Americans were physically attacked. The most famous riot was the Zoot Suit, or the Pachuco, riot of 1943. Zoot was a showy sartorial style of Mexican youth during the early 1940s, and Pachuco was the name adopted by some youth groups in Mexican neighborhoods. The precipitating events of the riot included the assault of several sailors stationed in Los Angeles by assailants that the servicemen identified as Mexicans. After the assault, a group of off-duty members of the Los Angeles police went to a Mexican neighborhood to punish the Zoot suiters, and a few days later a group of sailors in taxicabs cruised Mexican neighborhoods randomly beating Mexicans, searching for zoot suiters in movie theaters and restaurants. Los Angeles police failed to arrive at the scene on time to stop the attacks, few arrests were made, and no one was prosecuted. On the days that followed, the rampage by servicemen continued while major newspapers, some local government officials, and members of the Los Angeles police openly approved of and even encouraged the attacks (Escobar 1999). Prejudice and discrimination also contributed to the lynching of Mexican miners during the Gold Rush and to the Los Angeles riot in 1970.

Third, the types of occupations of many Mexican Americans, as well as illegal residents, create opportunities for severe exploitation and violence. Large numbers of Mexican Americans and, more particularly, Mexican immigrants, many without a legal status, in the United States work in the agricultural sector. In 1990, for example, 7.2 percent of Mexican Americans or Mexican immigrants had agricultural jobs, compared to 2.5 of all the population (Hraba 1994, 272). At the same time that the illegal status of some Mexican immigrants makes them vulnerable to deportation, fear of deportation tends to make them more controllable and exploitable. Agricultural jobs are traditionally the least legally protected, the lowest paid, and not infrequently, geographically isolated from urban centers. These conditions generate opportunities to control labor and to use violent means to an extent not present in urban and manufacturing jobs. Thus, episodes of unscrupulous employers and labor-recruiting entrepreneurs imprisoning workers, impeding their physical mobility, and using physical force to keep them attached to their jobs, though not frequent, have been recurrent throughout the history of Mexican Americans' relationship with the American majority.

See also Guadalupe Hidalgo, Treaty of; Hispanics, Prejudice and Discrimination against; Mexican-American War; Mexican Americans, Prejudice and Discrimination against; Zoot Suit Riots.

Further Reading

Escobar, Edward J. *Race, Police, and the Making of a Political Identity: Mexican Americans and the Los Angeles Police Department 1900–1945*. Berkeley: University of California Press, 1999.

Hero, Rodney E. *Latinos and the U.S. Political System: Two-Tiered Pluralism*. Philadelphia: Temple University Press, 1992.

Hraba, Joseph. *American Ethnicity*. Itasca, IL: F. E. Peacock Publishers, 1994.

Carmenza Gallo

Mexican Illegals, Labor Exploitation of

Since much of the Southwest of Mexico, including Arizona, Texas, New Mexico, and California, was annexed to the United States, the issue of Mexican immigration, and in particular, illegal or undocumented migration, has been a key aspect in border relations and in securing a cheap agricultural labor force. Illegal, or undocumented, Mexican immigrants have arrived in the United States in one of two ways. They have entered the country without inspection (illegal border or port-of-entry crossing by land, sea, or air, referred to as EWIs) or they have entered legally on a temporary basis through one of several types of visas and then have failed to leave within the allotted time period. Current estimates place the size of the undocumented immigrant population at 9.3 million, representing 26 percent of the total foreign-born population (Passel, Capps, and Fix 2004). It is estimated that approximately 5.7 million, or 57 percent, of the undocumented population is Mexican. The undocumented population is concentrated in several key states. Nearly two-thirds reside in just six states: California, Texas, Florida, New York, Illinois, and New Jersey.

The United States and Mexico share the longest border in the world. At 3,250 kilometers or 1,950 miles, the border serves as a boundary for four U.S. and six Mexican states. Entering the United States entails tremendous risk and hardship, as Mexicans will cross rivers, walk in desert conditions, travel in the trunks of cars or the backs of trucks, and sometimes run into traffic at official checkpoints in their efforts to cross the U.S.-Mexican border. A recent study conducted by Mexico's National Population Council has found that the number of Mexican illegals now exceeds one million on an annual basis. Moreover, approximately one-third, or 390,000 annually, of those who enter the United States illegally remain in the United States. The risks of crossing the border are significant, and hundreds die each year due to heat exhaustion, dehydration, drowning, or suffocation. These efforts to enter the United States illegally are coordinated and facilitated by human smugglers known as coyotes or *polleros*, who charge $2,000 to $6,000 for their assistance. Strategies to stem the flow of undocumented immigrants have included the construction of walls, enhanced Border Patrol, and the use of hi-tech equipment, including sensors and new unmanned aircrafts called drones that can identify "a potentially hostile target the size of a milk carton at an altitude of 60,000 feet."

The relationship between the United States and Mexico is defined by a high level of economic interdependence, and one aspect of this interdependence is the U.S. reliance on Mexican labor. The Bracero Program in place from 1942 to 1964, recruited about five million Mexican farm laborers to work in the developing agricultural industries of the Southwest. Implemented during a period of World War II labor shortages, this program was described as a form of "legalized slavery" by a U.S. Department of Labor official. The dependence of the United States on Mexican labor has not abated but has, in fact, expanded to include many other industries. The undocumented Mexican population is growing in the Northeast metropolitan region, including New York City, where they provide an indispensable labor force in construction, landscaping, personal services, restaurants, and downgraded manufacturing.

Many undocumented Mexican men are *jornaleros* (day laborers) and stand on street corners where they compete in an open market for daily employment. A particularly egregious incident in November 2000 underscores the dangers that day laborers face. In a suburban town on Long Island, New York, two undocumented Mexican immigrants accepted an offer to dig holes for fence posts. They were taken to an abandoned factory where their two "employers" attacked them with a shovel, a crowbar, and a knife. More frequent workplace abuses are hazardous job conditions such as the lack of proper equipment, training, or safety measures, which result in numerous fatal worksite accidents. Increasingly, ethnic organizations—for example, Asociacion Tepeyac de New York—have formed to advocate for undocumented Mexicans in cities with growing numbers of that population. Recognizing the growing share of the urban labor force that is undocumented, organized labor such as Janitors for Justice and the garment workers union, UNITE, have begun to mobilize undocumented Mexican workers.

Undocumented immigrants are often targeted as unfair competitors who drain taxpayer resources. Proposition 187, passed by 59 percent of California's voters, was a draconian statute that would have prevented state and local governments from providing nonemergency health care, social services, and public education to undocumented immigrants. Moreover, Proposition 187 would have required California law-enforcement, health, and social service agencies, as well as public-school officials, to report persons suspected of being undocumented. It was described on the official ballot as "the first giant stride in ultimately ending the illegal alien invasion." Attacked as unconstitutional in several lawsuits that were combined into two major suits, Proposition 187 was never implemented.

The debate on the costs and contributions of undocumented Mexican immigrants is ongoing. Central to this debate is the integral role of Mexican workers as a cheap labor source in the U.S. economy, the importance of remittances to the Mexican economy, the social and economic costs of immigrant marginalization, and the perceived and real effects of competition and downgraded labor standards. In January 2004, the Bush administration proposed granting temporary legal status to millions of illegal immigrants. Employed individuals who lack legal authorization would receive a renewable three-year work visa as long as they have a job. However, they would be required eventually to return to their home countries. To date, specific legislation has yet to be proposed by the Bush administration.

See also Bracero Program; Labor Movement, Racism in; Mexican Americans, Prejudice and Discrimination against; Mexican Americans, Violence against; Mexican Repatriations; Undocumented Immigrants; U.S. Border Patrol.

Further Reading

Camarota, Steven A. *Immigration from Mexico: Assessing the Impact on the United States*. Washington, DC: Center for Immigration Studies, 2001.

Johnson, Kevin R. "Proposition 187: The Nativist Campaign, the Impact on the Latino Community, and the Future." JSIR Research Report #15, The Julian Samora Research Institute, 1996.

Passel, Jeffrey S., Randolph Capps, and Michael E. Fix. *Undocumented Immigrants: Facts and Figures*. Washington, DC: The Urban Institute, 2004.

Tarry Hum

Mexican Repatriations

When there have been shortages of cheap labor in the United States, immigrants and foreign-born workers have been welcomed, but a poor economy and high rates of unemployment have narrowed the opening of the the door for immigration. This pattern has applied to all immigrants and especially to Mexicans. In one dramatic case, Mexicans not only were restricted from coming to the United States, Mexicans who were already in the United States were sent back to Mexico, and during the 1930s recession, a significant number of American-born Mexicans, American citizens, were repatriated. Because of the lack of economic opportunities during this period, some Mexican nationals went back to Mexico voluntarily. But those who remained were sent back to Mexico involuntarily. The U.S. government found that it might be less costly to the government to pay the transportation and other costs of sending them to Mexico than to maintain them on welfare rolls. Between 1931 and 1932, more than 200,000 Mexicans were deported to Mexico.

The repatriation program created a number of problems among Mexican Americans and Mexican descendants in the United States. It created panic within the Mexican American community. Mexican Americans who were naturalized citizens were frequently sent back to Mexico with other Mexican aliens. Many Mexican Americans were scrutinized and had to live in a state of anxiety due to the possibility of being "caught" and "repatriated." In some cases, Mexican American families were broken apart because some of their family members were sent back to Mexico while American-born spouses or children remained behind.

See also Mexican Americans, Prejudice and Discrimination against; Nativism and the Anti-immigrant Movements.

Heon Cheol Lee

Middle Easterners, Historical Precedents of Backlash against

The stereotype of Middle Easterners as terrorists, Muslim fundamentalists, and zealot nationalists has become so widespread in the United States that any time an act of terrorism is perpetrated against Americans around the world, Middle Eastern Americans suffer backlash. The 1993 bombing of the World Trade Center in New York City, which killed six people and injured thousands of others, and the subsequent conviction of four Muslims of Arab descent for masterminding the explosion, once again ingrained the terrorist stereotype in the average American's psyche. Thus, when the federal building in Oklahoma City was bombed on April 19, 1995, killing 168 innocent people, many Americans were quick to blame Middle Eastern Americans. These sentiments are perhaps best portrayed by the May 1, 1995, *Newsweek* headline, "Jumping to Conclusions: Many in the Press and Public were Quick to Assume the Crime had Mideast Origins. But 'John Doe' is One of Us."

The watershed in U.S.-Middle East relations was the 1967 Arab-Israeli war. In the decades that followed, events in the Middle East often reverberated as hate crimes, prejudice, and discrimination against people of Middle Eastern origin in the United States. Except for after major incidents, there is no sufficient evidence to indicate that every crisis resulted in a perceptible backlash against Middle Eastern Americans. Nonetheless, the cumulative effect of a continuing series of terrorist events manifested itself in a hostile attitude and the consolidation of stereotypes toward this group. The long list includes the 1973 Arab oil embargo, the 1979–1981 Iran Hostage Crisis, the 1982 explosion at Ankara Airport by the Armenian Secret Army for the Liberation of Armenia, the 1983 suicide bombing of the U.S. Marine barracks in Beirut, the 1985 hijacking of TWA flight 847 to Beirut, Libya's admission of the 1988 Pan Am bombing over Lockerbie, Scotland, and the 1990–1991 Gulf War.

For many Americans, the 1973 Arab oil embargo clinched the negative association between their pocketbooks and the Middle East, adding fuel to their already negative image of Middle Easterners. In response to the Arab defeat at the hands of Israel in the infamous Yom Kippur War, the Organization of the Petroleum Exporting Countries (OPEC), led by Saudi Arabia, announced that the Arab countries were cutting production and placing an embargo on shipments of crude oil to Western countries, including a complete boycott of Israel. As a result, oil prices skyrocketed to four times their previous levels. Arab princes (sheiks) were perceived as enriching themselves at the expense of common people in the West. By early 1974, most of the world was hit by the worst economic slump since the Great Depression. The oil crisis was soon followed by the Iranian Revolution, with its vehemently anti-American slogans, and in 1979 culminated in the taking of fifty-two Americans hostage for 444 days.

The political and social turmoil in the Middle East and the liberalizing of immigration laws have resulted in increased immigration to the United States since the 1970s. However, the situation in their homelands has adversely affected the reception Middle Eastern immigrants have received in the United States. Ironically, many of these immigrants are exiles or refugees. Even former college students from Arab countries and Iran who decided to settle in the United States permanently have on occasion felt unwelcome in the United States despite their tremendous educational and occupational achievements. When news of 9/11 broke out, the first thought that crossed the minds of many Americans was that Middle Easterners were somehow involved. This time, it was true. But rather than let negative perceptions persist, Middle Eastern Americans have instead begun to fight the stereotypes. Independent of their ancestral origins, they are forging a new image of their experience in the United States.

See also Government Initiatives after the September 11, 2001, Attack on the United States; "Green Menace"; Gulf War; Iran Hostage Crisis and Anti-Iranian Stereotypes; *Jihad*; Middle Easterners, Stereotypes of; Muslims, Prejudice and Discrimination against; Muslims, Terrorist Image of; September 11, 2001, Terrorism, Discriminatory Reactions to.

Mehdi Bozorgmehr and Anny Bakalian

Middle Easterners, Stereotypes of

Widespread stereotypes have been behind the discrimination and prejudice that Middle Eastern immigrants have experienced at various periods during their century-long history in the United States. The sources of these stereotypes, however, have changed over time. In the early period, Orientalist interpretations of Islam and the Arab world were dominant. In his seminal work, *Orientalism*, scholar Edward Said articulated how Occident (West) perceives the Orient (East) as beguiling, seductive, infantile, and inferior—a perspective that involves both a romanticization of the Orient and Islam and a fear of it. To the Orientalists, who run the gamut from writers to artists to political administrators, the Orient conjures up images of exotic lands, corrupt sultans, belly dancers, and the "infidels." Contemporary political crises in the Middle East have ushered in new stereotypes that include the religious zealot, the Islamic fundamentalist, the hostage taker, and the terrorist. The historical and current stereotypes of Middle Easterners stand apart from labels used to pigeonhole other ethnic groups in America. Ironically, the role of Arab and Muslim immigrants in perpetuating these stereotypes has been negligible.

In the beginning of the twentieth century, when large-scale immigration from the Middle East started, Middle Easterners' appearance (olive skin, dark eyes, black hair, and especially, their traditional outfits) set them apart. Children were harassed in schools by teachers for having unpronounceable names and by peers with such epithets as "camel jockey," "black," and most often "Turk." The Turk label was particularly infuriating to immigrants because they were fleeing the corrupt and decaying regime of the Ottoman Turks.

Stereotypes of Middle Easterners were also reflected in official governmental documents. In 1910, the U.S. Census Bureau classified Middle Easterners as "Asiatics" (i.e., nonwhite), making them ineligible for citizenship. Several cases came before the courts across the United States to argue that Syrio-Lebanese, Armenians, and other immigrants from the Middle East were Caucasians, or whites. The most notorious of these were probably the cases of *Re: Halladjian* (1909) in front of the U.S. Circuit Court of Massachusetts, which received expert testimony from renowned anthropologist Franz Boaz, and that of George Dow of Charleston, South Carolina, in 1915 (*Dow v. United States*). People of Middle Eastern ancestry are now officially classified as white, but ironically this has created a different type of misunderstanding and misrepresentation. Currently, persons of Middle Eastern origin are denied their identity by being omitted from official classifications in school, hospitals, job and loan applications, political caucuses, polls, market surveys, to name a few. This misclassification has also made them ineligible for receiving the benefits of affirmative action, although they have faced levels of prejudice and discrimination that could be considered high by any measure.

The popular media—Hollywood movies, inflammatory news shows, infomercials, and the tabloid press—has been especially prone to perpetuating stereotypes of Middle Easterners. Scholars have indicated that anti–Middle Eastern racism is more pervasive and institutionalized in the United States than in any other part of the world. These stereotypes are not only tolerated but also condoned and manipulated by the government and politicians in support of U.S. policy in the Middle East. Breakouts of violence (hijackings, bombings, etc.) in the Middle East often result in anti–Middle Eastern prejudice and discrimination in the United States because of the way the press covers the incidents. Since September 11, 2001, Middle Eastern (Arab, Muslim, etc.) community organizations have started to monitor and challenge these pejorative stereotypes in the media. These new stereotypes are particularly offensive to Middle Eastern immigrants because many are political refugees, asylees, and exiles who oppose the regimes in the countries they left behind. Additionally, the stereotypes often are not based in fact, because not all Middle Easterners are Muslim, nor are all Muslims Arabs.

See also Government Initiatives after the September 11, 2001, Attack on the United States; "Green Menace"; Gulf War; Iran Hostage Crisis and Anti-Iranian Stereotypes; *Jihad*; Middle Easterners, Historical Precedents of Backlash against Muslims, Prejudice and Discrimination against; Muslims, Terrorist Image of; September 11, 2001, Terrorism, Discriminatory Reactions to.

Further Reading

Abraham, Nabeel. "Anti-Arab Racism and Violence in the United States." In *The Development of Arab-American Identity*, edited by Ernest McCarus, 155–214. Ann Arbor: University of Michigan Press, 1994.

Said, Edward. *Orientalism.* New York: Random House, 1979.

Shaheen, Jack G. *Reel Bad Arabs: How Hollywood Vilifies a People.* New York: Olive Branch Press, 2001.

Mehdi Bozorgmehr and Anny Bakalian

Middleman Minorities

The term *middleman* refers to the stratum a group occupies between the elite and the masses in traditional societies. Middlemen minorities may also play a role between producers and consumers in modern economies when there is a status gap, or noticeable division. Ironically, the middleman status is itself a by-product of being discriminated economically in the first place. Unable to get decent jobs in the mainstream economy, some ethnic/religious groups specialize in specific occupational niches, such as trade, commerce, crafts, or the independent professions. Geographic mobility is an important characteristic of these occupations because middlemen minorities' structural position makes them vulnerable to economic and political crises in the host society. Jews, Armenians, and the Chinese are classic examples of middleman minorities, often spread out around the globe as a diaspora.

Middleman minorities are particularly prevalent in agricultural societies as intermediaries between the aristocracy and the peasantry. They sometimes continue to exist in postcolonial societies after the elites have been removed. (Some examples are the Chinese in southeast Asia, Asian Indians in Africa, and Parsees in India. In advanced industrial societies, they are called immigrant or ethnic entrepreneurs.) Under favorable historical circumstances, middleman minorities acquire special resources such as entrepreneurial values, beliefs, institutions, and social networks that enhance their financial success. These resources are often passed on to their descendants, who in turn continue the "family" tradition. In essence, their biggest asset is their cultural heritage of entrepreneurship. Bolstered by their international ties, middlemen minorities tend to thrive in business even after they migrate repeatedly.

Historically, middlemen minorities managed to form semiautonomous communities in host societies. They maintained their ancestral language and culture while adapting fairly successfully to their host society. A separate and distinctive group identity and a sojourner ideology made them turn inward for trust, mutual help, friendships and marriage partners. They developed an elaborate infrastructure for serving their community needs, whether for schools, press, houses of worship, or social and recreational associations. These activities made them highly visible and were the cause of accusations of being clannish and foreign.

The very factors that bestow economic success on middleman minorities (e.g., cohesion, outsider status, and business visibility) can provoke host hostility during turbulent periods. Middleman minorities are often hated by the majority population and envied by other minority groups in the host society. Because middleman minorities are numerically small, their livelihood depends on elite protection. When the elite is removed, as in times of political crisis, middleman minorities are likely to suffer reprisals by the masses, who begrudge them their economic success. The elite may also use them as a peon for their own gains, accusing them of disloyalty and of pilfering the country's resources. Hostile reactions to middleman minorities can run the gamut from boycotts to riots to expulsions and may even culminate in genocide. Extreme examples include the estimated 1.5 million Armenians who perished at the hands of the Ottoman and Young Turk regimes between 1915 and 1923 in Asia Minor; the Holocaust that killed more than six million Jews during Nazi Germany; and the expulsions of Indians from Uganda by Idi Amin in 1974. It is important to point out that the structural position of middleman minorities, and not their cultural traits, as it is popularly believed, accounts for their vulnerability.

Sociologists have argued that minorities frequently perform a middleman role because their "stranger" (outsider) status enables them to be objective and impersonal in business dealings. These very same advantages can, however, be a source of friction between the middleman minorities and the customers they serve, often resulting in all-out conflict and violence. But host hostility can actually reinforce the middleman minorities' ethnicity and group solidarity, locking them into their precarious position. Thus, what may have begun as a voluntary segregation can become a forced one. Relinquishing plans of eventual return to an ancestral homeland, as well as economic and social integration over several generations, remove the boundaries that make this group distinct. Inevitably, both cultural and structural forces contribute to the development, continuity, and eventual demise or assimilation of middleman minorities.

See also Black-Korean Conflicts; Jewish-Black Conflicts; Los Angeles Riots of 1992.

Further Reading

Blalock, Hubert. *Toward a Theory of Minority-Group Relations.* New York: John Wiley, 1967.

Bonacich, Edna. "A Theory of Middleman Minorities." *American Sociological Review* 38 (1973): 583–594.

Zenner, Walter. *Minorities in the Middle: A Cross-Cultural Analysis.* Albany: State University of New York Press, 1991.

Mehdi Bozorgmehr and Anny Bakalian

"Migrant Superordination and Indigenous Subordination"

Do race relations and intergroup inequality take on a substantially different pattern in societies where a migrating group arrives and then dominates an indigenous group than in societies where a migrating group arrives and then becomes a subordinate minority dominated by an indigenous group? Sociologist Stanley Lieberson contended that the outcome of intergroup contact would indeed vary, depending on whether a society's indigenous racial/ethnic group was able to remain dominant and in control over immigrants or, on the other hand, was subordinated by the newcomer racial/ethnic group. Lieberson presented this argument in a 1961 article, "A Societal Theory of Race and Ethnic Relations." His use of international comparative analysis and his greater emphasis on political and economic institutions than on prejudiced attitudes helped open new perspectives for social scientists interested in race and ethnicity.

Analysis of migration and colonization patterns occurring on several continents led Lieberson to the following three conclusions. First, when a newly arriving group conquers or subordinates the native group (a situation Lieberson calls "migrant superordination and indigenous subordination"), levels of initial violence or warfare and lingering conflict, hostility, and political dispute are much more severe than is the case in the opposite situation (where a migrant group voluntarily arrives and is incorporated as a subordinate or minority group). Specifically, the dominant colonizing migrants often kill large numbers of the indigenous group, bring about cultural upheaval, destroy traditional economic arrangements and sustenance systems, and fracture the political identities, boundaries, and institutions of the indigenous group.

Second, after "subduing" the native population, the dominant migrants often consider much of the remaining indigenous population untrustworthy for or incapable of anything but the most menial labor, or they regard the indigenous group as too decimated, dispirited, or disinclined to serve as a viable labor force, so the dominant migrant group begins importing additional new workers (often of a different racial/ethnic group) whom they expect to be more docile, reliable, efficient, or cheaper than the indigenous group. As white colonial employers introduced these additional groups (e.g., African slaves in the United States; Indian workers in South Africa and Fiji; Chinese and Filipino laborers in Hawaii), they produced highly stratified multiracial societies, well-developed racial/ethnic niches in the economy, and dominant ideologies that viewed nonwhites as inferior and incapable of assimilation.

Third, in societies where an indigenous population is initially subjugated by an in-migrating dominant group, Lieberson observed that little assimilation occurs and, instead, racial nationalism and warfare often develops years later in the cycle of group intergroup relations. As examples, he noted the late 1950s and early 1960s African and Asian anticolonial movements and their rhetoric of racial identity and pride. In contrast, Lieberson observed that more assimilation (in most dimensions) and less conflict are likely to occur in societies where voluntary migrants arrive and occupy subordinate, rather than dominant, positions.

In his article explicating this societal theory of race and ethnic relations, Lieberson also tried to explain the reasons for the patterns he observed, and he called for other researchers to do comparative cross-societal studies to test his theory's merits and limitations. However, no formal program designed to test his theory ensued, though his observations and the questions he raised about racial/ethnic dominance and subordination were widely discussed. Some of Lieberson's ideas about the results of migrant superordination and indigenous subordination resemble observations made later by social scientists who drew sharp contrasts between "colonized" and "immigrant" minorities and developed or made use of "internal colonialism" theories (e.g., Robert Blauner, John Ogbu). So it is possible that his "societal theory" did help stimulate further theorizing on racial/ethnic inequality and racism.

See also Colonized vs. Immigrant Minorities.

Further Reading

Blauner, Robert. *Racial Oppression in America*. New York: Harper & Row, 1972.

Lieberson, Stanley. "A Societal Theory of Race and Ethnic Relations." *American Sociological Review* 26 (1961): 902–910.

Staples, Robert. *The Urban Plantation: Racism and Colonialism in the Post Civil Rights Era*. Oakland, CA: The Black Scholar Press, 1987.

Charles Jaret

Militia Movement

See White-Supremacist Movement in the United States.

Million Man March on Washington

On October 16, 1995, more than a million black men from across the United States participated in a march on Washington in support of blacks and their families. The march, sponsored by Minister Louis Farrakhan of the Nation of Islam, was seen as controversial by some feminists and liberals because the Nation of Islam had asked black women to stay home and pray with their children on that day. Minister Farrakhan did not invite black women to the march because the main objective of the day was to ask black men to atone for their treatment of black women and their lack of support of the black family. Furthermore, since Farrakhan is a controversial public figure because of his radical position on political and racial issues, many people thought that the march was going to be another opportunity for him to criticize other groups in the country. However, to the surprise of the media and his critics, more than a million black men attended the march, and it attracted several prominent speakers, including Maya Angelou, Benjamin Davis (the head of the National Association for the Advancement of Colored People [NAACP] at that time), and civil rights icon Rosa Parks.

The million-man march on Washington made Farrakhan a major national fig-

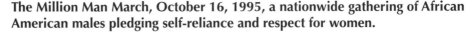

The Million Man March, October 16, 1995, a nationwide gathering of African American males pledging self-reliance and respect for women.

Photo by Cynthia Johnson/Time Life Pictures/Getty Images.

ure in the African-American community and the United States. The march was important because it proved the mobilizing power of the black community in the United States. This was the first time that more than a million African Americans congregated in Washington, the center of political power in the United States, to protest the conditions of African Americans in society. This march took place at a time when Congress was creating policy to dismantle the welfare state.

See also Farrakhan, Louis; March on Washington; March on Washington Movement; Nation of Islam; National Association for the Advancement of Colored People (NAACP); Parks, Rosa.

Francois Pierre-Louis

Minority Actors

See Hollywood and Minority Actors.

Minstrelsy

Minstrelsy was an early example of the entertainment industry perpetuating racial stereotypes and prejudice against African Americans. Minstrelsy was a popular form of entertainment in the nineteenth century. It refers to stage

William H. West's Big Minstrel Jubilee, 1899.

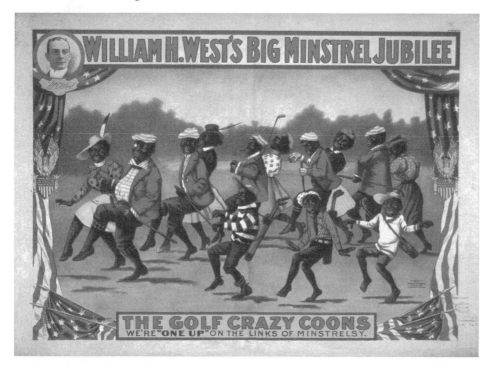

Courtesy Library of Congress.

performances in which white performers wore "blackface" make-up and performed grotesque caricatures of African Americans, who were often depicted as shifty, lazy, and comical figures. Minstrel shows incorporated aspects of dance, music, comedy, and outlandish wardrobe. Thomas Dartmouth Rice, considered the father of American minstrelsy, gave the first solo performance in blackface in 1828, introducing a popular song-and-dance routine in which he impersonated an old, crippled black slave named Jim Crow.

After the Civil War, African American entertainers began to form their own minstrel theatres, though they still wore blackface and acted out the caricatures and stereotypes created by the white performers. One of the first successful African American minstrel groups was Brooker and Clayton's Georgia Minstrels, whose advertising slogan was "The Only Simon Pure Negro Troupe in the World." In 1876, the African American group known as Callendar's Minstrels became the first black minstrel band to perform without blackface.

By the turn of the century, minstrelsy began to decline in popularity and soon gave way to more popular forms of entertainment such as vaudeville, motion pictures, and radio. However, the influence of minstrelsy could later be seen in stereotypical, or stock, African American characters, such as the large waddling mammy, the wide-eyed cowardly servant, or the shifty-eyed black hooligan, in film, radio, and television. Moreover, tap dance was developed in minstrel shows as a caricature of what was considered an African American man's clumsy shuffle.

See also Civil War and the Abolition of Slavery; Films and Racial Stereotypes; Jim Crow Laws; Reconstruction Era; Television and Racial Stereotypes.

Tracy Chu

Mismatch Hypothesis

Since the 1970s, the "mismatch" hypothesis has probably been the most prominent explanation social scientists have provided and debated on the subject of urban African Americans' employment and economic opportunities. Economist John Kain initiated this hypothesis with a 1968 article in the *Quarterly Journal of Economics*. He showed that many blacks in Chicago and Detroit were unemployed because racial residential segregation and discrimination prevented them from moving into parts of the metropolitan area where jobs were plentiful (e.g., more prosperous suburbs) and had to live in areas where job opportunities were declining, so they could not get to a job in a reasonably convenient way. In essence, the mismatch hypothesis is that there is a major disjunction or lack of a match between where people in need of jobs live and the locations of the jobs for which they are qualified. In other words, unemployment rates of blacks or other racial minorities might be high mainly because the jobs they could hold are not in close proximity; instead, they are in places that are inaccessible to them. This job inaccessibility is usually attributed to housing discrimination, lack of ownership of automobiles, lack of public transit that could move people from home to distant work locations quickly and at low cost, and lack of information on job openings in distant locales. Sociologist John Kasarda is a strong proponent of a mismatch explanation for black unemployment and slow economic progress. He argues that reductions in employment discrimination that may have occurred due to civil rights laws have been overshadowed by urban economic restructuring, in which business owners (1) eliminated manufacturing jobs that were accessible to black city neighborhoods and that paid good wages to relatively low-educated workers and (2) expanded job opportunities in light manufacturing, warehousing, retail, and personal services in suburban areas that were less accessible to blacks.

See also Deindustrialization and Racial Inequality.

Further Reading

Kain, John F. "Housing Segregation, Negro Employment, and Metropolitan Decentralization." *Quarterly Journal of Economics* 82, no. 2 (1968): 175–197.

Charles Jaret

Missouri Compromise

In 1820, when Missouri was ready to enter the Union, the important issue surrounding its admission was whether it was going to be a free state or a slave state. Representatives from the Northern states wanted it to enter as a free state to maintain the balance of power between North and South in Congress, while representatives from Southern slave states insisted on Missouri's admission as a slave state. As a compromise, Congress declared that Missouri should be admitted as a slave state but that slavery should be forever prohibited in all territory of the Louisiana Purchase north of the new state's southern boundary.

The Missouri Compromise was nullified in 1854 when the Kansas-Nebraska Act was passed. The new act allowed for the possibility of slavery in territories that the Missouri Compromise had closed to slavery. Passage of the Missouri Compromise contained the explosive issue of slavery expansion for almost thirty years; repeal of the Missouri Compromise intensified the growing debate on the issue that divided and embittered the North and the South in the decade before the Civil War.

See also Civil War and the Abolition of Slavery; Dred Scott Decision; Emancipation Proclamation; Guadalupe Hidalgo, Treaty of; Lincoln, Abraham, and the Emancipation of Slaves; Mexican-American War; Slavery in the Antebellum South.

Pyong Gap Min

Model Minority Thesis

In the United States, *model minority* usually refers to Asian Americans and is often understood or interpreted as referring to a socioeconomically successful minority, since *model* and success are often used as synonyms in this context (Kim and Hurh 1983).

The model-minority thesis was invented by Caucasian scholars and reporters in the mid-1960s, at the height of the civil rights movement, urban riots, and social unrest, to exemplify the socioeconomic success of Asian Americans, and their educational achievements, occupational mobility, rising income, and low rates of mental illness and crime. The term *model minority* was first coined to portray Japanese Americans and Chinese Americans, and starting in the 1980s, it was extended to Asian Americans as a whole.

Beginning in the late 1970s, scholars started to criticize the model-minority thesis. One of the major criticisms is that the model minority is a "myth" rather than a reality (e.g., Suzuki 1977; Takaki 1989). In other words, it has no factual basis. Another major criticism is that the model-minority concept is anti-Asian, or detrimental to Asian Americans. Despite these criticisms, the model-minority thesis has persisted until today.

Is the model minority a myth or reality? Empirical evidence suggests that the model minority image is not totally a myth, nor is it completely a reality. In other words, the model-minority image is not without any factual basis, but it inflates the success story of Asian Americans. Statistics show that Asian Americans generally fare better than blacks, Hispanics, and Native Americans in terms of all major socioeconomic indicators and even better than whites in education, occupational status, and family income. However, they lag behind whites in per capita earnings and wealth. They have not "outwhited whites."

Is the model-minority image beneficial or detrimental to Asian Americans? A thorough and impartial assessment of the model-minority thesis is in order. This seemingly positive image definitely has many negative effects on Asian Americans. First, the model-minority image conceals the diversity among Asian American groups and excludes the truly needy Asians, especially recent Asian immigrants and refugees, from receiving governmental assistance. Second, it downplays racial discrimination against Asian Americans. The message of the model-minority thesis is that Asian Americans have made it and have overcome discrimination through hard work. Hence, discrimination against Asian Americans is not insurmountable. Third, it may contribute to blaming other, less successful minority groups for their problems. The message of the model-minority thesis is that hard work and strong cultural values enable Asian Americans to succeed. Other minorities do not fare well because their cultures have problems or they do not try hard enough. If Asian Americans can make it without the government's assistance, why cannot blacks, Latinos, and Indians make it too? By emphasizing the importance of culture, the model-minority thesis contributes to the tendency to blame the victim for victimization. Fourth, it divides minority groups and pits one group against another. The concept implies that some minorities are model, or good, while other minorities are non model, or bad. In part, it serves an ideological purpose and is a way to control minorities. Fifth, the exaggeration of the success story of Asian Americans could partly spur anti-Asian resentment, especially on college campuses. Sixth, it serves to exclude Asian Americans from some social programs designed to help minorities, such as affirmative action, in some institutions. Finally, it puts undue pressures on Asian American students to do well in school.

Does the model-minority concept have any positive effects on Asian Americans? Scholars are usually silent about this. In reality, this image is not without its usefulness. Historically, it helped turn around the negative stereotypes of Asian Americans—for example, that they are unassimilable aliens and enhance the positive image of Asian Americans. It shows that Asians are not unassimilable but in fact have assimilated well into American society. In contemporary times, the model-minority image helps people recognize the remarkable achievements of Asian Americans, it helps people appreciate Asian cultures and traditions, and it may increase the acceptance of Asian Americans in school, employment, and residential neighborhoods.

In summary, the model minority is a new, positive stereotype of Asian Americans in contrast to old, negative ones. Although this concept has a statistical basis, it is an oversimplification and an exaggeration of the Asian American experience. It ignores the diversity among Asian groups: there is no single model minority (Cheng and Yang 1996). While its historical contribution to countering the negative stereotypes against Asian Americans and its contemporary utilities should not go unnoticed, its many problems or potential problems overshadow its positive lights.

Further Reading

Cheng, Lucie, and Philip Yang. "Asians: The 'Model Minority' Deconstructed." Chap. 11 in *Ethnic Los Angeles*, edited by Roger Waldinger and Mehdi Bozorgmehr. New York: Russell Sage Foundation, 1996.

Kim, Kwang Chung, and Won Moo Hurh. "Korean Americans and the 'Success' Image: A Critique." *Amerasia Journal* 10 (1983): 3-21.

Suzuki, Bob. "Education and the Socialization of Asian Americans: A Revisionist Analysis of the 'Model Minority' Thesis." *Amerasia Journal* 4 (1977): 23-51.

Takaki, Ronald. *Strangers from a Different Shore*. New York: Penguin Books, 1989.

Philip Yang

Modern Racism

Modern racism refers to subtle, conscious or unconscious prejudicial attitudes and behaviors that allow for the discrimination of people of color. Modern racism's development coincided with the demise of the Jim Crow South and the sharp decline in popularity of that era's supporting belief system, sometimes described as "old-fashioned racism," which incorporated a biologically based theory of African racial inferiority and support for racial segregation and formal racial discrimination. Modern racism may be defined as "the expression in terms of abstract ideological symbols and symbolic behaviors of the feeling that people of color are violating cherished values and making illegitimate demands for changes in the racial status quo." Modern racism is not often malicious by intent but is pernicious by effect.

In modern racism, prejudiced behavior is characterized by a subtlety that can make it much more difficult to identify—and to define as expressly and exclusively *racial* discrimination—than the older forms of racism. Modern racism perpetuates the idea that people of color are inferior to whites, although that idea is not extended into legal policies. It is thus a type of racism that cannot be undone by laws like the 1964 Civil Rights Act, but it allows for the perpetuation of individual acts of racism that have harmful effects. Indeed, while more difficult to detect, modern racism can have effects just as severe as overt racism.

Modern racism can take the following forms:

- *Avoidance of Contact.* Modern racism may be manifested in decisions, conscious or unconscious, not to have social or professional contact with people of color; in not making an effort to learn about communities of color; and in living in all-white communities, exercising the option not to be involved in the lives of people of color, the option that whites often have by virtue of economic privilege. Whites thereby maintain a lack of familiarity with members of other races that is self-perpetuating. A by-product is the likelihood of unconsciously discriminating against people of color, such as by seeing a person of color in one's neighborhood as being out of place.

- *Blaming the Victim.* In this modern form of racism, racist ideas are expressed by attributing the results of systemic oppression to the target group; ignoring the real impact of racism on the lives of people of color today; blaming people of color for troubled economic times; and subjecting successful target-group members to scrutiny or criticism that a similarly situated white would not have to confront.

- *Dysfunctional Rescuing.* This term, popularized by Valerie Batts, describes the "helping" of people of color when it is based on an assumption that they cannot help themselves. The "helped" person may be set up to fail by the situation the helper creates or may be treated by the helper in a patronizing or condescending manner. In this situation, the "helping" helps maintain the status quo with respect to the stratification of society. This "help that does not help" may be motivated out of guilt or shame but is carried out in a way that limits recipients' ability to help themselves.

- *Cultural and Religious Marginalization.* In this manifestation, modern racism involves the minimizing of obvious physical or behavioral differences between people and discounting the influence of culture or the experiences of people of color. Characterized by the phrase "color-blind," it ultimately has a pernicious effect on both the agent and the target. It masks the agent's discomfort with difference while undercutting the legitimacy of the target's lived experience.

See also Civil Rights Act of 1964; Color-Blind Racism; Jim Crow Laws; Tokenism.

Further Reading

Batts, Valerie. "Modern Racism: New Melody for the Same Old Tunes." Rocky Mount, NC: Visions Publication, 1989.

McConahay, J. B. "Modern Racism, Ambivalence, and the Modern Racism Scale." In *Prejudice, Discrimination, and Racism*, edited by J. F. Dovidio and S. L. Gaertner, 91–126. New York: Academic Press, 1986.

Khyati Joshi

Montgomery Bus Boycott

The Montgomery Bus Boycott was the grassroots African American mobilization effort that ignited a decade-long, nationwide civil rights struggle to end racial segregation. Even before the Montgomery Bus Boycott, Blacks had undertaken several mass boycotts against segregation. For example, in June 1953, the African American community in Baton Rouge, Louisiana, launched a mass boycott of the transport system under the leadership of the Rev. T. J. Jemison of the Mount Zion Baptist Church. However, the Baton Rouge boycott was settled by a compromise and so did not trigger a national movement.

The Montgomery Bus Boycott began with a black woman's undaunted defiance. On December 1, 1955, Rosa Parks, a forty-two-year-old African American seamstress, refused to give up her seat for a white passenger, hence violating the bus-segregation ordinance of the city of Montgomery, Alabama. The driver repeatedly told her to move and only received her answer: No. Even the threat of arrest did not stop her refusal. The driver called the police, and Parks was arrested. Her refusal to give up her seat was a conscious act of civil disobedience. Parks had been a member of the National Association for the Advancement of Colored People (NAACP) since 1943, had served as secretary of the Montgomery branch of the association, and had participated in the organization's voter-registration drives. About six months before her arrest, she wrote in a letter to the Highlander Folk School in Tennessee, a "modern American movement halfway house" attended by such noteworthy Civil Right activists as Martin Luther King Jr., and Stokely Carmichael, that she was "hoping to make a contribution to the fulfillment of complete freedom for all people."

The arrest of Parks prompted activists E. D. Nixon, a fellow member of the NAACP and Alabama branch president of Randolph's Brotherhood of Sleeping Car Porters, and Jo Ann Robinson, a professor at Alabama State College, the only institution for black students, and president of the Women's Political Council, to write a leaflet calling on the black community to stay off the buses on the day of Parks's trial. Student volunteers made thousands of copies of the leaflet and distributed them throughout the community. Black preachers Ralph D. Abernathy, secretary of the Baptist Ministers' Alliance, and Martin Luther King Jr. of the Dexter Avenue Baptist Church joined and made it possible to win the support of the wider African American community. On December 5, 1955, Montgomery blacks showed unprecedented solidarity, but the city commissioners rejected their modest demands such as the first-come first-served rule, politeness toward black passengers, and the hiring of black drivers for a community where 75 percent of passengers were black. White refusal

African Americans walk instead of riding the bus during an eventual 381-day bus boycott, Montgomery, Alabama, February 1956.

Photo by Don Cravens/Time Life Pictures/Getty Images.

and obscene resistance turned the one-day bus boycott into a yearlong struggle that demanded nothing less than total desegregation.

Black leaders established a new organization for campaign coordination called the Montgomery Improvement Association (MIA). The city commissioners had the grand jury indict the members of the MIA en masse. But it only reinforced the resolve of the African American community. The mass indictment and King's speech garnered attention from the national media. King's articulate message of nonviolent direct action for justice inspired some whites as well as blacks. King himself was indicted, found guilty, and fined. On June 7, 1956, however, the federal district court ruled that bus segregation was unconstitutional. The city commissioners tried to fight back with further lawsuits. But the U.S. Supreme Court on November 13 upheld the previous ruling. On December 21, Martin Luther King Jr. rode a desegregated Montgomery bus for the first time in history as the boycott was called off.

See also Civil Rights Movement; King, Martin Luther, Jr.; Parks, Rosa.

Further Reading

Eagles, Charles W. *The Civil Rights Movement in America*. Jackson: University Press of Mississippi, 1986.

Riches, William T. Martin. *The Civil Rights Movement*. New York: St. Martin's Press, 1997.

Dong-Ho Cho

Moorish Science Temple Movement

See the Nation of Islam.

Morrison, Toni (1931–)

Toni Morrison is a popular and highly regarded African American writer whose essays, plays, and novels chronicle the experiences of African Americans living with racism.

Morrison was born Chloe Anthony Wofford in Ohio in 1931. The author of seven novels and numerous essays and plays, Morrison has won the Pulitzer Prize (1988), the Nobel Prize in Literature (1993), the National Book Critics Award (1973), and the National Book Foundation Medal for Contribution to American Letters (1996), among other honors. Morrison, who holds degrees in English from Harvard University and Cornell University, was the first African American woman to receive the Nobel Prize in Literature. She has held several different academic appointments, including at Howard University, the State University of New York at Albany and Purchase, and Princeton Univer-

African American writer Toni Morrison receives the Nobel Prize in literature from King Carl XVI Gustaf of Sweden, December 10, 1993.

AP/Wide World Photos.

sity, where she became the first black woman to hold a named chair at an Ivy League university.

Morrison's first novel, *The Bluest Eye* (1970), was set in her hometown of Lorain, Ohio, and examines racialized beauty ideals, self-hatred, and internalized oppression. *Sula* (1973), nominated for a National Book Award, centers on the relationship between two Midwestern black women in the 1920s, friends since childhood, who struggle with issues of gender, race, poverty, and love. Her most famous work is *Beloved* (1987), which examines the life of an ex-slave, Sethe, who is haunted by the cruelty, torture, and sexual victimization of slave life, her journey to escape the South and, after her recapture, the infanticide of one of her children. For *Beloved*, Morrison won the Pulitzer Prize in 1988. Her most recent novel is *Paradise*, which examines the troubles of an all-black town in the Midwest in the 1970s.

Victoria Pitts

Mortgage Disinvestment

See Redlining.

Movies

See Films and Racial Stereotypes.

The Moynihan Report

See The Negro Family: The Case for National Action.

Muhammad, Elijah (1897–1975)

Born on October 7, 1897, as Elijah Poole in Sandersville, Georgia, Elijah Muhammad was the founder of the Nation of Islam. In 1923, he moved from Georgia to Detroit, Michigan, with his parents, as part of the Great Migration of African Americans from the South to the North. While living in Detroit, he met Fard Muhammad, who was going door to door preaching and inviting people to attend his mosque. Elijah Poole went to one of Fard Muhammad's sermons. He was so moved by Muhammad's preaching that he decided to convert to Islam.

Poole rejected his Christian name and adopted the name Muhammad to reflect the original name that blacks had before they were subjugated to slavery. After the mysterious disappearance of Fard Muhammad in the 1930s, Elijah Muhammad took over the leadership of the Nation of Islam. Under his leadership, the organization thrived and became an integral part of religious life among blacks in the United States. The Nation of Islam created its own schools and taught African Americans to be proud of themselves. It fought several battles with the FBI and the Justice Department, which perceived it as a threat.

Muhammad's greatest achievement was the recruitment of Malcolm X to the Nation of Islam. He quickly recognized the leadership of Malcolm X after he was released from jail and entrusted him with the development of the Nation of Islam. Within a short period of time, the Nation of Islam grew from several hundred members to a hundred thousand (Dyson 1995), and it had thirty temples nationwide. Harlem became the anchor temple for the Nation of Islam because of Malcolm X's speeches on black oppression in the United States. After several scandals within the Nation of Islam, Malcolm X broke away from Elijah Muhammad and founded his own mosque. Elijah Muhammad died in 1975.

See also Malcom X; Nation of Islam.

Francois Pierre-Louis

Mulatto

The term *mulatto* in the United States generally means an offspring of black and white parents. In other countries, such as Brazil, it could be the offspring of a light-skinned couple. However, this definition does not do justice to what the term *mulatto* connotes in U.S. society. Race, which is a social construct, is used in U.S. society to bestow privileges and power to certain groups while denying them to others. Therefore the closer a person is to being classified as white, the more likely that he or she might enjoy the privileges associated with whiteness. On a strict racial classification in the United States, a mulatto would be closer to whiteness than a person whose parents are both black.

The United States is the only country in the world that has a rigid racial classification system. Countries in the Americas that had a history of slavery invented various shades of color to classify people. Whereas in the United States a person was either black or white, in Latin America and the Caribbean, racial definition was more varied. The range of racial classification went from Octoroon, Quadroon to Mulatto and Marabou. The result of all these classifications is the division of oppressed people further on an imaginary color line.

See also Mestizo; Yellows.

Francois Pierre-Louis

Multiculturalism

The term *multiculturalism* is commonly used to refer to an ideology that emphasizes the importance of maintaining cultural diversity in the United States or the social movement organized to achieve such a culturally diverse society. *Multiculturalism* is also used to indicate the government policy aimed at facilitating the preservation of cultural diversity in the United States. As an ideology, multiculturalism demands that the unique cultures of African Americans, Asian Americans, Latinos/as, Native Americans, European Americans, and multiracial people be recognized and given a place in the curricula of schools and universities and in the societal contexts of the workplace. The multiculturalist ideology and the multicultural movement among minority members and women have led to changes in government policies, written and unwritten, on matters related to racial, gender, and sexual-identity diversity in the public sector.

Multiculturalism as an Ideology or a Social Movement

The ideological seeds of multiculturalism are found in the United States' formation myths of individual rights, human dignity, and social justice. Multiculturalism's response to the "melting pot" is the metaphor of the "salad bowl" or "mosaic." According to the multicultural ideology, immigrants and other minorities do not have to give up their values and traditions by assimilating *or* melting together. Rather, they can keep their unique cultural norms, traditions, and behaviors while still sharing common national values, goals, and institutions. The ideology of cultural pluralism can be traced to the writings of the Jewish philosopher Horace Kallen. Beginning in 1915, Kallen argued in favor of an ideology of cultural pluralism based on the belief that the members of every ethnic group in America should be free to participate in all of the society's major institutions, including education, employment, and governance, while they retain their own ethnic heritage.

Multiculturalism as a movement is an attempt to establish this ideology in the reality of contemporary America. It has since developed beyond the mere validation of diversity to encompass an agenda of reducing and ultimately eliminating racial oppression and inequalities that exist in contemporary American society. Multiculturalism's political coming of age can be traced to the 1960s, when a number of minority movements—the civil rights movement, the Black Nationalist movement, the Third World movement, the gay rights movement, and the women's movement—challenged the Euro-male-centric educational system and social fabric.

Black Nationalism that started in the late 1960s was the earliest expression of the multicultural ideology. Other social movements by people of color, such as Latinos' La Raza (the race) movement and the American Indian movement, also incorporated multiculturalist thought with a leftist political agenda. Simultaneously, the United States saw the growth of gender-related activism—including the successful advocacy of the Equal Pay Act of 1963 and the movement to pass the women's Equal Rights Amendment to the United States Constitution. Likewise, the Stonewall Riots of 1969 marked the beginning of the modern gay rights movement, which also incorporated elements of multiculturalist thought. The environmental movement, long present on the American stage, was revived at the same time, often around issues such as environmental justice for indigenous people, communities of color, and people in the developing world, who most often bear the brunt of toxic pollution.

Multiculturalism's rise was abetted by the evolution of the mass media, which made it possible for what were seen as local problems, like the early civil rights movement, to become national issues for debate. The sudden visibility of Jim Crow racism to political moderates and liberals in the North galvanized broad-based and national opposition to Southern segregationist policies and brought the issue of African Americans' rights—and their sociocultural uniqueness—to the forefront. The post–World War II changes in American demography and geography, and in particular the movement of American whites to the suburbs, caused issues such as redlining and white flight to become topics of broad discussion.

The educational arena is the multiculturalist movement's central forum. While decisions like *Brown v. Board of Education* and *Lau v. Nichols* affirmed a person's legal right to "equal educational opportunities" regardless of race or national origin, the process of enforcing such decisions against recalcitrant school districts has lasted decades. More important, the legal requirements of federal legislation and court opinions do not meet the standard that multiculturalism sets for schools: to be genuinely inclusive, to provide not only "opportunities" but also validation and visibility to ethnic, racial, religious, and social groups and pedagogy that addresses the marginalization and oppression of minority groups.

Contemporary multiculturalism in education is characterized by two modes of thought. The first and more widely known involves merely the appreciation and celebration of cultural diversity. Integrating the history and culture of dominated groups into public-school curricula and textbooks is an end unto itself, rather than a starting point toward empowering oppressed people and thereby achieving social change. The second mode of thought, which is becoming the subject of greater attention and support, incorporates the first but also looks to address prejudice and discrimination at the individual and institutional levels. This multiculturalism says that while celebration of diversity is essential, it alone is inadequate; schools should change their policy and pedagogy to examine and address injustice at all levels. Advocates of this multiculturalism criticize the earlier school as offering only "heroes and holidays"—the obligatory study of noted minorities in history and cursory celebration of non-Christian holidays—without addressing the societal and cultural patterns that perpetuate the very need to offer up such heroes and holidays every year. This mode of fostering multiculturalism calls for critical and multifaceted analysis of contemporary societal problems, and responses to those problems that unabashedly address white Christian dominance.

Colleges and universities have been battlefields in the war between multicultural education and Eurocentric education. The multicultural movement on college campuses can also be traced to the 1970s when the Third World Liberation Front, a student organization made up of African American, Asian American, Latino/a, and Native American students at San Francisco State University and the University of California at Berkeley, called a strike demanding a Third World, Ethnic Studies College. After months of protests, teach-ins, and strikes—during which authorities deployed as many as 10,000 armed men each day for nearly two months in an attempt to quell the uprising—San Francisco State University became the first university to establish a black studies department and a college of ethnic studies. Ethnic studies programs, along with women's studies and, later, queer studies programs, thereafter came to be established on other university campuses. Along with multicultural representation in academics, student organizations that focus on ethnicity, religion, gender, and sexual orientation were established on campuses; these organizations have engaged students, faculty, and school administrations in public events and debates on a plethora of issues related to multiculturalism.

Opponents of the multiculturalist ideology argue that the addition of non-European materials to the academic canon "waters down" curricula by spreading intellectual resources too thinly and by mandating less intellectually worthy pursuits. They also argue that it could "Balkanize" society by focusing individuals and communities on their respective dissimilarities and uniqueness, creating artificial interethnic competition, and damaging the cohesive effect of common "American culture."

Alongside the deep cultural changes already noted, multiculturalism seeks changes in the contemporary racial and cultural lexicon. Specifically, it advances the notion that any given group should be called by a name—a "label"—of its own choosing. Perhaps the best example of the effects of a group's deliberate attempt to name or "rename" itself is the evolution of the popular term for people of African heritage: from *Negro* in the middle of the twentieth century to *black*, *Afro-American*, and *African American* over the course of recent decades. Another example is the switch from *Oriental* to *Asian American* or *East Asian* to describe people of Japanese, Chinese, and Korean descent. The decision to name one's group is political as well as linguistic, and it responds to the need for group self-determination and autonomy.

Multiculturalism as Government Policy

Driven by the social movements of the modern age, government policy has changed from one of Anglo conformity to multiculturalism since the early 1970s. Fueled by the general social ferment of the civil rights movement and the war in Vietnam, the federal government enacted social and educational reform legislation in many areas related to multiculturalism. For example, the Voting Rights Act of 1963 eliminated race-based bars to suffrage, and the Equal Pay Act passed the same year required that men and women occupying the same position be paid equally. The Civil Rights Act was passed in 1964 to address discrimination in housing, employment, and education.

Again, the shift in government policy toward multiculturalism is particularly evident in the educational policy sector. Many civil rights–era legislative initiatives were aimed at past discrimination in the educational arena. Titles IV and VI of the Civil Rights Act aimed to end school segregation and provide authority for implementing the U.S. Supreme Court's decision in *Brown v. Board of Education*. The Bilingual Education Act of 1968 obligated schools to provide programs for children whose first language was not English. Title IX of the Education Amendments of 1972 prohibited gender-based discrimination against students and employees of educational institutions, and the Education of All Handicapped Children Act of 1975 required schools to assume the responsibility for education of all children in the least restrictive environment possible. In 1967, the U.S. Commission on Civil Rights was established to investigate complaints alleging violations of the Voting Rights and Civil Rights Acts. The Indian Education Act of 1972 provided financial assistance to local schools to develop programs to meet the "special" educational needs of Native American students, a response to a 1969 report condemning past discrimination against Native Americans.

Bilingual education, one of the most hotly debated topics related to multiculturalism, was officially born in 1974 when the U.S. Supreme Court issued its decision in *Lau v. Nichols*. In *Lau*, the high court ruled that the San Francisco public school system violated the Civil Rights Act of 1964 by denying non-English-speaking students of Chinese ancestry a meaningful opportunity to participate in the public educational program. The decision stated that "merely by providing students with the same facilities, textbooks, teachers, and curriculum," the school district was not meeting its obligation to ensure that they received an equal educational opportunity. The *Lau* decision was important because it extended civil rights protections to linguistic minorities, that is, to students who did not speak English, by applying the Civil Rights Act's prohibition on discrimination based on "national origin." Bilingual education continues to be a hotly debated topic as the number of immigrant students increases every year in public-school systems across the country.

Polices and practices related to multiculturalism are present at the local and state government levels in noneducational arenas as well. More recently, some states have directed resources to support "gay/straight alliances," organizations aimed at combating homophobia and ensuring equal educational access for gay, lesbian, bisexual, and transgendered students. State and local governments also have provided grants to programs that support the maintenance of different ethnic heritages. Government-supported social-service organizations have implemented translation programs to make sure all people get the services they need and that language is not a barrier. Vermont has enacted legislation giving gay couples rights substantially similar to those enjoyed by heterosexual married people, and Massachusetts has effectively been ordered to do the same by its state supreme court.

Of course, legal sanction does not equal social sanction. The legislation and court decisions described above did not guarantee social and educational equal opportunity to all. Historical disparities remain and are perpetuated by individual and institutional discrimination. American culture remains dominated by Anglo norms, and these lingering divisions still make structural pluralism a rarity in the early years of the twenty-first century. Multiculturalism—as an educational ideology and a social movement—will therefore remain a factor in contemporary education and public policy for years to come.

See also Anglo Conformity; Bilingual Education; *Brown v. Board of Education of Topeka*; Education and Racial Discrimination; *Lau v. Nichols*; Political Correctness (P.C.).

Further Reading

Banks, James, and Cherry McGee Banks, eds. *Handbooks on Research on Multicultural Education*. 2nd ed. San Francisco: Jossey-Bass, 2004.

McLemore, S. Dale, and Harriett D. Romo. *Racial and Ethnic Relations in America*. 5th ed. Boston: Allyn & Bacon, 1998.

Nieto, Sonia. *Affirming Diversity: The Sociopolitical Context for Multicultural Education*. 4th ed. White Plains, NY: Longman Publishers, 2003.

Spring, Joel. *Deculturalization and the Struggle for Equality: A Brief History of the Education of Dominated Cultures in the United States*. 4th ed. Boston: McGraw Hill, 2003.

Khyati Joshi

Music Industry, Racism in

Racism in the music industry cuts across the entire business spectrum: from exploitation of musicians to discrimination in the management of record labels to segregation within the musicians' union, the American Federation of Musicians. Racism in the music industry in the United States goes all the way back to the mid-nineteenth century minstrel shows in which white musicians and performing artists dressed in "blackface" and ridiculed African American culture. Racial discrimination in the music industry continued all the way through the twentieth century as black musicians created many popular music forms—including jazz, blues, rhythm and blues, and rock 'n' roll—but have never been compensated adequately for their work or creativity. White-owned record labels have been the beneficiaries of black creativity, and some have referred to the American music recording industry as a system of "black roots and white fruits."

Exploitation of black musicians by record labels happens in two ways. First, in the early years of the recording industry, black musicians were often denied "authorship" or copyrights to songs they composed and recorded. Under U.S. copyright law, when a musician writes a tune, he or she is entitled to the income derived from that song, which includes mechanical royalties—income based on record sales—and performance royalties—income based on the radio air play of the song or record. It was typical in the early days of the music recording industry for black musicians to compose and record a song for a record label, get paid a small fee for the work in the studio, and then lose the rights to the song because they were deceived by unscrupulous record-label owners and producers. Many African American recording artists were not aware of U.S. copyright law, and as a result most could be fooled into turning over their rights to the record label that recorded their songs. As a result, many black recording artists never received any royalties that they were entitled to under U.S. copyright law. Instead, record-label owners claimed that they were the "authors" of the songs, and they reaped all the royalty income. One notorious example was that of Fred Parris, who wrote the song "In the Still of the Night." Conservative estimates show that "In the Still of the Night" sold between 10 and 15 million copies. Based on those numbers, Parris should have received at least $100,000 in royalty payments, but because someone else was given credit for writing the song, Parris earned only $783 from the hit tune that he wrote. Another example of egregious racial discrimination in the music recording industry comes from an interview with Ahmet Ertegun, the founder of Atlantic records. Ertegun recalls a conversation he had with an executive at Columbia Records in the 1950s, who boasted to Ertegun that his label did not pay African American recording artists on his roster *any* royalties.

Second, another example of exploitation that became common in the 1950s was the practice of "covering" records or songs. White artists—such as Pat Boone, who started his own cover label called Dot Records—would cover or record a song originally written by a black artist, such as Little Richard. When Pat Boone covered "Tutti-Fruiti" by Little Richard, Boone was able to take advantage of the distribution system of the major record labels, whereas Little Richard's independent record label had a much smaller network of distribution and retail outlets. Radio listeners often did not know that records they were buying by white artists were records originally written and recorded by black artists. As a result, Pat Boone made many times more money than Little Richard off of sales of the single "Tutti-Fruiti" even though Little Richard wrote, recorded, and performed the song.

Racial discrimination also takes place in both the management operations of record labels and in the union that represents musicians in the United States, the American Federation of Musicians. In the 1980s, the National Association for the Advancement of Colored People (NAACP) conducted a study of the recording industry and found that African Americans were seriously underrepresented among management and professional positions in the industry. Most African Americans employed by record labels work in the A&R (artist and repertoire) departments, the lowest level of management. The NAACP found that the typical mid-sized record label has about thirty-five management positions and fills only four of those positions with African Americans. On the labor side, discrimination was widespread until 1964, when the American Federation of Musicians (AFM) was forced by the federal government to integrate its locals. Under the Civil Rights Act of 1964, labor unions were forced to end racial segregation. Before 1964, apart from a few exceptions like New York City, the majority of musicians' locals in the AFM chartered separate white and black locals. In most cases, the white locals monopolized the good jobs, excluding black musicians from the better-paying engagements in the cities or towns where they had jurisdiction. During the civil rights movement, black members of the AFM successfully challenged and defeated racial discrimination in the union by appealing to the 1964 Civil Rights Act.

Recent research on the music recording industry shows that racial discrimination continues to exist. According to Kelley (2002), rap and hip-hop music—a predominantly black musical form—is now the second largest musical genre in the United States, accounting for 13 percent of all record sales, but black musicians still earn a miniscule portion of the income from the music they produce. Worth more than $1.8 billion in annual sales, hip hop and rap music is still controlled by white-owned establishments. Compare that with the figure for the *entirety* of revenues generated by black-owned entertainment companies: $189 million dollars in the year 2000. There are a few profitable black-owned record labels in the industry such as Def Jam records, owned by Russell Simmons, and Bad Boy records, owned by Sean Combs. But even these labels are still dependent on white-owned and -controlled record companies for distribution. There are no fully independent, black-owned major record labels anymore since the 1993 sale of Motown records, which is now a subsidiary of the giant multinational corporate conglomerate Universal/Vivendi. Black musicians have made important gains in the recording industry, but discrimination remains a problem for future generations as they continue the struggle for equality in an industry that earns billions from their creativity.

See also Civil Rights Act of 1964; Films and Racial Stereotypes; Hollywood and Minority Actors; National Association for the Advancement of Colored People (NAACP); Television and Racial Stereotypes.

Further Reading

Garofalo, Reebee, and Steve Chapple. *Rock'n'Roll Is Here to Pay.* New York: Nelson-Hall, 1977.

George, Nelson. *The Death of Rhythm and Blues.* New York: Plume, 1988.

Kelley, Norman. *Rhythm and Business: The Political Economy of Black Music.* New York: Akashic Books, 2002.

Kofsky, Frank. *Black Music, White Business: Illuminating the History and Political Economy of Jazz.* New York: Pathfinder, 1998.

Michael Roberts

Muslim Philanthropic Organizations, Closure of after September 11, 2001

Philanthropy in Islamic communities has traditionally addressed needy Muslims and Muslim institutions. Since the late 1960s, Muslim Americans have raised funds for the development of a communal infrastructure in the United States as their numbers have increased as a result of immigration. Mosques, Islamic schools, social-service associations, and other institutions have been established to serve this new, rapidly expanding constituency. Muslim Americans have also contributed generously to needy Muslims overseas, notably the Palestinian refugees and victims of disasters and war, mostly in the Middle East and South Asia. After the September 11, 2001 attacks, Islamic charitable organizations in the United States that were registered with the Internal Revenue Service as tax-exempt associations were closely scrutinized, allegedly for laundering money for terrorist organizations in the Muslim world.

In December 2001, the U.S. government froze the assets of the Holy Land Foundation for Relief and Development (HLF), the Global Relief Foundation (GRF) and the Benevolence International Foundation (BIF). No criminal charges were filed against these organizations, but secret evidence was used in the prosecution of these cases, a violation of the Fifth Amendment. The 2002 report by the Council on American Islamic Relations (CAIR) on anti-Muslim actions in the United States in the year following 9/11 estimates that about 50,000 American Muslim donors were affected by the closures.

The HLF, established in 1989, was the first casualty on December 4, 2001. Federal agents closed down its headquarters in Richardson, Texas, and its three offices in Bridgeview, Illinois; Paterson, New Jersey; and San Diego, California. The HLF is the largest Muslim charity in the United States. It raised over $13 million from American Muslims in 2000, which HLF claims was spent on humanitarian causes in the West Bank and Gaza, on earthquake victims in Turkey, for refugees in Kosovo, Chechnya, Jordan, and Lebanon, and for various causes in the United States. The HLF released a statement denying the allegations that it had supported terrorist groups or individuals.

Following actions against the HLF, eight major national American Muslim organizations issued a joint statement asking President George W. Bush to reconsider his decision to freeze the assets of the charity, calling it "an unjust and counterproductive move." A few weeks after the closure of the HLF, the Treasury Department sanctioned two Illinois-based charities—the GRF and the BIF. Like HLF, both groups immediately denied ties to terrorism. Reporting $3.6 million in contributions for 2001, the BLF is also one of the largest Muslim charities in the United States. The founder of BLF, Enaam Arnaout, pleaded guilty to racketeering charges in February 2003. BLF entered a plea bargain to cooperate with the authorities, but it denied any ties to Al Qaeda, the Islamic group that took responsibility for the 9/11 attacks.

The U.S. government claimed that the money raised by the HLF was eventually used by Hamas to support schools that encourage children to become suicide bombers in Israel. However, defendants argued that HLF was a humanitarian and disaster-relief organization that had a solid track record in aiding widows and children and financing several development projects in Palestinian refugee camps through Hamas. Hamas encompasses a social-service arm, and it is difficult to separate its dual, often contradictory objectives. The GRF, which raised about $5 million in 2001, sent contributions to clinics in Israeli-occupied territories and to refugee camps in Kosovo. Many Muslim Americans viewed the U.S. Treasury's intensification of surveillance during the month of Ramadan (November–December 2001) as a highly provocative act. Muslims customarily contribute higher amounts during the holy month of fasting. Additionally, many of the Muslim charities under government surveillance do in fact accomplish their stated humanitarian missions.

The closure of Muslim charities curtails the ability of Muslim Americans to fulfill their *zakat* (alms-giving) duties. Giving alms is one of the five pillars of Islam and is a religious duty of all Muslims. Muslims are required to give charitable donations annually equaling 2.5 percent of their entire wealth, not just income. Muslim immigrants to the United States have brought with them not only their religious tenets but also their cultural practices. In the face-to-face social world of the Middle East and South Asia where most of them came from, alms were given mostly to local institutions and needy family or community members. With the exception of Islamic endowments, contributing to anonymous organizations remains an alien concept for many. It is therefore not surprising that Muslim Americans have continued their habits of giving to organizations they were familiar with and causes they espouse. Indeed, these motivations and practices are similar to those of all Americans; if anything, integration in the United States may encourage greater charitable giving.

See also Al Qaeda; Arab/Muslim American Advocacy Organizations, Responding to the Backlash; Government Initiatives after the September 11, 2001, Attack on the United States; Middle Easterners, Historical Precedents of Backlash against; Muslims, Prejudice and Discrimination against; Muslims, Terrorist Image of; September 11, 2001, Terrorism, Discriminatory Reactions to.

Mehdi Bozorgmehr and Anny Bakalian

Muslims, Prejudice and Discrimination against

In 2003, the U.S. Senate and House of Representatives both passed resolutions condemning bigotry and violence against Arab Americans, Muslim Americans, South Asian Americans, and Sikh Americans. These congressional actions were occasioned by a backlash among many Americans to the events of September 11, 2001, that resulted in prejudicial and discriminatory acts against Arabs, Muslims, and others who "looked like" Arabs or Muslims, thus the curious grouping of people in the resolutions. Prejudice, born of ignorance and spread by fear and hysteria, tends to stereotype and universalize without regard to fact. Many Americans do not know, for example, that the term *Arab* refers to Arabic-speaking people who may or may not be Muslims. In fact, there are many Christian Arabs. The term *Muslim*, on the other hand, refers to those who practice the religion of Islam, who may or may not be Arabs. In fact, most Muslims are not Arabs. In the parlance of prejudice, however, an "Arab" is a stereotype of a 9/11 hijacker, and they all look alike.

The Council on American Islamic Relations (CAIR), which collects and reports data on Muslim civil rights issues in the United States, noted that valid complaints, excluding those deemed to be backlash incidents, increased 43 percent from 366 in 2000–2001 to 525 in 2001–2002. These complaints included civil rights violations in workplaces, airports, schools, prisons, and public places where services or access were denied—all based on ethnicity or religion. The number of 9/11 backlash incidents, however, reached an alarming number, about eight times that of incidents reported after the Oklahoma City bombing, which had at first been thought to be the work of "Arab" terrorists. CAIR logged 1,717 incidents in these categories: hate messages or harassment, 687; violence, 303; false arrest/intimidation by authorities, 224; airport profiling, 191; workplace discrimination, 166; school discrimination, 74; and threats, 72.

From its point of view, CAIR found a number of troubling governmental policies and practices that endangered the civil rights of Muslims. The Patriot Act of 2001 had swept away some constitutional protections of citizens, allowing such changes as searches without probable cause to fight terrorism. Passenger profiling, the detention of non-U.S. nationals from Arab and Muslim countries, the closing of Muslim charities, the use of secret evidence; raids on Muslim homes and businesses, and interrogations of legal Muslim nationals: all these things singled out Muslims for discrimination.

The federal government, for its part, sought to stem the rising tide of discriminatory and illegal acts against "Arab, Muslim, Sikh, and South-Asian Americans, and those perceived to be members of these groups." Within the Justice Department's Civil Rights Division, the National Origin Working Group created its Initiative to Combat Post-9/11 Discriminatory Backlash. A priority was placed on cases involving discrimination against these groups in employment, housing, education, and access to public accommodations. Outreach and coordination programs within other government agencies were also established, prompting the investigation of 546 incidents, including "telephone, internet, mail, and face-to-face threats; minor assaults as well as assaults with dangerous weapons and assaults resulting in serious injury and death; and vandalism, shooting, arson and bombings directed at homes, businesses, and places of worship."

Civil Rights Division attorneys have assisted state and local prosecutors in 121 nonfederal cases. Thirteen federal cases have gone to trial with a 100 percent conviction rate. Among those convicted were four people who plotted to destroy the Islamic Education Center in St. Petersburg, Florida, and received a combined 285 months in prison. A man in Sacramento who shot a Sikh postal carrier with a high-powered pellet rifle paid $25,395 in restitution and was sentenced to seventy months in prison. In Des Moines, Iowa, Marriott International agreed to make a formal apology and set up a $100,000 scholarship fund to be administered by the Midwest Federation of American Syrian-Lebanese Clubs after that organization alleged discrimination when the local Marriott hotel revoked its offer to host that group's 2002 convention.

The U.S. Equal Employment Opportunity Commission (EEOC) is in charge of enforcing Title VII of the 1964 Civil Rights Act, which prohibits workplace discrimination based on religion, ethnicity, country of origin, race, and color in any aspect of employment. Harassment is also prohibited. Employers have an obligation to make reasonable accommodations for religious practices unless that obligation creates an undue hardship. The EEOC began tracking discrimination charges by "individuals who are—or are perceived to be—Muslim, Arab, Afghani, Middle Eastern or South Asian" after the 9/11 attacks and those who charged discrimination because of the 9/11 events. These were classified as "Process Type Z charges." From September 11, 2001, to September 10, 2002, 654 Process Type Z charges were filed against employers all over the country and in a large range of businesses, claiming violation of Title VII. Of the charges, 406 claimed wrongful discharge and 205 claimed harassment in the workplace. By October 1, 2002, sixty people had received nearly $680,000 in benefits as a result of the EEOC's efforts. Separate from the Process Type Z charges, the EEOC noted that charges of discrimination in the workplace based on Muslim religion nearly doubled to 706 for the September 11, 2001– September 10, 2002, period from the previous year's total of 323.

Clearly, U.S. society has not yet come to grips with its ingrained prejudice against its five to seven million Muslims, intensified by the fear of terrorism and the reality of war. The black civil rights movement proved that changing laws does not necessarily change people's hearts.

See also Al Qaeda; Arab/Muslim American Advocacy Organizations, Responding to the Backlash; Government Initiatives after the September 11, 2001, Attack on the United States; Middle Easterners, Historical Precedents of Backlash against; Muslim Philanthropic Organizations, Closure of after September 11, 2001; Muslims, Terrorist Image of; September 11, 2001, Terrorism, Discriminatory Reactions to.

Further Reading

The Status of Muslim Civil Rights in the United States, 2002. Washington, DC: Council on American Islamic Relations, 2002.

U.S. Department of Justice, Civil Rights Division. "Enforcement and Outreach Following the September 11 Terrorist Attacks," February 12, 2004. http://www.usdoj.gov/crt/legalinfo/discrimupdate.htm.

Benjamin F. Shearer

Muslims, Terrorist Image of

The image of Muslims as terrorists is not unfamiliar in the iconography of Western culture. European painters depicting the Crusades often used the same typology to portray the infidel Saracens, Moors, and Mohammedans as they did to portray Satan. Indeed, both the devil and the Muslims were believed to have a common objective—the downfall of Western civilization.

The fight to establish the state of Israel in 1948 saw the rebirth of the Muslim terrorist stereotype when Jewish "freedom fighters" battled displaced, stateless Palestinian "terrorists." Palestinians were all considered incorrectly to be Muslims in the public eye. These terrorist images were further enforced and ingrained into popular culture by highly visible terrorist attacks at the Munich Olympics in 1972, the bombing of the Marine Corps barracks in Lebanon in 1983, the bombing of the World Trade Center in 1993, the bombing of American embassies in Nairobi, Kenya, and Dar Es Salaam, Tanzania, in 1998, and finally, the attacks on Washington, DC, and New York City on September 11, 2001.

These events, along with numerous less sensational ones, have caused the happier but still stereotypical image of Muslims as rich, mysterious, turbaned sheikhs, as seen in Rudolph Valentino's 1921 silent movie *The Sheik*, to be replaced almost completely by the Muslim terrorist stereotype image. Replays of terrorist attacks appeared constantly on television, sometimes accompanied by jingoistic commentary and using the terms "Muslim terrorists" and "Arab terrorists" interchangeably. Characters in television dramas began fighting terrorists and even superheroes had to fight terrorists in comic books. These television and comic book terrorists always seemed to look Middle Eastern.

The human drama and experience of terrorism became excellent grist for the Hollywood mill. True to its tradition, Hollywood could make a lot of money out of stories in which good always triumphed over evil and stereotypical "bad guys" got their comeuppances. In World War II films, the bad guys were warmongering Germans and sneaky Japanese, only to be replaced during the Cold War by godless Russians. Now the bad guys became "Middle Eastern–looking" terrorists.

Actor Sean Connery discovered a terrorist plot to sell a Middle Eastern country a nuclear bomb in the 1981 film *Wrong Is Right*. *Wanted Dead or Alive* was updated in 1986 from a western to a tale about the deadly struggle between an ex-CIA man and an international terrorist. In the 1987 film *Death Before Dishonor*, Fred Dryer took on an entire group of terrorists who had stormed an American embassy in the Middle East and taken hostages. Arnold Schwarzenegger and Jamie Lee Curtis found themselves in the midst of an international terrorist crisis in the otherwise rather humorous *True Lies*, which came out in 1994. Two years later, Kurt Russell and Halle Berry saved the day in *Executive Decision*, after Islamic terrorists took control of an airplane filled with hundreds of people and bombs filled with nerve gas. Denzel Washington, Bruce Willis, and Annette Bening have rough going in *The Siege* (1998) when New York City is targeted for attacks by terrorists after U.S. military forces abduct a Muslim leader. In the 2000 film *Rules of Engagement*, Samuel L. Jackson saved the U.S. ambassador to Yemen and killed the terrorists and demonstrators who had invaded the embassy. When these films left theaters, they then went into American homes.

Organizations such as the Muslim Public Affairs Council, the American-Arab Anti-Discrimination Committee, and the Council on American Islamic Relations (CAIR) protested long before the 9/11 events that the constant bombardment of negative Arab and Muslim stereotypes was feeding the fire of prejudice against Arabs and Muslims in the United States. The civil rights of these groups were eroding in the face of it. Furthermore, the unceasing use of the terrorist stereotype throughout the media had falsely connected terrorism to the religion of Islam in the minds of many Americans. Because American media products are spread all around the world, the images of Arabs and Muslims were being damaged globally.

The problem had reached global proportions after 9/11, so the Arab League met in Cairo, gathering over seventy Islamic scholars from twenty countries to figure out how to present to the world a truer understanding of Islam. They were especially concerned about the well-being of Arabs and Muslims living in the West. There was general agreement that the chasm between Muslims and Christians, between East and West, which existed since the prophet Mohammed's time on earth, needed to be closed somehow. Muslim scholars and clerics had to spread the word of true Islam to non-Muslims in the West. Islam itself needed to be interpreted in one way, not many. It needed to be rejuvenated.

While the 9/11 tragedy provided spokespersons from Muslim and Islamic organizations in the United States with airtime on radio and television networks that were looking for experts, their efforts to separate a few militants from the mainstream of Islam may have fallen on deaf ears. The persistence of the terrorist stereotype and the anxiety of the moment inhibited any desire to see another side. And the stereotype will persist until Muslims and Arabs are integrated into the American fabric and not viewed as voices from the outside.

See also Al Qaeda; Arab/Muslim American Advocacy Organizations, Responding to the Backlash; Films and Racial Stereotypes; Government Initiatives after the September 11, 2001, Attack on the United States; Middle Easterners, Historical Precedents of Backlash against; Muslim Philanthropic Organizations, Closure of after 9/11; Muslims, Prejudice and Discrimination against; September 11, 2001, Terrorism, Discriminatory Reactions to; Television and Racial Stereotypes.

Benjamin F. Shearer

N

NAACP

See National Association for the Advancement of Colored People (NAACP).

Nation of Islam

The Nation of Islam, or Black Muslims, is an influential nationalistic religious movement, particularly among destitute blacks of the ghettos. The religion was founded by Wallace D. Fard, also known as Fard Muhhamed, who appeared in Detroit in 1930. Fard founded the Temple of Islam and assembled disciples but then mysteriously disappeared four years later. Elijah Pool, a former Baptist minister from Sandersville, Georgia, who became known as Elijah Muhammad, succeeded Fard in the leadership of the group, taking the title "Messenger of Allah."

While emphasizing solidarity with worldwide Islam, the Nation of Islam has some distinctive doctrines. The most important and controversial one is that the white race is the devil on earth. Whites are by nature evil, who are incapable of doing right and would soon be destroyed by God's righteous judgment.

Out of the weak individuals of the black race, Yacob, a mythical renegade black scientist, created the white race: "The human beast—the serpent, the dragon, the devil and Satan—all mean one and the same: the people or race known as the white or Caucasian race, sometimes called the European race. Since, by nature, they were created liars and murderers, they are the enemies of truth and righteousness, and the enemies of those who seek the truth." African Americans are the lost tribe of Shebazz. The salvation of blacks lies not in the white man's religion, Christianity, but the blacks' true religion, Mohammedanism.

The Nation of Islam movement advocated the sense of black pride, self-help, and the separation of the races, much like other Black Nationalist movements, such as Marcus Garvey's Universal Negro Improvement Association (UNIA) and the Moorish Science Temple founded by Noble Drew Ali in Newark, New Jersey. But unlike Garvey's UNIA, which focused on politics, the Nation of Islam and the Moorish Science Temple were religious movements more than anything else. The Moorish Science Temple movement was actually a forerunner of the Nation of Islam and contributed many members to the latter after the assassination of Noble Drew Ali. The Black Muslims are required to maintain a highly ascetic morality that forbids tobacco, drugs, extramarital sexual relationships, interracial marriage, dancing, movies, sports, laziness, lying, and other enticements. Garvey's movement had the political goal of returning black people to Africa and Africa to black people. On the contrary, the Nation of Islam has no explicit goal. Instead of returning to Africa, they rather call instead for a separate nation here in the United States and several states set aside for the purpose.

Black Muslims have been remarkably successful in rehabilitating ex-convicts and drug addicts and in building a strong economic base. The organization has enjoyed magnetic appeal to many blacks living without hope in urban ghettos. One of them was Malcolm X, the most famous convert and the spokesperson for the movement. But the influence of the Nation of Islam has gone beyond its membership. Its religiously tinged nationalistic doctrine gained a much wider audience within the Unites States and abroad. In par-

A member of the Nation of Islam stands in uniform in the Dag Hammarskjold Plaza, New York City, on October 16, 1996, the one-year anniversary of the Million Man March.

Photo by Stephen Ferry/Liaison/Getty Images.

ticular, Malcolm X's furious rhetoric against Christianity, the White civilization, and the racial integrationist movement stirred the world and irrevocably transformed racial consciousness. In the 1990s, Louis Farrakhan, a new leader, tried to revive the sense of black pride and the separatist ideology and organized a Million Man March in Washington.

See also Black Nationalist Movement; Farrakhan, Louis; Garvey, Marcus; Malcolm X; Million Man March on Washington; Muhammad, Elijah.

Further Reading

Baldwin, James. *The Fire Next Time.* New York: Dell, 1962.

Cone, James H. *Martin & Malcolm & America: A Dream or a Nightmare.* Maryknoll, NY: Orbis Books, 1991.

Essein-Udom. *Black Nationalism: The Search for an Identity in America.* Chicago: University of Chicago Press, 1962.

Lincoln, C. Eric. *The Black Muslims in America.* 1961. Rev. ed. Boston: Beacon Press, 1973.

————. *The Supreme Wisdom: The Solution to the So-Called Negroes' Problem.* Chicago: University of Islam, 1957.

Muhammad, Elijah. *Message to the Blackman in America.* Chicago: Muhammad Mosque of Islam No. 2, 1965.

Dong Ho Cho

National Advisory Commission on Civil Disorders

The National Advisory Commission on Civil Disorders, also referred to as the Kerner Commission, after chairman Otto Kerner, then governor of Illinois, was formed by President Lyndon B. Johnson on July 28, 1967, to investigate the causes and implications of full-scale urban riots in black sections of many major cities, including Los Angeles, Newark, Chicago, Cleveland, Atlanta, New York, and Detroit. The report, issued in 1968, stated that pervasive discrimination and segregation in employment, education, and housing had excluded African Americans from the benefits of economic progress. The commission warned that the United States was "moving toward two societies, one black, one white—separate and unequal," replete with a "system of apartheid" in which a largely poor and minority population would reside in the central cities while the more prosperous and predominantly white population would dwell in surrounding suburban rings. The commission argued that an intensification of racial divisions was not inevitable and called for a sweeping national action plan to set an alternative course for the country, including legislation to create jobs, job training, and affordable housing. The commission's recommendations were largely ignored by the president and Congress. One month after the release of the Kerner report in March 1968, rioting broke out in more than one hundred cities after the assassination of civil rights leader Martin Luther King Jr.

See also Kerner Commission Report; King, Martin Luther, Jr.; Race Riots.

Kenneth J. Guest

National Association for the Advancement of Colored People (NAACP)

The nation's oldest and largest civil rights organization, the National Association for the Advancement of Colored People (NAACP), was founded in 1909 by an interracial group of citizens in response to a 1908 race riot in Springfield, Illinois, home to President Abraham Lincoln for twenty-four years. Convening in New York City, sixty founding members signed a "Call" to form a racial justice organization to pursue and safeguard black civil and political rights. In 1911, the NAACP incorporated and commenced its work to end racial violence, abolish forced segregation, and promote equal education and civil rights. Only seven of the sixty founding members were African Americans, who included W.E.B. Du Bois, Ida B. Wells-Barnett, and Mary Church Terrell, but the proportion of African American members continuously increased to the extent that the organization became a largely African American civil rights organization. However, compared with Black Nationalist organizations, the NAACP has remained as a biracial organization, with many Jewish and other white members playing an active role, especially during the civil rights movement era.

Among the NAACP's immediate priorities was to end the horrific practice of lynching, and toward this goal the NAACP supported the federal Dyer bill introduced by Missouri Congressman Leonidas Dyer in 1918. The Dyer bill sought to punish those who participated in or failed to prosecute lynch mobs. Although the bill passed the House in 1922, a filibuster in the Senate halted its passage. The NAACP also published a comprehensive review of lynching records, "Thirty Years of Lynching in the United States, 1889–1919," which fueled much public debate and ultimately, helped to stem lynching. The NAACP employed a variety of strategies to combat racial discrimination in all spheres and institutions of civil society. These strategies included crusading against racial violence; petitioning and organizing for legal redress; publicizing African American achievements and excellence; studying socioeconomic conditions and migration patterns; publishing *The Crisis*, founded by W.E.B. Du Bois as a monthly magazine devoted to race topics; and holding mass meetings, sit-in demonstrations, and other public events (Price-Spratlen 2003, 306). Through these multiple and varied activities, the NAACP evolved into a formidable institution for racial and social change.

A cornerstone of NAACP accomplishments are legal victories fought in the court system such as the 1915 *Guinn v. United States*, which invalidated voter registration requirements that contained "grandfather clauses" requiring that registered voters be descendants of men who were enfranchised before the enactment of the Fifteenth Amendment. In addition to concerted legal action to obtain full citizenship rights for African Americans, the NAACP fought racial segregation in public schools in the landmark 1954 decision in the *Brown v. Board of Education* case and in residential neighborhoods by nullifying restrictive covenants, a clause in real estate deeds that prohibited a white buyer from selling the property to blacks. Thurgood Marshall (later, the first black U.S. Supreme Court justice) became the NAACP's special counsel, and in 1946, he founded the NAACP Legal Defense and Education Fund, which served as a model for civil rights organizations for other racial minorities, including Puerto Ricans, Mexicans, and Asian Americans.

Headquartered in Baltimore, Maryland, the NAACP is a network of more than 2,200 local branches in all fifty states and the District of Columbia. Local branches pay membership dues and are divided into seven regions that are managed and governed by a National Board of Directors. The chairman of the board in 2005 is Julian Bond, founder of the Student Nonviolent Coordinating Committee (SNCC), and the official NAACP spokesperson is president and CEO Kweisi Mfume, a former congressman from Baltimore, Maryland. The NAACP Washington Bureau represents one of the primary forces in civil rights lobbying, and its activities are directed primarily at Congress, the Executive Branch, and governmental agencies.

With around 9,000 members in 1917, NAACP's membership now exceeds 500,000. Recent issues include public safety and efforts to stem the influx of handguns into African American communities. The NAACP has been criticized for a top-down approach to organization building and a preference for elite leadership, and its influence may have waned since the 1950s and 1960s civil rights movement, particularly in light of its recent $4 million debt and the firing of its executive director, Benjamin F. Chavis Jr. Nevertheless, it remains an integral and reputable institution in the ongoing struggle for racial justice and equality.

See also Civil Rights Movement; Du Bois, W.E.B.

Further Reading

Price-Spratlen, Townsend. "The Urban Context of Historical Activism: NAACP Depression Era Insurgency and Organization Building Activity." *Sociological Quarterly* 44, no. 3 (2003).

Rudwick, Elliot. *W.E.B. Du Bois: Voice of the Black Protest Movement.* Champaign-Urbana: University of Illinois Press, 1960.

Tarry Hum

National Chicano Moratorium

On August 29, 1970, more than 25,000 protesters, mostly Mexican Americans, from all over Aztlan, marched down Whittier Boulevard through East Los Angeles, joining the first National Chicano Moratorium. It was the culmination of many smaller moratoriums held before on local levels. Youth, families, children and community organizers denounced the United States's involvement in the Vietnam War and pointed to racial oppression within the United States. They chanted the slogan "Nuestra Guerra es Aquil," meaning "Our War is not in Vietnam. It is here at home." Antiwar sentiment had escalated just prior to the National Chicano Moratorium, with huge demonstrations of 50,000 people occurring on the East Coast and 250,000 people in San Francisco.

Chicanos made up only 6 percent of the U.S. population but suffered 20 percent of the U.S. casualties in the Vietnam War. Many Chicano activists saw in the Vietnamese struggle against the United States their own struggle against internal colonialism as a subordinated nation. The Chicano Moratorium raised strong nationalism and demanded self-determination of Mexican Americans, an end to police and Immigration and Naturalization Service abuses and terror, relevant and bilingual education, no police state in the neighborhoods, and U.S. forces out of Latin America, the Middle East, the Philippines, and Columbia. Union jobs and decent wages, housing, and health care were also demanded. Many demonstrators were teargassed and beaten by Los Angeles police. Outspoken journalist Ruben Salazar, while relaxing with a beer in a café, was killed by a teargas projectile, which was shot into the bar at point-blank range.

See also War and Racial Inequality.

Dong-Ho Cho

National Congress of American Indians (NCAI)

The National Congress of American Indians (NCAI) was founded in 1944 as a result of the Indian New Deal, more formally known as the 1934 Indian Reorganization Act or the Wheeler-Howard Act. Most of the founders were Indians who had worked for the Bureau of Indian Affairs. With the formation of the NCAI, American Indian politics entered a new phase as leaders in the NCAI became skilled lobbyists and political advocates for Indian policies and issues at the national level.

The NCAI emphasized the need for unity and cooperation among tribal governments for the protection of their treaty and sovereign rights in response to assimilation policies that the United States forced on the tribal governments, often in contradiction of their treaty rights and status. Since 1944, the NCAI has worked to inform the public and Congress of the sovereign rights of American Indians and to serve as a forum for consensus-based policy development among its membership of more than 250 tribal governments. The NCAI has also monitored federal policies that affect tribal-government interests.

The NCAI, however, did not gain widespread support within the Native American community until the early 1950s, when it became the center of organized opposition to the termination of American Indian treaty rights. The NCAI was different from earlier Native American groups, such as the Society of American Indians, in that it maintained its focus as a national lobby and advocated for Indian issues in Washington, DC. In the 1960s, the NCAI was often criticized by younger activists groups, such as the National Indian Youth Council and the American Indian Movement, because the NCAI's activities are limited to lobbying and advocating.

See also American Indian Movement (AIM); Indian Reorganization Act of 1934 (IRA); Red Power Movement.

Sookhee Oh

National Crime Victimization Survey (NCVS)

The National Crime Victimization Survey (NCVS) is an annual, nationally representative survey of 42,000 households meant to determine the frequency, characteristics, and consequences of various kinds of crimes in the United States. The results can be sorted and analyzed with regard to gender, race, age, and urbanization. The Bureau of Justice Statistics (BJS) has administered this survey since 1973. The data collected through this survey is available to researchers and has resulted in many published books and articles addressing crime, changes in crime rates over time, and the relationship between crime rates and race. Preliminary analyses of this survey are also published by the BJS, allowing those without advanced statistical training to gain access to the data and findings.

Since 1997, as part of this NCVS, the BJS and the FBI have been collecting data about hate crimes. These are the first significant data on hate crimes broken down by race available in the United States, and so the NCVS has been important both in terms of research and public policy with regard to these crimes. The numbers found in this survey have forced both academia and lawmakers to take note of hate crimes as a serious social problem. The study has also revealed such surprising findings as African Americans being disproportionately represented among those charged with hate crimes, particularly against whites.

Mikaila Mariel Lemonik Arthur

National Labor Relations Act

See Wagner Act.

National Origins Act of 1924

The National Origins Act of 1924 severely restricted the flow of immigrants to the United States and marked the culmination of forty years of anti-immigrant legislation. Also known as the Immigration Act of 1924 or the National Origins Quota Act of 1924, the National Origins Act was designed to preserve the existing ethnic makeup of the population, which was dominated by western and northern Europeans.

Millions of new immigrants arrived in the United States between 1880 and 1924, dramatically changing the nation's demography. The vast majority of these newcomers hailed from southern Europe, particularly Italy, and Eastern Europe, including a large number of Jews from Poland and Russia. At the same time, rising nativism in the United States began to find expression in a series of laws designed to limit and control the ethnic and racial composition of the U.S. population. The Chinese Exclusion Act of 1882 initiated the use of national origins to restrict immigration, barring Chinese laborers. Later legislation expanded and extended this exclusion, which remained in place until 1943. The Immigration Act of 1907 doubled the head tax on immigrants from $2 to $4 and granted the president powers to block immigration. In 1911, the U.S. Immigration Commission, also known as the Dillingham Commission, embraced the psuedoscience of the eugenics movement. It argued that immigrants from southern and eastern Europe were inferior to other races and as such were degenerate and unassimilable, becoming the source of many social problems. The commission proposed a bill based on national origins to limit this immigration, though it was not enacted into law.

World War I saw a decrease in immigration to the United States and a rise in out-migration, as many immigrants left the country in the face of intense Americanization crusades. At the conclusion of the war, the Immigration Act of 1917 continued the restriction trend by requiring language literacy for immigrants over the age of sixteen and creating an Asian "barred zone" extending exclusion to India, Burma, Malaysia, Arabia, Afghanistan, and parts of Russia. Despite attempts to impose stricter limits, immigration rates began to rise again in the postwar period. In response, Congress passed the National Origins Act of 1921, establishing temporary immigration quotas of three percent of each foreign-born nationality living in the United States based on the 1910 census, with a ceiling of 350,000 European immigrants. Originally enacted for one year, in 1922 it was extended for two more. Also in 1922, Congress passed a punitive and discriminatory law removing citizenship from any U.S.-born woman who married an alien ineligible for citizenship.

The National Origins Act of 1924 set a new temporary annual quota of two percent of the foreign-born members of each nationality living in the United States in 1890. Setting the bar at this historically low point intentionally excluded southern and eastern Europeans, who immigrated in much larger numbers after 1890. The act further placed a ceiling of 150,000 total immigrants from Eastern Hemisphere countries, placed no quotas on Western Hemisphere nations, and completely excluded Asian immigration (with the exception of the U.S. colony in the Philippines). Exempted from the quotas were nuclear family members, ministers, professors, students, and women who had lost their citizenship through marriage to an alien. Within the quotas, preferences were given to parents, spouses, and unmarried children under age twenty-one, as well as to skilled agricultural workers and their families. The act also shifted the administration of the immigration process to U.S. consular officials abroad.

The temporary quotas of the 1924 act were made permanent in 1929, and the 1920 census was established as the basis for their calculation. The 1929 revisions also expanded the notion of national origins to a percentage of "national stock," incorporating native and foreign-born Americans. The National Origins Act and its 1929 revisions gave clear preference to immigrants from northern and western Europe, who in the ensuing years received 83 percent of all visas, compared to 15 percent for those from southern and eastern Europe and 2 percent from the rest of the world.

In 1921, then vice president Calvin Coolidge stated, "America must be kept American." The National Origins Act of 1924 succeeded in codifying the nativist and anti-immigrant sentiments of the age, including a belief in Nordic superiority and a fear of race mixing. As a result, the United States enacted the most restrictive and comprehensive immigration laws in its history and provided the foundation of immigration policy until 1965.

See also Asiatic Barred Zone; Chinese Exclusion Act of 1882; Dillingham Report; Eugenics Movement; Nativism and the Anti-immigrant Movements.

Further Reading

Foner, Nancy. *From Ellis Island to JFK: New York's Two Great Waves of Immigration.* New Haven, CT: Yale University Press, 2002.

Salyer, Lucy E. *Laws Harsh as Tigers: Chinese Immigrants and the Shaping of Modern Immigration Law*. Chapel Hill: University of North Carolina Press, 1995.

Kenneth J. Guest

National Origins Quota Act

See National Origins Act of 1924.

Native Americans

See Indian Allotment Act of 1887; Indian Citizenship Act of 1924; Indian Claims Commission (ICC); Indian Occupation of Alcatraz Island; Indian Reorganization Act of 1934 (IRA); Indian Reservations; Indian Self-Determination and Education Assistance Act of 1975 (ISDEAA); Native Americans, Conquest of; Red Power Movement; Slavery and American Indians.

Native Americans, Conquest of

The continent of North America was a peaceable place where Native Americans lived in harmony with nature, before white settlers arrived there. Those first people had migrated from Asia across Beringia, a land that then connected Siberia to present-day Alaska, following the large animal herds at least 15,000 years ago. They spread over what is now the Americas, ranging from the Arctic to the southern tip of South America, and created hundreds of Indian nations with different languages and unique cultures. Italian explorer Christopher Columbus's arrival in the Bahamas in 1492 marked the European intrusion into the existence of these indigenous people. The Indian population in 1492 was at least 72 million in the Western Hemisphere, with more than five million of them living in what eventually became the United States. After the onset of European contacts and colonization, the Indian population of North America decreased tremendously, to 600,000 by 1800 and to 250,000 by the 1890s. European diseases, warfare, and the U.S. government's geographical removal and relocation caused the deaths of many Indians and the destruction of their ways of life. The history of Indians in the United States has been a history of conquest.

Attacks on Indians by British Settlers during the Colonial Period

After Columbus landed in the New World, European explorers, Jesuit priests, and slave hunters swarmed to the Americas in the seventeenth century. They were anxious to find gold, convert the "savages," and capture the natives and sell them as slaves. At first, the Indians helped Europeans settle down in the New World by providing food, shelter, and land and by teaching them how to grow crops and how to fish and catch wild animals. But European settlers treated Indians as "savages" and tried to exterminate them by using all kinds of methods, including spreading diseases through blankets contaminated with germs and killing them by swords and guns.

Hernando De Soto, Francisco Vasquez Coronado, and Hernando Cortez each explored Florida, New Mexico and California to find gold but could not find any. However, the Spanish government was successful in converting Indians to Catholics. Unlike the Spaniards, whose goal was to find gold and other riches of the Indians, and the French, who concentrated on the fur trade, the British used every method to take away land from Indians. When English settlers landed in Jamestown, Virginia, in 1607, they were well received by Powhatans. But, as settlers started to take Indian land, as well as their crops and games, Indians became vigilant against the Europeans' greed and hostility. The tensions between the Europeans and Indians grew deeper, which made warfare unavoidable. Only thirty-seven years after welcoming the first English settlers in Jamestown, the Powhatans were defeated by the English.

The pilgrims who arrived in Plymouth on the *Mayflower* in 1620 were well received by the Wampanoags, led by Massasoit. After Massasoit celebrated the first Thanksgiving with the pilgrims in 1621, more and more settlers came to the New England shore from England. From 1630 on, England sent more than one thousand English settlers to Massachusetts with a slogan "to build a perfect Christian Society in the New World." They were eager to buy or take lands from the Indians because land meant commodity, wealth, and security for them. Indians, who had no concept of land ownership, considered land as a gift from god to be shared by everybody, so Massasoit signed the papers when the English wanted any land. Problems occurred when the English forbade Indians to hunt and fish in the land that Massasoit had allowed settlers to use. When Massasoit died and his second son, Metacomet (Europeans called him King Philip) became the chief, he prepared for war against the British as more and more settlers moved into Wampanoag territory and killed Indians. In 1675, Metacomet and his warriors destroyed twelve English colonies out of fifty-two with the help of other allied Indian tribes. But after the several months of prolonged warfare, Metacomet's warriors were defeated and Metacomet was killed. Finally, the British soldiers defeated the Wampanoags.

In the early eighteenth century, the British colonists, who tried to expand their territory from the Atlantic coast to the West, came into contact with the French in the Mississippi area. After ten years of warfare, the British defeated the French in 1763 by winning Montreal and occupied Canada and the vast Indian land from the Appalachians to the Mississippi River. After the war, the British Parliament started to collect money from the new colony to offset the financial deficit incurred by the war against France.

Broken Treaties, 1778–1871

When the colonies became an independent nation in 1776, Indians hoped to maintain better relations with Anglos after the British, the French, and the Spanish left. However, Indians were forced to live under even more aggravated circumstances. The U.S. government signed treaties with Indian nations and then broke them to take Indian land and distribute it to white settlers. After frontiersman Daniel Boone invaded Indian land and built a village called Boone's Borough in the West, poor farmers and laborers who did not own any land wanted to go west. As tens of thousands of white settlers moved west of the Mississippi River, they killed Indians, destroyed their ways of life, and took their lands. For example, when the Shawnees tried to make the Ohio River the permanent boundary between the U.S. and Indian land, William

Henry Harrison's troops destroyed the Prophetstown founded by the Shawnee Chief Tecumseh in 1812. General Andrew Jackson and his army slaughtered more than ten thousand Creek Indians during the Creek War of 1813–1814 and took 14 million acres—two-thirds of their land.

When Andrew Jackson became the president of the United States in 1828, he started an aggressive policy toward Indians by using the power of the U.S. Army. With the Indian Removal Act passed by Congress, the U.S. government massively removed Indian tribes from their native lands and forcefully relocated them to unfamiliar and barren land in the West. In 1834, Indian Territory was created, including present-day Kansas, most of Oklahoma, and parts of Nebraska, Colorado, and Wyoming, which continued to be reduced until it eventually became the size of present-day Oklahoma. The U.S. government forced Indian tribes to move to Indian Territory, but the removal and relocation of the Cherokees from Northern Georgia to Oklahoma between 1838 and 1839 was especially tragic.

After gold was found in the Cherokee land in Northern Georgia, the state of Georgia claimed jurisdiction over a part of the Cherokee land. The Cherokees resisted the pressures to cede their land and move west of the Mississippi River. After the Treaty of New Echota was signed between the U.S. government and some Cherokee people, Chief John Ross and other leaders protested. However, General Winfield Scott and his army invaded the Cherokee Nation and forced them to move out of their land. Chief John Ross and almost seventeen thousand Cherokees were held in stockades until they finally removed themselves into thirteen groups and traveled north and west from Georgia to the Indian Territory in Oklahoma. They marched one thousand miles, riding on horses or wagons or walking in freezing rains and blizzards for five months until they reached their destination. During this long march, approximately four thousand Cherokee Indians were reported to have died from starvation and disease. Also, about eight thousand Navajos were forced to walk three hundred miles from Arizona to a reservation in New Mexico by Kit Carson and his troops.

After removing Indians from their nations, the federal government started driving Indians into reservations. When the transcontinental railroad linking the East and West coasts was completed in 1869, the settlers took a lot of vast Indian hunting grounds and slaughtered a large number of buffalo. Plains Indians lost their supply of buffalo, which they needed for food, tents, and other necessities while those in the Indian Territories were forced onto smaller and smaller plots of poor lands unfit for cultivation. White settlers continued to demand more land, and the Indian reservations shrank rapidly.

Terminating the Identity and Culture of Indians through Military Campaigns

After the U.S. troops forcefully removed Indians from their native and sacred land to unfamiliar and barren Indian territories and relocated them on tiny reservations, the federal government made every effort to eradicate Indian identity and culture. With the Indian Appropriation Act of 1871, the U.S. government ceased recognizing Indian tribes as sovereign nations and forbade them to leave the reservations without permission.

When gold was discovered on the Cheyenne reservations in the Black Hills of South Dakota, General George Custer and his army attacked Sioux, Cheyenne, and Arapaho in the Little Big Horn Valley in his campaign to force them into reservations. The U.S. government drove the surviving Indians to reservations and took most of the Sioux land from the Indians. The U.S. Army also chased approximately eight hundred fleeing Nez Perce Indians and forced them onto a reservation and sent the survivors to Indian Territory in Oklahoma. The Black Hills in Dakota had been a sacred land for the Sioux Indians for many years. But, white miners invaded the Black Hills to find gold, with about fifteen thousand miners swarming to this area in 1875. The federal government asked the Sioux to sell the Black Hills, but they refused and decided to fight for the sacred land in late 1875 under the command of the great warrior Sitting Bull. In this battle, Indians had achieved their greatest victory yet, but after General Custer was killed in the battle, white people demanded harsh revenge against Indians. They redrew the boundary lines of the Black Hills, placing it outside the reservation and open to white settlement. Within a year, the Sioux nation was defeated and broken.

After losing the Black Hills as well as other lands, the Sioux people became dependent upon the U.S. government for food, clothing, and other things. Encountering starvation, fatal diseases, and reduced rations, they desperately needed hopes and dreams. The Ghost Dance Religion initiated by the prophet Wovoka was spreading among northern Plains Indians. Ghost dancers wore a spiritual shirt, believing that it would protect them from white people's bullets. They also believed that the Great Spirit would protect Indians from the white power and revive the Indians who were killed. In 1890, the Sioux people were totally enthralled to this religion. Even Sitting Bull learned this dance and taught it to other Sioux Indians. On the other hand, white settlers believed the rumor that Ghost Dance believers would kill the settlers. Upon receiving the petition from the settlers, the U.S. army marched through the Plains to arrest Sitting Bull. After Sitting Bull was shot during a violent fight between the Indian police and the followers of Sitting Bull, some Sioux Indians joined Big Foot, the leader of the Miniconjou Sioux.

The military captured Big Foot, known as the Ghost Dance leader, and his followers, and took them to Wounded Knee Creek. There were 470 soldiers and around 350 Indians, including women, old men, and children. The military was going to disarm Big Foot's warriors before removing them by trains to the Cheyenne River Reservation. But when some warriors fired at the soldiers, they fired back and killed one-half of the warriors in one volley. The combat between the soldiers and the warriors continued, and thirty-one soldiers and about three hundred Indians were killed during this massacre. The troops had stripped the Ghost Dance shirts off the dead bodies and shoved the remaining bodies into the trench and buried them. This was the last resistance of the Sioux Indians, which completed the European Conquest of Indians.

Conclusion

There are several indigenous peoples around the world, who make up about 5 percent of the total population of the globe, but no other indigenous group has been so cruelly massacred and terminated than Indians in the United

States. During the colonial period, English settlers were more cruel to Native Americans than Spanish or French settlers had been. As noted, the U.S. government's changing policies toward Native Americans contributed to the extermination of Indians, appropriation of their vast land, and destruction of their culture and religion. The surviving Indians in the United States (approximately 2.4 million in 2000), whether living in reservations or cities, in general maintain a low standard of living and poor health conditions comparable to African Americans. But partly because of a relatively small population and partly because of Americans' amnesia regarding history, neither scholars nor policymakers have paid enough attention to "Indian issues."

See also American Indian Movement (AIM); Columbus Day Controversy; Ghost Dance Religion; Indian Allotment Act of 1887; Indian Occupation of Alcatraz Island; Indian Reservations; Native Americans, Forced Relocation of; Native Americans, Prejudice and Discrimination against; Noble Savage; Red Power Movement; Sioux Outbreak of 1890.

Further Reading

Bragdon, Kathleen Joan. *The Columbia Guide to American Indians of the Northeast*. New York: Columbia University Press, 2001.

"Cherokee Indians Forcibly Removed from North Georgia." http://ngeorgia.com/history/hghisttt.html.

Cothran, Helen, ed. *The Conquest of the New World*. San Diego: Greenhaven Press, 2002.

————, ed. *Early American Civilization and Exploration—1607*. San Diego: Greenhaven Press, 2003.

Jones, Constance. *The European Conquest of North America*. New York: Facts On File, 1995.

Sheppard, Donald E. @NACC. (Native American Consulting Committee). *Native American Conquest*. American History for Teens. http://e-student.net/inset32.html.

Thornton, Russell. *American Indian Holocaust and Survival: A Population History since 1492*. Norman: University of Oklahoma Press, 1987.

On Kyung Joo

Native Americans, Forced Relocation of

Andrew Jackson, as the seventh president of the United States (1829–1837) introduced the Indian Removal bill, enacted in 1830, which made it possible to legally force all tribes remaining east of the Mississippi River to relocate west of the river. The Indian Removal bill, the first step toward the creation of a national reservation system, designated Indian Territory in the present-day states of Iowa, Kansas, Oklahoma, and Arkansas and required Native Americans to move there. The bill specified that tribes should be paid for their lands through negotiation. Resistance to the sale and relocation, however, was met with force to gain the tribes' compliance.

Jackson's removal policy was directed primarily against Native Americans who preferred to live in traditional ways under their own tribal government.

The Indian Removal bill permitted members of these tribes to stay in the Southeast only if they agreed to live in the manner of white settlers. This meant that the tribe had to agree to divide the land into allotments to farm, become "civilized," and abide by the laws of the states they lived in.

By the time this bill was passed, the white population of the United States had increased to nearly 13 million. More land was needed to accommodate their needs. There was also growing animosity toward tribes as European settlement in the Southeast increased rapidly in the 1820s. At the same time, the government wanted to hold a buffer zone between United States and European holdings in the western part of the continent by moving eastern American Indians. This plan would allow for American expansion westward from the original colonies to the Mississippi River.

Five tribes of the Southeast—the Cherokees, Creeks, Chickasaws, Choctaws, and Seminoles—who already had begun assimilating, also had to sign treaties and move west to the Indian Territory under military escort. Under the terms of the treaties, the U.S. government promised that it would pay for tribal lands if the tribe gave up their eastern territory. It also promised to pay the cost of relocating and to support Native Americans for one year after relocation. After the treaties had been signed, some bands of the five "civilized" tribes decided to start for Indian Territory as soon as possible, hoping to obtain the best land. Other bands were determined to stay on in their ancestral homelands until the army forced them to leave.

In 1838, the last group of Cherokees began their journey on what became known as the Trail of Tears. Because most Cherokees had refused to abandon their land until the government demanded it, they did not have time to prepare for the trip. They suffered from disease and hunger, and out of 180,000 people who set out on the Trail of Tears, only about 140,000 (78 percent) reached the Indian Territory in Oklahoma. The figures do not measure the grief they felt about leaving their homes. This forced relocation also involved an eight-year war between the U.S. government and bands of Seminoles led by Chief Osceola. The Seminoles won the war, escaping into the Florida Everglades, out of reach of government troops. There they made a new life for their people.

Native Americans who survived the journey to Indian Territory found adapting to reservation life difficult. The main challenge, besides the unfamiliar environment, was frequent trouble with indigenous local tribes whose ways of life were quite different from theirs. The local tribes moved from place to place to hunt buffalo. As the buffalo population decreased and more Native Americans moved to Indian Territory, conflicts over hunting rights and dwelling resources increased among tribes. In addition, the U.S. government often failed to keep the promise that they would provide food, goods, and money and to protect them from attack by other tribes and white settlers. As more displaced Native Americans crowded into the Indian Territory, the government required them to live on smaller reservations. By the mid-1840s, most of the Native Americans who had lived east of the Mississippi River were gone. Between 1830 and 1850, the United States had forced at least 100,000 Native Americans to relocate to western reservations.

See also American Indian Movement (AIM); Columbus Day Controversy; Ghost Dance Religion; Indian Allotment Act of 1887; Indian Occupation of Alcatraz Island; Indian Reservations; Native Americans, Conquest of; Native Americans, Prejudice and Discrimination against; Noble Savage; Red Power Movement; Sioux Outbreak of 1890.

Further Reading

Forman, Grant. *Indian Removal: The Emigration of the Five Civilized Tribes of Indians*. Norman: University of Oklahoma Press, 1953.

Sokolow, Gary. *Native Americans and the Law: A Dictionary*. Santa Barbara, CA: ABC-CLIO, 2000.

Sookhee Oh

Native Americans, Prejudice and Discrimination against

Native Americans, the original inhabitants of the Americas, have been subjected to the systemic violence of extermination and subordination by white invaders since the fateful encounter in the late fifteenth century. America's westward expansion meant genocide and land thievery to these indigenous populations. The completion of the continental expansion put the surviving natives in isolated reservations. Whites' racial prejudice toward Native Americans has justified the acts of conquest and domination. The foundation myth of America glorified the massacre of Indians and the taking of their land as a civilizing mission. Indian killers became folk heroes. The indigenous people of America became, in the eyes of white settlers, subhuman savages who had to be annihilated for the progress of civilization and empire. To many white settlers, the best Indians were dead Indians.

The prejudice against Native Americans consists, first of all, in the European invention of the term *Indians*. The use of the generic category has erased at one stroke the rich diversity of hundreds of tribes or nations that had or have different languages, social forms, and levels of civilization. And it created and has perpetuated the fictitious impression that those native tribes share the same basic qualities. Europeans defined the "Indian" qualities invariably as the other of their own self-image, Christians and the representatives of morality and civilization. Like any stereotype, the Indian images were constructed by wrenching some characteristics of a few tribes out of cultural and historical contexts and generalizing them as the common traits inherent to "Indians." The racist images, thus fabricated, were loaded with strong moral judgment, usually negative, but often positive. It can be said, therefore, that the racial prejudice toward Native Americans tells more about the bearers of prejudice than about the objects thereof.

One popular "Indian" image is that of a bloodthirsty savage. In fact, however, most Indian tribes sought to avoid conflict wherever possible, although some intertribal rivalries existed. European colonizers often took advantage of such conflicts. Scalping was not common. It was practiced, when practiced at all, within the limit of retributive justice that a wrong must be paid by equal measure. Scalping spread all over the country when white settlers started paying huge sums of money for killed Indians. Indian scalps served as effective proof of dead Indians. A male Indian scalp was rewarded with $134 in mid-eighteenth-century Pennsylvania. Some whites found a great business opportunity in butchering defenseless natives of old age. The image of the cruel savage was in fact the projection of European invaders' disavowed aggressiveness.

The opposite image of a noble savage has long quenched the nostalgic thirst of European Americans for the supposedly innocent and uncorrupted world before the coming of civilization. This image, too, although positive, is remote from the reality of Native American life, and merely contributes to the public ignorance. Moreover, the innocent, simple, and naturalist way of life is always presented as a vanishing culture. "Real" Indians are, in whites' minds, destined to disappear either by annihilation or by assimilation.

The mass media, particularly western-themed movies, reproduce these images over and over again and eternalize them as changeless entities, although the catastrophic contact of some four centuries has irrevocably transformed the lives of Native Americans. The continuous stereotyping blinds the general public to the current plight of Native American reservation life as well as to the centuries-long violence and discrimination that produced the plight.

See also American Indian Movement (AIM); Columbus Day Controversy; Ghost Dance Religion; Indian Allotment Act of 1887; Indian Occupation of Alcatraz Island; Indian Reservations; Native Americans, Conquest of; Native Americans, Forced Relocation of; Noble Savage; Red Power Movement; Sioux Outbreak of 1890; Sports Mascots.

Further Reading

Berkhoffer, Robert F., Jr. *The White Man's Indian: Images of the American Indian from Columbus to the Present*. New York: Knopf, 1978.

Drinnon, Richard. *Facing West: The Metaphysics of Indian Hating and Empire-Building*. Minneapolis: University of Minnesota Press, 1980.

Huhndorf, Shari M. *Going Native: Indians in the American Cultural Imagination*. Ithaca, NY: Cornell University Press, 2001.

Pearce, Roy Harvey. *Savagism and Civilization: A Study of the Indian and the American Mind*. Berkeley: University of California, 1988.

Dong-Ho Cho

Nativism and the Anti-Immigrant Movements

The United States has been a nation of immigrants and for immigrants. From the earliest settlers to the latest newcomers, millions of immigrants have arrived, settled, and contributed to the building of the nation. And yet, it has also been a nation of anti-immigrant movements. Immigrants often have been reviled as sources of political, economic, and social problems. Discriminatory laws against immigrants have been enacted; their fundamental rights have been denied; and they have even been physically assaulted. The overall attitudes and actions toward immigrants have oscillated between welcoming new immigrants and restricting them.

This ambivalent attitude toward immigrants started after white Anglo-Saxon Protestants established themselves as a dominant host group and became the "native." Since then, the category of the native has expanded to white Protestants and then to all whites in contemporary America. As the category of the native has changed, the targets of anti-immigrant movements have also changed from non-Anglo-Saxons to non-Protestants and now to non-white immigrants.

Conditions Fostering Anti-Immigrant Movements

The anti-immigrant movements have not been constant. They have surged and receded. What factors account for the rise of anti-immigrant movements? Despite the differences in different historical periods, some general patterns can be discerned. It seems obvious that when a large number of immigrants came to the United States, it created a conducive condition for the surge of nativism. When new waves of immigrants arrived on American shores during the periods of 1880–1924 and 1970–2003, anti-immigrant movements arose in America.

The volume of immigrants is just one condition. More importantly, nativist reactions have surged when a large number of new immigrants were physically and culturally different from the dominant native-born Americans. Such differences or perceived differences provided a fertile ground for anti-immigrant movements. During the 1880–1924 periods, Italian, Irish, Jewish, and eastern European immigrants, as well as Asian immigrants, were thought to be significantly different from the dominant "native" Anglo-Saxon Americans. These latest immigrants from southern and eastern Europe differed from the previous immigrants, and it was widely claimed that they were much more difficult to assimilate. Some nativists believed that they were even "racially" different from and inferior to the native-born whites, who were said to be of "Nordic" racial stock.

Since the late 1960s, there has been similar concern about the different national origins of the newest immigrants. Immigrants from Latin America, Asia, and the Caribbean make up the vast majority of these new immigrant groups. To the natives, they are too different and too diverse to be assimilated into American culture and to become Americans. In this regard, it should be noted that, in the United States, nativism has often taken the form of racism.

The third condition that has contributed to the anti-immigrant movements is the existence of economic, political, and social problems in the United States. In other words, the anti-immigrant sentiments have surged not only because of the large number and characteristics of immigrants but because of when the existing social, political, and economic conditions of the United States were more severe. When the United States has been at war with other countries, its economy has been contracting and in recession, and/or it has been divided by controversial social issues such as slavery, anti-immigrant activities arose and strengthened. Such conditions often led to the targeting of immigrants as scapegoats for the hardships and fears of Americans.

Different Forms of Nativism

Throughout U.S. history, nativism has been manifested in many different ways and taken a variety of forms. People organized themselves, creating anti-immigrant ideologies, publishing anti-immigrant materials, spreading anti-immigrant sentiment, and taking collective actions against immigrants, their descendants, and future immigrants. The Immigration Restriction League of 1894 and The Federation for American Immigration Reform of 1992 are two typical examples of such organizations. Nativists sometimes took violent actions against immigrants, as can be seen in the case of anti-Catholicism in the United States. Another extreme example of anti-immigrant sentiment was the Mexican Repatriation that was undertaken during the 1930s. In 1871, sixty-two Irish Catholics were killed and one hundred others injured when they protested against a militantly anti-Catholic Orange Order.

However, the most effective anti-immigrant nativist strategy was to lobby politicians to enact laws to bar or restrict the immigration of "undesirable" people. The most notorious example of such restrictive immigration laws was the Immigration Act of 1924, better known as the National Origins Act or the National Origins Quota Act. The U.S. Congress passed this law after many white supremacists, including influential scholars, such as Henry Goddard and Madison Grant, had emphasized the inferiority of non-Protestant immigrant groups. Beginning with the Chinese Exclusion Act of 1882, Congress passed a number of laws in the late nineteenth and early twentieth centuries whose chief purpose was to exclude Asian immigrants. They include the Gentlemen's Agreement of 1907 and 1908 (which banned the immigration of Japanese laborers), the 1917 Immigration Act (which barred the immigration of laborers from the Asiatic Barred Zone), and the National Origin Quota Act of 1924 (which provided for the permanent exclusion of any alien ineligible for citizenship). Since a 1790 statute made only "Caucasians" eligible for citizenship, Asians and other people from non-European countries were ineligible for citizenship and could not immigrate to the United States. Thus, anti-immigration laws restricted immigration based on race or national origin.

In the post–1965 era too, many outspoken individuals and groups have emphasized the inassimilability of Third World immigrants and have lobbied for laws to reduce immigration generally and/or change the ethnic and racial composition of immigrants. However, their efforts have not been successful. In fact, the Immigration Act of 1990 increased the number of preference immigrants by 40 percent, to 675,000 per year. No individual or group can now persuasively argue for the restriction of immigration from particular countries or regions of the world, mainly because the Immigration Act of 1965 abolished the discrimination in immigration based on national origin or race. Instead, in the post–1965 era, the general public and government of the United States are both far more concerned about the flow of illegal aliens. Most Americans think that the influx of illegal aliens has contributed to the increase in crime, welfare, job competition, and housing difficulties. As a result, in 1994 California passed a referendum that was to make illegal residents and their children ineligible for the benefits of free public education and health care. The U.S. federal government, too, tried to restrict the flow of illegal immigration by reducing illegal entry and visa overstay through more effective border patrol and enforcement of the laws on the one hand and by sanctioning employers who hire illegal residents on the other (the Immigration Reform and Control Act of 1986 and the Immigration Act of 1990).

The nativists also reacted to the influx of immigrants by lobbying for an assimilationist policy to make immigrants and their children give up their cultural traditions as soon as possible and acculturate to the American fabric along the Anglo-Saxon line. However, the pursuit of assimilationist policy also has been much less successful in the post–1965 era than in the beginning of the twentieth century. In the first two decades of the twentieth century, federal and local governments, following the nativist, ethnocentric rhetoric, tried to coerce immigrants to give up their old-world cultural orientation and attachments to their homelands. The main mission of public schools at that time was to Americanize the children of immigrants by replacing their language and cultures with English and Anglo-Saxon customs, values, and habits. But similar arguments for the one-sided assimilationist policy have not gained much support from policymakers in the post–1965 era. African American and other minority leaders and feminists had already started the multicultural movement emphasizing cultural diversity in the 1960s, concurrently with, or even before, the massive immigration of Third World immigrants began. Since the early 1970s, the U.S. government has gradually replaced the policy of Anglo-conformity with that of cultural pluralism. The change in the government's policy has been in its reaction to the multicultural movement and to the influx of new immigrants who have entirely different cultural traditions. Nativists have been successful in getting English-only laws passed in several states, but these laws making English the standard language have had little practical impact on the lives of immigrants.

Nativists have provided various arguments as to why immigration should be restricted and/or immigrants should be assimilated. Charles Jaret (2002) analyzed in detail the variety of claims on the negative impact of new immigrants. One of the most persistent arguments has been that immigrants pose a threat to the U.S. economy and place a burden on government resources. Nativists have claimed that the immigrant workers take jobs away from native-born American workers. Since immigrants are willing to accept lower wages and work under worse conditions, nativists argue, they have negative effects on American workers' ability to protect their jobs, maintain wage levels, and ensure acceptable working conditions. Thus, immigrant workers have been labeled "wage-bursters" or "wage-downers."

Nativist arguments by white workers about the negative effects of immigrants on the American labor market were typified by the anti-Chinese movement at the end of the nineteenth century. The nativists repeatedly insisted that the Chinese workers lowered wages and, consequently, the American standard of living. Led by Denis Kearney, the Workingman's Party argued that "The Chinese laborer is a curse to our land, is degrading to our morals, is a menace to our liberties, and should be restricted and forever abolished." Thus, the argument of white labor leaders about Chinese workers' "excessive competition," as well as anti-Chinese prejudice, was the major factor that contributed to the passage of the Chinese Exclusion Act by the U.S. Congress, the nation's first immigration restriction against a particular group on the basis of national origin.

In the post–1965 era, proponents of immigration restriction have used the economic-burden argument more often than the economic-threat argument. They have argued that the newest immigrants pose a greater economic burden, especially because their skills and education levels are lower than those of previous immigrants. Nativists argue that the overall economic impact of immigrants has been negative and that immigrants often aggravate the government's "fiscal crisis" because of the direct and indirect costs to the government. Under such circumstances, nativists assert that immigration is a drain on public resources and a drag on the economy. Especially in California, where large numbers of Mexican and other immigrants of generally lower economic status are settled, the economic-burden argument has gained popularity. In 1994, the anti-immigrant forces were mobilized and California voters approved Proposition 187, the enforcement of which would have deprived undocumented residents and their children of free education and medical treatment. Although it was eventually ruled unconstitutional, a few similar measures were incorporated in the Welfare Reform Law passed in 1996.

In the present era, "a new form of nativism" has emerged over the ownership of small business, which has always been the route for immigrants' upward mobility. Rooted in anger over economic disadvantage and exploitation, some native-born African Americans have targeted immigrants who own businesses in their neighborhoods, arguing that they are deprived of economic opportunities due to unfair competition from new immigrant entrepreneurs. Korean American merchants in Los Angeles have often been the victims of violent acts resulting in injuries and property damage caused by disgruntled Blacks.

These arguments against immigration have been countered by the number of studies that conclude that immigration has a positive impact on the U.S. economy. Michael Fix and Jeffrey Passel (1994) reexamined the economic effects of recent immigrants and concluded that the cost of providing welfare benefits to legal immigrants is lower than has been claimed and that the impact of immigration on job displacement and wages is far more modest than it is widely perceived to be. Furthermore, immigrants contribute to economic growth by providing inexpensive labor, being willing to work hard, and taking risks as business entrepreneurs. Proponents of immigration argue that immigrants should not be blamed for problems such as the sluggish economy, when the source of the problem lies elsewhere.

Another common argument against immigrants has been that immigrants are threats to American identity and cultural unity. The nativists assert that certain types of immigrants undermine American identity and cultural unity—common values, a common language, and common political institutions. They are, culturally, too different from the "American mainstream" to be Americanized and too diverse among themselves to be culturally unified. The nativists assert that diverse immigrants are a direct threat to American identity and may lead U.S. society to cultural fragmentation.

Such an argument has a long historical precedent. In the 1830s–1840s, when large numbers of Irish and German Catholic immigrants arrived, anti-Catholic activities surged in the United States to protect Protestant America from these "un-American" foreigners. Later, a similar argument was used to protect against the "unassimilable" Chinese. For the same reason, the alien land laws were passed in California in 1913 and 1920 to prevent "un-American" Japanese immigrants from owning American agricultural land. The effort of keeping America as it was defined by nativists resulted in the enactment of anti-immigrant laws like the National Origins Quota Act of 1924.

The same argument—immigrants' threats to American identity and cultural unity—has been used again against recent immigrants. These recent waves of immigrants have been physically and culturally diverse among themselves and different from dominant white America, altering the nation's ethnic mix significantly. White Americans were again threatened by the influx of "different" people, mostly coming from Latin America and Asia. The nativists once again assert that America is going through an identity crisis and "disuniting of America" (Schlesinger 1991). They warn that these newest immigrants, in conjunction with the upsurge in ethnic awareness, may cause the fragmentation of American society and a national identity crisis.

Based on the fear of such cultural fragmentation, in the early 1980s, nativists launched a movement to restrict the language of government to English only. The campaign won broad support among Americans who believe that cultural unity is necessary to maintain the United States as a nation-state. Nativists also argued that immigrants needed to learn English for their own survival. But, in fact, the legislative means were often punitive, blocking essential services to immigrants and their children, such as driver's-license exams. For this purpose, nativists argue that the overall level of immigration should be reduced to "digest" the previous wave of immigrants and to assimilate them successfully into the American nation. Furthermore, in schools and elsewhere, they argue that diversity should be deemphasized and common values should be emphasized more.

Critics of the cultural-unity argument indicate that fears of excessive diversity amount to a new form of racism. They recall earlier episodes of xenophobia and racism in anti-immigrant movements. They believe that the key motif behind the resurgence of nativism in the contemporary United States is to keep America as the nativists define it: white. The American is tacitly understood to be of European descent. Among some whites, anxieties over losing their majority-race status have led them to anti-immigrant movements. Groups, such as the National Organization for European American Rights (NOFEAR), formed by former Klansman David Duke, and the Council of Conservative Citizens, overtly promote racial hatred, using vicious language to attack immigrants. As indicated before, critics argue that such anti-immigrant movements do nothing to address the root causes of social, economic, and political problems in the United States. Furthermore, critics argue that it would be a serious mistake to fix American identity without permitting the evolutionary change that additional diversity brings.

Another argument used against immigration has been that immigrants are threats to the political system and stability. During the early period of nation building, politically active immigrants from Europe were regarded as radical subversives threatening the stability of the new nation. They were portrayed as rabble-rousers threatening a stable republican form of government in the United States with revolutionary anarchy and mob violence. Their presence "was a menace to American institutions and American liberty" (Billington 1974, 45). The nativist Federalists succeeded in passing the Alien and Sedition Acts of 1798, giving the president arbitrary powers to exclude or deport foreigners deemed subversive and to prosecute anyone who criticized the government. The new Naturalization Act of 1790 sought to limit immigrants' political influence by extending the waiting period for citizenship to fourteen years. The act dealt with the government's policy toward naturalization, but one can argue that one of the primary purposes of the act was to control immigration and that it was the beginning of the U.S. nativist, anti-immigrant movement to control immigration because of a perceived political threat.

Another example from history was the threat supposedly posed by Catholic immigrants who were alleged to be agents of a foreign power that wanted to conquer and seize political control of the United States. In the 1830s–1850s, the large wave of Irish and German immigrants who arrived were labeled "Papists" who followed the authoritarian leader. Catholic immigrants became scapegoats for economic insecurity and division on the slavery issue. Such charges against newcomers were common when there was an international conflict and political insecurity in America. Anti-German movements during World War I and anti-Japanese activities during World War II were notable cases of the fear and suspicion of various immigrant groups' loyalty to the United States.

Such suspicion of immigrants' loyalty to the United States and their threat to national security resurfaced again after the terrorist attacks of September 11, 2001. Arab and South Asian immigrants were stereotyped as potential terrorists as the violent acts of a few extremists were blamed on all Arab immigrants. Once again, the U.S. government resorted to legal means and enacted a law, the Patriot Act of 2001. The ensuing enforcement of the act led to the arrest and imprisonment of many innocent South Asian and Middle Eastern Muslims.

A new argument has emerged recently against immigration. The current nativists assert that immigrants are threats to the natural environment of the United States. They argue that population growth and new immigrants' different lifestyles will eventually create harmful effects on the natural environment of the United States. Some environmental organizations have urged a drastic reduction of immigrants on the basis of their concern over the long-term effect of overpopulation on the natural environment. This sentiment needs to be monitored in the future to track how it will affect U.S. immigration policy.

See also Americanization Movement; Anglo Conformity; Anti-Catholicism in the United States; Anti-Semitism in the United States; Asiatic Barred Zone; Biological Racism; English-Only Movement; Duke, David; Government Initiatives after the September 11, 2001, Attack on the United States; Irish Immigrants, Prejudice and Discrimination against; Japanese American Internment; Know-

Nothing Party; Ku Klux Klan (KKK); National Origins Act of 1924; Naturalization Act of 1790; Nordic Superiority.

Further Reading

Billington, R. A. *The Origins of Nativism in the United States, 1800–1844.* 1933. Reprint, New York: Arno Press, 1974.

Crawford, James. *Hold Your Tongue: Bilingualism and the Politics of "English Only."* Boston: Addison-Wesley, 1992.

Dinnerstein, Leonard, Roger L. Nichols, and David M. Reimers. *Natives and Strangers: A Multicultural History of Americans.* New York: Oxford University Press, 1996.

Feagin, Joe R. "Old Poison in New Bottles: The Deep Roots of Modern Nativism." In *Immigrants Out! The New Nativism and the Anti-immigrant Impulse in the United States*, edited by J. F. Perea, 13–43. New York: New York University Press, 1997.

Fix, Michael, and Jeffrey Passel. *Immigration Today: Myths and Realities.* Washington, DC: The Urban Institute, 1994.

Higham, John. *Strangers in the Land: Patterns of American Nativism, 1860–1925.* 2nd ed. New Brunswick, NJ: Rutgers University Press, 1988.

Jaret, Charles. "Troubled by Newcomers: Anti-immigrant Attitudes and Actions during Two Eras of Mass Migration." In *Mass Migration to the United States: Classical and Contemporary Periods*, edited by Pyong Gap Min, 21–63. New York: AltaMira, 2002.

Jones, Maldwyn Allen. *American Immigration.* 2nd ed. Chicago: University of Chicago Press, 1992.

Schlesinger, Arthur M., Jr. *The Disuniting of America.* New York: Norton, 1991.

Heon Cheol Lee

Naturalization Act of 1790

The Naturalization Act of 1790 was the first federal law concerning naturalization of immigrants. Based on the power given to Congress by the U.S. Constitution, the First Congress established a uniform rule of naturalization to be followed by all of the United States. It provided the first rules and procedures to be followed in granting U.S. citizenship to the foreign born. It stipulated that "any free white person" who had resided in the United States for two years could apply for citizenship. Thus, by that stipulation, slaves, Indians, and indentured servants were excluded as potential citizens. The act also ruled out applicants who were not of "good moral character."

The Naturalization Act of 1790 employed explicit racial criteria by limiting citizenship to free white persons. The act dealt with only the government's policy toward naturalization, but since immigration and naturalization are so closely linked, it had a significant impact on the immigration of nonwhite persons to the United States. One can argue that one of the primary purposes of the Naturalization Act of 1790 was to discourage the immigration of nonwhite persons to the United States.

The history of U.S. naturalization since that date has been the effort to realize uniformity in practice, procedure, and principle. It is from this structure of steps and requirements that U.S. naturalization laws evolved. While government policy still requires new naturalized citizens to be persons of "good moral character," limitations based on gender or race eventually disappeared and new requirements have been introduced by subsequent legislation.

See also National Origins Act of 1924.

Heon Cheol Lee

Nature of Prejudice, The

First published in 1954, *The Nature of Prejudice* by Gordon Allport has influenced and guided the study of prejudice in many disciplines, particularly social psychology, for nearly fifty years. Allport's definition of prejudice has become the fundamental building block of the Human-Relations movement, better known today as the multiculturalism movement. *The Nature of Prejudice* was written during and for a turbulent period in U.S. history to address particular aspects and dimensions of prejudices brought about by economic, legal, political, and social inequality. Allport's book was monumental in that it was published just before the Supreme Court's historic decision overturning the legality of "separate but equal" public facilities: *Brown v. Board of Education*.

Allport defined prejudice as "an aversive or hostile attitude toward a person who belongs to a group, simply because he belongs to that group, and is therefore presumed to have the objectionable qualities ascribed to the group," and as "an antipathy based upon a faulty and inflexible generalization" (Allport 1954). Allport notes that human rivalries and hatreds are omnipresent.

The Nature of Prejudice explores racial, religious, ethnic, economic, and sexual prejudice while focusing on strategies for ameliorating the devastating effects of discrimination. Many of Allport's foundational concepts and theories for addressing social problems can now be found in the literature of various disciplines with new labels and more nuanced meanings. Allport was also one of the first scholars to substantively discuss anti-Semitism.

Among the book's most important theoretical contributions concerning the source of prejudice is the "frustration-aggression/scapegoat" hypothesis. Allport described how frustration over issues involving family, personal characteristics, and other social factors in the community can develop into "reactive aggression," which is then directed toward an "out-group." This out-group becomes a scapegoat as the negative qualities that cause guilt in some prejudiced people are repressed and "displaced" onto the targeted population.

Further Reading

Allport, Gordon W. *The Nature of Prejudice*. Unabridged 25th anniversary ed. New York: Perseus Books Group, 1979.

Khyati Joshi

NCAI

See National Congress of American Indians (NCAI).

NCVS

See National Crime Victimization Survey (NCVS).

Negative Self-Image among Minorities

Negative self-image is the negative feeling that minority members develop toward their physical, mental, or intellectual appearance and capacity. People with a negative self-image are often unable to function properly in society because it limits their capacity to move forward or assume challenging responsibilities. The media and those in power usually contribute to people's development of negative self-images through images and words that reinforce racial and physical stereotypes.

Blacks in the United States have historically suffered from a negative self-image because of racism and discrimination. One of the effects of a negative self-image is self-hatred. Since race is perceived to be the most salient dimension of a person's characteristics in the United States, it is difficult for people of color to assume other aspects of their lives that make up their personality. Often a negative self-image is developed early on in a person's life. Several studies reported that black children were more likely to play with white dolls than black ones because they thought they were better. This reflection further reinforces the negative self-image of African Americans. Furthermore, everything that is associated with whiteness is projected in a positive light, while blackness is always associated with negative feelings and experiences.

Francois Pierre-Louis

The Negro Family: The Case for National Action

This 1965 report by the then-senator Daniel Patrick Moynihan (D-NY) blamed the breakdown of the African American family for the poverty and social problems experienced by African Americans after the civil rights movement. It took the form of a call to action to create policies that would help to strengthen African American families and reduce teenage and out-of-wedlock pregnancies as well as youth delinquency and crime. While Moynihan did suggest that white society should take the blame for the roots of the problems (slavery, urbanization, and employment discrimination, for example): he said that there is a "tangle of pathology" that keeps African Americans impoverished. Moynihan wrote that not only did the government have to work to reduce the problems African Americans face; African Americans must take part of the responsibility for ensuring that they have stable family lives and bring up their children well. Often referred to as *The Moynihan Report*, this work has, since its publication, been at the center of a national debate about the causes of the black underclass. The ideas it put forth have continued to guide debate on and implementation of governmental policies, most notably welfare reform.

See also Black Family Instability Thesis.

Further Reading

Moynihan, Daniel Patrick. *The Negro Family: The Case for National Action.* Washington, DC: The U.S. Department of Labor, 1965.

Mikaila Mariel Lemonik Arthur

Neocolonialism

Neocolonialism describes the continuing reality of domination, although in a new form, in the newly independent countries of Africa, Asia, and Latin America by their former colonizers. Although the former colonies did attain nominal political sovereignty after the end of the World War II, they are still the providers of cheap labor and raw materials for the markets of the advanced industrial economies. Unequal exchange and superexploitation in the global capitalist economy exacerbates the economic instability and poverty of those countries in the periphery. Economic development has been aborted in most of the Third World countries, except South Korea, Taiwan, and Singapore. In particular, neoliberal economic policy has had a devastating effect on farmers and the middle class in Latin America. As popular resistance grows, political oppression also intensifies. Often, the superpowers intervene in the internal political affairs under the guise of the war-on-drugs, human-rights advocacy, democracy initiatives, and so forth, negating even the nominal sovereignty of the countries.

Poverty and political instability in those countries push a large population out of the countries into the wealthy countries, and this global inequality accounts for why even the most restrictive immigration policy of the United States cannot stop the inflow of immigrants, legal and illegal, from Latin America.

Once these immigrants arrive in the United States or other wealthy countries, they are often concentrated in the lowest-paying and menial jobs and generally live in the most undesirable neighborhoods. They are more likely to suffer racial discrimination. The surge of anti-immigration sentiment in recent years has largely been targeted toward non-European immigrants. To the extent that neocolonialism contributes to global inequality, it also contributes to the reproduction of ethnic inequality and racism in the Unites States.

See also Internal Colonialism.

Dong-Ho Cho

Neo-Nazism

Neo-Nazi groups find their basis in a perverted hatred of Jews that often extends to homosexuals and other minorities. Neo-Nazis associate themselves with Nazi Germany and Adolph Hitler and believe that Jews somehow control the government which they refer to as the Zionist Occupied Government (ZOG). Additionally, they believe in a widespread Jewish conspiracy and blame the Jewish people for many social problems. Neo-Nazi groups generally do not accept exceedingly well documented facts about the Holocaust, often arguing that the Holocaust was a myth or a gross exaggeration conceived to gain sympathy for Jews. In 2000, the Southern Poverty Law Center identified 220 active neo-Nazi groups in the United States.

Neo-Nazism in the United States began with the American Nazi Party, founded in 1958 by George Lincoln Rockwell. Rockwell was assassinated in 1967, and the party broke off into various branches. The New Order, formerly the National Socialist White People's Party, is the offshoot of the earlier Nazi Party. Matthias Koehl leads the party in 2005. He maintains international contacts and is strongly committed to Nazi philosophy.

Other groups that have been associated with neo-Nazis include the National Alliance (formerly headed by William Pierce), Aryan Nations (although they are also associated with the Christian Identity Church Movement), and skinheads. Skinheads are among the most violent of the neo-Nazi groups. At the present time, it is estimated that there are several thousand skinheads in the United States. They are easily identified by their hate music known as "oi," and they often use the Internet in an attempt to spread their message of hate. Other hate groups, such as Hammerskin Nation, have been generated from the skinheads.

See also Aryan Nations; Skinheads; White-Supremacist Movement in the United States; White-Supremacist Underground.

John Eterno

Newark Riot of 1967

In the summer of 1967, a black cab driver named John Smith drove around a police car that was double parked on the corner of Seventh Street and Fifteenth Avenue in Newark, New Jersey. The driver was subsequently stopped, interrogated, and then taken to the local precinct, where he was severely beaten by the arresting police officers. The news of the arrest spread throughout the community, and in a matter of minutes a large crowd gathered outside the precinct. Civil rights leaders were allowed to see Smith and upon viewing his injuries, demanded that he be taken to a hospital. The crowed outside was growing restless as false rumors spread that Smith had died. The crowd then began throwing rocks at the police precinct, and when the police dispersed the crowd, the violence spread throughout the neighborhood and sparked six days of rioting in Newark that ended with 23 people dead and 725 seriously injured.

The Newark riots were among the many race riots of the late 1960s that all shared similar conditions. The underlying causes of the Newark riots, like the other urban riots during the period, were police brutality against African Americans, exclusion of blacks from local politics, urban-renewal projects that devastated black neighborhoods, disproportionate unemployment of blacks, and lack of affordable housing in black neighborhoods. Police brutality was the catalyst for the riot, but discontent had been brewing for years prior to the riot, and African Americans struggled against a system of discrimination and exploitation. The race riots of the 1960s forced the federal government to look into the serious problems faced by blacks living in the urban ghettos of the United States.

National Guardsmen search African American men at bayonet point following the riots in Newark, New Jersey, July 17, 1967.

AP/Wide World Photos.

See also Bellingham Riots; Detroit Race Riot of 1943; Harlem Riot of 1964; Los Angeles Riots of 1871; Memphis Race Riot of 1866; Race Riots; St. Louis Riot of 1917.

Michael Roberts

Niagara Movement

The Niagara movement was founded in 1905 by W.E.B. Du Bois and twenty-nine other prominent African Americans, mostly intellectuals. It called for full civil rights for all African Americans, including full male suffrage. Annual meetings were held in symbolic locations such as Harper's Ferry, Virginia, the site of James Brown's raid to free the slaves in 1859. A lack of funds and organizational weakness prevented the organization from gaining mass support, though it did establish thirty local branches and achieve some local civil rights victories. Its key local projects were voting rights, school desegregation, and the election of candidates who would fight racism. The organization disbanded in 1910, though many of its members became part of the core group that founded the National Association for the Advancement of Colored People (NAACP).

This organization was particularly important because it broke with the views of Booker T. Washington, one of the leading African American public figures of the late nineteenth century. He believed that vocational education and economic security were far more important than political rights and de-segregation.

See also Du Bois, W.E.B; National Association for the Advancement of Colored People (NAACP).

Mikaila Mariel Lemonik Arthur

Nigger

Nigger is the most offensive word that a white person can use today to insult an African American. The word has evolved greatly since it was first used in the sixteenth century to describe a black person. Both African American and White American authors used the word in literature for much of the eighteenth and nineteenth centuries. Its derogatory aspect was accentuated in the twentieth century through the media. The word became an offensive expression of hatred by whites toward blacks, and this was emphasized in films, plays, and music in which whites were portrayed as being superior to blacks. Television programs around the country often showed statements by public officials who used the word *nigger* to demean African Americans who were protesting against white supremacists. Movies such as *Gone with the Wind*, *Roots*, and *Glory* further reinforced the pejorative connotation of the word.

Although blacks are offended when whites use the word *nigger* to refer to or attack them, it is a common occurrence for blacks to greet each other using that word. The word *nigger* is becoming acceptable again in American society, given the prevalence of black actors, artists, authors, and public personalities who use it to celebrate African American life. The late rapper Tupac Shakur and comedian Chris Rock have used the word to express both the sorrow and the greatness of African Americans.

See also Derogatory Terms; Films and Racial Stereotypes; Journalism and Racial Stereotypes; Television and Racial Stereotypes.

Francois Pierre-Louis

9/11

See Al Qaeda; Arab/Muslim American Advocacy Organizations, Responding to the Backlash; Government Initiatives after the September 11, 2001, Attack on the United States; "Green Menace"; Gulf War; Middle Easterners, Historical Precedents of Backlash against; Muslim Philanthropic Organizations, Closure of after September 11, 2001; Muslims, Prejudice and Discrimination against; Muslims, Terrorist Image of; September 11, 2001, Terrorism, Discriminatory Reactions to.

Noble Savage

The term *noble savage* refers to a romantic view of indigenous peoples as more natural, authentic, and communal than Europeans. The "noble savage," as seen in colonial and postcolonial history, popular culture, and mythology, is a character who lives simply and in harmony with his or her natural environment. The mythology of the noble savage, closely linked to primitivism, developed during the time of European colonial expansion into Africa, the Americas, and elsewhere.

Even as colonized cultures were being destroyed with increasing brutality, Europeans and white Americans romanticized them as more ecologically sensitive, more exciting, and even more sexually pleasured. Such notions essentialize indigenous people and circulate negative stereotypes about the relative intelligence, sophistication, and sexual mores of whole groups of people who have faced colonization by Westerners. According to postcolonial scholars, the concept of the noble savage is also a nostalgic one, reflecting the West's longstanding unease with its own technological advances, ecological destruction, and cultural homogenization. For at least two centuries, Western culture generated images of noble savagery that suggest alternative, more traditionally rooted modes of living with nature that are perceived as symbolic alternatives to Western problems. In recent manifestations, primitivism is seen as a way of life, a set of values and relationships that can be experienced even within Western cultures through the appropriation of indigenous rituals, ceremonies, and spiritual and body practices.

See also Native Americans, Prejudice and Discrimination against.

Victoria Pitts

Non-Judeo-Christian Immigrant Groups, Violence against

Notwithstanding the American myth of flight from religious persecution, the United States, from its beginnings, has a history of religious intolerance. Native Americans, Catholics, Quakers, Mennonites, and Eastern Orthodox Christians faced religious persecution in eighteenth- and nineteenth-century America. Anti-Semitism, born on European soil, also took its place in American history and culture. Today, the followers of Sikhism, Islam, Hinduism, Buddhism, and other non-Western faith traditions encounter prejudice and discrimination because of the religion to which they subscribe. It was after the passage of the Immigration and Nationality Act of 1965, although the worshippers of these non-Christian religions were present in the United States before that time, that these populations grew to a size where they and their houses of worship became visible in many American cities and towns.

Along with the growing presence of these religious groups has come an increase in violence against individual members and houses of worship. Such violence occurs on both ideological and physical levels. Ideologically, these religions are compared with Christianity, and in particular to the Protestant Christianity that is the unofficial state religion of the United States. Because of Christianity's historic and continuing dominance in American culture,

Christian groups, individuals, and organizations possess the power and privilege to define religious normalcy. To be religiously "different" in the United States is to be theologically inferior to Protestant Christianity. This phenomenon also perpetuates the invisibility of minority religions in the cultural discourse. America's linguistic and symbolic vocabulary of faith, practice, prayer, belief, edifice, and history largely ignores the existence of other religions, despite the fact that most of these "new" American religions are older than Christianity. Christianity in America is normative; non-Christians are asked, "What is 'your Bible'? What is 'your Christmas'?" Adherents of non-Judeo-Christian faiths have been accused of devil worship and paganism, and the religions themselves are often misunderstood and mistaken for each other.

Ideological violence can also become the basis for discrimination at the policy level. For example, zoning variances that might be forthcoming to a church or synagogue are not made available when a mosque or *mandir* (Hindu temple) is planned. The Christian power to define normalcy was in stark display in San Jose, California, in 1997, when the Sikh community encountered opposition when attempting to build a *gurudwaras* (Sikh temple) in one neighborhood. Non-Sikh residents objected, saying they did not want to have a "Taj Mahal"-like structure built because the neighborhood would turn into "a kind of religious Disney World."

Likewise, the constant association of Islam with terrorism in the media and popular culture—and the dearth of dialogue about Islam that does *not* relate to terrorism—creates and perpetuates a fear of American Muslims and is what most frequently results in physical violence. As a result, Muslim communities have encountered hostility when attempting to erect *masjids* (Muslim houses of worship) in towns across America even when they were going to be built in areas designated by special zoning ordinances that help create a safe space for "churches" and worshippers.

The religious-minority status of non-Judeo-Christians in contemporary America is further affected by the fact that they are disproportionately *racial* minorities as well. These "double minorities," including Arab American Muslims, South Asian American Hindus, Sikhs and Muslims, and Asian American Buddhists, among others, encounter overt and covert discrimination on racial and religious levels. In such situations, it is often difficult or impossible to separate the racial animus from the religious animus that caused the attack. Nor is it necessary to do so; the better approach is to see the targeting of racial and religious minorities as a compound problem involving both racial and religious oppression. Both types of oppression should be considered and addressed, and the interplay between them should be recognized as a new element of the post–1965 phenomenon of discrimination.

The combination of racial visibility and religious misunderstanding can lead to what might be called "misdirected" racial violence. For example, after the attacks of September 11, 2001, many South Asian Americans became targets of anti-Muslim violence, yet the victims were often not Muslim but Sikh, Hindu, or even Christian. The most pronounced example of this phenomenon involves religiously observant Sikh males, who wear turbans. While the turbans are Sikh religious objects to their wearers, they have an association in the American mind with the turbans worn by some Muslims in Afghanistan and Iran. In Phoenix, Arizona, on September 15, 2001, Balbar Singh Sodhi, a turban-wearing Sikh gas station owner, was murdered; he was just one of hundreds of Sikhs and other South Asians hurt or killed in post–9/11 "anti-Muslim" attacks. However, violence against these groups is not only a post–9/11 phenomenon. Moreover, violence against non-Judeo-Christians can also happen at the collective level, such as when a Sikh house of worship, a mosque or a Hindu temple is vandalized.

See also Government Initiatives after the September 11, 2001, Attack on the United States; Religion and Racism; September 11, 2001, Terrorism, Discriminatory Reactions to.

Further Reading

Eck, Diana. *A New Religious America: How a Christian Country Has Now Become the World's Most Religiously Diverse Nation*. San Francisco: HarperCollins, 2001.

Joshi, K. Y. *Patterns and Paths: Ethnic Identity Development in Second Generation Indian Americans*. PhD diss., University of Massachusetts, Amherst, 2001.

Singh, J. "The Racialization of Minoritized Religious Identity: Constructing Sacred Sites at the Intersection of White and Christian Supremacy." In *Revealing the Sacred in Asian and Pacific America*, edited by Jane Iwamura and Paul Spickard, 87–106. New York: Routledge, 2003.

Khyati Joshi

Nonwhite Racism

Racism is a belief system designed to entrench inequalities on the basis of race. In the United States, it has usually been seen as a tool of the majority white population to be wielded against various minority groups. However, nonwhite racism—racism perpetuated by persons who do not identify themselves as white—has also had a significant and complex effect on American race relations and politics.

There are a couple of possible explanations for the development of nonwhite racism in the American context. The first lies in the complexity of social stratification itself. Minority groups are not evenly distributed across the economic or social ladder, and thus their relation to whites, and to each other, may be profoundly different based on where they are positioned. For example, Native Americans in the late eighteenth and early nineteenth centuries were known to have held racist views against black slaves. Scholars argue that some Native American groups developed a racist ideology to distinguish themselves from blacks, at a time when whites were increasingly eroding away Native American livelihoods. Thus, nonwhite racism in this instance may have been a way of protecting their marginally better status vis-à-vis slavery.

Nonwhite racism can also be a consequence of the "middleman" syndrome. Middleman minorities usually occupy an intermediate place in the ethnic hierarchy and take on intermediary occupational roles, such as shopkeepers, moneylenders, or traders. In the United States at varying times, Jews, Koreans, Asian Indians, and Pakistanis have been part of the middleman group. Because of their intermediate position, middleman groups can sometimes find themselves the target of racial hostility by either the dominant or subordinate groups. Subordinate groups may feel that middleman minorities perpetuate their own kind of racism, through their exploitative labor and business practices, and their cultural insularity. Such anger can coalesce in times of severe social stress, such as after the infamous Rodney King trial in 1992. In the riots that ensued in Los Angeles, Korean stores were targeted by angry black mobs, exposing ethnic tension, stereotyping, and discrimination that could not be explained simply by a black-white dynamic.

A recent manifestation of nonwhite racism that has bearing on contemporary racial politics is anti-Semitism. This can, on the one hand, be seen as an attempt to subvert traditional racial hierarchies, in that it is directed against people who in some measure have been associated with the "white" majority group. However, others have considered anti-Semitism to have its roots in the middleman syndrome, because Jews in America had historically played a middleman role, particularly in urban centers that have a large black underclass. Intellectuals such as Leonard Jeffries and Tony Martin have been accused of anti-Semitism, in part because of their contentious views regarding Jewish involvement in the African slave trade. Louis Farrakhan and the Nation of Islam have also been charged with fanning the flames of anti-Semitism among blacks.

Nonwhite racism should be seen as both similar to and separate from the historic American pattern of white racism against nonwhite groups. Like white racism, nonwhite racism can inflict tremendous psychological, social, and material damage. Nonwhite racism is also similarly built on a foundation of internalized racial hierarchy and privilege and can be encouraged through stereotypical portrayal of certain groups in media and popular culture. However, certain distinctions from "traditional" racism need to be emphasized. In some respects, nonwhite racism serves the interests of the dominant group because it is often enacted between subordinate groups, thereby preventing any economic or ideological alliance. Also, because minority groups do not have the same access to institutional and ideological power structures in America as the dominant group, one can argue that nonwhite racism has a less pernicious and widespread effect. So, although it can be said that white racism historically became manifested, and entrenched, in the system of slavery and segregation, little parallel exists with nonwhite racism, at least on the level of scale. However, the implications of nonwhite racism should not be underestimated. As minority groups increasingly take center stage in a more multicultural political and economic environment, such racist beliefs may wield considerable power in the future.

See also Black Anti-Semitism; Black-Korean Conflicts; Jewish-Black Conflicts.

Further Reading

Blalock, Hubert M., Jr. *Toward a Theory of Minority-Group Relations*. New York: John Wiley, 1967.

Bonacich, Edna. "A Theory of Middleman Minorities." *American Sociological Review* 35 (1973): 583–594.

Marger, Martin. *Race and Ethnic Relations: American and Global Perspectives*. 6th ed. Belmont, CA: Wadsworth, 2003.

Rebekah Lee

Nordic Superiority

Nordic superiority is a version of the "master race" theory used and popularized by the Nazi Party in Germany under Adolf Hitler. In 1853, Count Arthur de Gobineau first developed the "master race" concept, which states that there exists a "race" of people that is genetically superior to all others. Gobineau argued that a race "degenerates" when it mixes with others. In particular, it was thought that people of southern Europe had mixed with "inferior" people of Africa, while people of northern Europe remained pure and, therefore, "superior." Between the years of Gobineau and Hitler, various versions of eugenics—the study of genetic heredity—argued for the superiority of one race or another; most eugenicists argued for the superiority of white Europeans of upper-class background. The Nazis developed their particular form of eugenic ideology referred to as "Nordic Superiority" by distorting the philosophy of the German Friedrich Nietzsche, who made references to the "blonde beasts" of the north in his magnum opus, *The Genealogy of Morals*. Nietzsche himself was not an anti-Semite. On the contrary, he criticized anti-Semitism. Nietzsche had used the concept "blonde beast" as a *cultural* ideal type. But the Nazis misinterpreted this as a *biological* concept. Thus, the Nazis took the concept to mean that those from a Nordic-German background were a superior race. People with "Nordic" features, such as tall height, narrow heads, blond hair, and light skin, were said to be the master race of all peoples.

Hitler plunged the world into war, and his people were disgraced when the Allied troops discovered the death camps in Auschwitz, Poland, and other German-controlled cities where millions of Jews of varying descent were exterminated following the distorted logic of "Nordic superiority." The ideology of Nordic superiority has since been thoroughly debunked by geneticists and social scientists, but it exists in underground racist movements in Germany and the United States, especially among so-called skin-head groups who continue to propagate the ideology of white supremacy.

See also Aryan Nations; Biological Racism; Eugenics Movement; Neo-Nazism; White-Supremacist Movement in the United States; White-Supremacist Underground.

Michael Roberts

O

OAAU

See Organization of Afro-American Unity (OAAU).

"Obsession with Race"

See American "Obsession with Race."

OCA

See Organization of Chinese Americans (OCA).

Oklahoma City Federal Building Bombing

On April 19, 1995, the Alfred P. Murrah Federal Building in Oklahoma City was bombed by right-wing extremist Timothy McVeigh and his accomplice, Terry Nichols. They used a rented truck with 4,800 pounds of homemade plastic explosives (C4). The bombing killed 191 men, women, and children and injured hundreds of others. The Oklahoma City bombing is generally regarded as the most destructive terrorist act by domestic terrorists and the second most destructive terrorist incident within the United States, with the September 11, 2001, attacks being the worst.

McVeigh was apparently influenced by the domestic white supremacist movement. A page from the book *The Turner Diaries*, written by William Pierce under the pseudonym Andrew McDonald, was found on McVeigh when he was arrested for the attack. Pierce was the leader of the National Alliance (NA), a neo-Nazi hate group. The novel portrays white supremacists as exceedingly agitated over federal gun-control legislation, which leads the characters to conduct a series of terrorist attacks, including the bombing of FBI Headquarters. Pierce, who died on July 23, 2002, denied any involvement with the bombing.

Domestic terrorists, such as McVeigh and Nichols, have a familiarity with the laws, practices, and vulnerabilities in the United States that international terrorists may not have. Nevertheless, the similarities among domestic and international terrorists are striking: distorted views, overwhelming hatred of various people and the U.S. government, a total lack of respect for human life, and the unrestricted use of violence.

See also Neo-Nazism; White-Supremacist Movement in the United States; White-Supremacist Underground.

Further Reading

Brodie, Renee. "The Aryan New Era: Apocalyptic Realizations in *The Turner Diaries*." *Journal of American Culture* 21, no. 3 (1998): 13–32.

John Eterno

One-Drop Rule

The "one-drop rule," or the Rule of Hypo-Descent, is the name given to the historical practice of determining racial classifications based on a remote biological connection to persons of African descent. According to this rule, one drop of African blood identifies a person as "black." Thus if one of sixty-four of a person's ancestors is black (i.e., a person who is one-sixteenth black), he or she is black. Consequently, based on this ideological practice, once one is considered "black," six generations of nonblack ancestors would be required to alter one's race. The one-drop rule is rooted in the race ideology and racism in the United States. Historically, the one-drop rule represented attempts by segments of white society to minimize race mixing or miscegenation, especially relationships between blacks and whites. In addition, the rule is an effort to establish a dominant racial in-group and subordinate out-groups for the purpose of ascribing tangible and intangible rewards and penalties. The one-drop rule has been strictly applied in the United States, more than in other multiracial societies such as Brazil and the Caribbean Islands; is used solely to identify persons of African descent; and reflects greater prejudice against and social distance from blacks, in terms of friendship and intermarriage.

The notion of "race" was originally considered in biology to classify groups of people based on commonly held physical characteristics. Over time, the term has come to be used as an overarching trait, not only to describe groups of people, but also to evaluate their character and worth. Increasingly, social scientists are acknowledging the socially constructed nature of the concept "race" and question its appropriateness as an accurate descriptive. As a method to phenotypically classify persons, race is inaccurate, due to a history of "race mixing." Furthermore, its validity as a descriptive tool is questioned because of the various ways in which it is understood and appropriated across cultures and nations, and because of intra-group differences. Although race has been found to be a less-than-accurate trait to describe groups, it continues to influence the economic, political, social, and psychological experiences of a myriad of persons, especially blacks.

The concept of race as a mechanism to delineate phenotypically different groups was rooted in European colonization and the attempt to identify persons of European descent as superior to others and to protect in-group privileges. Despite sexual encounters with black slaves that were initiated by whites, political and social sanctions existed to discourage race mixing (interracial unions continued to be illegal in parts of the United States until 1967). Slaves, and later freed persons, could meet violent ends if suspected of initiating race mixing. In this context, the one-drop rule discouraged black-initiated sexual interaction with whites but also ensured that the progeny of slave and slave master would be black and thus also considered slaves. A perceived economic necessity precipitated continued sexual relationships between some white males and black females after slavery, but white society continued to fear black-initiated race mixing. White males were most concerned about sexual relationships involving white females and black males.

The ideology of race in the United States places whiteness at the center as the ideal and "black" as the negative extreme, and so the one-drop rule can be linked to a race-based hierarchy of penalties and rewards in the United States that continues to stigmatize blacks. Based on the possible economic, political, social, and psychological benefits often afforded to whites in society, and the corresponding history of racism and discrimination experienced by many blacks, race mixing, although not legally barred, continues to be discouraged. The one-drop rule also undermines the ability to acknowledge a multiracial identity. For example, it is common for blacks of mixed lineage who embrace their white heritage to be viewed suspiciously by some blacks as attempting to distance themselves from being black and aligning with the dominate racial group. Given that whites are less likely than blacks to accept race mixing and less likely to acknowledge their mixed lineage—especially when it includes African blood—this suggests that the one-drop rule continues to undermine an appreciation for racial diversity. However, social changes such as the inclusion of racial/ethnic categories and a multiracial classification option on the 2000 census and the growing tendency for multiracial persons to embrace their identity suggests that the validity of the one-drop rule continues to be questioned.

See also Intermarriage.

Further Reading

Davis, James. *Who Is Black? One Nation's Definition*. University Park: Pennsylvania State University Press, 1991.

Gallagher, Charles, ed. *Rethinking the Color Line: Readings in Race and Ethnicity*. San Francisco: Mayfield Publishing Company, 1991.

West, Cornel. *Race Matters*. Boston: Beacon Press, 1993.

Sandra L. Barnes

Operation Wetback

In July 1954, the United States Immigration and Naturalization Service (INS) launched the controversial paramilitary repatriation program "Operation Wetback," which, as implied by the racist title, targeted Mexicans working illegally in the agricultural industry in the Southwest region of the U.S. *Wetback* is a racial slur, first used in the United States to describe immigrants who cross the border illegally, usually by crossing rivers or streams. The term *wetback* for Mexican Americans is as offensive as the term *nigger* is for Americans of African descent. The officially stated purpose of the operation was border patrol, but it became a paramilitary operation as armed officers implemented racial profiling and surprise raids, which in many cases violated with impunity the civil rights of legal immigrants and Mexican American citizens.

Before Operation Wetback, in 1942, the U.S. and Mexican governments had implemented the Bracero Program, which was designed to bring a large number of Mexicans to the United States as temporary workers. To have Mexicans working in the U.S. agricultural industry was viewed by both countries as mutually beneficial. The Bracero Program was successful and popular throughout the 1940s, but by the early 1950s, a backlash against Mexican immigrants emerged and Operation Wetback was the result. The anti-Mexican hysteria that swept across the Southwest in the early 1950s was a reaction to what was to become known as the "decade of the Wetback," the years between 1942 and 1954, when the number of illegal Mexican immigrants approached one million.

During the summer of 1954, INS officials swarmed Mexican neighborhoods all over the Southwest, capturing and deporting some eighty thousand allegedly illegal immigrants. In some cases, children of immigrants who were born in the United States, and therefore citizens, were sent back to Mexico with their parents. The paramilitary practices of Operation Wetback outraged U.S. citizens who were of Mexican descent. They complained that American growers in the agricultural industry benefited from the influx of inexpensive labor from Mexico and that all immigrants deserved protection regardless of their legal status. It was not until the early 1980s that illegal immigrants from Mexico were given certain rights protected by the courts, so that now, BCIS officials are subject to litigation if they violate the rights of illegal immigrants. On the other hand, anti-Mexican sentiment is alive and well in the American Southwest as many, including radio talk show host Rush Limbaugh, have called for Operation Wetback II. In certain parts of Texas, rogue vigilantes loosely organized as the group "Ranch Rescue" roam privately held lands in search of illegal immigrants.

See also Bracero Program; Mexican Americans, Prejudice and Discrimination against; Mexican Illegals, Labor Exploitation of; Undocumented Immigrants; U.S. Border Patrol.

Michael Roberts

Oppositional Identity

Anthropologist John Ogbu and his associates coined the term "oppositional identities" or "oppositional youth culture" to explain the low school performance of African American children compared with that of white children and the children of immigrants. They theorize that, as involuntary minorities,

African American students often adopt an oppositional identity that holds an inherent distrust for mainstream white authority and rejects mainstream values such as hard work and educational achievement. To adopt the mainstream value system and excel in school would be a form of "acting white," which is interpreted as a betrayal of black group solidarity and racial identity. To gain popularity among their peers, many African American children deliberately neglect their schoolwork by cutting class and not listening to white teachers. Thus, their attempt to maintain black identity hurts their academic performance. This explanation is a kind of cultural explanation in the sense that it focuses on African American students' negative attitudes toward the school system and their low motivation to explain their poor school performance. But it is also a structural explanation in that Ogbu and his associates have interpreted African American children's alienation and distrust for the mainstream society as reactions to historical and contemporary discrimination.

According to Ogbu and his associates, the children of immigrants tend to be more successful than involuntary minorities, regardless of their class or race, although they also face social barriers. For example, in the United States, Afro-Caribbean immigrants are often able to achieve greater success than even middle-class blacks born in the United States. They argue that this is because the lineage of historical and social forces that mediate their cultural orientation is so different from that of minorities who were forcibly brought to the country. Immigrants do not have a long history of discrimination over generations and thus experience American society as a new social environment. As voluntary minorities, they have a greater degree of trust for members of the dominant group and the institutions that they control. Thus, they do not overreact to unfair treatment they get from members of the dominant group. They develop a social identity based on premigrant culture and history rather than develop it in opposition to the social identity of the dominant group of the host society. As a result, they are not as afraid of "acting white" as are involuntary minorities. They rather often see their cultural and linguistic differences from the dominant group as barriers that they have to overcome. They immigrate to the United States largely with the mentality of wanting to embrace American society, and its educational system, as a means of achieving social mobility.

Mary Waters and other researchers who have studied the children of contemporary immigrants have applied the concept of oppositional youth culture to the children of Caribbean lower-class black immigrants. According to these scholars, when lower-class black immigrants from the Caribbean Islands settle in African American neighborhoods, their children develop oppositional identities through their interactions with African American children. As a result, the black children focus on their identity as a black person and emphasize their racial characteristic as the main barrier to their success in school and social mobility. They reject their immigrant parents' message that they can achieve social mobility through education and hard work. By contrast, Water has found that the children of Caribbean middle-class immigrants who live in white neighborhoods emphasize their ethnic identity rather than racial identity and tend to accept education as the channel for social mobility. The major findings from her study suggest that the children of black immigrants, as long as they have frequent contact with African American children, can be acculturated into black youth culture quickly.

See also Black Identities:West Indian Immigrant Dreams and American Realities; Colonized versus Immigrant Minorities; Segmented-Assimilation Theory.

Further Reading

Fordham, Signithia, and John U. Ogbu. "Black Students' School Success: Coping with the Burden of 'Acting White.' " *The Urban Review* 18, no. 3 (1986): 176–206.

Gibson, Margaret, and John Ogbu, eds. *Minority Status and Schooling: A Comparative Study of Immigrant and Involuntary Minorities*. New York: Garland, 1991.

Waters, Mary. *Black Identities:West Indian Immigrant Dreams and American Realities*. Cambridge, MA: Harvard University Press, 1999.

Pyong Gap Min

Organization of Afro-American Unity (OAAU)

The Organization of Afro-American Unity (OAAU) was founded in 1964 by Malcolm X, after his break with the Nation of Islam. It was formed to coordinate political action and self-organization among blacks toward the goal of racial equality. Its secular character and more inclusivist ideology distanced the OAAU somewhat from the black militancy espoused by the Nation of Islam. However, the OAAU's mission to restore African identity and an ethos of self-determination to black people in America remains relevant to this day, despite Malcolm X's assassination in 1965.

At its core, the OAAU saw slavery as having robbed blacks of their connection to an African sense of culture and history, and their links to each other. The OAAU resolved to foster unity among blacks through a platform that embraced pan-Africanism, education, and political militancy. The OAAU advocated a "Basic Unity Program," which included the restoration of cultural links to and knowledge of Africa; reorientation to include a larger pan-African consciousness and agenda; education designed to free blacks from "mental bondage," programs to promote economic security; and self-defense against white domination.

The OAAU's political agenda can be seen as an outgrowth of Malcolm X's own evolving politics. Although calling for black self-organization and militant black action, the OAAU did not advocate black separatism as an end in itself but as the only means necessary to achieve full racial equality. However, the OAAU's acceptance of a multiethnic "future" needs to be seen alongside its fervent commitment to an African-centered cultural, political, and spiritual restoration project.

See also Black Nationalist Movement; Malcolm X.

Rebekah Lee

Organization of Chinese Americans (OCA)

The Organization of Chinese Americans (OCA) is a national nonprofit, nonpartisan advocacy organization of concerned Chinese and Asian Americans.

Founded in 1973, OCA is devoted to protecting the rights of American citizens and permanent residents of Chinese and Asian descent through legislative and policy initiatives at all levels of the government.

The primary objectives of OCA include promoting active participation of Asian Americans in both civic and national matters; securing social justice, equal opportunity, and equal treatment of Asian Americans; eliminating prejudices, stereotypes, and ignorance of Asian Americans; and promoting the cultural heritage of Chinese and other Asian Americans. Current issues concerning OCA include affirmative action, appointments of Asian Pacific Americans (APAs) in governments, campaign finance, APA participation in the census, education, hate crimes, immigration and welfare reform, media image and representation, racial profiling, redistricting, and voting. OCA holds an annual convention. Other programs include the APA College Leadership Training Conference, a variety of scholarships (e.g., Avon Scholarship, UPS Gold MountainVerizon Scholarship, Gates Millennium Scholarship), Brands National Essay Contests, Hate Crime projects, and internships. OCA publishes *Image* magazine, which serves as a communication link between chapter members and a source of information on federal and legislative initiatives and policies relevant to the Chinese American and Asian American communities.

OCA bases its national office in Washington, DC, and has forty-four chapters across the United States plus a Hong Kong chapter. Membership is open to any U.S. citizen or permanent resident aged eighteen or above regardless of race, sex, religion, education, profession, or national origin. Associate membership is open to anyone who is not a U.S. citizen or permanent resident but intends to become one in the future.

Philip Yang

Oriental Exclusion Act of 1924

See National Origins Act of 1924.

Orientalism

Orientalism is the long-held Western ideological bias that view Eastern societies and cultures as inferior, exotic, and erotic. Noted intellectual Edward W. Said first introduced the term in his classic book, *Orientalism*, published in 1979. He used this term to conceptualize in the framework of traditional scholarly thinking the relationship of power and knowledge between the "Occidental" colonizer and the "Oriental" colonized.

According to Said, the Orientalist scholars sharply divided the "Occident" as the West—in particular, England, France and the United States—and the "Orient" as the romantic, imaginative, and exotic Middle East and Far East. By making a comparative review of European colonial arts and literature on the peoples of the Middle East, Said argued that Occidental scholarship had conflated a myriad of cultures of the East into a single, cohesive whole of the "Orient" or subjugated "Others." In this discourse, the Orientalist scholars used dominating and sexual terms to describe Eastern cultures; by doing so, the

West and the East were dichotomously identified from a viewpoint of the Occidental.

The concept of Orientalism has greatly contributed to various academic areas by transforming scholarly views toward the East. Through the late twentieth century, the postmodernist critique of Orientalism highlighted that the Orient is not a single, monolithic region but rather a broad area encompassing multiple civilizations. This intellectual discourse has encouraged academic institutions in North America to replace "Oriental" studies with "Asian" studies. This transformation has included a scholarly acknowledgment of the diversity of Eastern cultures and a localization of focus to specific regions, such as the Middle East, South Asia, and East Asia, in the postcolonial studies of the East.

The idea of Orientalism has also revolutionized scholarly thinking among postmodernists and conflict theorists of race. Referring to Said's work, many scholars now contend that the West's idea of itself during the colonial period was constructed largely by saying what others were not. The Orientalist studies imposed a homogenous image of a prototypical Oriental on the East by considering it biologically inferior and culturally backward, peculiar and static. In this way, the Occidentals enabled themselves to define the West as powerful, civilized, and superior, in striking contrast to the East in its image, idea, personality, and experience. This ideological framework by Orientalists helped to justify the political imperialism of Europe in the East during the colonial period. Scholars in this area also highlight that this historical discourse has led to Western dominance over other parts of the world in international politics and economics through the contemporary global age.

Social scientists in Asian American studies have pointed out that Orientalism has conceptualized the negative cliché fantasies of Asians and the stereotypical imagery of Asian immigrants and Asian Americans by European Americans. The Orientalist novelists and filmmakers, especially in the early twentieth century, portrayed Oriental men as feminine, weak, cunning, ugly, and dangerous villains, as characterized by "Yellow Perils/Hordes" and "Fu Manchu." Likewise, women in non-Western cultures were typically depicted as erotic, mysterious, and objects for conquest, as illustrated by the images of the "harem" in Arab society and the "geisha" in Japan. Taking a more recent example, the Broadway musical, *Miss Saigon*, and such Disney films as *Pocahontas* and *Aladdin* are often criticized for their Orientalist stereotypes and assumptions about non-Western women and cultures as a whole. Scholars in Asian American Studies claim that these negative images of Asians are inseparably tied to discrimination and prejudice that Asian immigrants and Asian Americans have experienced in reality.

In addition, it is important to note that although the concept of Orientalism originated as a critique of Western views of the Orient, recent studies of Asians and Asian Americans have revealed that Orientalism is prevalent even among postmodern Asian and Asian American writers. On close examination, popular fictions by such writers as Maxine Hong Kingston, Amy Tan, and Frank Chin have used the Orientalist views of Eastern histories and minority cultures. It reflects the writers' unconscious deployment of the Orientalist stereotypes that have been built upon the enduring Western cultural hegemony.

See also Asian Americans, Discrimination against; Derogatory Terms; Fu Manchu.

Further Reading

Lee, Robert G. *Orientals: Asian Americans in Popular Culture*. Philadelphia: Temple University Press, 2000.

Ma, Sheng-Mei. *The Deathly Embrace: Orientalism and Asian American Identity*. Minneapolis: University of Minnesota Press, 2000.

Macfie, Alexander Lyon. *Orientalism: A Reader*. New York: New York University Press, 2001.

Said, Edward W. *Orientalism*. New York: Vintage Books, 1979.

———. Culture and Imperialism. New York: Vintage Books, 1994.

Tchen, John Kuo Wei. *New York before Chinatown: Orientalism and the Shaping of American Culture, 1776–1882*. Baltimore: Johns Hopkins University Press, 1999.

Yu, Henry. *Thinking Orientals: Migration, Contact, and Exoticism in Modern America*. New York: Oxford University Press, 2002.

Etsuko Maruoka-Ng

"Origin of Ethnic Stratification"

Sociologist Donald Noel developed a theory of the origin of ethnic stratification in his article published in *Social Problems* in 1968. In this now classic article, "Origin of Ethnic Stratification," Noel identified both the preconditions and necessary and sufficient causes of ethnic stratification.

According to Noel, for ethnic stratification to arise, there must be two preconditions. First, there must be two or more ethnic groups in a society. If only one ethnic group exists, there will be no ethnic stratification since the same group will be at the top and at the bottom of the social hierarchy. Second, different groups must have a period of continuous contact in the same society. If there is no group interaction, there will be no stratification. However, recurrent contact between two or more ethnic groups does not necessarily lead to ethnic stratification. The outcome could be ethnic equality.

Noel identified three conditions that cause the emergence of ethnic stratification. First, there must be ethnocentrism. Ethnocentrism refers to the tendency to judge other groups by the standards of one's own group. That is, one's own group is the center and the standard. Norms, values, and behaviors of other groups that are consistent with those of one's own group would be viewed as normal; those that deviate would be deemed abnormal or inferior. Ethnocentrism helps create ethnic boundaries, identities, and a sense of community; justify a double standard of morality for in-group members and for outsiders, in which insiders are not subject to the normal rules concerning dishonesty, cheating, exploitation, and killing; and legitimize actions against other supposedly inferior groups. Hence, ethnocentrism explains whom to dominate.

Second, there must be competition for the same scarce resources (e.g., land, water, jobs, money, prestige, and power) among ethnic groups. One ethnic group is motivated to subordinate another group because this subordination gives the first group advantages over the second group in gaining scarce resources that both groups compete for. Even though two groups are not in direct competition, ethnic subordination could occur if one group has certain resources (e.g., labor, land) desired by the other group. Hence, competition for scarce resources explains why one group seeks to dominate another.

Finally, there must be differential power between ethnic groups. Power includes physical or military strength; technological advantages; possession of wealth, land, natural resources, special job skills or labor power, and valuable information; political power; group size; degree of organization and so forth. One group must be powerful enough to dominate the others. If no group has enough power to control others, ethnic stratification will not occur. Unequal power is probably the most crucial factor, and it is unequal power that explains how to dominate.

Noel argued that only when all three conditions are present together will ethnic stratification emerge. Without ethnocentrism the groups would quickly merge and competition would not be structured along ethnic lines. Without competition, there would be no motivation and no rationale for instituting stratification along ethnic lines. Without differential power, it would simply be impossible for one group to achieve dominance and to impose its wills and ideals upon the others.

Noel then applied this theory to explaining the origin of black slavery—manifestation of black-white stratification. He concluded that ethnocentrism toward blacks who were clearly different from their English colonists in terms of physical or cultural criteria, led to the selection of them as the target of subordination; competition for labor utilized to achieve wealth and prestige provided a rationale to institutionalize slavery; and blacks' lack of power made their enslavement inevitable.

To a great extent, Noel's theory is a synthesis of some valuable ideas from a number of approaches, and it provides a more plausible explanation for the emergence of ethnic stratification. However, Noel's theory is not flawless. Class complicates the causal relationships (Yang 2000).

Further Reading

Noel, Donald. "A Theory of the Origin of Ethnic Stratification." *Social Problems* 16 (1968): 157–172.

Yang, Philip. *Ethnic Studies: Issues and Approaches*. Albany: State University of New York Press, 2000.

Philip Yang

Osama Bin Laden

See Al Qaeda.

Overt Discrimination

See Covert versus Overt Discrimination.

Ozawa v. United States (1922)

Ozawa v. United States was a U.S. Supreme Court case in the fall of 1922 that addressed the question of whether a Japanese person was eligible for citizenship in the United States in light of the 1906 Naturalization Act, which specified that its provisions apply to free white persons and those of African descent. The point on which this case turned was the fact that this act had been edited extensively since its passage to make it quite clear that only free white persons, those of African descent, and other individuals who had served three years or more in the U.S. armed forces were eligible for citizenship. The Court then turned to examining what the definition of a "free white person" is, and came to the conclusion that making clear boundaries for this term is very difficult, but that a Japanese person certainly is not white. Therefore, the Court concluded, Japanese individuals are ineligible for citizenship. They were careful to mention that this case has nothing to say about racial superiority or individual worthiness, particularly in light of the improved state of diplomatic relations with Japan at the time and the numerous briefs describing the accomplishments of Japanese art and culture submitted to the court.

This case paved the way for *United States v. Thind* later, which aimed to determine just what the limits of whiteness were. It also established Japanese Americans as an ethnic group entirely unable to become citizens and thus subject to many forms of discrimination, particularly in terms of ownership laws and employment practices.

See also Asian Americans, Discrimination against; *U.S. v. Thind.*

Mikaila Mariel Lemonik Arthur

P

Paine, Thomas (1737–1809)

Thomas Paine, known as a founding father of the United States and a prominent pamphleteer in the age of the American Revolution, denounced the slavery system in America to be the most monstrous crime against humanity and
conscience. He was born in England, had been raised among commoners, and
had received little formal education. But he belonged to a debating club called
the Headstrong Club. Upon immigrating to America in 1774, he began publicly
expressing his thoughts on religion, politics, and social issues in accessible language. He believed that the age of myth and superstition had gone and a new
age of reason had come. Reason was something bestowed to every human
being without distinctions by the Creator of the Universe. Justice based on
common sense—reason and conscience—would abolish all conventional privileges, including monarchy and hereditary aristocracy. People would govern
themselves in a representative government. His *Common Sense*, published in
1776, inspired thousands of Americans, including Thomas Jefferson and George
Washington, and helped to shape the Declaration of Independence. He is also
the one who conceived the name the United States of America. In the second
part of *Rights of Men*, Paine proposed progressive taxation, funds for social
protection of the poor, family allowances, publicly funded general education,
and old-age pensions, "not as a matter of grace and favor, but of right."

It is no surprise that such an egalitarian spirit debunked the evil of slavery
in his tract "African Slavery in America." To Paine, it was so unnatural that
human beings were sold as commodities, and he called slave traders "men-
stealers." Africans had been industrious farmers, peace-loving people inhabit-
ing fertile lands, "before the Europeans debauched them with liquors, and
bribed them against one another; and that these inoffensive people are
brought into slavery, by stealing them, tempting Kings to sell subjects, which

they can have right to do, and hiring one tribe to war against another, to catch prisoners." Buying slaves is no less criminal than selling them, insofar as they are ill-gotten goods. Slaves themselves are true owners of their freedom. For the already enslaved, Paine proposed, besides emancipation, humane treatment of aging slaves, granting land at reasonable rent, paying reasonable wages, helping all build up some property, having families living together, and settling on the frontiers. He thought these measures would lead them to active participation in public affairs.

See also Abolitionist Movement.

Further Reading

Fruchtman, Jack, Jr. *Thomas Paine: Apostle of Freedom*. New York: Four Walls Eight Windows, 1994.

Dong-Ho Cho

Palestinian Islamic Jihad

See Islamic Jihad.

Pan-Asian Solidarity

Asian Americans (about eleven million according to the 2000 census data) consist of fifteen or more national-origin groups that have different languages, religions, and historical traditions. Despite their diversity, Asian Americans share common experiences mainly because they are treated as one group by government agencies and the general public alike. The U.S. Census Bureau classified all Asian and Pacific Islander groups together in 1980 and 1990. Following census classification, local and federal government agencies, public school districts, and colleges/universities lumped all Asian Americans and Pacific Islanders together for policy and resource-allocation purposes. Therefore, all Asian and Pacific Islander ethnic groups needed to make concerted efforts to protect their interests in welfare, health, education, and so forth. Asian (and Pacific Islander) American studies programs that had mushroomed since the early 1970s emphasized the common fate of Asian Americans or Asian Pacific Islander Americans.

Since Pacific Islanders composed a tiny fraction (about 5 percent in 1990) of Asian and Pacific Islander Americans in the 1990 census, the classification of the Asian and Pacific Islander populations in the same category mainly contributed to pan-Asian solidarity. In the 2000 census, the U.S. Census Bureau tabulated Asian Americans and Pacific Islanders separately. This may lead other government agencies and schools to tabulate Asian Americans and Pacific Islander separately. This change in classification system is likely to further enhance pan-Asian solidarity. Because government and schools have allocated for resources for Asian Americans as one group, several pan-Asian organizations, such as the Asian American Mental Health Center and Asian American Bilingual Resource Center, have been established in Los Angeles, New York, and other large metropolitan areas.

In addition to the tabulation of Asian Americans into the same category by government agencies and schools, most Americans have difficulty in distinguishing members of various Asian ethnic groups, despite some observable physical differences. Thus, in 1982, two white Americans in Detroit murdered a Chinese American man, Vincent Chin, with a baseball bat, because they mistook him for a Japanese American. In 1990, a Vietnamese immigrant was severely beaten by black gangs in Brooklyn because they thought he was a Korean. Each incident led Asian Americans to realize that they could be targets of attack by non–Asian Americans simply because they share Asian American physical characteristics. Thus, each incident enhanced pan-Asian unity. When Judge Charles Kaufman gave the two white criminals only three years of probation, the Asian American community formed American Citizens for Justice to protest the lenient sentence. Asian Americans across the country also sent letters of protest to the judge's office.

The practical need of Asian Americans to make pan-Asian coalitions to protect their political and economic interests is another factor that has contributed to pan-Asian solidarity. With the exception of Japanese Americans in Hawaii, no Asian ethnic group in any metropolitan area has a population that is large enough to elect its candidate as a mayor or even as a city council member. But the Asian American population in many West Coast cities and New York City is large enough to influence city politics with a pan-Asian coalition. Thus, Asian Americans in many cities have made pan-Asian coalitions for political purposes. For example, Japanese Americans in Monterey Park, California, mostly native born, made a coalition with Chinese immigrants in the 1980s and 1990s to elect Asian American candidates for mayors and city council members.

In 2000, Jon Liu, a Chinese American, was elected as the first Asian American council member in New York City, representing the Flushing district. He was reelected in 2003. Again, without a broad pan-Asian coalition in the Flushing area, involving Chinese, Korean, and Indian immigrants, he could not have been elected.

See also Pan-ethnic Movements.

Further Reading

Espiritu, Yen Le. *Asian American Panethnicity: Bridging Institutions and Identities.* Philadelphia: Temple University Press, 1992.

We, William. *The Asian American Movement.* Philadelphia: Temple University Press.

Pyong Gap Min

Pan-ethnic Movements

Pan-ethnicity is a created ethnic identity that draws together diverse groups of people who differ in their language, national origin, religion, culture, immigration history, and other facets of identity but who nonetheless view themselves as part of the same group. In many cases, this identity is first a categorization developed externally; for example, by the U.S. Census Bureau.

At other times, the identity is created by groups of individuals themselves as they search for those with whom they identify. Examples of pan-ethnic identities are Asian American, Latino/a, South Asian, or Caribbean. As is evidenced by these types of names, the groups that make up a pan-ethnic identity can come from an area as broad as a continent or as small as a group of islands. They can speak many different languages or just a few. The most important point is that they belong to different specific ethnicities but have come together to form a common identity.

The creation of a pan-ethnic identity involves the following elements: the construction of a common history and of a unified symbolic culture (often involving elements common across the participant ethnicities, such as food, religion, or language); the development of a political ideology that mobilizes participants; the organization of groups and organizations that represent the pan-ethnic identity to the outside world (such as political action committees and campus student groups); and the recognition of the pan-ethnic identity by the outside world (in many cases, this is an easy task, since the outside world is often the force to first apply the pan-ethnic label). In many cases, it was necessary for particular descent groups to live in the United States for multiple generations before their members could reach beyond national memories of conflict with their new "partner" groups to pan-ethnic identities. Of course, pan-ethnic groups still face internal divisions over specific aspects of ethnic identity, histories of national conflict, gender, social class, and other factors.

Pan-ethnic identities are largely political in nature, and this means that they are likely to act in a political way and to develop social movements around their identity. These movements are, in the broad sense, civil rights movements. They fight for political representation of their constituents, educational policies that help their constituents succeed, employment practices that do not discriminate against them, and public awareness of the issues and problems that they face. Choosing to employ pan-ethnic definitions and identities in these movements has been helpful as it allows them to present, in their activism, a unified front and a face consistent with outsider definitions. The development of pan-ethnic identities and pan-ethnic movements was also an important precursor to the establishment of ethnic-studies departments and student centers on campuses, as these departments and centers speak to wide groups of students rather than those descended from particular nations and backgrounds.

The particular demands and outcomes of different pan-ethnic movements have, of course, varied. In addition, there are constant struggles within movements over how they will define themselves and who counts as a part of the movement (for instance, should there be an Asian Pacific American movement and identity, an Asian American one, or an East Asian American and South Asian American duality?). Movements also struggle with one another over the limited resources provided by the wider society for dealing with their needs and the demands that they press. Finally, the gains that movements do make are not guaranteed to be permanent, as the continued reorganization and reassessment of various affirmative action programs can demonstrate.

See also Black Nationalist Movement; Pan-Asian Solidarity; Red Power Movement; "Third World Movement" of the 1960s.

Further Reading

Ackah, William B. *Pan-Africanism: Exploring the Contradictions: Politics, Identity, and Development in Africa and the African Diaspora.* Brookfield, VT: Ashgate, 1999.

Espiritu, Yen Le. *Asian American Panethnicity: Bridging Institutions and Identities.* Philadelphia: Temple University Press, 1992.

Hertzberg, Hazel W. *The Search for an American Indian Identity: Modern Pan-Indian Movements.* Syracuse, NY: Syracuse University Press, 1971.

Morales, Ed. *Living in Spanglish: The Search for a New Latino Identity in America.* New York: St. Martin's Press, 2002.

Mikaila Mariel Lemonik Arthur

Panic-peddling

See Block-busting.

Park, Robert

See Race-Relations Cycle.

Parks, Rosa (1913–)

Often referred to as the "Mother of the Civil Rights Movement," Rosa Parks is credited with personifying and galvanizing forces during the early period of the civil rights movement in general and during the Montgomery Bus Boycott in particular. Parks is a civil rights activist and speaker, seamstress, and author. She was born in Tuskegee, Alabama on February 4, 1913, to James and Leona McCauley and is the granddaughter of former slaves. Her father was a carpenter and her mother was a teacher. Parks was raised by her mother and grandparents on a farm in Pine Level, Alabama. At the age of eleven, Parks attended the Industrial School for Girls and later attended the Alabama State Teachers College. In 1932, she married Raymond Parks, a barber, and they lived in Montgomery, Alabama. Due to discrimination and Jim Crow laws in the South, the only jobs many black women could hold were as domestics in white homes. Parks' training in sewing enabled her to locate part-time employment as a seamstress. She would later become a tailor's assistant at a local department store. Parks also became a member of the local chapter of the National Association for the Advancement of Colored People (NAACP), where she was trained in the art of nonviolent protest. As a member, she was also involved in voter-registration drives and later became the secretary of the Montgomery branch of the NAACP.

On December 1, 1955, Parks became famous when she refused to give up her seat on a crowded bus. Although she was seated in the "Blacks Only" section, because the bus was crowded and a white passenger wished to sit, she was asked to move. With her refusal, she was arrested for violating segregation laws. The treatment of Rosa Park ignited local civil rights leaders, who formed the Montgomery Improvement Association and, under the leadership of Rev. Martin Luther King Jr. and Ralph D. Abernathy, organized the Mont-

Rosa Parks sits in a 1950s-era bus in Montgomery, Alabama, during the 40th anniversary celebration of the Montgomery bus boycott, December 2, 1995.

AP/Wide World Photos.

gomery Bus Boycott. For 382 days, blacks refused to ride Montgomery public buses. Approximately 42,000 people took part in the boycott. The boycott received national media attention and spurred a civil rights legal battle that reached the U.S. Supreme Court, which ruled that segregation on public buses and in public facilities was unconstitutional.

Parks's involvement in the boycott was later met with harassment by whites in Montgomery, and she was subsequently fired from her job. She and her husband eventually relocated to Detroit, Michigan, where Parks resumed work as a seamstress and dressmaker. She would later become a staff person for U.S. Representative John Conyers (D-MI) and a public speaker on civil rights. In 1987, Parks founded the Rosa and Raymond Parks Institute for Self-Development that sponsors annual outings to educate youth about the civil rights movement. In 1996, Parks was awarded the Presidential Medal of Freedom: the highest honor the U.S. government can bestow on a nonmilitary citizen. Her four books, *Rosa Parks: My Story*, *Dear Mrs. Parks: A Dialogue with Today's Youth*, *Quiet Strength*, and *I Am Rosa Parks* chronicle her personal experiences living in a segregated society and her involvement in the civil rights movement.

See also Civil Rights Movement; Jim Crow Laws; King, Martin Luther, Jr.; Montgomery Bus Boycott; National Association for the Advancement of Colored People (NAACP).

Further Reading

Brinkley, Douglas. *Rosa Parks*. New York: Viking Press, 2000.

Parks, Rosa. *Rosa Parks: My Story*. New York: Dial Books, 1992.

Quarles, Benjamin. *The Negro in the Making of America*. New York: Simon & Schuster, 1987.

Sandra L. Barnes

Passing of the Great Race, The

Madison Grant (1865–1937) and his most widely read book, *The Passing of the Great Race* (1916), were influential in shaping American attitudes and social policies about race, immigration, and eugenics in the first third of the twentieth century. He was well educated, had strong affiliations and influential positions with prestigious scientific institutions (he was a founder and chairman of the New York Zoological Society as well as a trustee of the American Museum of Natural History), and he was well connected to many members of the Northeast's upper-class elite. Grant was convinced that racial differences among the world's peoples were the most powerful causal factor determining not only their appearance, but their intelligence, work ethic, and other social and psychological characteristics. His racist theorizing included ideas about a "superior race" and a need for that race and its "most fit" members to out-reproduce the lower classes and inferior races. Clearly his ideas and those of other scholars of his era with similar views (e.g., Lothrop T. Stoddard, and Henry Fairchild Osborn), were opposed to those scientists who were formulating environmentalist theories stipulating that social conditioning, cultural milieu, and agents of socialization were more influential than "race" or simple genetic inheritance.

Grant argued in essays, lectures, and several books (especially *The Passing of the Great Race*) that there was a "Nordic race," and that this race was superior to all others on the most important physical traits, mental abilities, and characteristics of temperament that lead to human progress or advancement. Grant contended, in *The Passing of the Great Race*, that Nordic founders and "Nordic blood" were what made several ancient civilizations great, and in this regard his writing resembles ideas of earlier racists Joseph Arthur Gobineau or Houston S. Chamberlain. Moreover, he argued that it was the special *racial* qualities of the early Nordic settlers and immigrants in the U.S. from Great Britain and northwestern Europe (and their "pure-blood" descendants) that were responsible for producing the outstanding political, cultural, economic, and scientific institutions of American life.

Despite the qualities of genius and strength that Grant attributed to the "Nordic race," he was deeply worried, even pessimistic, about its future in the United States. In *The Passing of the Great Race*, he expressed fear that the high civilization that Nordics built (which he considered one of mankind's greatest achievements) was threatened with racial and reproductive threats that might destroy it. He wrote of three threats. One was racial intermarriage between Nordics and members of "less fit races." He feared this because he believed, erroneously, that the offspring of such intermarriages inherit the traits of the inferior or weaker parent. He therefore urged the United States to strengthen or expand its state laws against racial intermarriage to avoid what he called "racial degeneration." Grant's second fear was the heavy immigration arriving in the United States from countries of southern and eastern Europe. His theory was that people from these countries were mainly from the backward or primitive "Alpine" and "Mediterranean" races, and that as millions and millions of them arrived, Nordic American society would be overrun with inferiors who could neither appreciate nor assimilate into it. For this reason, Grant campaigned strongly for drastic reductions in the number of southern and eastern European immigrants allowed to enter the United States. Indeed, he consulted with a leading congressional sponsor of immigration-restriction legislation (Albert Johnson of Washington) in devising a quota system that would reduce the flow of newcomers from that region.

Grant's third fear arose out of his understanding of the newly developed field of eugenics. He believed that members of the upper class (to which his family had belonged for several generations) were genetically "more fit" or superior to members of the middle and lower classes in regard to intelligence, industriousness, and many other important characteristics. Given this attitude, a demographic pattern alarmed him: upper-class families were having fewer children than were lower-class families. He believed this was the main cause of increases in crime, poverty, alcoholism, and feeblemindedness. To save the nation from those problems, Grant endorsed the proposals of the eugenics movement, that upper-class "Nordic Americans" have more children and that the least capable and least productive segment of the lower classes, especially those from racial/ethnic minorities, be sterilized so that they could not reproduce. Some states did pass sterilization laws and this practice was adopted in Nazi Germany.

Grant rejected both the idea of racial equality and the notion of America as a mixture of many people and cultures from around the world as "maudlin sentimentalism" and naïve idealism that was misguided and would lead to disastrous consequences. Actually, his racist ideas, which are based more on myth and ethnocentrism than on scientific facts, have led to monumental suffering and disaster, and yet numerous groups, including those espousing white supremacy, still voice the same myths, exaggerations, and distortions that Grant asserted.

See also Academic Racism; Biological Racism; Nordic Superiority.

Further Reading

Gossett, Thomas F. *Race: The History of an Idea in America*. Dallas: Southern Methodist University Press, 1963.

Grant, Madison. *The Passing of the Great Race*. New York: Scribner & Sons, 1916.

Charles Jaret

Passing, Psychosocial

Historically, *passing* most commonly referred to the phenomenon in which people of African ancestry who had a phenotypical likeness to whites (generally because of mixed ancestry), assumed a white racial identity. This phenomenon is unique in U.S. history because the very presence of light-skinned African Americans speaks to the taboo of interracial relations between blacks and whites and the often unacknowledged but widespread practice of white masters having sex with their female slaves. This type of passing became a particularly important issue during the post–Civil War era, when the advent of antimiscegenation laws and "one-drop" legal designations of blackness made passing one of the few viable paths to social and economic mobility for African Americans.

At present, passing is discussed as a psychosocial phenomenon in which minority members, regardless of what they look like, adopt the cultural norms and the political ideology of the mainstream society. In this context, passing stems from the conscious or unconscious desire of minority members to be accepted by white society. Prominent African American conservatives, such as Supreme Court Justice Clarence Thomas, are often criticized as trying to pass for white because their political values and beliefs are so incongruent with what are considered to be larger African American political and social interests.

Passing is almost always considered a derogatory act, especially when it involves individuals from minority groups that have their own defined cultural norms and value systems. Their "passing" is often considered an abandonment of their native culture in favor of "acting white." The feeling of betrayal is especially sharp among minority groups that have been systematically oppressed by the white majority, such as African Americans and American Indians, because often much of the group's cultural identity and attitudes have developed in response to this oppression. Such minorities are characterized as possessing what anthropologist John Ogbu terms a "secondary cultural system," in which cultural differences arise in a state of subordination. For example, African Americans and American Indians have a long history of having their native culture and language subordinated and disvalued. Though they may understand the adoption of white practices and behavior as a means to succeeding in school and in the job market, they may feel resentful that these requirements are being imposed on them by the dominant society. Also, their differences in culture and language often represent boundary-maintaining symbols of identity to be preserved because it gives them a sense of collectivity and self-worth. Thus, when such individuals "pass" as white they are not only viewed as being disloyal to their cultural heritage, but as actively "going over to the enemy."

There are many areas of social life in which passing may be exhibited—in politics (e.g., when an African American identifies him/herself politically as a conservative Republican), employment (e.g., when an Asian immigrant attempts to enter into a largely white corporate field rather than partake in an ethnic business), and personal relations (e.g., when a member of a minority group has a white spouse). One of the most extensively researched and discussed areas in which passing can be an issue is within the framework of educational achievement. Here, conflicting cultural systems and the fear of "acting white" often cause minority students, especially African American and Latinos, to fail school rather than adopt the mainstream white ideology of "achievement through educational advancement" and be seen as trying to pass as white.

Among immigrant groups, such as Asian immigrants, educational achievement is not necessarily such a contested area, since many immigrant groups stress educational achievement similar to whites. Nevertheless, many immigrant parents lament that their children are becoming "too American" in their lax work habits, in their behavior, and in their disrespectful attitude toward authority. Among their ethnic peers, immigrant children who "hang out" with white friends, who eschew speaking their native language, as well as their native music and cultural institutions (e.g., churches and other ethnic organizations), are often thought to be trying to pass as white.

See also "Acting White" Stage of Life; Black Conservatives; Colonized versus Immigrant Minorities; Oppositional Identity; Thomas, Clarence.

Further Reading

Ogbu, John U. "Immigrant and Involuntary Minorities in Comparative Perspective." In Margaret Gibson and John Ogbu, ed., *Minority Status and Schooling: A Comparative Study of Immigrant and Involuntary Minorities*, 3–33. New York: Garland Publishing, Inc., 1991.

Russell, Kathy, Midge Wilson, and Ronald Hall. *The Color Complex: The Politics of Skin Color among African Americans*. New York: Anchor Books, 1992.

Tracy Chu

Paternalistic Race Relations

See Race Relations, Paternalistic versus Competitive.

Patriot Act

See Government Initiatives after the September 11, 2001, Attack on the United States; September 11, 2001, Terrorism, Discriminatory Reactions to.

P.C.

See Political Correctness (P.C.).

Peculiar Institution: Slavery in the Ante-bellum South, The

The publication in 1956 of Kenneth Stampp's monumental work, *The Peculiar Institution: Slavery in the Ante-bellum South*, heralded the beginning of a significant revision of the history of slavery. Until then, historians generally held that slavery was a "civilized" institution borne out of the cultural and racial mores of the South. Stampp's work was influential in that it rejected the notion of the civilizing influence of slavery. Slavery was not seen as a benign, paternalistic system, but rather as a coercive and profit-seeking regime. His emphasis on viewing slavery in economic rather than cultural terms allowed him to address in specific ways the mechanisms through which slave labor was controlled and exploited. For example, his careful description of the myriad slave codes that developed in the South showed the extent to which the most coercive aspects of slavery were institutionalized through legal statute.

Stampp's work also shed new light on the slave experience itself. *The Peculiar Institution* revealed the plantation as a scene of constant conflict and social tension, rather than a serene haven of Southern culture. Stampp dealt at length with some of the more troublesome aspects of slave life, such as the breakup of slave families and white fears of rebellion and miscegenation. His study paved the way for later research that more completely conveyed the experiences of slaves through the testimonies of slaves themselves.

The phrase "peculiar institution" refers to the institution of slavery in the antebellum South. Its origins derive from the Latin *peculiaris*, which means "of or relating to private property." Because slaves were considered "chattel personal," or private property, this term for slavery was particularly apt.

See also Plantation System; Slave Auctions; Slave Codes; Slave Families; Slave Revolts and White Attacks on Black Slaves; Slave Trade; Slavery in the Antebellum South; Underground Railroad.

Further Reading

Stampp, Kenneth. *The Peculiar Institution: Slavery in the Ante-bellum South*. New York: Vintage Books, 1956.

Rebekah Lee

Phenotype

See Genotype v. Phenotype.

Philippine-American War

The United States invaded the Philippines on May 1, 1898, when, under the pretext of the Spanish-American War, Commodore George Dewey led a squadron of American warships into Manila Bay, destroyed the Spanish war fleet stationed there, and established a beachhead on Philippine soil. On December 21, 1898, the United States unilaterally annexed the Philippines when President William McKinley declared the U.S. possession of the islands and a corresponding policy of Benevolent Assimilation. But this unilateral annexation of the Philippines led to a war between American forces and the Philippine revolutionary army between February 1899 and July 1902.

Emilio Aguinaldo and his forces had sought independence from Spain beginning in 1896, only to be exiled to Hong Kong in 1897 when the insurgency failed. Commodore Dewey invited Aguinaldo to return to the Philippines, landing him and his troops on Luzon. Aguinaldo believed that the United States would support his revolution. He soon controlled the islands, except for

Manila, and declared independence on June 12, 1898. Late in July, twelve thousand U.S. soldiers had arrived, and an uneasy peace developed between them and Aguinaldo's forces. Aguinaldo's friends, however, went on to convene a congress at Malolos in September and approve a constitution in November. On January 23, 1899, Aguinaldo was inaugurated as president.

In less than two weeks, war broke out when two American soldiers killed three Filipino soldiers outside of Manila. By November, after experiencing numerous defeats, Aguinaldo had to dissolve his army and attempted to continue fighting a guerilla war. This too failed eventually. Aguinaldo was captured in March of 1901, swore allegiance to the United States, and asked his revolutionaries to cease fighting. Some resistance continued until 1903 and in the Muslim Moro province, until 1914. The war had cost the lives of 4,234 U.S. soldiers, 16,000 Filipino soldiers, and some 200,000 Filipino civilians. The United States had squashed the native rebellion against colonial rule.

The Philippine Organic Act of 1902 reorganized the U.S. administration of the islands. Elections to a two-house legislature were to be held when peace finally arrived and the Bill of Rights was extended to Filipinos. William Howard Taft, the first civilian governor, declared that his measure of any rules and regulations would simply be the welfare of the people. Under his guidance, a free system of elementary education was broadened, an economic development plan was established, and Catholic Church lands were purchased for resale to Filipinos, since the Organic Act had taken away the Church's status as the state religion. In July 1907, elections for the assembly were held.

The Jones Act replaced the 1902 Organic Act in 1916. It promised independence as soon as the government stabilized. Previous to this, only the House had been popularly elected, and the Philippines Commission acted as the Senate. Now the people would elect the Senate too, but executive functions still belonged to Americans. The independence movement picked up in the United States during the Depression, when an unlikely coalition of farmers and labor unions pushed for Philippine independence to protect themselves from cheap agricultural goods and cheap labor. Congress passed a bill in January 1933, over President Herbert Hoover's veto, that protected American trade interests, excluded Filipino immigrants, and retained the U.S. military bases on the islands in return for Filipino independence. The Philippine legislature, however, would not agree to it.

The Tydings-McDuffie Act, passed in March 1934, was a compromise. The Commonwealth of the Philippines would be established during a ten year transition period, after which independence would follow. During the transition, the United States would be in charge of foreign policy, and the president would have to approve any laws regarding currency, foreign trade, and immigration. The United States got what it wanted. only fifty Filipino immigrants to the United States a year were permitted, but Americans could enter and reside in the Philippines at will; tariffs on Philippine goods gradually increased to 100 percent in 1946 after an initial five year standstill, but American goods could enter the Philippines duty-free for a full ten years; and the United States could retain a naval base and stations for fueling. After the devastating occupation of the Philippines by Japan from 1942 to 1945, the United States again took possession of the islands, and Philippine independence finally came about on July 4, 1946.

Most Americans are aware of the Spanish-American war, which lasted less than a year. But few Americans seem to remember the Philippine-American War, which lasted three years and claimed 200,000 Filipino lives. Furthermore, many Americans who know of the U.S. involvement in the Philippines still seem to accept the myth that Americans went to the Philippines to liberate it from the Spanish colonization. Contrary to the myth, the U.S. occupation of the Philippines at the end of the nineteenth and beginning of the twentieth century was an imperialist war that crushed hundreds of thousands of Filipino nationalists who fought for self-rule. The ensuing forty-five-year U.S. rule was as devastating to the Philippines and its people as the military conquest of the islands. Even since its independence in 1946, the Filipino economy has continued to be dominated by U.S.-based multinational corporations. Moreover, the immigration of Filipinos to the United States and the identity of Filipino Americans have never ceased to be influenced by the legacy of colonization.

See also Manifest Destiny; Spanish-American War.

Further Reading

"Essays into American Empire in the Philippines." Special issue, *Amera Journal* 24, no. 2, 1998.

Feuer, A. B., ed. *America at War: The Philippines, 1898–1913*. Westport, CT: Praeger, 2002.

Tan, Samuel K. *The Filipino-American War, 1899–1913*. Quezon City: University Press of the Philippines, 2002.

Benjamin F. Shearer

Philippines, U.S. Rule in

See Philippine-American War.

PIJ

See Islamic Jihad.

Plantation System

The plantation system was a system of capitalist agriculture that developed in the Americas in the late seventeenth and early eighteenth centuries. It was based on the acquisition of large plots of land, an organized pool of labor, and technological investment. The plantation system of agriculture represented a significant shift from the traditional yeoman style of farming that existed in the colonies of the New World previously. The development of plantation economies had a significant impact on the course of slavery in America.

Plantation economies were cash-crop economies, dependent in large part on single commodities that required intensive labor to produce tobacco, cotton, rice, hemp, and sugar. Plantation economies were dependent on the subordination of a consistent, cheap, and large supply of labor to maximize profits. Slavery provided a convenient solution to this dilemma. In the balmy

Plantation slaves in Beaufort, South Carolina, circa 1862.

Courtesy Library of Congress.

climates of the South (particularly the Deep South), where cash crops had the best chance for success, plantation slavery reached its zenith. Though debate exists as to the extent of the shift from small agricultural units to large plantations, it is clear that by 1860, most slaves were concentrated among plantations of varying sizes in the South.

Plantations operated in a highly organized and coercive manner. Plantations needed to run efficiently, thus slaves operated under a hierarchical system designed to train and discipline them. At the top of the hierarchy was the slaveowner and his family. If the owner had a large number of slaves and a sizable plantation, he often hired an overseer to look after the day-to-day management of the plantation and to ensure that slaves were obedient and productive. Overseers were a diverse group. They were sometimes familial relations of the owners, or sometimes semiprofessional overseers who expected to oversee as a career for life, or in hopes of eventually buying land of their own.

"Field" slaves usually worked under the supervision of a slave "driver," normally a slave appointed to act as foreman of field labor and supervisor of living quarters. Drivers helped manage slave training and supervised agricultural activities, from planting to cotton-ginning, curing tobacco, and boiling sugar. "House" slaves tended to the maintenance of the owner's domestic quarters and gardens and were usually under the supervision of the slaveowner's wife. In a large plantation, slaves were also employed as blacksmiths, carpenters, and other craftsmen.

Considerable scholarship has helped debunk the myth of the plantation system as a benign, paternalistic institution. The image of the "genteel" Southern plantation, where planter-owners leisurely pursued a "civilized" existence had little resemblance to slaves' experience of plantation life. Though significant variations existed in the level of coercion experienced by slaves, there is little doubt that slaves survived through a regimented, and often brutal, existence. Plantation owners in the South lived in perpetual fear of slave revolts and required maximum productivity, and thus maximum obedience, from their slaves. Thus, every aspect of a slave's life was regulated. Slaves toiled year-round, with precious little time for leisure or their own personal lives. Overseers often brutally beat their slaves into submission, with little fear of punishment because of the protection the slave codes provided. These coercive features gave the plantation system the characteristics of a "total institution."

Some scholars argue that slaves ultimately suffered because of the shift to a plantation style of agriculture in the South. They argue that slaves led a less regulated existence under yeoman farming, because farms' smaller size and diversified agricultural output meant that a hierarchical division of labor could not become entrenched. There was less social distance between slaves and their owners, and sometimes owners participated in farming activities alongside their slaves. However, the importance of this distinction should not be overstated. Plantation slavery certainly introduced new mechanisms for the coercion and oppression of slaves. But conversely, because plantation slaves were able to live together in large numbers in slave quarters, away from the eyes of their masters, slave culture found room to flourish in ways not possible under yeoman farming.

See also The Peculiar Institution: Slavery in the Ante-bellum South; Slave Auctions; Slave Codes; Slave Families; Slave Revolts and White Attacks on Black Slaves; Slave Trade; Slavery in the Antebellum South; Underground Railroad.

Further Reading

Blassingame, John. *The Slave Community: Plantation Life in the Antebellum South*. New York: Oxford University Press, 1979.

Genovese, Eugene. *Roll, Jordan, Roll: The World the Slaves Made*. New York: Pantheon, 1974.

Stampp, Kenneth. *The Peculiar Institution: Slavery in the Ante-Bellum South*. New York: Vintage Books, 1956.

Rebekah Lee

Plessy v. Ferguson

See Separate but Equal Doctrine.

Political Correctness (P.C.)

The term political correctness is most often used as a negative description of attempts to change the way issues are talked about, particularly issues of race and gender, and to avoid stereotyping. It gained prominence in the late 1980s and 1990s in response to social movements that sought to change the language used to discuss politically important and often controversial issues. A central assumption of those who advocated such changes is that everyday language can bring with it power dynamics that work against particular groups, particularly those that are already marginalized.

For example, some activists argued that labeling people "disabled" implied that they were less able than others and that the term *disability* was purely negative. In place of that term, some activists suggested that *physically challenged* or *differently abled* be used because they lack the negative connotations of *disabled* and, it was argued, more accurately reflect the experience of individuals being described and do not imply a deficit. Many of the terms called into question are related to race. For example, some terms such as *Negro* and *Oriental* are outdated and carry with them strongly negative connotations and stereotypes. Similarly, the use of the term *Indian* to refer to people indigenous to the Americas is incorrect and reflects historical inaccuracies. Activists promoted the use of more neutral terms, such as African American, Asian, and Native American.

Critics of so-called political correctness argue that being forced to use the new terms amounts to censorship and mangles the English language by replacing commonly accepted terms, such as disabled, with more cumbersome terms, such as *differently abled*. But the most cumbersome of the new terms will most likely fall out of use and others may simply appear cumbersome as we adjust to them. Therefore, in some cases, concerns about verbal censorship and mangling of the English language may be misplaced. The language may simply be catching up to new social realities.

Concerns about free speech and censorship, however, are more valid. Arguments over language can be used to stifle the voices of groups who voice unpopular or dissenting views. Ironically, this argument against political correctness draws on the fundamental insight of many of its early proponents: Language is powerful, and the privileging of some terms over others has political consequences. Battles over supposedly politically correct terms are often battles to define the nature of a situation. Although most charges of political correctness are made by the political right against the political left, Christian fundamentalists have also faced charges that they are stifling debate—particularly in school textbooks—by being politically correct. Left-wing critics have also convincingly argued that the term *politically correct* is itself used to stifle debate and to discredit the arguments of those who wish to challenge the power assumptions implicit in everyday language.

Although the argument over political correctness cooled in the late 1990s, the fundamental issues remain. How is a language that accurately describes the experience of all groups in a multicultural society created? How is civil debate encouraged without encroaching on free speech? When, if ever, does one person's right to his or her opinion infringe on another person's right not to live or work in a hostile environment? How should government and educational institutions weigh the rights of various groups when they come into conflict? How should this translate into the language used within these institutions? Perhaps one of the most dangerous aspects of the arguments over political correctness in the 1990s was that these vital and complex issues were trivialized.

See also Education and Racial Discrimination; Multiculturalism.

Further Reading

D'Souza, Dinesh. *Illiberal Education: The Politics of Race and Sex on Campus*. New York: Free Press, 1998.

Wilson, John K. *The Myth of Political Correctness: The Conservative Attack on Higher Education*. Durham, NC: Duke University Press, 1995.

Robin Roger-Dillon

Poll Tax

A poll tax was a fee charged to citizens who wanted to vote during the segregation era. Poll taxes created a barrier to poor people voting, but they were often used in the rural South to limit the voting power of African Americans, who as a group were disproportionately poor. In 1964, the United States ratified the Twenty-Fourth Amendment to the constitution, which made poll taxes illegal in federal elections. The Twenty-Fourth Amendment states, "The right of citizens of the United States to vote in any primary or other election for President or Vice President, for electors for President or Vice President, or for Senator or Representative in Congress, shall not be denied or abridged by the United States or any State by reason of failure to pay any poll tax or other tax." In 1966, the U.S. Supreme Court ruled that poll taxes were illegal in all elections because they violated the equal-protection clause of the Fourteenth Amendment to the Constitution. Although the poll tax in the United States had the effect—and intent—of disenfranchising many African Americans, it also affected poor whites and other economically disadvantaged groups.

See also Black Political Disenfranchisement; Fourteenth Amendment; Literacy Test.

Robin Roger-Dillon

Poole, Elijah

See Muhammad, Elijah.

Poverty

See Culture of Poverty Thesis; Racial Difference in Poverty Rate.

Powell, Colin (1937–)

First-term secretary of state under George W. Bush, Colin Powell, the son of Jamaican immigrants, was born in New York City on April 5, 1937, and was raised in the South Bronx. Powell was educated in New York City public

Colin Powell, the first African American secretary of state, January 2001.

Courtesy State Department.

schools and graduated from the City College of New York (CCNY), where he earned a bachelor's degree in geology. He also participated in ROTC at CCNY and received a commission as an Army second lieutenant upon graduation in June 1958. Powell was sent to a training school in Fort Benning, Georgia, where he had an awakening in the form of black and white military segregation, which led him to become an admirer of Martin Luther King Jr. He went on to earn a master of business administration degree from George Washington University.

Powell was a professional soldier for thirty-five years, during which time he held many command and staff positions and rose to the rank of four-star general. He was assistant to the president for national security affairs from 1987 to 1989. Powell served as the twelfth chairman of the joint chiefs of staff, the highest military position in the Department of Defense, from 1989 to 1993, under presidents George H. Bush and Bill Clinton. During this time, he oversaw twenty-eight military crises, including Operation Desert Storm in the 1991 Persian Gulf War. On January 20, 2001, he became the sixty-fifth secretary of state, in the George W. Bush administration. Powell is the first African American to hold this high office in the U.S. government. During his career, he has made many speeches and challenged young black Americans to hold high expectations for their lives and to realize those expectations through character-building activities and hard work.

See also Gulf War; War and Racial Inequality.

Sookhee Oh

Prejudice, Cognitive and Emotional Dimensions of

Prejudice usually refers to negative attitudes or beliefs toward a group and its members that are based on faulty or inadequate information. Prejudice may in fact be manifested in positive attitudes or opinions, but scholars usually avert positive prejudice and focus on negative attitudes and beliefs because negative attitudes and beliefs overshadow positive ones in frequency and intensity, and because scholars are most concerned about the consequences of negative attitudes and beliefs and how to deal with them. It is this negativity that defines prejudice. Moreover, prejudice is a prejudgment based on wrong or inadequate information. It is a categorical judgment based on the group membership of individuals.

Prejudice includes cognitive and emotional dimensions. The cognitive dimension of prejudice refers to false beliefs about a group based on faulty or insufficient information. The most typical form of cognitive prejudice is stereotype, which is an overgeneralization or exaggeration about the characteristics of a particular group that ignores individual differences within the group. Examples of stereotyping: African Americans are oversexed; Indians are drunkards; Asian Americans are treacherous; Italian Americans are associated with the Mafia; and Jews are money hungry. These stereotypes are false characterizations of these groups.

The emotional (or affective) dimension refers to negative feelings about a group, such as fear, hatred, dislike, disgust, uneasiness, contempt, or suspicion. It has to do with sentiments, emotions, or feelings. The cognitive and emotional dimensions of prejudice may be intertwined. For example, a feeling of dislike or uneasiness toward another group may be associated with a person's stereotype toward that group.

Philip Yang

Property Holding

See Racial Differences in Property Holding.

Proposition 187

See California Ballot Proposition 187.

Proposition 209

See California Ballot Proposition 209.

Proposition 227

See California Ballot Proposition 227.

Proximal Host

The proximal host is a concept that David Mittleberg and Mary Waters first used in 1992 to explain how new immigrant groups come to be identified in American society with the native group that is closest to it ethnically and racially. When members of a new immigrant group arrive in the United States, Americans tend to classify the new group on the basis of the racial/ethnic category that already exists, even when the new immigrant group may not fit into that classification. This new identity may strain relations between the newcomers and the native population.

African Americans in the United States find themselves identified as the proximal host of Caribbean blacks by Americans, even though they come from different regions in the Caribbean and do not base their identity and culture on skin pigmentation. Therefore, they are often reluctant to be identified as African American in the United States. In a comparative study of Haitian and Israeli immigrants, Mittelberg and Waters noted that even though Haitian middle-class immigrants prefer not to be classified as African Americans in the United States, they often find themselves classified in that category by U.S. officials. Although Israeli immigrants living in the United States prefer to maintain their identity as such and practice Judaism in their own way, they find themselves being identified with American Jewry, which has a different meaning than being a national of Israel.

New immigrants may resist being classified in a new racial/ethnic group because they want to preserve their culture, language, and religion. New immigrants from Mexico who move to states that have a large Mexican American population often prefer to maintain a separate religious and cultural identity from the established Mexican group because they believe that Mexican Americans are too far removed from Mexico's culture and religion. There are also instances in which an ethnic group may prefer to be associated with the proximal host if such an association can help it acquire resources and status to further increase its economic standing in the United States. Polish immigrants, for example, may not resent being considered part of the Polish American community because this gives them access to employment, resources, and services in neighborhoods that already have an established Polish American community.

Even when Caribbean immigrants resent being identified as African Americans, their proximal host, they have limited options because race plays an important role in group identification in the United States. Whereas an Israeli immigrant who chooses not to identify with the American Jewry can change his religion, intermarry, or move away from communities that have a large Jewish concentration, this distancing is not as easily available to Haitians, Jamaicans, Ghanaians, or Nigerians. As blacks, they are often forced to live in minority neighborhoods, and they suffer the same racial prejudice that African Americans encounter in their daily lives.

See also Caribbean Immigrants, Attitudes toward African Americans; Caribbean Immigrants, Experience of Racial Discrimination.

Further Reading

Mittelberg, David, and Mary Waters. "The Process of Ethnogenesis among Haitian and Israeli immigrants in the United States." *Ethnic and Racial Studies* 15 (1992): 412–435.

Warner, Stephen R., and Judith G. Wittner, ed. *Gatherings in the Diaspora, Religious Communities and the New Iimmigration.* Philadelphia: Temple University Press, 1998.

Watkins-Owens, Irma. *Blood Relations: Caribbean Immigrants and the Harlem Community, 1900–1930.* Bloomington: Indiana University Press, 1996.

Francois Pierre-Louis

Q, R

Quota Act of 1924

See National Origins Act of 1924.

Race Card in Political Campaigns

The "race card," in political campaigns, is the use of coded words, racial stereo-types, and issues by white candidates against blacks and other minority candidates. The most typical example of using the race card in a political campaign to appeal to white voters was seen in 1988. Michael Dukakis was nominated as the Democratic Party candidate to challenge Vice President George Bush for the presidency. Bush attacked Dukakis for being too soft on crime and used as an example of his liberal view the parole of Willie Horton, an African American who was convicted of rape in the state of Massachusetts. While he was released on a furlough program, Horton traveled to Maryland, where he robbed a house and raped a white woman. Capitalizing on whites' fear of crime and of African Americans, Bush's campaign mounted several advertising programs in which a black man was shown going through a revolving door and accusing Dukakis of being too soft on crime, particularly crime committed by blacks. As white America is afraid of black crimes associated with assault, robbery, and rape, the publicity around the release of Horton further alienated voters from Dukakis.

Politicians do not explicitly mention it. But it is a common understanding that even when speaking of combating crime they are specifically appealing to white voters who think that blacks are the cause of this problem. Since the passage of the Civil Rights Act of 1964, politicians, the media, and those who harbor the white-supremacist viewpoint have found different ways to make race a salient issue in American politics without ever mentioning it.

See also Civil Rights Act of 1964; Liberal and Conservative Views of Racial Inequality.

Francois Pierre-Louis

Race Matters

Published in 1994, *Race Matters* is a social commentary on contemporary race relations in the United States written by Cornell West, scholar, theologian, author, minister, activist, and public intellectual. The author addressed the role of race in shaping the experiences of Blacks in the United States, especially poor and disenfranchised inner-city residents. According to West, "race" continues to matter economically (government cutbacks of aid to the poor), spiritually (stereotypes and negative portrayals of black culture), and politically (black leaders coopting for profit and publicity). He acknowledges the importance of social policy to address poverty as well as individual initiative to reject controlling influences and counterproductive behavior. But he contends that liberal and conservative rhetoric have only minimized the complexity of racial issues and the long-term effects of racism in the United States that include poverty and growing nihilism and angst in black America. He is especially critical of black political and intellectual leaders who possess the socioeconomic status and resources to effectively serve as activists but who instead become coopted by personal ambition. The current tenure of U.S. race relations that views blacks as the "problem" rather than as citizens who face problems has resulted in the collective inability of citizens to acknowledge common Americanness and humanness. *Race Matters* has achieved national acclaim because it has informed both academic and mainstream audiences about the negative effects of racism and strained race relations in the United States. West was formally trained at Harvard University and Union Theological Seminary. He is currently the Class of 1943 University Professor of Religion at Princeton University.

Further Reading

West, Cornel. *Race Matters*. New York: Vintage Books, 1994.

Sandra L. Barnes

Race Relations, Paternalistic versus Competitive

To explain changing patterns of black-white race relations, Belgian sociologist Pierre van de Berghe made a distinction between paternalistic and competitive race relations. Each pattern reflects a specific historical moment that is linked to the existing economic and social structures present in that society. Paternalistic race relations prevail in an agrarian society not transitioned to the industrial base of production. In paternalistic race relations, the mass of the labor force consists of unspecialized, servile, or docile peasantry. There may be considerable differentiation among workers because one group may have specific skills that allow it to monopolize a branch of the production process. For example, one might find a group of workers who dominate the handicraft production while another group finds its niche in trading, thereby creating a merchant class.

Despite the specific skills of the labor force, the division of labor in paternalistic race relations is based strictly on racial lines. Black slaves, indentured servants, or quasi-servile laborers usually perform heavy work that involves manual labor. The dominant white upper class in the paternalistic race relation confines itself to professions that have a higher social status and that depend less on manual labor. Members of the upper-class are often found in the priesthood, government, supervision of labor, law, and commerce.

Social relations in the paternalistic race relation are sharply defined through an elaborate and rigid etiquette of racial rules and status. Spatial segregation in paternalistic race relations is minimal and it does not pose any danger for the dominant class because each group is well aware of its status vis-à-vis the other. Slaves and servants may live in the same household with their masters without any incident since they know their limits and are "accommodated" to their inferior status. Moreover, slave owners develop attitudes and stereotypes that present the slaves as immature, childlike, fun-loving, and good humored to placate them and to justify the treatment that they forced on them.

Although the upper class may present the lower class as lovable and fun loving, this does not prevent it from inflicting heavy corporal punishment on it whenever the lower class attempts to rebel. In the Southern states of the United States, where paternalistic race relations existed during slavery, slave masters never hesitated to inflict severe corporal punishments on their slaves whenever there was an attempt by them to rebel against the institution.

Competitive race relation is usually found in the large-scale manufacturing economy of industrial capitalism. In a competitive race relation, most of the labor force is skilled; technical competence and efficiency become the most important criteria for employment. As a result, any rigid racial division of labor that is based on ascription or racial prejudice has to be discarded if the society is to maintain a competitive edge in the market economy. Although racial prejudice and discrimination may exist as it did in the United States before the 1960s, it is not sanctioned by the state. In many instances, the state becomes an important agent in promoting good race relations since it knows the devastating impact that racial tension can have on the economy of the country. When racial barriers become an obstacle to the functioning of the economy, the state intervenes to assure that businesses are not adversely affected. Laws against racial discrimination are passed to assure a minimum level of competition among people of all backgrounds and races.

Social and racial differences do not necessarily end in competitive race relations. They are usually expressed through geographic segregation, level of education, income, and living standards, as well as disparity in health care and mortality rate. However, in competitive race relations, members of the lower class may have the opportunity to move upward by changing employment, attending better schools, or relocating to other residential neighborhoods. Since racial roles in competitive race relations are fluid and ill defined, members of the lower class may take initiatives that would have been off limits in a paternalistic race relation. The fluidity of racial relations may also create doubt among members of the lower-class since they are unsure of what is expected of them by the upper-class.

The breakdown of traditional racial barriers in competitive race relations does not mean that the upper class loses control over members of the lower class. Overt violence such as lynching and torture that took place in the South during the paternalistic race relation era may be replaced by rational-legal methods that achieve the same result. For example, there are more blacks in prison in the United States today than before the civil rights movement of the 1960s. Official discrimination against blacks has been banned in the United States, but stereotypes of blacks as lazy, dirty, immature, and fun loving continue to be disseminated by the dominant class.

Van de Berghe claimed that the form of government found in competitive race relations is generally a restricted or partial democracy in which members of the lower class are prevented from participating through various mechanisms that are rational and legal. At one time in the United States, blacks were prevented from participating in the political process through the imposition of poll taxes, literacy tests, and the grandfather clause.

See also Civil Rights Movement.

Further Reading

Pierre L. Van den Berghe. *The Ethnic Phenomenon*. New York: Elsevier, 1981.

———. *Race and Racism: A Comparative Perspective*. 2nd ed. New York: John Wiley, 1978.

Francois Pierre-Louis

Race-Relations Cycle

In the 1920s, after a large number of new immigrants from southern and eastern European countries had arrived, settled, and formed their own ethnic communities in urban America, many social scientists were interested in their adjustment process in the new land. What happens when new immigrant groups come, meet, and interact with other groups? Are ethnic and racial conflicts inevitable? Will new immigrant groups assimilate to the Anglo-centered mainstream America? Robert Park was one of the first sociologists to be concerned with such questions.

Park proposed a theory of race relations cycle. According to him, immigrant groups would pass through a sequence of stages: contact, competition, accommodation, and eventual assimilation. Different groups of people first come into contact through migration. Once they are in contact, they compete for scarce resources, such as land, educational opportunities and/or jobs, and competition often develops into conflict. But, as time passes, overt conflict is less frequent, and these groups gradually learn how to accommodate each other. Park argued that the members of minority groups, especially new immigrant groups, would gradually learn the language, customs, manners, and beliefs of the dominant group.

Over several generations, such acculturation occurs, structural integration in schools and workplaces is complete, group boundaries break down, and the society becomes more blended. The cycle completes itself with "eventual assimilation." To Park, this cycle of race relations is inevitable and "progressive and irreversible." Furthermore, the process of assimilation is also universal. He asserts that "the processes by which the integration of peoples and cultures has always and everywhere taken place." Since the term *race* was used much more broadly in Park's day than now, *race* may refer to both racial and ethnic groups.

Park's theory was popular until the 1960s, but it has been subject to severe criticism since the late 1960s. One major criticism is that his theory is not an explanation of historical reality on race relations but in fact an ideology advocating assimilation as a desirable end-state of American society. He seems to promote the full assimilation and amalgamation as an ideal pattern of race relations when he asserts: "Because the tendencies to the assimilation and eventual amalgamation of races exist, they should not be resisted and, if possible, altogether inhibited." The theory, according to his critics, is an ideology justifying one particular model of assimilation in the United States: the Anglo-conformity model. It is a tacit endorsement of assimilation to the dominant white Anglo-American culture and institutions. His theory of the race relations cycle might have represented the prevailing thought on race relations during the 1920s in the United States.

Furthermore, his race relations cycle may describe and explain fairly well the experiences of white European immigrants in the United States, especially those who settled in the Chicago area. But, his critics argue, his theory is not applicable to the experiences of racial minorities with distinctive physical markers such as Native Americans, African Americans, Hispanic Americans, and Asian Americans. Their experiences seemed to diverge from Park's cycle as they encountered relocation, genocide, exclusion, segregation and continued conflict. Although African Americans have lived in the United States for many generations, they have never achieved the type of full assimilation Park envisioned. Moreover, his theory ignores the possibility of maintaining stable race relations with different arrangements, such as cultural pluralism that do not lead to complete assimilation.

Another problem in his theory is that the hypothesis of an inevitable cycle is not empirically testable. If assimilation and eventual amalgamation do not occur, it would be explained as the result of obstacles or interference of the process. There is no way to prove or disprove the validity of his theory empirically. In fact, such race relations cycles are rarely complete.

Another problem in Park's race relations cycle is the universality of conflict in race relations. There are cases in history where conflict and competition did not occur when different groups came into contact. Brazil and Hawaii are two examples of ethnically diverse societies where relatively peaceful and harmonious interactions have existed between different groups of people.

The key problem in his theory is that he ignored several significant variables that could affect the assimilation processes of diverse groups differently. Some of these factors are the context of migration and contact (voluntary versus involuntary), the size and dispersion of a particular group, its cultural similarity to the dominant group, and its physical distinctiveness. The dominant group's willingness to accept the subordinate group also affects the assimilation process. Such situational variables affect the group's assimilation. Historically, racial minorities in the United Stated have been excluded, segregated, and prevented from full assimilation in the United States.

See also Anglo Conformity; Assimilation Theory.

Further Reading

Park, Robert E. *Race and Culture*. 1950. Reprint, New York: The Free Press, 1964.

Shibutani, Tamotsu, and Kian M. Kwan. *Ethnic Stratification: A Comparative Approach*. New York: Macmillan, 1965.

Heon Cheol Lee

Race Riots

The history of race relations in the United States is marked by recurring patterns of violence, and race riots are one of the most frequent, and tragic expressions of racially motivated violence that scars our past. Race riots go all the way back to the origins of the United States, but the modern, more lethal form of race riots emerged after Reconstruction as the processes of urbanization, monopolization of capital, and industrialization transformed both the geographic and social landscapes of the country. These macro-level structural changes in the economy and polity had a significant impact on race relations, and they help to explain why race riots occurred in the ways and places that they did. In the years after the Second World War, the reasons for race riots changed as the civil rights movement altered the context in which race riots occurred.

In the United States it is generally *mis*understood that African Americans are responsible for race riots, because the descriptive modifier *race* is usually ascribed to minority groups rather than whites. The concept of whiteness persists to this day as the invisible, or race-*less*, norm in America. In reality, however, whites have been the perpetrators of the most deadly race riots in U.S. history, but the media, in various ways, has diverted public attention away from white violence. (Smith McKoy 2001). To compound the problem of correctly understanding the phenomenon in historical accounts that describe in a linear, progressive framework the social history of the United States as the story of the steady, constant expansion of democracy and freedom, race riots continue to be incorrectly explained as *aberrations*. But the frequency and *intensity* of race riots in the United States calls into question the mainstream explanation of these events as well as the teleological perspective of American history in general. (Ginzburg 1997).

The regularity of race riots in American history is compounded by the variety of their causes and the diversity of their participants on all sides of the racial and ethnic divides. Therefore, it would be more accurate to use an explanatory framework that emphasizes discontinuity and interruption by drawing more attention to the specificity of the conditions that give rise to race riots. This would correct the mistakes of a linear, "progressive" analytic framework that downplays race riots as temporary sidetracks or minor deviations in a mainly progressive story about the evolution of race relations in America. Race riots are not temporary setbacks or minor deviations but rather major events or fissures that send the history of race relations in different directions.

In most cases, modern race riots have involved violence between whites and blacks, but there are also many examples of race riots where white mobs have attacked Chinese (the Los Angeles Riot of 1871), Filipino and Asian Indian (the Bellingham Riots of 1907), and Mexican American communities (the Zoot Suit Riot of 1943). Indeed, it is no exaggeration to say that the "native" white population has made use of the riot as one of many ways to attack nearly every minority group in the United States.

Riots as a Specific Pattern of Racially Motivated, Violent Collective Behavior

Racially motivated acts of violence can take many forms. In the United States, the most common forms of racially motivated patterns of organized violence have been lynching and riots. While riots have oftentimes involved lynching, riots are distinguished from lynching in that the target of violence in a race riot is an entire racial or ethnic *community*, whereas lynching usually targets one or a handful of individuals.

Riots in general and race riots in particular are usually understood to be expressions of irrational mob behavior, and more to the point, as *aberrations* in search of explanation. For example, many of the mayors of major cities where riots have taken place have insisted that riots are no more than the product of a collection of thoughtless, random *individual* criminal acts perpetrated by the undesirable elements of society (Folgelson 1971). Because there is rarely a spokesperson or representative who speaks for rioters, it is assumed that riots, by definition, have no meaning or rational purpose. This point of view became known as the "riff-raff" theory of race riots. Upon closer examination, however, race riots have proven to be a much more complicated kind of riot.

Beginning in the late 1960s, the perspective on race riots began to change as researchers debated the usefulness even of the term *riot* as a way to describe this particular type of racially motivated, violent, collective behavior. While the catalyst for many race riots involves elements of the irrational—especially rumor—and while there are both victims and perpetrators of violence on either side of the racial divide, race riots are characterized by distinct patterns of collective behavior, and the violence usually has a recognizable *direction* depending on which racial group takes the lead in the riot. The initial goal of a race riot is often irrational, but the means to achieve the goal involve rational choice. When one group attacks another group out of fear and misunderstanding it is not rational, but *how* a group goes about attacking another involves the use of reason. For instance, some have argued that in many cases of coordinated group violence, *massacre* would be a more accurate term than *riot*, as several of the race riots led by whites in the United States have involved the *systematic* destruction of entire neighborhoods, resulting in hundreds of deaths and thousands of injuries. The Tulsa race riot in 1921 has the infamous distinction of being the first time Americans dropped bombs on themselves from airplanes; angry whites hijacked crop dusters to conduct aerial bombardments of black neighborhoods. The organization of aerial bombardments indicates planned, rational organization of behavior, rather than thoughtless, random mob activity. Once a riot begins, the systematic destruction of an entire racial or ethnic community suggests that the perpetrators of violence act in a rational manner rather than an irrational one, and the frequency of white mob violence contradicts the notion that race riots exist merely as temporary—however tragic—deviations from the progressive, linear path toward freedom and equality in America. Therefore, the term *massacre* is sometimes applied as a conceptual modifier for race riots instigated by "white" racial groups.

On the other hand, recent research has characterized many of the more recent race riots instigated by blacks between the end of World War II and the 1960s as rebellions, or protests, rather than riots. In these cases, race riots are understood as articulate protests, expressions of resistance by oppressed racial groups against the system of racial and ethnic discrimination in the United States (Gale 1996). This point of view rejects the so-called riff-raff theory that explains race riots as the result of a collection of random, mindless individual acts of pillage and looting. Close examination of race riots in the 1960s revealed that at least 10–20 percent of ghetto residents engaged in the civil disorders of the 1960s—as opposed to the 1–2 percent in official police reports—and that a majority of the participants were of middle- and working-class backgrounds, suggesting that the rioters were representative of the community as a whole rather than merely a rag-tag group of hoodlums (Fogelson 1971). Among those residents who did not participate in the riots, it was found that most were sympathetic with the rioters, suggesting again that there was a rational meaning to be drawn from the activity of rioting.

The researchers concluded that long-term deterioration of urban ghettos—economic deprivation, racial discrimination, decay of housing stock, consumer exploitation, political corruption, and inferior education—prohibited the gradual improvement of living conditions and closed down conventional institutional channels for the expression of legitimate grievances by ghetto residents. Furthermore, it was argued that civil disorders in the 1960s, while violent, were nonetheless meaningful protests because the violence was focused on specific targets and, perhaps more importantly, the violence was *restrained*. Rioters looted stores but did not damage schools, homes, churches or other institutions. The stores that were burned were targeted because they were perceived to be exploiting ghetto residents by selling inferior goods at inflated prices. While a handful of the thousands of white passersby in the postwar riots were the victims of brutal attacks, the number of whites who died at the hands of African Americans pales in comparison to the thousands of blacks massacred by whites in the prewar riots. In these ways, it has been argued, mob violence takes the form of articulate protest, since the collective behavior is specific, restrained, and *meaningful* (Fogelson 1971).

In sum, there are competing explanations for the conditions that give rise to race riots, and each perspective has a specific way to frame the content

Children cross the street in front of a storefront covered with graffiti from the 1965 Watts riots.

Photo by Bill Ray/Time Life Pictures/Getty Images.

and meaning of a race riot. The term *massacre* has been used to describe riots instigated by whites against blacks, while the term *rebellion* has been used to describe the black-instigated urban riots that took place during the civil rights era.

Two Types of Race Riots in Two Separate Historical Periods

Race riots occur within particular social contexts that are themselves the product of larger, structural shifts in the economy and polity. In other words, there are identifiable reasons why riots occur and how they occur. Race riots in the modern era can be broken down into two distinct historical periods. The periods are separated by different conditions that gave rise to race riots, and the riots in the two different periods had opposing goals. The *individual* race riots in each period share certain characteristics, such as macroeconomic, structural conditions that set the stage for riot, and patterns of behavior that determine the direction and meaning of the riot, but the reasons for the race riots in the early period are different from the reasons for race riots in the second period. Also, the actions of the participants in race riots differ in important ways from one era to the next.

The first period spans the years between the Wilmington, Delaware riot of 1898 and the Detroit riot of 1943, and is characterized by white-on-black violence. These riots were reactionary in nature, the expression of white mobs that wanted to maintain the status quo of Jim Crow. White mob violence reached a peak in the summer of 1919 when there were at least twenty-five incidents or major racial conflicts throughout the country. The first cycle of modern race riots that emerged after Reconstruction shares most of the following conditions:

- White workers, and in some cases their union representatives, created a climate of fear among their ranks that blacks were coming North to take their jobs and homes
- Employers used black strike breakers in periods of labor strife to encourage racial conflicts as a way to undermine unions
- Politicians looked for ways to use race riots to solidify their power
- Rumors were spread that a white woman was assaulted by a black man
- Sensationalist press coverage included unverified—and in most cases false—reports that blacks were heavily armed and preparing for conflict prior to the riot
- Violence during the riots was directed at people rather than property
- Police failed to adequately restrain white rioters
- Federal soldiers and sailors participated as rioters in a few cases

The later period of riots began after World War II, continued through the civil rights movement, and erupted again in the early 1980s. These riots were extensions of waves of protests against discrimination and racism in the United States. The second cycle of race riots in America emerged in a different social context from the first. The race riots since the World War II occurred within the context of a social movement—the civil rights movement—and they expressed a desire to change the social relations of society and end discrimination, rather than to preserve the status quo of racial discrimination, as was the case in the first wave of race riots, in the earlier period. Causal factors in the second cycle of urban race riots included the following:

- Decimated housing stock in the ghetto
- Lack of good-paying jobs/high unemployment in central cities
- Widespread police brutality in the ghetto
- Inadequate city services for African Americans living in the ghetto
- Dysfunctional education system in the inner city

Incidents of police brutality were usually the *immediate* cause of race riots in the 1960s, but the other factors contributed to long-term discontent.

Analyses of Differences between the Two Types of Riots

An important difference in the direction and content of race riots between the two cycles is that in the first era of race riots the target of violence was people, whereas in the second wave of race riots, the target of violence was property. Both cycles of race riots share a few characteristics, including the element of rumor, although rumors were much more prevalent in the white-led riots of the earlier era. In the first period of race riots, it was often falsely rumored that a black man had sexually assaulted a white woman, or that African Americans were arming themselves in preparation for a race war. These particular rumors were the spark that ignited many of the early race riots. In the second cycle of race riots, rumor usually involved a story about rogue white cops beating or killing black ghetto residents. While in many cases the specific details of the rumors were untrue, some were true, and more to the point, police brutality was a *real* problem for blacks living in the ghetto (Knopf 1975).

The first period of race riots occurred in a period of radical economic changes that broke down the existing social relations of production that were partly structured along racial lines. The development of assembly-line production in the modern factories that made mass production possible completely transformed the labor process. Skilled workers—who were almost exclusively white—lost control over the shop floor as new technologies transferred the orientation of production from the hand to the mind. New machine technology increased both the pace and intensity of production and displaced skilled workers, allowing manufacturing corporations to replace expensive, skilled union labor with relatively unskilled workers. At the time, "skilled" and "unskilled" worker was code for "white" and "black" worker.

However, the emergence of a strong industrial economy in the Northeast, combined with declining economic opportunities for work in the South contributed to the mass migration of blacks from rural areas in the South to large cities in the North. Between 1900 and 1941, the number of blacks living in Northern cities tripled. For the first time in the United States, blacks were living, in large numbers, in close proximity to whites in Northern cities. Once there, many blacks found themselves competing with whites for relatively good-paying factory jobs and for decent housing in the urban centers. The interracial competition for jobs and housing was one of the main contributing factors in the race riots of the early period. As the demand for labor increased sharply during World War I—blacks were enjoying relative success in landing blue-collar jobs as the United States boosted production to fuel the war—so did interracial disturbances. Racial tension increased when white GIs returned from World War I, expecting preferential treatment from employers in the growing industrial sectors of the economy. Between 1915 and 1919 there were eighteen race riots in the United States. One of the worst occurred in St. Louis in 1917. The reasons for the race riot in St. Louis were typical of many of the racial disturbances between 1898 and 1943 and include many of the causal factors already listed.

The Newark riots were among the many race riots of the late 1960s that all shared similar conditions. The underlying causes of the Newark riots, like the other urban riots during the period, were police brutality against African Americans, exclusion of blacks from local politics, urban-renewal projects that devastated black neighborhoods, disproportionate unemployment of blacks, and lack of affordable housing in black neighborhoods. Police brutality was the catalyst for the riot, but discontent had been brewing for years prior to the riot, and African Americans struggled against a system of discrimination and exploitation. The race riots of the 1960s forced the federal government to look into the serious problems faced by blacks living in the urban ghettos of the United States.

See also Bellingham Riots; Detroit Race Riot of 1943; Detroit Race Riot of 1967; Draft Riot of 1863; Los Angeles Riot of 1871; Los Angeles Riot of 1992; Memphis Race Riot of 1866; Newark Riot of 1967; St. Louis Riot of 1917; Zoot Suit Riots.

Further Reading

Comp Boesel, David. *Cities Under Siege: An Anatomy of the Ghetto Riots, 1964–1968.* New York: Basic Books, 1971.

Ellsworth, Scott, and John Hope Franklin. *Death in a Promised Land: The Tulsa Riot of 1921.* Baton Rouge: Louisiana State University Press, 1982.

Fogelson, Robert M. *Violence as Protest: A Study of Riots and Ghettos.* New York: Doubleday, 1971.

Gale, Dennis E. *Understanding Urban Unrest: From Reverend King to Rodney King.* Thousand Oaks, CA: Sage Publications, 1996.

Ginzburg, Ralph. *100 Years of Lynchings.* New York: Black Classic Press, 1997.

Horne, Gerald. *Fire This Time: The Watts Uprising and the 1960s.* New York: DaCapo Press, 1997.

Knopf, Terry Ann. *Rumors, Race and Riots.* New Brunswick, NJ: Transaction Publication, 1975.

Madagan, Tim. *The Burning: Massacre, Destruction and the Tulsa Riot of 1921.* New York: St. Martin's Press, 2001.

McKoy, Sheila Smith. *When Whites Riot: Writing Race and Violence in American and South African Culture.* Madison: University of Wisconsin Press, 2001.

Rudwick, Elliot. *Race Riot at East St. Louis.* Champaign: University of Illinois Press, 1982.

Stockley, Grif. *Blood in Their Eyes: The Elaine Race Massacre of 1919.* Little Rock: University of Arkansas Press, 2001.

Michael Roberts

Racial Classification of Population

The racial classification of the population by the U.S. Census Bureau is premised on a question on the decennial census that asks for self-identification and selection among several racial categories that were codified by the Office of Management and Budget's (OMB) Directive 15 in 1977. The data are used for social analysis in the areas of health and education and for policy, legislative, and judicial actions regarding civil rights, voting rights and legislative redistricting, allocation of federal resources, federal and private-sector affirmative action programs, school desegregation, minority business development, and fair housing. The history and process of racial classification, however, are based on social constructions, as new categories have been created, existing ones have been modified, and the location of groups have shifted from one category to another as a result of political claims and advocacy (Espiritu and Omi 2000, 43). It has been noted that "the great irony is that the American government gathers data on people's race through a more or less slippery and subjective procedure of self-identification and then must use these counts as the basis of legal status in an important domain of law and administrative regulation—namely, civil rights" (Perlmann and Waters 2000, 11).

Since census enumerations began, racial classifications have changed and expanded, reflecting the evolution of the social meaning of race in the United States. "The Bureau's description of the race question reveals the subjective nature of the racial data it was collecting and the general ambivalence, and touchiness, about the intellectual standing of the material" (Perlmann and Waters 2002, 10). In 1970, a Hispanic-origin question was added to the long form sent to a sample of respondents; and in 1980, this question was included on the short form sent to the entire population. The Hispanic-origin question replaced the Spanish-speaking question to capture information about Hispanics who speak Spanish.

A significant change in the race question in the 2000 census allows individuals to "check one or more" from the following six race categories: white; black, African American or Negro; American Indian or Alaska native; Asian; Native Hawaiian and Other Pacific Islander; and Some other race. This option resulted in sixty-four mutually exclusive race/Hispanic categories, marking a significant change from the 1990 census, when just five categories existed for race, with no option for tabulating multirace responses. As Perlmann and Waters wrote in their recent volume on the multirace category, "By allowing individuals to report identification with more than one race, the census challenges long-held fictions and strongly defended benefits about the very nature and definition of race in our society" (1). The OMB, which has the task of deciding how multiracial individuals will be counted, has ruled that for the purposes of enforcing civil rights legislation, multiracial individuals will be counted in the minority category.

See also Social Construction of Whiteness.

Further Reading

Espiritu, Yen Le, and Michael Omi. *"Who are You Calling Asian?": Shifting Identity Claims, Racial Classifications, and the Census in Transforming Race Relations; A Public Policy Report* ed., Paul Ong, LEAP Asian Pacific American Public Policy Institute and UCLA Asian American Studies Center, Los Angeles, CA, 2000.

Perlmann, Joel, and Mary C. Waters. *The New Race Question: How the Census Counts Multiracial Individuals.* New York: Russell Sage Foundation, 2002.

Rodriguez, Clara E. *Changing Race: Latinos, the Census, and the History of Ethnicity in the United States.* New York: New York University Press, 2000.

Tarry Hum

Racial Difference in Poverty Rate

Poverty occurs when an individual or group lacks socially acceptable amounts of money or material possessions to meet basic living needs. In the United States, poverty is determined based on the official poverty line formulated in

1964 by the Social Security Administration. This threshold reflects a set of rock-bottom allowances that includes a certain proportion of yearly costs for food. An individual is officially considered poor if his or her personal family income falls below this governmental standard. In 1975, the poverty line for a nonfarm family of four was $5,500. In 2002, the threshold for a family of four was approximately $18,556. Although the poverty line has been criticized for excluding in-kind government transfers in its income calculation and for strict income cut-offs, it is a commonly implemented threshold for comparing basic quality-of-life measures across various groups.

Poverty rates differ dramatically by racial/ethnic group, and these differentials have been consistent over many decades. In 2001, approximately 11.7 percent of the U.S. population lived in poverty, a significant decrease from 15.1 percent in 1993. Poverty rates for African Americans and Hispanics were 22.7 percent and 21.4 percent, respectively, in 2001, compared with 9.9 percent for whites and 10.2 percent for Asians and Pacific Islanders. In addition, poverty rates are highest for families headed by single women, especially Hispanic and African American women. In 2001, only 4.9 percent of married-couple families and 13.1 percent of male-headed families lived in poverty. By contrast, the rate was 26.4 percent for female-headed families, and rates for African American and Hispanic female-headed families exceeded 35 percent. Given the high incidence of poverty among female-headed families, it is not surprising that children are also disproportionately represented among the U.S. poor. Although children composed about 25.6 percent of the total population, about 35.7 percent of them lived in poverty. Increasingly, younger children are experiencing the most poverty, especially if they are part of single female–headed families. In 2001, about 18.2 percent of children under age six were living in poverty. However, about 48.9 percent of children younger than age six who lived in female-headed families were poor. Factors such as deindustrialization, racism, disparate marriage rates, housing discrimination and segregation, unemployment, and inadequate educational systems have contributed to continued racial differentials in poverty rates. The vast majority of poor racial/ethnic minorities live in urban areas.

See also Culture of Poverty Thesis.

Sandra L. Barnes

Racial Differences in Property Holding

There are large differences in the wealth and property holding between white and black families in America. These differences go far beyond differences in earned income and account for some of the differences in social and economic outcomes for black and white children from families with comparable household incomes and parental educational levels. For example, low-income black families, those with incomes less than $15,000 per year, often hold no assets, while low-income white families typically have assets of around $10,000. Information about high-income families, those with incomes above $75,000, reveals a similar pattern, with white families having assets around $300,000 and equivalent black families having assets of around $100,000.

Melvin Oliver and Thomas Shapiro's *Black Wealth, White Wealth* (1995) first brought attention to the vast differences in wealth between white and black Americans, even among those with comparable incomes, and the systemic barriers that foster that gap. In the late 1990s, Sociologist Dalton Conley further analyzed these differences in his book *Being Black, Living in the Red* (1999). These books documented the pervasiveness and importance of racial differences in property holding. Persistent differences in wealth are largely due to intergenerational transference of assets. Typically, each generation must earn its own income independently of the last generation. Social advantages such as education can be transferred between generations, but there is very little direct transfer of income: children do not inherit their mother or father's paycheck. In contrast, wealth is often directly transferred from one generation to the next in the form of inheritance, such as a house or lump sum of money, or gifts, such as the down payment for a house or money for college tuition. Racial differences in property holding are one mechanism that perpetuates racial disadvantage across generations.

See also Black Wealth/White Wealth: A New Perspective on Racial Inequality.

Robin Roger-Dillon

Racial Earnings Gap

There has been a large racial gap in earnings in the United States for some time. African American, Latino, and Native American workers have earned much less than white workers, and the racial gap has been much greater for men than for women. For example, according to 2001 census data, African American men earned on average approximately 78 percent ($30,409) of white men's earnings ($38,869), and Latino men earned only 63 percent ($24,638). The racial gap in earnings has been shrinking between African American and white men but growing between Latino and white men. Asian American men earned slightly more ($40,946) than white men on average.

In 2001, African American women earned on average about 90 percent ($25,117) of white women's earnings ($28,080), while Latino women earned 72 percent (20,527). Asian American women earned more than ($31,156) white women. To consider race and gender together, white women earned 72 percent of white men's earnings, while African American, Latino, and Asian American women earned 64 percent, 52 percent, and 80 percent, respectively.

What factors contribute to the big racial gap in earnings? One explanation for the racial differences in earnings is the racial gap in education. African American and Latino workers on average have attained substantially lower educational levels than white workers, while Asian American workers have attained a substantially higher educational level than whites. However, analyses of census data show that minority workers earn less than white workers with the same educational level. This means that minority workers receive a lower return for their educational investment than white workers because of racial discrimination.

The gender gap in earnings is narrower for African Americans than for white and for other minority groups. This can be explained partly by African American women's higher level of education than African American men and partly by their experience with lower levels of labor market discrimination than African American men. African American men may experience a higher level of discrimination in the labor market than African American women in part because white men consider African American men rather than African American women as a threat to their occupations. Although Asian American workers earn more than white workers, the rate of return for their educational credentials is not as great as that for white workers. This suggests that other minority workers, in addition to African American workers, are subject to racial discrimination in the labor market.

Still, it is necessary to analyze the discrimination, which contributes to racial earnings gaps. First, past discrimination, which was more blatant in form, has lingering effects. Past instances of discrimination and labor-market segregation may result in creating a pool of minority workers who are less experienced and less skilled than white workers, because they have not had the same opportunities. Older minority workers will continue to experience significant wage gaps, since their base rate of pay may have been established when it was acceptable to pay racial minority workers less than white workers.

Second, the impact of nonmarket discrimination must be considered. Factors such as education, region, and residential segregation also influence wages. Minority workers are more likely to live in racially segregated neighborhoods with depressed economies and jobs that offer lower wages. Minority-dense communities were especially hard hit by job loss when manufacturing companies left central-city areas for more space and lower taxes in the suburbs. The industries, which replaced the manufacturing industries, are typically service oriented or white collar in nature and often do not match the skills of the residents in central-city areas.

Finally, instances of current discrimination must be examined. This form of discrimination must be subtle, given that laws have been established (Civil Rights Act of 1964) that make it illegal to discriminate in the labor market based on race, among other factors. These subtle practices include occupational segregation, quality of employment differences (fewer hours, lower wages, fewer benefits, less training, less prestige), higher rates of and longer periods of unemployment, and lower hire rates for racial minorities.

Recent evidence indicates that a dual labor market has emerged in the United States. Minorities have historically been excluded from certain occupations, and they continue to encounter barriers to entering many prestigious occupations. When minorities are able to break into these formerly "reserved" occupations, they frequently have difficulties accessing the better-caliber jobs within the field. Minorities with an immigrant background in particular are likely to work in the secondary, rather than the primary, labor market.

The greater earnings gap between whites and Latinos than that between whites and African Americans is due mainly to the heavily immigrant background of Latino workers. Minorities who are also immigrants may experience certain challenges or disadvantages in the labor market, because they are usually not proficient in English and may be unfamiliar with the social-network practices in the mainstream, or primary, labor market. Lacking knowledge about how social networks operate could prevent minority members with an immigrant background from obtaining information about employment opportunities. Some immigrants are forced to re-establish their educational credentials, since degrees they have earned at institutions in their home countries are not always recognized in the United States. Finally, illegal immigrants are generally exploited by employers, who hire them to work cheaply (below market rates) in exchange for not reporting their illegal status.

See also "Cost of Being a Negro"; Dual Housing Markets.

Further Reading

Hacker, Andrew. *Two Nations: Black and White, Separate, Hostile, Unequal.* New York: Scribner, 2003.

National Committee on Pay Equity. "The Wage Gap by Education, Race and Gender." U.S. Census Bureau, Current Population Survey, March 2001.

Siegel, Paul. "The Cost of Being a Negro." *Sociological Inquiry* 35 (1965): 41–57.

Romney S. Norwood

Racial Epithets

See Derogatory Terms.

Racial Formation in the United States: From the 1960s to the 1980s

Published in 1986 by sociologists Michael Omi of the University of California, Berkeley, and Howard Winant of the University of California, Santa Barbara, *Racial Formation in the United States: From the 1960s to the 1980s* is a groundbreaking work on racial theory. Recognizing the fact that race is a fundamental dimension of social organizations and cultural meaning in the United States, this book critiques three paradigmatic approaches to race and race relations that are based on ethnicity, class, and nation. It then develops an alternative racial-formation theory based on the idea that the concepts of race are always politically constructed and contested, and that the state is the preeminent site of racial contestation. Guided by the racial formation theory, the book analyzes postwar U.S. racial politics from the 1960s to the 1980s.

Since the publication of its first edition, this highly acclaimed book has become an instant classic in racial and ethnic studies and in the social sciences and humanities in general. Influenced by the racial-formation approach, the idea of the social construction of race has been widely accepted in the academy.

In 1994, Omi and Winant released the second edition of this book. The new edition further elaborates on the racial-formation theory by detailing the racial-formation processes. It also offers new materials on the historical development of race, racism, race-class-gender interrelations, everyday life, and hegemony. It updates the developments of racial formation in the United States to the early

1990s, covering such events as the 1992 presidential election, the Los Angeles riots, and the racial politics and policies of the Clinton administration.

See also Pan-ethnic Movements.

Further Reading

Omi, Michael, and Howard Winant. *Racial Formation in the United States: From the 1960s to the 1980s.* 2nd ed. New York: Routledge, 1994.

Philip Yang

Racial Ghettoes

The term *ghetto*, meaning "gated," originally referred to efforts to residentially isolate Jews in Italy using brick fortifications. The term has now come to be associated with severely impoverished inner cities in which a disproportionate percentage of African Americans reside. Barrios are considered poor urban areas where the majority of residents are Hispanic. Dramatic population shifts occurred during the Great Migrations of the early and mid-twentieth century as African Americans exited the rural South for Northern states such as New York, Illinois, Pennsylvania, and Michigan to seek employment and escape discrimination. Persons of Hispanic descent migrated to cities such as Chicago, New York, and Miami from Mexico, Puerto Rico, Cuba, and Central and South America for similar reasons. Cities provided manufacturing jobs, and it was common to relocate to places where family members had already settled. By the mid-twentieth century, American cities had experienced significant in-migration by members of racial/ethnic minorities coupled with out-migration of whites to suburban areas.

After World War II, globalization and deindustrialization resulted in a dramatic decline in the need for manufacturing workers—many of whom were minorities. These jobs were replaced with lower-paying service occupations. And many urbanites were ill-prepared to compete for new technology-oriented opportunities. Thus, large segments of African Americans and Hispanics experienced downward economic mobility. In addition, out-migration of middle-class white families and businesses exacerbated urban unemployment, poverty, and crime. Historic and current racism and discrimination and residential segregation are other factors that have resulted in urban ghettos. Critics suggest that because most residents in ghettos are minorities, the government is less willing to support initiatives to combat urban poverty.

See also Barrios; Colonized vs. Immigrant Minorities; Housing Discrimination.

Sandra L. Barnes

Racial Inequality

See Capitalism and Racial Inequality; Capital Punishment and Racial Inequality; Deindustrialization and Racial Inequality; Liberal and Conservative Views of Racial Inequality; War and Racial Inequality.

Racialism

The term *racialism*, as commonly used in the United States, refers to a preoccupation with racial issues and the constant filtering of events, experiences, and decisions through the lens of race. In other words, racialism gives race an important (if not paramount) role in making sense of life, classifying people into groups, and determining how to arrange the social world. Many social thinkers make the point that the United States is a particularly racialist society, as demonstrated by the fact that race is often the dominant characteristic that people use to differentiate each other and that racial categories are very rigid and hierarchical. Additionally, racialist thought makes it impossible to perceive alternatives to the essentialist and hierarchical system of racial categories in place in the particular racialist society. This can be compared with the situation in other societies such as in the Caribbean and Latin America, where distinctions between people and groups are based on more gradual color-based classifications as well as on nonracial identities such as social class. *Racialism* can be used as a derogatory term against African American groups when whites accuse African Americans of believing that all negative occurrences in their lives are racially motivated.

Racialism has an additional meaning, more common in the United Kingdom, which is synonymous with *racism*. This term has been picked up on by many white supremacist groups, who use it to describe their ideology. Since *racialist* is not a common word, these groups can use it to describe what they believe in without encountering the same angry responses that might emerge if a group described itself as actively racist.

See also American "Obsession with Race."

Mikaila Mariel Lemonik Arthur

Racialization

Racialization is the extension of racial meaning to a previously racially unclassified relationship, social practice, or group. Racialization has been characterized as an ideological process shaped by history, prejudice, and the human tendency to use conceptual categories to simplify their ascription of meaning to nonidentical experiences. Among other things, racialization involves the attribution of undifferentiated identities, cultures, and behaviors to individuals based on their membership in a racialized group. While the characteristics so attributed are not always negative per se—take, for example, the association of Asian Americans with academic success—they are pernicious in that they replace individual uniqueness with facile assumptions about motives, background, conduct, and interests.

Racial difference as such is not at the root of racialization. Within the unique context of their own time and place, human beings ascribe social meaning to certain biological characteristics to differentiate, to exclude, and to dominate. Reinventing the ideation of "race," individuals create a racialized other and simultaneously racialize themselves. This process occurs not in a vacuum but in the context of the historical moment; social values and political presumptions are connected to the racialized object. Racialization is most obvious when its effect is directed at groups that are visibly—phenotypically—different from others, but "invisible" minorities are equally vulnerable to being racialized. The racist imagination views these minorities' nonvisibility as the proof of their "essential" but concealed difference; this difference is then signified by a socially imposed mark. While the term "racialization" is most often used to describe this phenomenon, similar processes may be found to occur with respect to ethnicity, religion, gender, sexual orientation, political affiliation, and other characteristics.

See also Social Construction of Whiteness.

Further Reading

Omi, Michael, and Howard Winant. *Racial Formation in the United States: From the 1960s to the 1980s.* 2nd ed. New York: Routledge, 1994.

Khyati Joshi

Racial Oppression in America

Robert Blauner's 1972 book *Racial Oppression in America* challenged the traditional theoretical paradigm of racial relations in the United States—that is, the classic assimilation theory—and proposed a new one, the so-called internal-colonialism paradigm. He emphasized that the patterns of entry, movement, job mobility, and racial discrimination were not the same with all ethic groups. White European ethnics voluntarily came to the United States, moved with no significant restriction, achieved upward mobility within two or three generations, and suffered lesser racial discrimination. On the contrary, the people of color, particularly Native Americans, African Americans, and Chicanos, were forcefully brought or incorporated into the United States, confined to certain geographical locations, stuck at the bottom of the occupational ladder for generations, and victimized by harsher forms of racism. The former were voluntary immigrant groups, while the latter were involuntary or colonized groups. Race relations in the United States reproduced the colonization of the Third World peoples by the West outside the United States. Hence, he referred to the internal-colonization paradigm as the Third World perspective. The internal-colonization paradigm best explains the earlier experience of Native Americans and Afro-Americans, but less that of Chicanos and Asians. Also controversial is whether the paradigm is still relevant to the recent experience of these people, particularly after the civil rights movement of the 1960s. In the new and expanded edition of the book, newly entitled *Still the Big News* (2001), Blauner admitted that the contrast between European white ethnic and minority racial groups was too sharply drawn and that class analysis had more potential for coalition politics.

See also Colonized versus Immigrant Minorities; Internal Colonialism.

Further Reading

Blauner, Robert. *Still the Big News*. Philadelphia: Temple University Press, 2001.

Dong-Ho Cho

Racial Preferences

See Racial Segregation, White and Black Preferences as a Cause of.

Racial Privacy Initiative

See California Ballot Proposition 54.

Racial Purity

Racial purity refers to the idea that "races" should be kept biologically separate from one another. This idea is based on the false assumption that racial groups are fundamentally different and that it is unnatural or harmful for racial groups to blend. Proponents of racial purity often view racial groups as being similar to different species of animals, a notion that is rejected by contemporary science. Antimiscegenation laws, which outlawed interracial marriage primarily to prohibit mixed-race children, were common in the United States until they were found unconstitutional in 1967. Defining who belonged to a particular race was a particular challenge for those that promoted the idea of racial purity. Areas in the American South maintained the infamous "one-drop rule" for many years. Under this rule, any black ancestor—one drop of "black blood"—meant a person was not white. In contrast, a person could have one Native American ancestor and still be classified as white. Other countries have also attempted to maintain racial purity. Most notoriously, Nazi Germany committed genocide in the name of racial purification. It is still common for countries, including Japan, to have intricate laws determining who is truly Japanese. Therefore, while American antimiscegenation laws were struck down by the Supreme Court long ago and the term *racial purity* is now used primarily by fringe groups, the underlying concept that racial and ethnic groups are biologically different and should not mix still remains powerful. Nonetheless, it has no scientific basis.

See also Intermarriage; One-Drop Rule.

Robin Roger-Dillon

Racial Segregation, White and Black Preferences as a Cause of

Three hypotheses may explain the persistence of residential segregation between blacks and whites in the United States: economic differentials, discrimination in housing and lending markets, and neighborhood preferences. The view that economic differentials and institutional discrimination have attributed to residential segregation has been undeniable. But apparently, people choose where to live. The preference hypothesis posits that segregation re-sults not so much from discriminatory practices or economic difference but mainly from blacks' and whites' own preferences. According to this view, both races desire to live in racially homogenous neighborhoods; with similar in-comes and assets and without racial discrimination in the housing market, blacks and whites would live in different communities.

Scholars who investigate racial segregation differ significantly in their as-sumptions about what underlies these preferences. Some argue that racial pref-erences are derived from "neutral preference." These scholars believe that residential segregation is the consequence of a desire among whites and blacks to live "with their own kind." Such preferences could presumably arise from a widespread desire to preserve common family, church, and cultural ties. Oth-ers argue that racial preferences are largely an outcome of each group's con-cerns about possible hostility in neighborhoods where either group is the minority. These preferences reflect an unwillingness to confront the expected antagonism of the community. Preferences, then, are both a cause and an ef-fect of racial discrimination and can thus be seen as a part of the web of si-multaneous forces generating and maintaining residential segregation.

National surveys asking whites about their preferences for the principle of residential integration began in the early 1940s. Whites were asked about their preferred neighborhood racial composition; whether it would make a differ-ence to them if a black family with income and education similar to theirs moved onto their block. In 1942, 65 percent said that it would make a differ-ence, but by the 1970s, just 15 percent of whites said it would make a differ-ence. Such survey of blacks' preferences began much later. One early effort was the 1976 Detroit Area Study, which assessed the preferences of blacks and whites. Findings from this study have frequently been cited as supporting the hypothesis that blacks' and whites' residential preferences do not overlap.

According to the study, 42 percent of whites said that they would feel un-comfortable if blacks constituted 20 percent of their neighborhood, and 25 percent said they would try to move away in such a circumstance. Whites were unwilling to move into integrated neighborhoods. In contrast, Detroit-area blacks overwhelmingly preferred integrated neighborhoods, specifically, those in which there were roughly equal numbers of blacks and whites; 82 percent of black respondents said that they prefer neighborhoods containing equal numbers of blacks and whites. Findings from a second Detroit Area Study conducted in 1992 showed a considerable moderation of whites' pref-erences relative to 1976. Forty percent of white respondents, however, still indicated that they would not move into neighborhoods where blacks con-stitute 20 percent of the population.

The findings from the two Detroit studies suggested that "white preference" played a major role in segregation. Many whites resisted integration and indi-cated that they would move out of their neighborhood if it became integrated. The preference hypothesis, therefore, suggests that residential segregation should be determined not by the preferences of one population group but rather by the relationship of preferences across groups. Many scholars fre-quently use the original Detroit study to set the issues of preference within the context of avoidance rather than preference, emphasizing white avoidance as the central cause of persistent residential segregation.

Recently, Farley (1997) addressed the danger of generalizing from the Detroit study and emphasized the idea that preferences differ significantly from one metropolitan area to another. Preferences clearly are relevant in generating and maintaining de facto residential segregation. But looking at preferences leaves many questions about racial segregation unanswered. Any consideration of residential segregation must also take into account other forces, such as the historical and spatial contexts, institutional practices, and governmental policies.

See also Residential Segregation.

Further Reading

Bobo, Lawrence, and Camille Zubrinsky. "Attitudes on Residential Integration: Perceived Status Differences, Mere In-Group Preferences, or Racial Prejudice." *Social Forces* 74, no. 3 (1996): 883–909.

Farley, Reynolds, Elaine Fielding, and Maria Krysan. "The Residential Preferences of Blacks and Whites: A Four-Metropolis Analysis." *Housing Policy Debate* 8, no. 4 (1997): 763–800.

Schnare, Ann Burnet. *The Persistence of Racial Segregation in Housing.* New York: Urban Institute, 1978.

Sookhee Oh

Racial Socialization

Racial minority children, especially African American children, in the United States, are expected to experience different forms of racism in the contexts of school, neighborhood, workplace, and street. Therefore, parents and teachers need to provide racial socialization to prepare their children psychologically to resist and endure racial subordination. Racial socialization refers to race-related socialization that transmits knowledge about racial identity, racial discrimination, and race relations. Racial socialization serves to forewarn children about the nature of their racial reality and teach them what to expect and how to develop adaptive techniques to resist negative forces of racial devaluation.

Some upper-middle-class African Americans live in predominantly white neighborhoods and send their children to a predominantly white private school. They may never talk to their children about racial barriers and disadvantages encountered by African Americans. They emphasize that if their children have high motivations and work hard, they can achieve any goal. This kind of color-blind child socialization is naïve and unhealthy. It can leave children at a disadvantage when they grow up and encounter racism. Personal narratives by black college students reveal that when black students are not prepared for racial reality, they often have psychological problems and may experience an identity crisis.

Frustrated by experiences with racism over many years, some African American parents in lower socioeconomic groups go to the other extreme in their children's socialization by overemphasizing racial barriers encountered by African Americans. They blame racism for their failure. They again and again send the message that no matter how hard their children work, they cannot make it in this country because of racial discrimination. This kind of cynical racial socialization can destroy or at least weaken their children's motivation to work hard to resist racial adversity. Instead, it is seen that African American parents should emphasize that because of disadvantages, their children need to work much harder than white children to achieve the same goals. Moreover, they need to teach their children to develop their racial pride and strategies to resist and protect themselves from racially biased treatment.

Further Reading

Bowman, P.J., and C. Howard. "Race-Related Socialization, Motivation, and Academic Achievement: A Study of Black Youth in Three-Generation Families." *Journal of the American Academy of Child Psychiatry* 24: 134–141.

Garrod, Andrew, Janie Victoria Ward, Trancy Robinson, and Robert Kilkenny, eds. *Souls Looking Back: Life Stories of Growing up Black*. New York: Routledge, 1999.

Pyong Gap Min

Racial Stereotypes

See Films and Racial Stereotypes; Journalism and Racial Stereotypes; Television and Racial Stereotypes.

Racial Stigmatization

A stigma is an attribute considered to be socially undesirable. The attribute itself may not be harmful or negative, but the *social reaction* to that attribute is negative. Racial stigmatization occurs when a racial group or groups are considered to be less desirable than other groups. This is not because of any fundamental difference between groups (in fact, there is considerable scientific debate over whether racial classifications are biologically meaningful), but rather because of the social reaction of others. The sociologist Erving Goffman separated stigmatized people into two categories, the discredited and the discreditable. The discredited are those whose stigma is immediately known to others; for example, someone in a wheelchair has a visible stigma and therefore is considered discredited. The discreditable refers to those whose stigma is not visible, such as ex-convicts. The terms *stigma*, *discredited*, and *discreditable* refer only to the negative *social* reaction; they do not represent personal judgments about the desirability of the attribute itself.

Racial stigmatization is for the most part visible; therefore, those in racially stigmatized groups often have to counter the negative assumptions that others make about them in everyday interactions. Young African Americans, for example, often find themselves watched more carefully in stores than are whites. Racial stigmatization makes others assume that they are more likely to shoplift than their white counterparts. Because racial stigmatization is based on social reaction, it varies from place to place. Members of particular racial groups may find themselves stigmatized in some countries, regions, or even neighborhoods, but not in others. Racial stigmatization can make it more difficult for some groups to advance socially or economically. Employers often prefer some racial and ethnic groups to others. Similarly, at one point, banks routinely refused to make loans in neighborhoods dominated by blacks and Latinos. That practice has a name: redlining. Research now suggests that the stress of racial stigmatization can even result in physical health problems. Racial stigmatization can greatly affect many aspects of an individual's life.

Robin Roger-Dillon

Racism

See Modern Racism; Racism, Aversive versus Dominative.

Racism, Aversive versus Dominative

Racism may be expressed in various forms. One way to characterize this variability involves the dichotomy between dominative and aversive racism. Dominative racism involves subjugation of the oppressed through slavery and other means of control. This was the prevailing mode of racism in the South before the Civil War. In the post–Civil War South and in the North, racism typically transpired in less blatant forms: aversive racism. Aversive racism, in its original sense, involves social and physical distancing initiated by the oppressors toward the oppressed. School and residential segregation, for example, are forms of aversive racism. In recent decades, through such social and political actions as the civil rights movements, Americans have begun to consider systematically delivered aversive racism (e.g., segregation) to be both unethical and illegal. Reflecting such transitions, aversive racism is now defined as subtler and often unintended forms of racism, typically observed among white Americans who ostensibly hold racially egalitarian values. Racism among such individuals is usually expressed in ways in which they can maintain the egalitarian images of themselves.

For example, a recent series of social-psychological experiments demonstrate that when white American and African American job candidates have identical qualifications, white American employers tend to hire white American candidates over African American candidates. Four decades after the emergence of the civil rights movements, aversive racism remains prevalent in our society.

See also Civil Rights Movement; Civil War and the Abolition of Slavery.

Daisuke Akiba

Rainbow Coalition

The Rainbow Coalition is an organization founded in 1985 by Rev. Jesse Jackson with the goal of "uniting people of diverse ethnic, religious, economic, and political backgrounds" in a push for "social, racial, and economic justice" through political empowerment and changes in public policy. It sees itself as a child of the civil rights movement, using demonstrations and boycotts as well as litigation and lobbying to promote its interests. Since its founding, the Rainbow Coalition has been active in voter registration, getting people of color elected, lobbying for equal-opportunity employment in various industries, and bringing attention to U.S. foreign policy in South Africa and Haiti.

In 1996, the Rainbow Coalition merged with People United to Serve Humanity (PUSH), another organization that Jackson founded in 1971 to expand educational and employment opportunities for disadvantaged people of color. The united single organization is referred to as the Rainbow/PUSH Coalition. Rainbow/PUSH currently focuses on HIV/AIDS issues, advocating for minority and women-owned businesses, linkages between black churches, local civil rights issues, voter registration, prison ministry and services for prisoners, and health insurance for children.

See also Civil Rights Movement; Jackson, Jesse.

Mikaila Mariel Lemonik Arthur

Randolph, A. Philip (1889–1979)

Asa Philip Randolph was an African American activist leader in the labor movement and the civil rights movement for the black American community. In 1917, when the United States declared war on Germany during World War I, Randolph founded a radical Harlem magazine, *The Messenger* (the name was changed to *Black Worker* in 1929), with his old friend, Chandler Owen, and advocated increasing the number of positions in the war industry and the armed forces available to blacks. In 1925, he successfully established the first black trade union, the Brotherhood of Sleeping Car Porters. Gaining support from the American Federation of Labor, in 1937 Randolph led the Brotherhood to win a major contract for black laborers with the Pullman Company.

In 1941, Randolph planned a protest march of thousands of black workers in Washington, DC. When Randolph warned President Franklin D. Roosevelt, Roosevelt issued Executive Order 8802, which banned discrimination against blacks in defense industries and federal bureaus and created the Fair Employment Practices Committee. In 1947, Randolph also founded the Committee against Jim Crow in Military Service (later renamed the League for Nonviolent Civil Disobedience against Military Segregation). This organization also led President Harry S. Truman to issue Executive Order 9981 in 1948, which prohibited segregation of racial minorities in the armed forces. In 1963, Randolph helped Martin Luther King Jr. organize the March on Washington for Jobs and Freedom. This protest brought more than 200,000 demonstrators to the capital to support civil rights measures for black Americans. Randolph, Martin Luther King Jr., and other activist leaders met with President John F. Kennedy after the march. A series of these actions greatly gave impetus to the passage of the Civil Rights Act in the following year (1964).

Etsuko Maruoka-Ng

Rape and Racism

Rape is a violent crime. According to the FBI, 95,136 forcible rapes were reported in the United States in 2002, but federal crime-victimization surveys indicate that number to be nearly three times higher because only about one in three rapes is reported. Women are 91 percent of the victims and men are 99 percent of the offenders. The vast majority of rapes against women are perpetrated by offenders of the same race, with about 81 percent of the victims being white. Certainly gender stereotyping—the dominant male and the submissive female—plays a part in many cases of rape, but in cases of interracial rape, the addition of racial stereotypes born of racial prejudices creates a complex set of circumstances that affect both victims and offenders.

When the U.S. Constitution was hammered out by the white Founding Fathers, it institutionalized the racist ideology by counting black slaves as three-fifths of a person. The prevailing white belief that blacks were not just unequal to whites but somehow subhuman, led to stereotyping black males as animals with insatiable sex drives and black females as readily available for the pleasure of white men without consequence to the men. This gave rise to, among other things, the myth of the black rapist. Thus, before the Civil War, many Southern states punished rape offenders by race rather than by deed. A black man who raped a white woman would be sentenced to death, but a white man who raped a white woman might get two to twenty years in prison. Raping a black woman might get a fine or some jail time, but only if the court so decided.

The persistence of these stereotypes has led to countless travesties of justice. Charges of rape were used to prop up white supremacy and to provide a ready excuse to lynch black men. Black women victimized by rape were victimized again in judicial hearings. A violent crime against a black woman was not considered as something serious by judges or juries, just evidence of the way blacks lived everyday life. How could a subhuman be violated? Not surprisingly, many black women chose not to report the crime at all. One of the best-known examples of functional racism in rape cases was the case of the "Scottsboro Boys" in Alabama. Two young white women accused nine black teenagers who were removed from a Southern Railroad freight train of gang rape. All but one of the nine, a twelve-year-old, were convicted of rape and sentenced to death in the course of a few weeks after their arrest, but only after the governor of Alabama called in the National Guard to save them from a lynch mob. It turned out that the rape had never occurred. It took twenty years, countless court battles, and intervention from national organizations like the National Association for the Advancement of Colored People (NAACP) to put an end to the injustice.

The fate of the Scottsboro Boys did not end racism in rape cases. Long after that, juries continued to convict black men alleged to have committed rape at higher rates than white men accused of rape. Black women who alleged rape, on the other hand, tended not to be believed, even after having suffered the incredulity of police and the skepticism of the medical establishment to pursue a case. And even then, prosecutors were less likely to take their case to court, a case they had a good chance of losing. Latino women, who like blacks were stereotyped as members of a culture that tolerated all kinds of violence, including rape, had similar experiences.

In more recent times, as women and minorities have found their rightful political power and voice, the old racial, sexual stereotypes are collapsing if not being reversed. Many social observers saw a larger message in the jury's innocent verdict that ended the 1995 murder trial of O. J. Simpson. A racially diverse jury seemed to be announcing to the nation that the days of racial discrimination in court proceedings were over, no matter how solid the physical evidence and no matter what the alleged crime. A sense of guilt on the part of whites for the documented mistreatment of blacks through American judicial history suggested a bias for innocence. This was the so-called race card. Too many black men had been victimized by the U.S. criminal justice and judicial systems for too many years. That was also the message of Kobe Bryant's attorneys when the basketball star was accused of rape by a white woman. There was nothing deviant and certainly nothing illegal about a black man and a white woman having consensual sex. Yet no matter what the Simpson jury's intentions were, there was an immediate backlash to it, notably among whites, who believed that justice had not been served. The evidence against Simpson was too clear and obvious.

For example, a 2002 study of college students found that racial factors determined victim blaming. Men's scores on the Modern Racism Scale were correlated positively with victim blaming in all rapes. The conclusion of the study was that racial stereotyping in rape cases persists and directly influences judicial outcomes.

See also National Association for the Advancement of Colored People (NAACP); War and Racial Inequality.

Further Reading

Davis, Angela. "Rape, Racism, and the Myth of the Black Rapist." In *Feminism and "Race,"* edited by Bhavnani, Kum-Kum, 50–64. New York: Oxford University Press, 2001.

George, William H., and Lorraine J. Martinez. "Victim Blaming in Rape Effects and Perpetrator Race, Type of Rape, and Participant Racism." *Psychology of Women Quarterly* 26 (June 2002): 110–119.

Hacker, Andrew. *Two Nations: Black and White, Separate, Hostile, Unequal.* New York: Scribner, 1992.

Benjamin F. Shearer

Reconstruction Era

The Reconstruction era (1865–1877) is the period after the American Civil War, during which the North tried to restore political order to the South and to integrate the newly freed slaves into civil society. Reconstruction was a difficult and chaotic time. Much of the Southern economy had been based on the slave system that was abolished with the Civil War. In addition to the end of slavery, the South had been economically and socially devastated by the

Reconstruction of the South.

Courtesy Library of Congress.

war. Many families had lost husbands and sons. Other men had come home from war disabled. For the North, too, there had been considerable loss of life. During Reconstruction, the United States faced the task of rebuilding after a brutal civil war had almost torn it apart.

One of the first tasks of the United States was to integrate the newly freed slaves into civil society. In 1866, the United States ratified the Thirteenth Amendment, which granted citizenship to freed slaves. In 1867 and 1870, respectively, the Fourteenth and Fifteenth Amendments to the Constitution were ratified. Together, these amendments granted freed slaves citizenship and gave black men, but not yet women, the right to vote.

The freed slaves faced considerable difficulties in both the South, in which many whites were reluctant to accept the North's victory, and the North, where economic difficulties and racism often created hostile and dangerous environments for blacks. Laws known as "Black Codes" that limited the freedom of blacks were passed in numerous Southern states. The social advances of African Americans during this time were dramatic, but they were also marred by race riots against blacks and attempts to limit their newly gained constitutional rights, particularly the right to vote through mechanisms such as poll taxes. The Ku Klux Klan was also established at this time to oppose African American citizenship.

In 1877, federal troops pulled out of the South and left Southern elites to govern as they wished. The federal pullout was part of a deal, known as the Hayes-Tilden Compromise, reached to settle the contested 1876 presidential election. After 1877, African Americans lost even more of the ground they had gained through the constitutional amendments. Jim Crow laws and court rulings limited the legal freedoms that African Americans had gained during Reconstruction. Nonetheless, the Thirteenth, Fourteenth, and Fifteenth Amendments laid the constitutional groundwork for many of the successes of the civil rights movement in the twentieth century.

The Civil War is sometimes portrayed as a war waged by the antislavery North against the slave-holding South. Although it is true that slavery was more fundamental to the Southern economy and way of life and that conflict over slavery fueled the war, historians also suggest that shifts in the Northern economy to an industrial base and the North's increasing interest in having a strong federal government to buffer its interactions and trade with Europe, created economic and political conflicts with the still agriculturally based South, which preferred to retain local governance. The Civil War, therefore, was a war over the nature of the United States as a country as well as one over the institution of slavery.

The Reconstruction era was a time of great leaps forward legally for African Americans. Much of this advancement, however, was opposed by whites at the local level who responded with violence and legal challenges. Many of the legal victories were rolled back in the following decades. It took many years for the ideals of equal citizenship for all to begin to become a reality. Even today, there are still heated conflicts over the root causes of racial inequality and the role of the government in assuring full social and political rights for all.

See also Civil War and the Abolition of Slavery; Emancipation Proclamation; Fourteenth Amendment; Hayes-Tilden Compromise of 1877; Jim Crow Laws; Ku Klux Klan (KKK).

Further Reading

Louisiana State Museum. *Reconstruction: A State Divided*. http://lsm.crt.state.la.us/cabildo/cab11.ht.

Maltz, Earl. *Civil Rights, the Constitution and Congress, 1863–1869*. Lawrence: University Press of Kansas, 1990.

Ward, Geoffrey, Ken Burns, and Ric Burns. *The Civil War: An Illustrated History*. New York: Knopf, 1992.

Robin Roger-Dillon

Redistricting

When new census data becomes available every ten years, the redrawing of voting districts is required under the equal-protection clause of the Constitution to assure equal representation of voters living in the districts. The Voting Rights Act of 1965 sought to eliminate discriminatory election processes by declaring in Section 2 that "no voting qualification or prerequisite to voting or standard practice or procedure shall be imposed or applied . . . in a manner which results in a denial or abridgement of the right of any citizen of the United States to vote on account of race or color. . . ." This meant that the old tradition of racial gerrymandering, prevalent in the South, could be illegal. No longer could black voters be packed into a particular district or split among districts to dilute their votes. The act also placed districts with a history of voting discrimination under federal supervision for redistricting or any other changes in voting law.

The 1982 amendments to the Voting Rights Act allowed so-called minority-majority districts to be created, which gave concentrated minorities in those districts the power to elect their own candidates. Congress specifically stated, however, that these amendments did not imply proportional representation: that is, there was no intention to legislate a mandate that a minority with 10 percent of the total population should elect 10 percent of the representatives. With these new rules, minority representation in Congress increased dramatically in the 1992 elections.

The law affecting redistricting remains in flux as cases make their way through the courts. The U.S. Supreme Court has made it clear, however, that drawing districts on the basis of race, any race, is illegal. Yet communities of interest are to be left intact. The Court has also found that drawing district boundaries for purely political reasons, including the reelection of incumbents, is legal.

See also Voting Rights Act of 1965; Voting Rights Amendments of 1975.

Benjamin F. Shearer

Redlining

Redlining, also known as "mortgage disinvestment," is a discriminatory practice that occurs when mortgage lenders refuse to make loans in neighborhoods for racially motivated reasons. The process was termed redlining because lenders would literally draw "lines" around certain locales on city maps (usually urban areas) to identify acceptable and unacceptable markets. It was safe to provide loans in areas identified in "green," "yellow" areas were considered questionable, and "red" areas were considered unsafe. Once an area had been redlined, no mortgage or property improvement loans were extended to its residents, even persons who were creditworthy. Redlining was most likely to occur in African American neighborhoods. Banks and other lending institutions feared extending credit in areas believed to be undergoing racial transition—especially when the in-migrating group was African American—for fear that such areas would decline economically. Ironically, by refusing credit in such neighborhoods, lenders initiated a self-fulfilling prophecy as residents had difficulty maintaining their homes or getting fair market value for them.

The resulting devalued areas then stood as "evidence" to justify continued redlining. Similar forms of discrimination also occurred among federal housing agencies. Such practices and lending disparities were discovered during the community-reinvestment movement of the 1970s, and activists sued agencies responsible for policing fair-banking practices. Several national laws were instituted to address discriminatory lending practices. In 1976, Congress passed the Home Mortgage Disclosure Act, which requires banks to make their lending data public. In 1978, the Community Reinvestment Act (CRA) was passed, which requires banking institutions to address the lending needs of communities in which they serve.

See also Financial Institutions and Racial Discrimination; Housing Discrimination.

Sandra L. Barnes

Redress Movement

See Japanese American, Redress Movement for.

Red Power Movement

The Red Power movement, similar to the Black Power movement, stresses the ideas of self-determination and cultural pride. Several Native American groups that were part of a Pan-Indian movement were dedicated to the preservation of the Native American identity and gaining a bigger voice in politics. Pan-Indianism is a social movement that attempts to establish a collective Native American ethnic identity, not just a single tribal identity. Pan-Indianism served the youth who found comfort in each other's presence. Before 1960, individual tribes were trying to negotiate with the federal government. After years of failed attempts, Native Americans banded together to approach the government as a pan-Indian organization.

The phrase *red power* was first introduced at the convention of the National Congress of American Indians (NCAI) in 1966. Since then, several other pan-Indian groups have emerged to spread the message of red power. These groups include the Society of American Indians (SAI), National Indian Youth Council (NIYC), the American Indian Movement (AIM), and the Indians of All Tribes. The SAI and the NCAI were the first pan-Indian groups to organize. Founded in 1944 in Denver, the NCAI consists of members of tribes, bands, or groups recognized by the federal government, and other people of Indian ancestry. Today, the NCAI is a major lobbyist group for Indian legislation in Washington. There is some controversy surrounding the group because some think the group is too conservative because its members, representing various Indian reservations, only concern themselves with reservation problems. Urban Indians and nonreservation rural Indians have put pressure on the NCAI to change its membership restrictions to include all types of Indians.

The NIYC was created from the Chicago Conference of national Indian representatives, which was held to review Indian policies in June 1964. A group of Indian college students was displeased with what went on in the meeting and decided to form their own national group that would use white political tactics to achieve their goals. The NIYC created scholarship opportunities for Native Americans and also staged illegal fish-ins in Washington State to protest treaty violations of Native American rights.

The AIM was created in the summer of 1968 in Minneapolis by Dennis Banks and George Mitchell. It started as a volunteer citizen patrol developed in response to the numerous complaints of police harassment and brutality against

Indians. By 1971, AIM was reported to have eighteen chapters across the nation, with twelve in urban areas and six on reservations. About two hundred members of AIM participated in seizing control of the village of Wounded Knee, South Dakota, on February 27, 1973. The location of Wounded Knee was the site of the last Native American resistance in 1890 when one hundred and fifty Miniconjou Sioux from the Cheyenne River Reservation were killed by the U.S. Calvary. The siege lasted seventy-one days and was a staged media event to direct attention to the plight of Native Americans. Some Native American leaders were against the takeover, but most sympathized with it.

In November 1969, the Indians of All Tribes arrived on Alcatraz Island to demand that the island be seen as Indian land. The goal of the seizing of Alcatraz was to turn the island into an Indian cultural and education center. The occupation lasted almost two years before the remaining occupants were surprised by federal marshals and escorted off the island. The occupation succeeded in getting the federal government to allow Indian self-determination and tribal self-rule. President Richard M. Nixon increased funds for health care, education, economic development, expanded housing, and other programs.

The pan-Indian movement was not accepted by all Indians, even young ones. Many Native Americans prefer to preserve their separate tribal identities instead of a unified tribal group. These Native Americans focus on preserving tribal pride by teaching their people arts and crafts and establishing cultural centers to exhibit and sell their work.

See also American Indian Movement (AIM); Indian Reservations; National Congress of American Indians (NCAI); Native Americans, Prejudice and Discrimination against.

Further Reading

Healey, Joseph F. *Race, Ethnicity, Gender, and Class.* Thousand Oaks, CA: Pine Forge Press, 1998.

Parillo, Vincent N. *Strangers to These Shores: Race and Ethnic Relations in the United States.* Boston: Allyn & Bacon, 2000.

Tiffany Vélez

Regents of the University of California v. Bakke

The decision in the 1978 U.S. Supreme Court case *Regents of the University of California v. Bakke* represented the first time that the Court upheld the concept of affirmative action and its goal of remedying past discrimination against members of minority groups and women. When Allan Bakke's application to the University of California Davis, Medical School was denied a second time, Bakke, a white man, charged that he had been passed over in favor of less qualified African American applicants. Claiming he was a victim of reverse discrimination, Bakke argued that the decision to deny him admission was based solely on his race, since his academic credentials were better than some African Americans who were admitted to the UC Davis Medical School. Bakke filed a suit against the Regents of University of California, claiming that

his constitutional right to equal protection under the Fourteenth Amendment
had been violated.

During the 1970s, the UC Davis Medical School employed a dual admissions
process: a regular admissions program in which applicants with a grade-point
average of 2.5 or lower on a scale of 4 were automatically rejected, and a special admissions program to increase the representation among the student
body of minorities and other "disadvantaged" groups. Special-admissions applicants did not need to have maintained a 2.5 GPA. Of the 100 spaces available in each class, sixteen were reserved for special-admissions applicants. The
Court ruled by five to four that the use of quotas in affirmative action programs was unconstitutional and hence, not permissible. As a result, Bakke was
admitted to the medical school, and he graduated in 1992. However, writing
the decision of a closely divided Supreme Court, Justice Lewis F. Powell (who
died in August 1998) also held that race, along with other factors, could be
used as a "plus" factor in admissions decisions. Interestingly, in a subsequent
law suit filed against the University of Michigan in 2003, the U.S. Supreme
Court offered a similar ruling that rejected the university's undergraduate admission system based on a quota for minority students but accepted its use
of race as one criterion for admission to the law school.

Allan Bakke is trailed by reporters after attending his first day at University of California, Davis, Medical School.

AP/Wide World Photos.

See also Affirmative Action; Affirmative Action, University of Michigan Ruling on; *Affirmative Discrimination: Ethnic Inequality and Public Policy*; Fourteenth Amendment; Legacy of Past Discrimination Argument for Affirmative Action; Reverse Discrimination; Role-Model Argument for Affirmative Action.

Tarry Hum

Religion and Racism

Throughout American history, religious institutions and theologies have interacted symbiotically with the social phenomenon of color hierarchy and with institutionalized discrimination, such as the slave trade and Jim Crow legislation. Put simply, white racism and white Christianity, particularly Protestant Christianity, are foundational elements of American society and culture, and each has served the other since the colonial era.

Given the parallels between Christian theological concepts of exclusivity and the "in-group/out-group" dynamic of racial discrimination, this interrelation is perhaps not surprising. Its transcendent philosophy notwithstanding, religion and its institutions reflect the society in which they exist. As institutions with social power, Christian churches in the United States buttressed the institution of slavery, provided a "higher" logic to explain the plight of African Americans during the Jim Crow era, and in contemporary times, fuel discrimination against non-Christian communities of color. (At times in history, some white Christian churches have also applied the power of their moral influence in opposition of racial and religious discrimination.)

Beginning even before the founding of the United States, racism interacted with Christian supremacy as both causes and characteristics of the slave trade: Africans "were beings apart" because they "were not merely black, they were black *and* heathen" (Lincoln 1999). Non-Christian Africans' "depraved condition"—a condition that their enslavement both rescued them from and condemned them to—thereby explained their place in society as slaves. At the same time, in a reflection of political institutions' role in spreading the dominant religious doctrine, many slave traders sought to convert their slaves to Christianity. Whites used purportedly Christian doctrines both to rationalize slavery to themselves (by invoking the necessity of controlling African slaves whose "heathen rituals" showed their low intelligence) and to the slaves (describing to Christian blacks their slave status as the "destiny" God intended for them).

However, racial minorities were not the only targets of religion-based racism. Jewish and Catholic immigrants in the late nineteenth and early twentieth centuries, who traced their origins to central, eastern, and southern Europe and to Ireland, were victims as well. Although both groups have since been accepted as whites, they were treated as racial minority groups at the time of their arrival. The confluence of their non-Protestant religious identities and, in some cases, of their darker coloration (as compared with the northern European majority of the time) made them targets.

One lasting result of Christianity/slavery symbiosis has been the creation of separate church institutions by and for black American Christians. This was a response to the way white churches perpetuated and acted out society's racial hierarchy, with blacks forced to sit in rear pews or in "nigger heaven" (church balconies, often with separate entrances) rather than in the company of their white "brethren." Notwithstanding Christian theology that could be interpreted as racially egalitarian, "a racial tribalism [among whites] . . . militated against sharing a common experience with blacks as equals under any circumstances, religious or otherwise." Historical black institutions, like the African Methodist Episcopal Church and the National Baptist Convention, are examples of black Christian denominations that developed in this manner.

While churches, both black and white, were a major venue for progressive social activism during the civil rights era, other churches fomented opposition to the civil rights movement. To this day, the Creativity movement (formerly known as the World Church of the Creator) and other white supremacist organizations use Christian scripture and imagery to call for "RAHOWA"—a RAcial HOly WAr—against racial minorities and Jews.

Race-based exclusions remained common in some American Christian institutional policies into recent decades. For example, the Church of Jesus Christ of Latter Day Saints (the "Mormons") did not permit African Americans to become clergy until 1978 and attribute blacks' misfortune to a holy curse. Similarly, it was not until the late 1990s that a major white Christian denomination issued a statement repudiating slavery.

In recent decades, the interaction between American Christianity and racist oppression has transformed in response to new immigration patterns. White American society's acceptance of theological anti-Semitism shrank dramatically in the post–World War II era, a reaction to the horror of the Holocaust, which was also reflected in the Catholic Church's *Nostra Aetate* proclamation in 1965 that Jews "remain very dear to God." At virtually the same moment, the Immigration Act of 1965 resulted in a dramatic increase in the size and geographic dispersion of religious minority communities previously unknown in the United States, including Muslims, Hindus, Sikhs, Jains, animists, and others from Asia, Africa, and the Middle East. As racial and religious minorities, these communities are experiencing new manifestations of the combined prejudice once directed at African slaves.

When Franklin Graham, son of the famous white Baptist preacher Rev. Billy Graham, described Islam as a "very evil and wicked religion" in 2001, it can hardly be doubted that his statement was meant and understood to have racial overtones as well. Although most American Muslims are not Arab (most are African American), the contemporary American mental image of Muslims—and, by extension, of Islam—is the nineteen Saudi, Egyptian, and United Arab Emirates hijackers who committed the terrorist attacks of September 11, 2001. In a fresh manifestation of centuries-old views about the "depraved condition" of African animist slaves, the line between Muslims' theological inadequacy and their racial and ethnic status in the view of white American Christians is vague and porous.

In another reflection of contemporary religious racism, the Southern Baptist Convention's program to convert Hindus away from the "spiritual darkness" of Hinduism announced during the Hindu holiday Diwali in 1999, was directed at an American minority community made up almost entirely of brown-skinned South Asians. The Convention proclaimed that there is "no salvation apart from . . . Jesus Christ as . . . Lord and Savior" or without baptism in the church, a theological litmus test which neither Hindus nor Jews nor the Amish "pass"; the organization's decision to focus on Hindus reflects the greater acceptability, even today, of targeting racial minorities with charges of religious inadequacy. This is the continuing legacy of the interaction of religion and racism that has characterized the United States since its colonial beginnings, notwithstanding its creation myth of religious freedom and equality.

See also Anti-Catholicism in the United States; Anti-Semitism in the United States; Black Anti-Semitism; Ghost Dance Religion; Non-Judeo-Christian Immigrant Groups, Violence against; Religious Right; *United States v. Thind*.

Further Reading

Lincoln, C. Eric. *Race, Religion, and the Continuing American Dilemma*. New York: Hill and Wang, 1999.

Khyati Joshi

Religious Right

What is referred to as the "religious right" is that subset of the American polity characterized by political conservatism grounded in the rhetoric of evangelical Christianity. Although religious rightists can be found in every state and in most ethnic groups, their demographic characteristics skew toward predominantly white rural or suburban communities in the American South and Midwest. These demographic epicenters are reflected in the political positions of religious rightists, which envision an idyllic and mythologized image of pre-civil rights era white communities undisturbed by crime, poverty, and ethnic and religious diversity.

Most religious rightists do not espouse the violent and overt racism and White supremacy that characterized the Jim Crow era but support instead legislation that and political candidates who wield the language of modern racism. Religious rightists' aspiration for America manifests an ethos of color-blind racism, which identifies those who are outside acceptable norms of morality and family values to include "welfare moms," "illegal aliens," lesbians and gay men of all races, beneficiaries of affirmative action, and others whose identities define them in the religious rightist mind as living an "un-American" life. At the "right" edge of religious right ideology are the virulently and violently racist and anti-Semitic groups, such as neo-Nazis and the Christian Identity Movement, which use Christian religious themes and concepts in presenting and spreading their ideology of race- and religion-based hatred and violence.

While purportedly populist, religious rightist ideology privileges the culture of white northern Europeans at the expense of diversity and a pluralistic model of democracy. Members of other religious minority groups, such as Muslims, Hindus, and Sikhs—who are also disproportionately likely to be people of color—are portrayed as morally suspect and less deserving of the benefits of residency and citizenship in the United States. The religious right believes women should adopt "traditional" roles that are secondary and submissive to men. Its call to make the United States a "Christian nation" and to press the secular government into service of overt Christian ideals implies that non-Christians are second-class citizens. Notwithstanding the expressly Christian orientation of religious rightists, however, Jews are accepted as allies to the extent that they adopt the Right's agenda.

See also Civil Rights Movement; Jim Crow Laws; Liberal and Conservative Views of Racial Inequality; Non-Judeo-Christian Immigrant Groups, Violence against.

Khyati Joshi

Reparations for African Americans

Slavery reparations, or acts of making amends for the injustices of slavery, may take many forms: an apology, monetary rewards, land redistribution, or the creation of social programs and policies. The main criterion is that they serve as a comparable form of repayment for the impact of almost 250 years of legalized slave trade and the subsequent years of second-class status experienced by many African Americans after the abolition of slavery. The modern-day discussions of reparations for slavery are at least thirty years old, but there is evidence that the quest for slavery reparations is more than a hundred years old.

After the Civil War there was some discussion of compensating ex-slaves for their losses, but President Andrew Johnson vetoed the legislation that would have made this possible. Instead, the Southern Homestead Act, which allowed ex-slaves to purchase land at relatively low rates without competition from whites and outside investors, emerged. The drawback to this plan was that few former slaves had enough resources to take advantage of this opportunity, and those who did found themselves the proud owners of decrepit land. Legislation that acknowledges the "fundamental injustice, cruelty, brutality and inhumanity of slavery" and calls for the creation of a commission to examine the institution of slavery and to make recommendations on appropriate remedies, has been introduced every year since 1989 by Congressman John Conyers (D-MI), but this bill has not gone beyond the committee level.

The debate over reparations for slavery is twofold. First, there is considerable division about whether repayment is warranted. The second part of the argument revolves around whether it is feasible to administer reparations at this point in time. Opponents of the reparations movement contend that slavery took place so long ago that it could not possibly have any impact on the lives of Americans today. This argument is usually accompanied by the belief that today's citizens should not be held responsible for what their forefathers did.

In discussing whether reparations should be made for slavery, the conversation usually turns to how impractical such a plan would be, given the difficulty in determining who is a descendent of slaves, how much that person is owed, and who will pay for the reparations. Historians have pointed out that slavery was not a race-specific crime. People from many racial/ethnic backgrounds were sold into slavery and people of all races owned slaves. This evidence supports those who believe that race-specific policies, such as reparations for African Americans, are not warranted. Some who are opposed to administering cash reparations to African Americans argue that reparations have already been given to African Americans in the form of Affirmative Action policies, scholarships, and empowerment zones. There is also some concern that implementing a slavery reparations policy could create hostility between African Americans and other Americans.

Advocates of the reparations movement argue that indeed the effects of slavery and its successor, segregation, are quite strong today. Disparities in health, wealth, and social status are offered as evidence of the lingering effects of slavery and the policies established in subsequent years. Reparations advocates also contend that today's citizens continue to benefit from the transgressions of their ancestors in a multitude of ways, such as using infrastructure that was built with slave labor or inheriting fortunes that were built on the backs of slaves.

There is also the problem of record keeping and determining who is entitled to receive slavery reparations. Since slaves were not allowed to read or write and had no safe place to maintain documents, it is not likely that people would be able to produce evidence to support a case for their entitlement. The slave owners themselves had little incentive to keep detailed records on the slaves as individuals, and even if such documents ever existed, it would prove difficult to acquire them for systematic use in the courtroom.

Reparations advocates also point out that slavery reparations may not seem feasible, but reparations for Native Americans and Japanese Americans seemed impractical at one time; however, after resources were committed to developing a strategy for repayment, a feasible plan emerged. They contend that the same would be true for African American reparations, even if a commitment were made only to studying the impact of slavery and the need for reparations.

The American public seems to be quite divided on the subject of reparations. About 33 percent of whites feel that corporations that benefited from slavery should provide an apology to African Americans, while 66 percent of African Americans share this view. What is most striking about this debate is the unwillingness to create a national dialogue about whether reparations are warranted. This reticence to discuss slavery reparations suggests that although slavery ended 138 years ago, Americans are still uncomfortable discussing its impact.

See also Japanese Americans, Redress Movement for; Slavery in the Antebellum South.

Further Reading

Robinson, Randall. *The Debt: What America Owes to Blacks.* New York: Penguin Putnam, 2000.

Winbush, Raymond, ed. *Should America Pay?: Slavery and the Raging Debate on Reparations.* New York: Amistad, 2003.

Romney S. Norwood

Residential Segregation

The term *residential segregation* is used to describe the creation and maintenance of separate neighborhoods for various racial and ethnic groups. Segregation can be either voluntary or involuntary. Involuntary segregation occurs when members of a minority group are forced to live in segregated neighborhoods against their will. There is a long history of racial residential segregation in the United States. Despite some modest to moderate declines in levels of segregation, racially separate neighborhoods remain quite common in the United States. African Americans, in particular, still maintain a high level of involuntary segregation partly because of various forms of housing discrimination and mainly because of the tendency of white Americans to avoid contact with them. The persistence of racial residential segregation among African Americans and other racial minority groups has some serious negative implications for the quality of their lives.

Current Trends

Sociologists have created the dissimilarity index to measure the level of segregation. The scores for the dissimilarity index range from 0 to 100. A score closer to 0 suggests that the two groups are almost completely integrated, while a score closer to 100 indicates that they are almost completely segregated. A dissimilarity index of 0.5 between African Americans and whites means that one-half of the African American population should move to white neighborhoods to achieve complete residential integration between the two groups.

Most measures indicate that residential segregation has declined for African Americans in the last two decades. Even with these moderate declines, segregation levels for African Americans remain high. In 2000, the dissimilarity index for African Americans was .640, which represents a 12 percent decline since 1980. An exceptionally high level of overall segregation for African Americans is partly the function of their high concentration in major American cities, as the level of segregation is highly correlated with the level of the population concentration.

Since the 1970s, African Americans, like all Americans, have been steadily increasing their presence in the suburbs. This suburban movement has contributed to the modest declines in segregation levels for African Americans. Nevertheless, the levels of residential segregation for African Americans remain high, because even in the suburbs they remain isolated from other racial groups, especially whites. African Americans tend to reside in older suburbs that have been abandoned by whites. Even wealthier African Americans who do reside in new suburban communities tend to reside in predominantly African American communities in an effort to avoid harassment from white neighbors who may not be pleased to have them as neighbors.

Most of the indices used to measure residential segregation indicate an increase for Hispanic Americans between 1980 and 2000. The dissimilarity index for Hispanic and Latino Americans in 2000 was .509, which represents a 1.5 percent increase since 1980. This is not a large increase and mostly represents

voluntary segregation among recent Hispanic immigrants who settle in ethnic enclaves that have an abundance of resources for new immigrants. Hispanics who were born in the United States and reside in medium to large
cities have experienced steadily lower levels of residential segregation than
Hispanic immigrants.

Most of the sizable concentrations of Asians and Pacific Islanders are found
on the West Coast. Several measures of residential segregation indicate increases in segregation for both groups since the 1980s. The greater the percentage of the population accounted for by Asians and Pacific Islanders in a
metropolitan area, the more isolated they are and the more likely they are to
live together. The various segregation indices suggest that Asians are more segregated than Pacific Islanders. Based on the dissimilarity-index estimate, the
segregation of Asian Americans increased by 14 percent between 1980 and
2000 to .411, but it is not high, compared with African Americans and Hispanics.

These lower levels of segregation among Asian Americans are in great part
due to the ability of Asian immigrants to bring enough economic resources to
the United States to purchase the American dream house in the suburbs. Asian
Americans have moved into the suburbs of U.S. metropolitan areas at a great
rate. This high level of suburbanization for Asian Americans also reflects the
low level of resistance they received from white suburban dwellers upon moving into predominantly white neighborhoods.

Levels of residential segregation for Hispanics and Asian Americans are not
explained by the attitudes of whites to the same extent that segregation levels for African Americans are. Many Hispanic and Asian Americans voluntarily
segregate themselves by establishing enclaves. In the enclave, they can associate with others who share a similar background and have access to the resources and commodities that they are accustomed to in their home countries.
New and recent immigrants find living and working in these communities to
be extremely beneficial because they are able to establish social networks,
which help them to navigate their new environs.

Since the early 1980s, Native Americans have experienced an 11 percent
nationwide decline in residential segregation, with mid-size metropolitan areas
having less residential segregation than large and small ones. The dissimilarity
index for Native Americans in all metropolitan areas in 2000 was .333, which
is not indicative of drastic segregation, as only 33 percent of the population
would have to move to achieve complete integration.

The low levels of residential segregation for Native Americans in metropolitan areas generally reflect lower levels of prejudice toward Native Americans compared with African Americans. The rate of intermarriage between
Native Americans and whites is quite high, especially in comparison to the
level of intermarriage between African Americans and whites. The levels of
residential segregation for Native Americans and their levels of intermarriage
with white Americans suggest that Native Americans are much more accepted
by white Americans than are African Americans. The Native American population in urban areas is quite small as well, so it is easy for the population to
be dispersed in metropolitan areas. The lack of concentrated Native American

communities in urban areas prevents other Americans from feeling threatened by their presence.

Causes of Residential Segregation

White Prejudice and White Preference. The hierarchy of residential settlement patterns suggests that white Americans are most comfortable living in neighborhoods where they are in the majority. When nonwhite families move into their neighborhoods, they are most at ease with the presence of Asian Americans, followed by Hispanics, and are most uncomfortable with African Americans.

Attitudes toward integrated housing have changed considerably over the last several decades. Many whites cite concerns about higher levels of crime, lower property values, and a lack of respect for culture as reasons for their reluctance to live in neighborhoods with large numbers of minority members in general and African Americans in particular. Gradually, the tipping point or the percentage of African American households in a white neighborhood that would lead whites to leave, also known as "white flight," has increased over time. In 1976, 7 percent of whites said they would move if one of fifteen homes in their neighborhood were occupied by African Americans, but by 1992 only 4 percent indicated this neighborhood composition would motivate them to move.

Whites' attitudes regarding neighborhood composition have changed considerably over time. In 1976, only 16 percent of whites were willing to move into a neighborhood where 53 percent of the homes were black. By 1992, 29 percent of whites were willing to move into such a neighborhood. By contrast, almost all blacks preferred to live in such a racially mixed neighborhood in the two time periods (99 percent in 1976 and 98 percent in 1992). Despite moderate changes in whites' attitudes over the years, there is still a big difference between African Americans and whites in the type of neighborhood they find most comfortable. Also notable is the decline from 1976 to 1992 in the percentage of African Americans who were willing to move into all-white neighborhoods (from 38 percent to 31 percent) and the increase in the percentage of African Americans who were willing to live in all-black neighborhoods (from 69 percent to 75 percent). Apparently, some African Americans have given up the idea of racially integrated neighborhoods, but why?

African Americans express serious concerns about moving into predominantly white communities. They fear that white neighbors may display hostile attitudes or even threaten them with physical harm. Attitudes have changed, but the change has been slow and attitudes do not always match actions. Despite more tolerance among white Americans for integrated neighborhoods and a desire among African Americans for more integrated communities, measures indicate high levels of residential segregation for African Americans. In fact, whites and African Americans are more segregated from each other than any other two groups.

Economic Factors. Recent research indicates that the primary determinant of residential segregation is one's economic status. This literature suggests that rather than choosing where to live based on one's racial status, the financially better off isolate themselves from the economically disadvantaged regardless of race. Still, there are considerable differences in wealth between whites and racial minorities. The average net financial worth of whites is considerably more than that of African Americans and Hispanic Americans. Racial minorities are a disproportionate share of the low-income population. The economic disparity between whites and racial minorities does translate into real differences in terms of buying power when it comes to choosing a neighborhood and contributes to African Americans' and Hispanics' much lower rates of home ownership when compared to whites. So, opportunities for whites and minorities to live together are constrained due to disparities in wealth.

The economic explanation for residential segregation patterns that implies that rich whites and rich people of color will live together, while poor people regardless of race will live together has largely been discounted, because upper- and middle-class minorities, especially African Americans, have a difficult time establishing separate residential communities from poor minorities. Meanwhile, wealthy whites certainly do not often share their zip code with poor whites.

Housing Discrimination

There is a long legacy of separate living communities for whites and people of color in the United States. After slavery was abolished, separate communities for whites and African Americans were established. This separation was further encouraged by housing laws and policies. Zoning laws and ordinances prevented mixed-race residential areas or subtly discouraged them by regulating the sizes of houses and lots that could be built in certain neighborhoods. Today, many communities have restrictions that prohibit the erection of multiple-dweller units, such as apartments and duplexes, which might be more economically feasible for some minority families. American housing laws have also served to limit the range of possible neighborhoods available to Asian Americans. Anti-immigration policies, such as the Alien Land Law, which were introduced in the western states during the twentieth century, extended to housing policies, precluding Asian immigrants from settling in certain areas.

The 1934 Federal Housing Act established the Federal Housing Administration (FHA) to insure private mortgage loans and provide protection to lenders against losses on loans for residential properties. In its early years, this agency primarily worked to stabilize the housing industry, which had experienced some serious downturns after the Great Depression. The FHA also financed the development of military housing and created programs to facilitate home-ownership for military veterans. In 1965, the goals of this agency shifted considerably when it was consolidated into the Department of Housing and Urban Development's (HUD) Office of Housing. Its primary responsibility continued to be providing opportunities for affordable homeownership and developing healthy and prosperous communities, but once the 1968 Fair Housing Act was enacted, HUD also assumed the responsibility for ensuring that housing-related transactions were not affected by discriminatory practices.

Federal housing laws actually condoned separate housing, if not explicitly, until the 1968 Fair Housing Act was passed. The Fair Housing Act, also known as Title VIII of the 1968 Civil Rights Act, bans discrimination when selling, renting, or financing dwellings or in conducting any housing-related transactions, based on race, color, national origins, religion, sex, family status, or disability. Subsequently, several amendments to this act have been passed to enhance the effectiveness of the policy and to promote enforcing the act.

Despite the passage of the Fair Housing Act of 1968, discrimination in the housing industry is quite prevalent. The housing choices of minorities are restricted unofficially by the practices of real estate agents, such as steering minorities to neighborhoods that are less integrated, providing poor service in the form of showing fewer properties, making minorities wait longer, asking them fewer questions about specific needs and more questions about income, making fewer positive comments and fewer follow-up calls, and giving different price quotes to racial minorities. Apartment managers have also been known to claim there are no vacant units to avoid renting to racial minorities. Local leaders and politicians in predominantly white communities may promote policies such as zoning laws and restrictive covenants that discourage or prohibit racial minorities from moving into certain neighborhoods. Racial minorities may also hesitate to move into predominantly white areas because of concerns about being harassed by white residents who would resent their presence.

Some commercial banks hinder the house-search process for minorities by establishing different standards for loan qualifications. Other factors that restrict members of minority groups, especially African Americans, in choosing housing include racially motivated site selection in public and government subsidized housing, as well as, in the establishment of urban-renewal programs, the implementation of zoning and annexation laws that promote racial segregation, the attachment of restrictive covenants to housing deeds that prohibit the sale of property to certain ethnic groups, the exclusion of African American real estate agents from realty associations and multiple-listing services, and financial institution policies that discourage developers from building racially integrated housing and force African Americans to live in neighborhoods that are predominantly African American if they desire to receive loans.

Impact of Residential Segregation

Residential segregation remains a volatile topic, because of the practical implications associated with residential communities separated by race. Predominantly racial minority communities tend to have much higher levels of poverty than predominantly white or even mixed-race communities. Not only are minorities in racially segregated neighborhoods isolated from other racial groups, they also face a greater likelihood of living in concentrated poverty. Living in communities where poverty is concentrated is associated with a seemingly never-ending list of social ills, including high unemployment rates, dilapidated buildings, housing abandonment, low housing values, higher mortality rates, higher crime rates, toxic environments, poor education facilities, low educational achievement, family instability, and welfare dependency. Clearly, the consequences of racial residential segregation are considerable and the impact is most heavily felt in the African American community.

Most African Americans continue to live in neighborhoods that are predominantly African American, closer to the central city, and have lower property values than the neighborhoods of their white counterparts who earn about the same level of income. African American neighborhoods are more likely to be in transition and are characterized by higher rates of poverty, crime, substance abuse, and mortality. Although trends suggest that segregation has declined modestly in the last two decades, African Americans are the most isolated of all ethnic minority groups in America.

African Americans tend not only to live in more isolated communities but to live in communities with a lower resource stock. The resources available in African American neighborhoods are dwarfed by those available in white or mixed neighborhoods. Schools are poorer and fewer. Roads and infrastructure are allowed to deteriorate well beyond levels of safety or repair. Grocery stores are not well stocked or conveniently located. Hospitals are understaffed and underbudgeted. All of this makes African American neighborhoods quite unattractive, so it is understandable that whites and other ethnic groups do not wish to move into these areas. Even African Americans would prefer not to move into these types of neighborhoods, but they are often prevented from moving into the types of neighborhoods they would prefer to live in, so African Americans frequently must make due with the second-class neighborhoods that are open to them.

The social ills associated with concentrated poverty due to residential segregation also serve to discourage property owners from investing in real estate in predominantly African American areas. Property owners who are already invested in these areas look for ways to divest from the community, leading to further deterioration of neighborhood buildings. More subtle social problems that emerge due to the concentration of poverty in African American neighborhoods include social disorders such as street-corner drinking, catcalling, sexual harassment, graffiti, and littering. On the surface, these disorders do not seem that harmful, but over time they lead neighbors to become distrustful of each other. To avoid these situations, many residents will withdraw from the community and opt to stay indoors when possible. This strategy may be effective for individuals or families, but for the broader community it further weakens social control in the neighborhood. Ultimately, these small social-order violations create conditions conducive to the perpetration of more serious crimes.

It is not only low-income African Americans who are subjected to these substandard living conditions. Recent research indicates that middle-class African Americans are much more likely than middle-class whites to live in resource-poor neighborhoods. Even high-status blacks are frequently unable to settle in neighborhoods that befit their level of income, education, and social prestige. Beyond the physical and material disparities, continued levels of moderate to high residential segregation based on race diminish efforts to create racial and social harmony in the United States.

See also Closed Doors, Opportunities Lost: The Continuing Costs of Housing Discrimination; Dual Housing Markets; De Jure and De Facto Segregation; Fair Housing Act of 1968; Fair Housing Amendments Act of 1988; "Fair Housing Audit"; Federal Housing Administration (FHA); Housing Discrimination;

Racial Segregation, White and Black Preferences as a Cause of; Redlining; Restrictive Covenants; U.S. Department of Housing and Urban Development (HUD); White Flight.

Further Reading

Farley, Reynolds, Charlotte Steeh, Maria Krysan, Tara Jackson, and Keith Reeves. "Stereotypes and Segregation: Neighborhoods in the Detroit Area." *American Journal of Sociology* 100 (1994): 750–780.

Jargowsky, Paul. "Take the Money and Run: Economic Segregation in U.S. Metropolitan Areas." *American Sociological Review* 61 (1996): 984–998.

Massey, Douglas S., and Nancy A. Denton. *American Apartheid, Segregation and the Making of the Underclass*. Cambridge, MA: Harvard University Press, 1993.

Oliver, Melvin, and Thomas Shapiro. *Black Wealth/White Wealth: A New Perspective on Racial Inequality*. New York: Routledge, 1995.

U.S. Census Bureau. "Housing Patterns." June 18, 2002. http://www.census.gov/hhes/www/housing/resseg/.

Yinger, John. *Closed Doors, Opportunities Lost: The Continuing Costs of Housing Discrimination*. New York: Russell Sage Foundation, 1995.

Zhou, Min, and John R. Logan. "In and Out of Chinatown: Residential Mobility and Segregation of New York City's Chinese." *Social Forces* 70 (1991): 387–407.

Romney S. Norwood

Restrictive Covenants

Restrictive covenants in housing are private mutual agreements that regulate the size, appearance, occupants, and/or other features of a dwelling unit or the area immediately around it. During the first half of the twentieth century, restrictive covenants were used in many parts of the United States to prevent blacks or other racial/ethnic minorities from living in the same residential areas as whites. These racially restrictive covenants were signed private agreements among white property owners or neighborhood association members. They stipulated that the homes or apartments were only to be sold, rented, owned, or occupied by members of the "Caucasian race," although sometimes the names of the prohibited or excluded groups were explicitly listed in a clause of the restrictive covenant. Whites used this device to maintain segregation, to avoid unwanted social contact with people they believed to be inferior, to maintain the prestige and property value of their area, and to reproduce their socioeconomic dominance and privilege.

Some cities tried to control the racial composition of urban areas by using zoning codes to designate "white" or "colored" districts, but in 1917, the U.S. Supreme Court ruled that it was unconstitutional for state or local governments to use zoning ordinances to dictate what races may occupy certain areas (*Buchanan v. Warley*). Whites then used private racially restrictive covenants as a common device to accomplish discrimination in housing. Civil rights activists challenged the legality of racially restrictive covenants and, in 1948, the U.S. Supreme Court ruled (*Shelley v. Kraemer*) that the equal-protection clause of the Fourteenth Amendment to the Constitution prevents courts from enforcing racially restrictive covenants in housing. Since then, whites often have relied on other mechanisms to exclude unwanted groups (e.g., informal unwritten agreements about who to sell or rent to; "steering" by accommodating real estate agents), which were not made illegal until legislation and judicial rulings in the 1960s.

See also Housing Discrimination; *Shelley v. Kraemer.*

Charles Jaret

Reverse Discrimination

Discrimination can be defined as "the denial of opportunities and equal rights to individuals and groups based on some type of arbitrary bias" (Schaffer 2001, 264). Normally, the target of discrimination is associated with a minority group. That is, discrimination in American society is generally seen as being practiced by those in a dominant power position, white males, against other groups, such as blacks, Hispanics, Asians, American Indians, and women. Some examples of discriminatory behavior include a minority member being denied a job, a promotion, or admission into a college because of that person's race or ethnicity. Egregious examples of discrimination are seen in the practices of white supremacist groups such as the Ku Klux Klan (e.g., lynchings).

Reverse discrimination can be seen as the other side of the coin. The *American Heritage Dictionary* (2nd college ed.) defines it as "discrimination against members of a dominant group, especially discrimination against whites or males in employment." In general, reverse discrimination has been claimed by whites who argue that affirmative action programs, which are aimed at correcting past discrimination against minority groups, are now discriminating against them.

The American public is quite divided about whether affirmative action programs should be considered reverse discrimination. Two recent opinion polls help to see this division. In the New Democratic Electorate Survey, conducted in 1997 with 1,009 registered voters participating, 50 percent of the respondents agreed with the statement, "Affirmative action programs are no longer necessary and are a form of reverse discrimination that should be ended." In that same survey, 43 percent agreed with the statement, "Affirmative action programs are needed to promote diversity and to ensure that minorities have access to college, job promotions, and government contracts." Thus, half of those surveyed thought that affirmative action was a form of reverse discrimination, while the other half thought that affirmative action was necessary and was not reverse discrimination. This certainly revealed a divided America.

Another survey, the NBC News/Wall Street Journal Poll, conducted in 1995 with 1,005 American adults participating, showed a racial divide on this issue. Fifty-seven percent of respondents thought that "federal affirmative action programs that give preferences to women and minorities [should] . . . be continued but reformed to prevent reverse discrimination." However, in that same survey, a large portion of black respondents thought that such programs should be left unchanged. Indeed, 31 percent of blacks responded that "federal affirmative action programs that give preferences to women and minorities [should] . . . be continued as they are." Other groups did not even come close to this: whites, 10 percent; Hispanics, 19 percent; females, 13 percent; Asians, 12 percent. The results clearly indicate a racial divide among the American public on this issue. Perhaps this is because Blacks continue to feel discriminated against.

In fact, some scholarly literature shows evidence of continued discrimination against minorities. For example, one study (Tsang and Dietz 2001) examined the impact of affirmative action programs on Americans, using data collected from 1979 to 1994 from the National Longitudinal Survey of Youth. This cohort data included a sample of 12,686 people aged 14 to 22 in 1979. It was found that "women and ethnic minorities continue to earn less . . . [and] race played an increasingly important role in determining one's economic success in contemporary America" (75). These results suggest that reverse discrimination is not occurring and that affirmative action programs are still widely necessary. For another viewpoint, however, see Lerner and Nagai (2000).

See also Affirmative Action; *Affirmative Discrimination: Ethnic Inequality and Public Policy*; Ku Klux Klan (KKK).

Further Reading

Lerner, Robert, and Althea K. Nagai. "Reverse Discrimination by the Numbers." *Academic Questions* 13, no. 3 (2000): 71–84.

Schaefer, Richard T. *Sociology.* 7th ed. New York: McGraw-Hill, 2001.

Tsang, Chiu-Wai Rita, and Tracy Dietz. "The Unrelenting Significance of Minority Statuses: Gender, Ethnicity, and Economic Attainment Since Affirmative Action." *Sociological Spectrum* 21 (2001): 61–80.

John Eterno

Richmond v. Croson

In *City of Richmond v. J. A. Croson Company*, 488 U.S. 469, the U.S. Supreme Court ruled on January 23, 1989, that the City of Richmond's "Minority Business Enterprise" (MBE) program, an affirmative action program, violated the equal-protection clause of the U.S. Constitution's Fourteenth Amendment. To promote minority participation in city construction contracts, the City of Richmond, Virginia, had adopted in 1983 a minority business utilization "set-aside" plan, which required successful bidders on government contracts to subcontract at least 30 percent of the dollars to minority owned firms. The city refused the only bidder, J. A. Croson Company, on a project for the provision and installation of certain plumbing fixtures in the city jail on the grounds that the company did not meet the requirement. J. A. Croson sued the city, claiming that the MBE program violated the equal-protection clause. The District Court upheld the city's ordinance in all respects. The Court of Appeal initially affirmed the ruling but later reversed it upon the Supreme Court's order of reconsideration. On appeal, the Supreme Court affirmed the reversion in a

6-to-3 vote. The Court ruled that an affirmative action program must be targeted to proven discrimination against minorities within the Richmond area. It made clear that "generalized assertions" of past racial discrimination could not justify "rigid" racial quotas for the awarding of public contracts.

Some, including Justice Thurgood Marshall, took the ruling as a setback in the affirmative action policy. Others said that the ruling did not overthrow affirmative action itself but specified the standards by which an affirmative action program could be considered legitimate. The decision, they argued, would strengthen rather than weaken affirmative action. In the decade after the ruling, local governments created more than one hundred new MEB programs.

See also Affirmative Action; *Regents of the University of California v. Bakke.*

Dong-Ho Cho

Robinson, Jackie (1919–1972)

Born in Cairo, Georgia, on January 31, 1919, Jack Roosevelt Robinson would become Major League Baseball's first black player. He grew up in Pasadena, California, not segregated Georgia, because his mother moved to California after his father abandoned the family. He attended integrated schools and ex-

Dodger Jackie Robinson at bat.

Photo by Francis Miller/Time Life Pictures/Getty Images.

celled at sports. Robinson's athletic abilities helped him to get into UCLA, where he received national attention in football and track. He served in the Army during World War II and was exonerated in a court-martial proceeding that resulted from an incident on a segregated bus.

After completing his service, he joined the Kansas City Monarchs of the Negro National League. From there, he was signed to a Major League Baseball contract in 1946. In 1947, Robinson played for the Brooklyn Dodgers becoming the first black major-league player. His outstanding talent as a ballplayer earned him the honor of being named Rookie of the Year and helped to bring a pennant to the Dodgers. These were, however, difficult years, as racial tensions ran high in many places where the Dodgers played ball. Robinson overcame the barrier through his athletic skill and mental toughness—a truly remarkable feat. Within a few years, most ball clubs followed suit, accepting blacks onto their teams. In 1949, he was the league's Most Valuable Player. He retired from baseball in 1956 and in 1962 was elected to the Baseball Hall of Fame. In 1972, at the World Series, baseball honored Robinson on the twenty-fifth anniversary of his entry into Major League Baseball. At the time, he argued for black managers in baseball. Three years later, in 1975, Frank Robinson (no relation) became the first black manager.

Robinson died on October 24, 1972. His accomplishments at a time of Jim Crow laws in the South and widespread individual discrimination against blacks have etched the trail that he blazed into both baseball history and American history.

See also Sports and Racism.

John Eterno

Rodney King Beating

The beating of Rodney King by police in Los Angeles in 1991 is often cited as a classic example of police brutality in the United States. On March 3, 1991, officers in the Los Angeles Police Department pursued Rodney King for speeding. He refused to pull over, and after a lengthy car chase through Los Angeles streets, King's vehicle was finally stopped. More than twenty officers surrounded King. At least two officers used batons, or nightsticks, a stun gun, and physical force, beating King repeatedly. The others, including police supervisors, simply looked on. The officers did not stop, even though King was apparently subdued. A nearby apartment dweller caught the incident on videotape. The videotaped beating was seen over and over again on the news and in various media outlets.

There were two trials associated with the beating. In the first trial, in a California state court, the officers were acquitted by the jury. The officers claimed that they had acted appropriately in that they were responding to King's resisting arrest. All the jurors viewed the videotape and still came to that verdict for all four defendants. The not-guilty verdict led to civil disobedience in Los Angeles as riots broke out in April 1992. The police response to those riots has also been the subject of criticism in that they were very slow to react. Even before the riots, police were making fewer arrests. Some claim this was because of the publicity of the King case, specifically, fear of retaliation by the media or the public. Nevertheless, the officers were put on trial again, this time in federal court on civil rights charges, for which two of the officers were found guilty.

See also Criminal Justice System and Racial Discrimination; Los Angeles Riots of 1992.

John Eterno

Role-Model Argument for Affirmative Action

Reflecting the complexity of the issues surrounding affirmative action, scholars and politicians have posed various arguments to support or to refute increasing diversity in schools and workplaces through this particular means. The role-model argument for affirmative action is among the most frequently cited; at the same time, it may also be among the most misunderstood arguments in support of affirmative action. In most educational and professional fields, such as academia and medicine, people of color have historically been underrepresented. Among these are a variety of causes of this phenomenon, discriminatory practices in school and by employers, as well as a long history of racism depriving people of color of adequate social capital (e.g., social networks), have perhaps been the most widely discussed. Affirmative action has primarily been designed to address these systemic problems, but the role-model argument reminds us that affirmative action also promotes equality by enhancing the collective self-efficacy of people of color. Due to the history of racism in the United States, the members of many ethnic groups have grown skeptical about their roles in occupational areas in which they have historically faced discrimination. As a result, they may not think they belong in those fields, which would discourage them from entering these professions or pursuing an education leading to such careers. It is therefore not surprising that researchers frequently cite this disillusionment as a contributing factor to the apathy toward school among many children of color.

Rodney King displays his bruises, March 6, 1991.

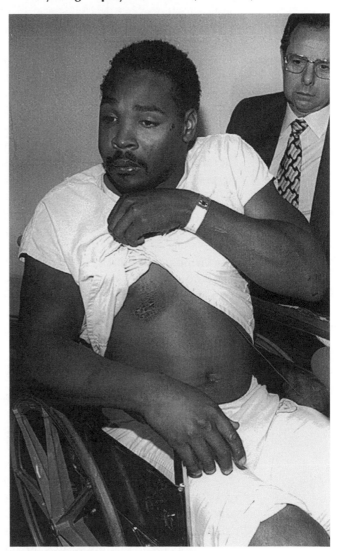

AP/Wide World Photos.

The role-model argument for affirmative action essentially posits that programs fostering cultural inclusion in various fields—either through the hiring of authority figures of color or through enhancing the educational opportunities for students of color to eventually gain professional visibility—will allow individuals from traditionally underrepresented groups to serve as role models. It is argued that their presence will decrease the feelings of detachment, disillusionment, and apathy among the members of underrepresented groups, including women, which is likely to encourage their current and future participation in the field. This, in turn, is believed to be beneficial to the society at large because it would gradually promote equality by allowing more members of underrepresented groups to enjoy a variety of options as productive members of the society.

For example, an African American mathematics college professor may serve as an exemplary figure for African American students, not only by demonstrating that African Americans can indeed be successful in such a field despite their historical underrepresentation in it, but also by providing the opportunities for mentorship without ethnic power differentials. She would accomplish this primarily—though not exclusively—by performing her duties as a mathematics professor, as any other mathematics professors would do regardless of their backgrounds. Thus, despite common beliefs, her primary role does not involve advocating for the rights of the people who share her racial or ethnic background. The role-model argument additionally contends that the individuals of color she inspires will then proceed to obtain positions of power, further widening the circle of participation by people of color.

The "population specificity" of the role-model argument is that its primary focus is to have people of color serve as mentors to the members of their own communities. But this has sometimes limited the legal strengths of affirmative action programs. For instance, in *Wygant v. Jackson Board of Education* (1986), the U.S. Supreme Court rejected the board's hiring policy of increasing the number of African American teachers in their districts, whose student bodies were predominantly African American. Justice Lewis F. Powell Jr. condemned this practice, citing that hiring African American teachers to serve as role models for African American children would provide a justification for segregation.

Many scholars dispute Justice Powell's reasoning and argue that, since great inequality already exists, the current racial injustice will be perpetuated without some corrective measures, such as welcoming role models with whom people of color can culturally identify. By allowing people of color to serve as role models, the foundation may be built toward expanding the collective social mobility of the members of underrepresented communities. While the role-model argument for affirmative action presents a compelling case, it needs to be accepted with caution. The primary responsibility of role models of color is not to salvage their communities but to perform their duties like their European American colleagues do. Expectations for the role models of color, therefore, should not revolve primarily around their cultural backgrounds. Such expectations may (1) lead to the perception that role models of color are recruited solely based on their color and not on their achievements and (2) cause added pressure for the role models to perform tasks that are not inherent in particular positions. Also, the successes of some role models should not reflect badly on other members of their group who do not enjoy similar success. The presence of role models represents only a single factor within a set of complex systems of social injustice within which individuals of color live. Also, individuals vary greatly in their affective, cognitive, and behavioral characteristics. Thus, success cannot be expected to take exactly the same form from individual to individual.

See also Affirmative Action.

Further Reading

Carroll, Grace, Karolyn Tyson, and Bernadette Lumas. "Those Who Got in the Door: The University of California-Berkeley's Affirmative Action Success Story." *The Journal of Negro Education* 69, no. 1–2 (2000): 128–144.

Nan, Carlos J. "Adding Salt to the Wound: Affirmative Action and Critical Race Theory." *Law and Inequality: A Journal of Theory and Practice* 12 (1994): 553–572.

Daisuke Akiba

Roots

Published in 1976, *Roots: The Saga of an American Family* was presented as the semiautobiographical history of author Alex Haley's family. The novel was written from the perspective of one of Haley's ancestors, a slave known as Kunta Kinte. Haley's epic story followed the African Kunta Kinte as he was forced to board a slave ship to America and documented his experiences in the New World, including his purchase by white slave masters, life on the plantation, and family formation patterns.

Roots received much media attention and critical acclaim, which culminated with Haley's receipt of a Pulitzer Prize in 1977. In that same year, the novel was optioned for a television film. It became an epic miniseries, which garnered for ABC what remain among the highest television ratings ever. For five nights, most American households tuned in to see the history of slavery in America dramatized. This was significant, not only because ABC had expected the movie to be a ratings bust but also because the movie brought the horrors

LeVar Burton in the television miniseries *Roots*, which achieved some of the highest ratings ever.

© Bettman/CORBIS.

of slavery and its aftermath into the homes of a country that had a history of silence on the subject.

The movie gave its audience common ground and served as a starting point for conversations about the impact of slavery on America and on the black family specifically. Although initially the book and the movie were lauded as American treasures, ultimately Haley's novel became the target of skepticism due to charges of plagiarism and fabrication. In response to these charges, Haley referred to his work as 'faction'—part fact, part fiction. Despite these allegations, in celebration of the twenty-fifth anniversary of the first airing of *Roots*, the miniseries was rerun in the fall of 2002.

See also Films and Racial Stereotypes; Slave Families; Slavery in the Antebellum South; Television and Racial Stereotypes.

Romney S. Norwood

Rule of Hypo-Descent

See One-Drop Rule.